Fruits Basket™

Volume 15

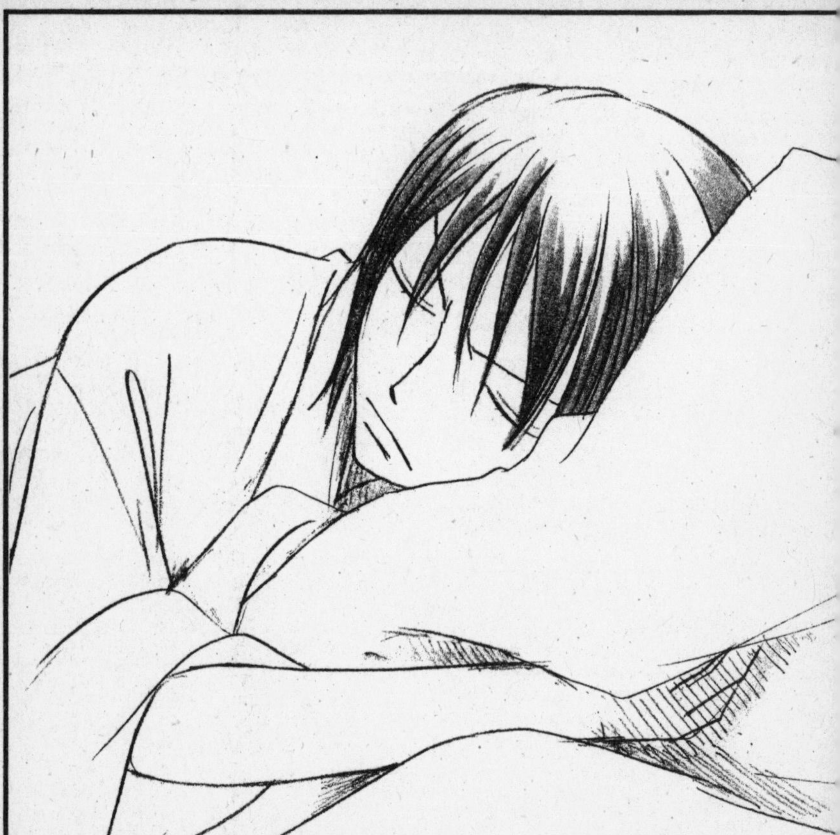

Natsuki Takaya

Fruits Basket Vol. 15
Created by Natsuki Takaya

Translation - Alethea Nibley and Athena Nibley
English Adaptation - Lianne Sentar
Associate Editor - Peter Ahlstrom
Retouch and Lettering - Dongjin Oh
Production Artist - Jihye "Sophia" Hong
Cover Design - Christian Lownds

Editor - Paul Morrissey
Digital Imaging Manager - Chris Buford
Pre-Production Supervisor - Erika Terriquez
Art Director - Anne Marie Horne
Production Manager - Liz Brizzi
Managing Editor - Vy Nguyen
VP of Production - Ron Klamert
Editor-In-Chief - Rob Tokar
Publisher - Mike Kiley
President and C.O.O. - John Parker
C.E.O. and Chief Creative Officer - Stuart Levy

A 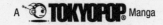 Manga

TOKYOPOP Inc.
5900 Wilshire Blvd. Suite 2000
Los Angeles, CA 90036

E-mail: info@TOKYOPOP.com
Come visit us online at www.TOKYOPOP.com

FRUITS BASKET Vol. 15 by Natsuki Takaya
© 2003 Natsuki Takaya. All rights reserved.
First published in Japan in 2004 by
HAKUSENSHA, INC., Tokyo. English language
translation rights in the United States
of America, Canada and the United Kingdom
arranged with HAKUSENSHA, INC., Tokyo through
Tuttle-Mori Agency Inc., Tokyo.
English text copyright © 2006 TOKYOPOP Inc.

All rights reserved. No portion of this book may be
reproduced or transmitted in any form or by any means
without written permission from the copyright holders.
This manga is a work of fiction. Any resemblance to
actual events or locales or persons, living or dead, is
entirely coincidental.

ISBN: 1-59816-023-0

First TOKYOPOP printing: December 2006
10 9 8 7 6 5 4 3 2 1
Printed in the USA

Fruits Basket™

Volume 15

By
Natsuki Takaya

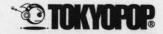

HAMBURG // LONDON // LOS ANGELES // TOKYO

Fruits Basket ™

Table of Contents

STORY SO FAR...

Hello, I'm Tohru Honda and I have come to know a terrible secret. After the death of my mother, I was living by myself in a tent, when the Sohma family took me in. I soon learned that the Sohma family lives with a curse! Each family member is possessed by the vengeful spirit of an animal from the Chinese Zodiac. Whenever one of them becomes weak or is hugged by a member of the opposite sex, they change into their Zodiac animal!

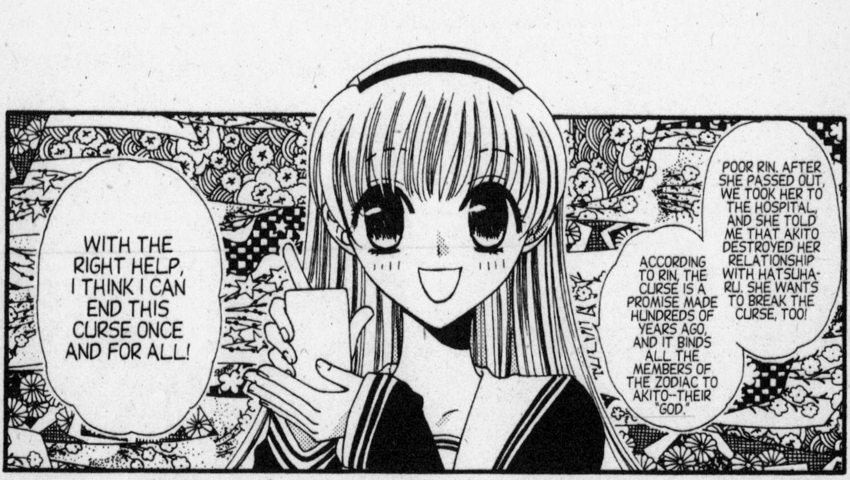
POOR RIN. AFTER SHE PASSED OUT, WE TOOK HER TO THE HOSPITAL, AND SHE TOLD ME THAT AKITO DESTROYED HER RELATIONSHIP WITH HATSUHARU. SHE WANTS TO BREAK THE CURSE, TOO!
ACCORDING TO RIN, THE CURSE IS A PROMISE MADE HUNDREDS OF YEARS AGO, AND IT BINDS ALL THE MEMBERS OF THE ZODIAC TO AKITO--THEIR "GOD."
WITH THE RIGHT HELP, I THINK I CAN END THIS CURSE ONCE AND FOR ALL!

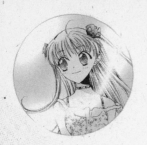

Tohru Honda

The ever-optimistic hero of our story.
An orphan, she now lives in Shigure's
house, along with Yuki and Kyo, and
is the only person outside of the family
who knows the Sohma family's curse.

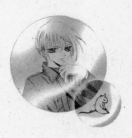

Yuki Sohma, the Rat

Soft-spoken. Self-esteem issues.
At school he's called "Prince Yuki."

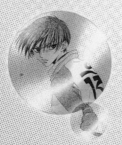

Kyo Sohma, the Cat

The Cat who was left out of the Zodiac.
Hates Yuki, leeks and miso. But mostly
Yuki.

Kagura Sohma, the Boar

Bashful, yet headstrong. Determined to
marry Kyo, even if it kills him.

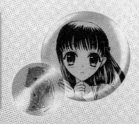

Fruits Basket Characters

Mabudachi Trio

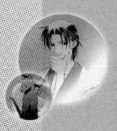

Shigure Sohma, the Dog

Enigmatic, mischievous and a little perverted. A popular novelist.

Hatori Sohma, the Dragon

Family doctor to the Sohmas. Only thing he can't cure is his broken heart.

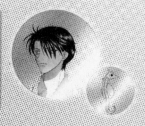

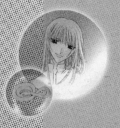

Ayame Sohma, the Snake

Yuki's older brother. A proud and playful drama queen...er, king. Runs a costume shop.

Saki Hanajima

"Hana-chan." Can sense people's "waves." Goth demeanor scares her classmates.

Arisa Uotani

"Uo-chan." A tough-talking "Yankee" who looks out for her friends.

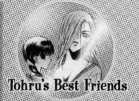

Tohru's Best Friends

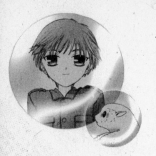

Hiro Sohma, the Ram (or sheep)

This caustic tyke is skilled at throwing verbal barbs, but he has a soft spot for Kisa.

Momiji Sohma, the Rabbit

Half-German. He's older than he looks. His mother rejected him because of the Sohma curse. His little sister, Momo, has been kept from him most of her life.

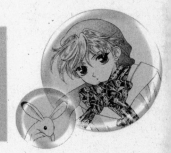

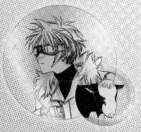

Hatsuharu Sohma, the Ox

The nicest of guys, except when he goes "Black." Then you'd better watch out. He was once in a relationship with Rin.

Kisa Sohma, the Tiger

Kisa became shy and self-conscious due to constant teasing by her classmates. Yuki, who has similar insecurities, feels particularly close to Kisa.

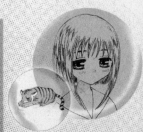

Fruits Basket Characters

Isuzu "Rin" Sohma, the Horse

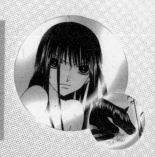

She was once in a relationship with Hatsuharu (Haru)...and Tohru leaves her rather cold. Rin is full of pride, and she can't stand the amount of deference the other Sohma family members give Akito.

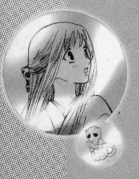

Ritsu Sohma, the Monkey

This shy kimono-wearing member of the Sohma family is gorgeous. But this "she" is really a he!! Crossdressing calms his nerves.

Akito Sohma

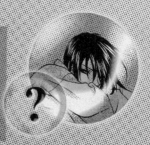

The head of the Sohma clan. A dark figure of many secrets. Treated with fear and reverence.

Filler Sketch

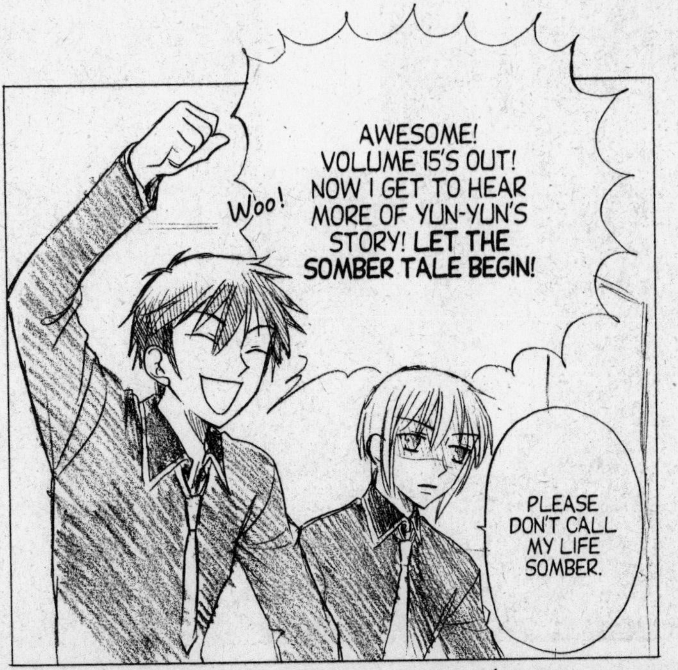
AWESOME! VOLUME 15'S OUT! NOW I GET TO HEAR MORE OF YUN-YUN'S STORY! LET THE SOMBER TALE BEGIN!
Woo!
PLEASE DON'T CALL MY LIFE SOMBER.

Sorry for the delay.

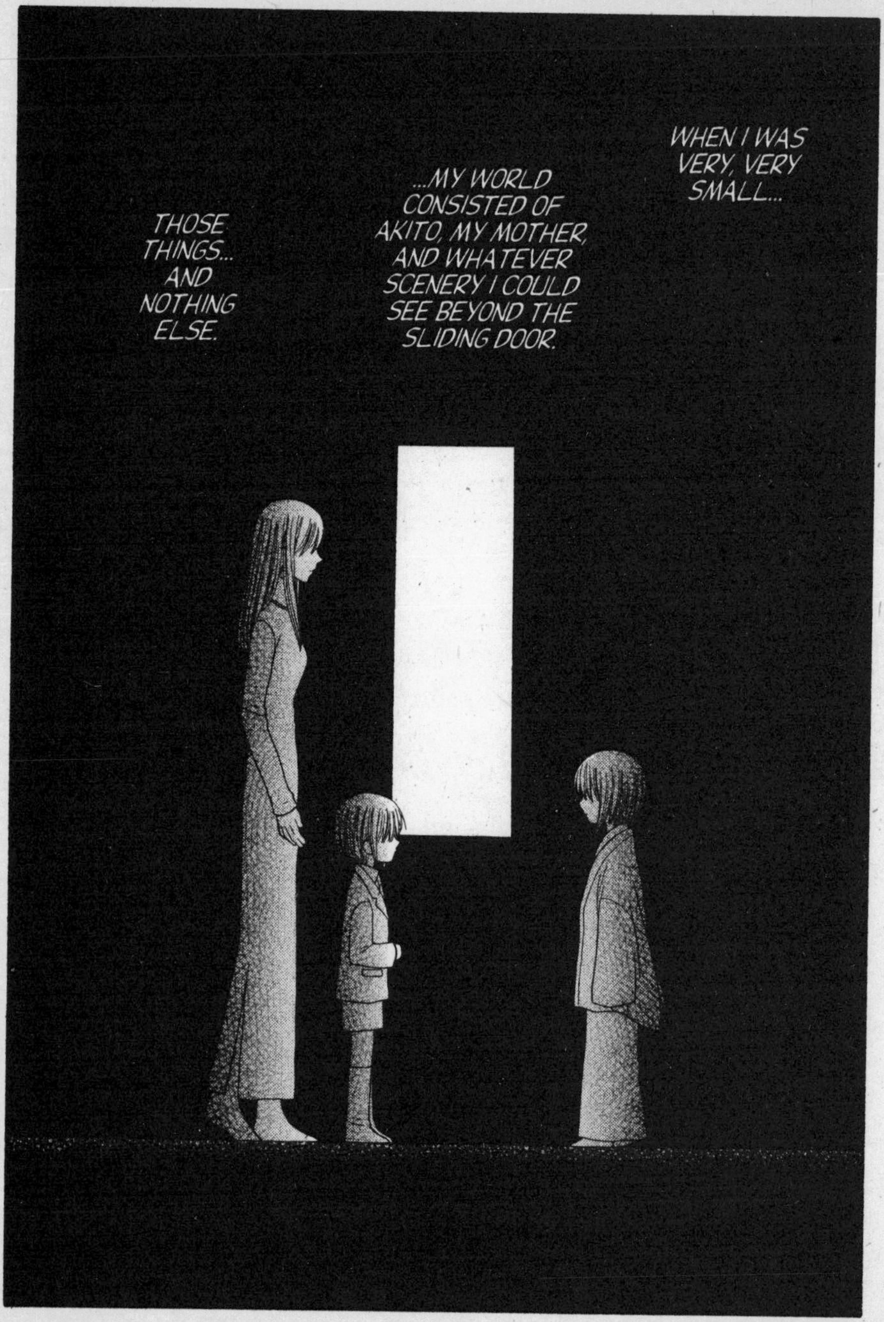
WHEN I WAS VERY, VERY SMALL...
...MY WORLD CONSISTED OF AKITO, MY MOTHER, AND WHATEVER SCENERY I COULD SEE BEYOND THE SLIDING DOOR.
THOSE THINGS... AND NOTHING ELSE.

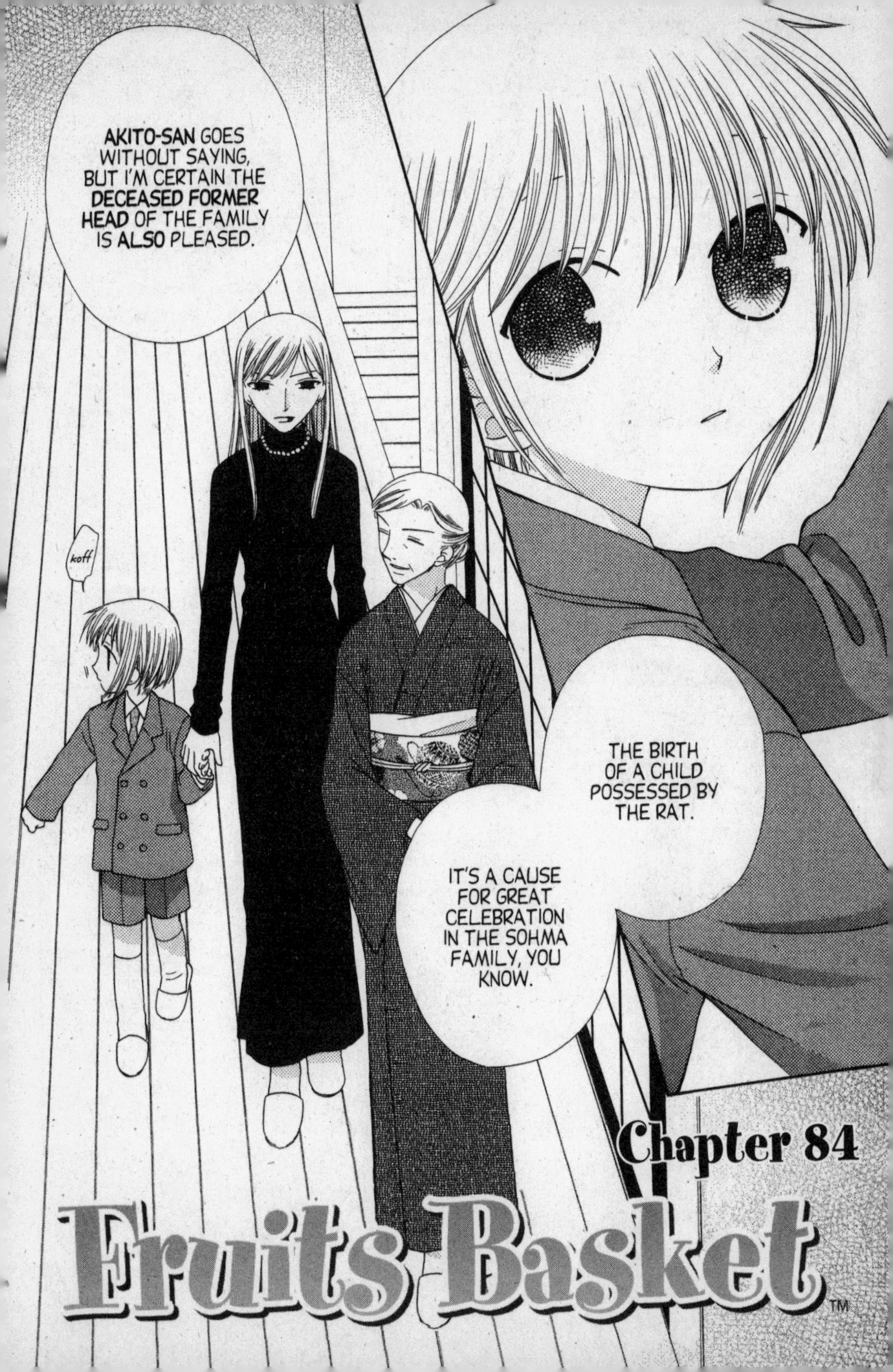
THE BIRTH OF A CHILD POSSESSED BY THE RAT.
IT'S A CAUSE FOR GREAT CELEBRATION IN THE SOHMA FAMILY, YOU KNOW.
AKITO-SAN GOES WITHOUT SAYING, BUT I'M CERTAIN THE DECEASED FORMER HEAD OF THE FAMILY IS ALSO PLEASED.
koff
Chapter 84
Fruits Basket™

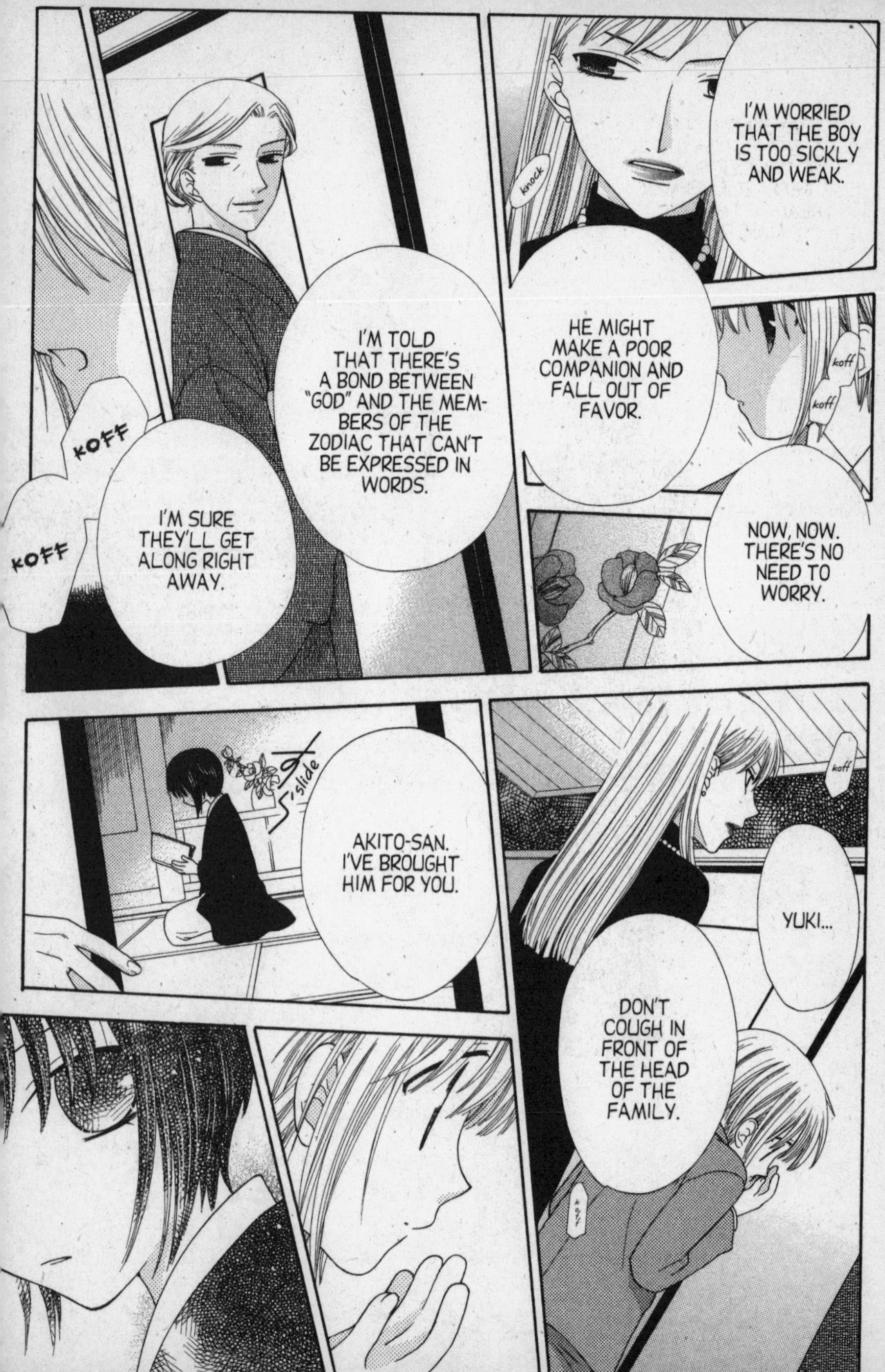
knock
I'M WORRIED THAT THE BOY IS TOO SICKLY AND WEAK.
HE MIGHT MAKE A POOR COMPANION AND FALL OUT OF FAVOR.
koff
koff
NOW, NOW. THERE'S NO NEED TO WORRY.
I'M TOLD THAT THERE'S A BOND BETWEEN "GOD" AND THE MEMBERS OF THE ZODIAC THAT CAN'T BE EXPRESSED IN WORDS.
I'M SURE THEY'LL GET ALONG RIGHT AWAY.
KOFF
KOFF
koff
YUKI...
DON'T COUGH IN FRONT OF THE HEAD OF THE FAMILY.
koff
slide
AKITO-SAN. I'VE BROUGHT HIM FOR YOU.

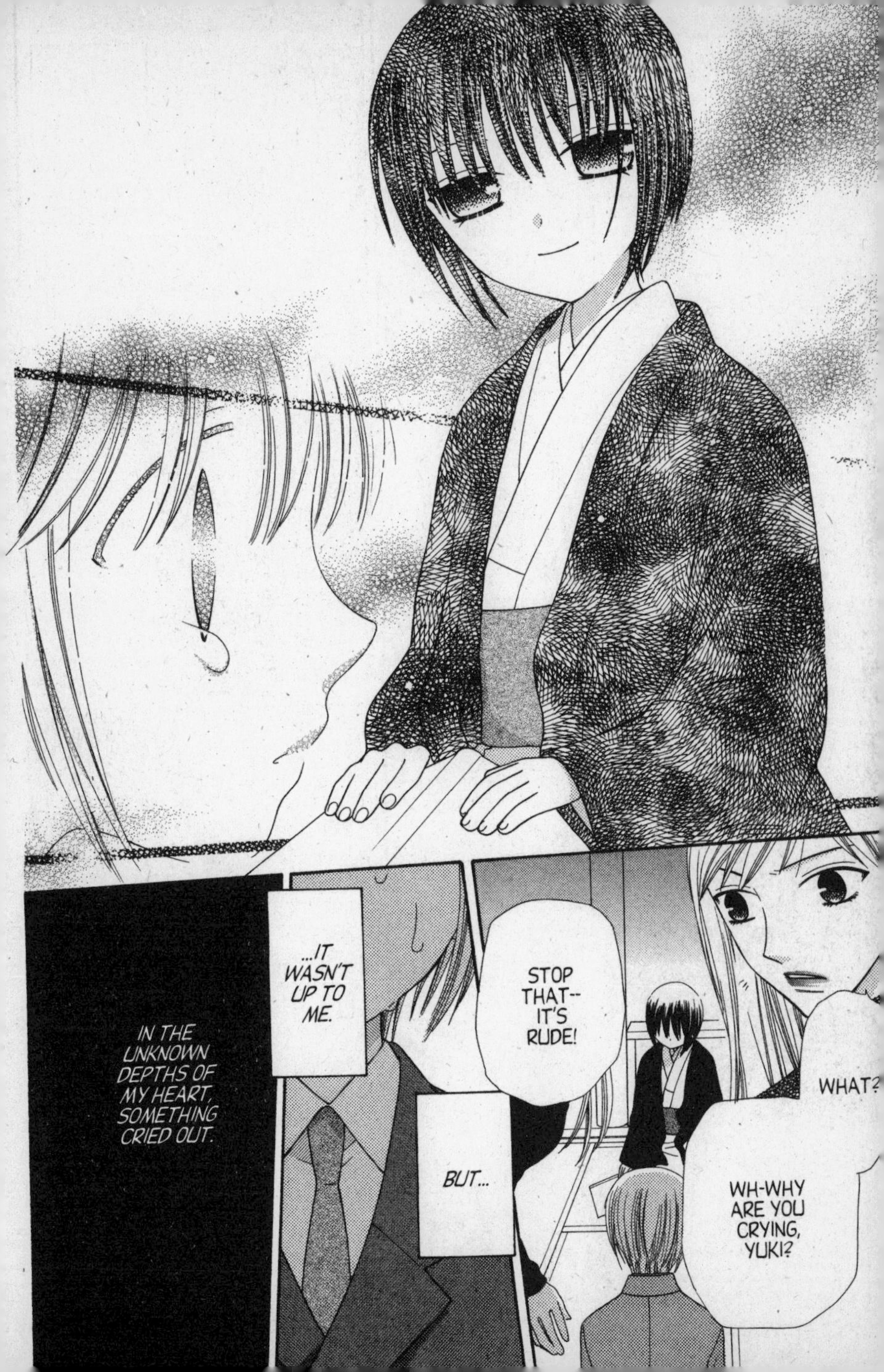
WHAT?
STOP THAT-- IT'S RUDE!
WH-WHY ARE YOU CRYING, YUKI?
...IT WASN'T UP TO ME.
BUT...
IN THE UNKNOWN DEPTHS OF MY HEART, SOMETHING CRIED OUT.

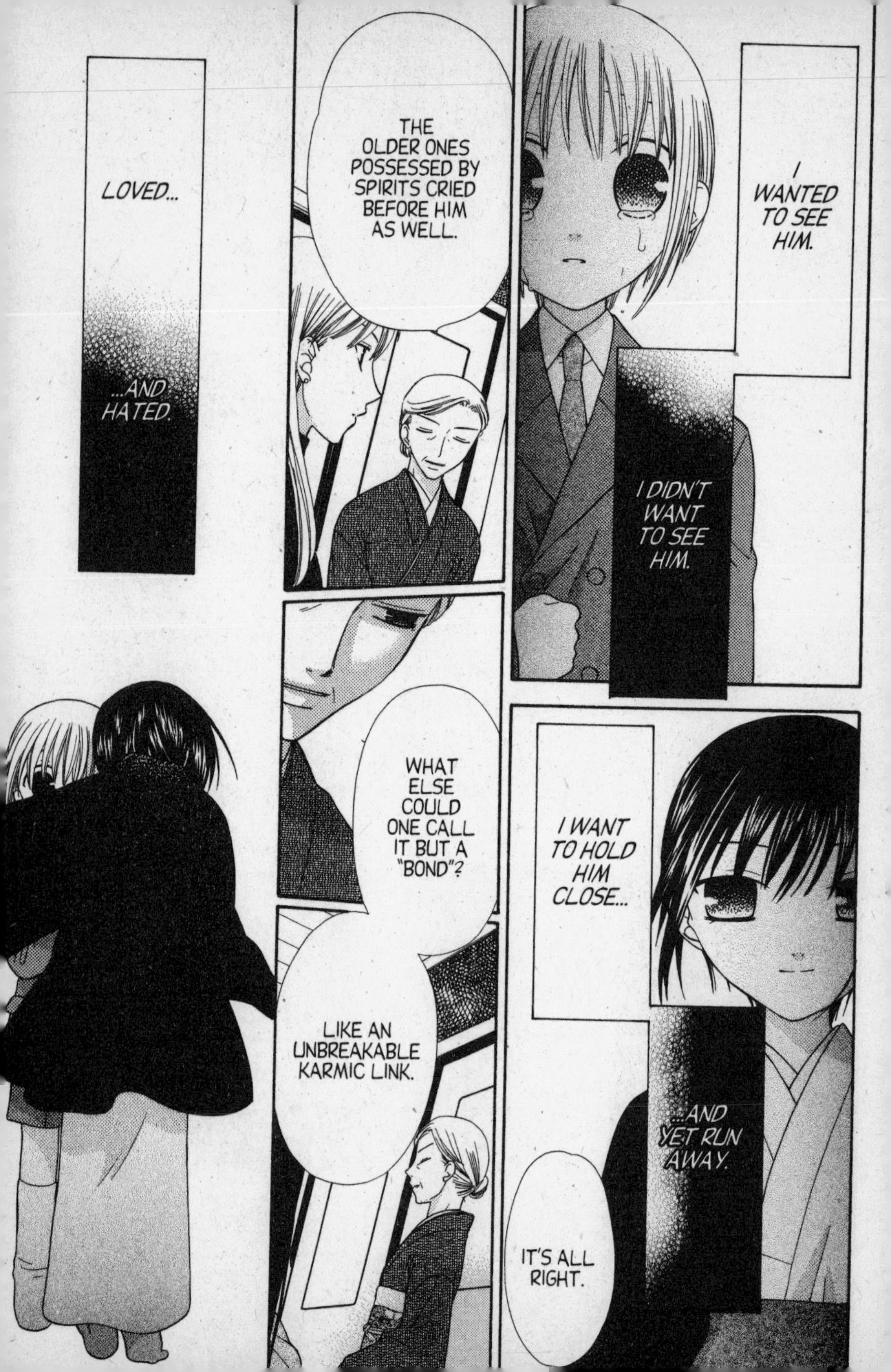
I WANTED TO SEE HIM.
I DIDN'T WANT TO SEE HIM.
THE OLDER ONES POSSESSED BY SPIRITS CRIED BEFORE HIM AS WELL.
LOVED...
...AND HATED.
I WANT TO HOLD HIM CLOSE...
...AND YET RUN AWAY.
IT'S ALL RIGHT.
WHAT ELSE COULD ONE CALL IT BUT A "BOND"?
LIKE AN UNBREAKABLE KARMIC LINK.

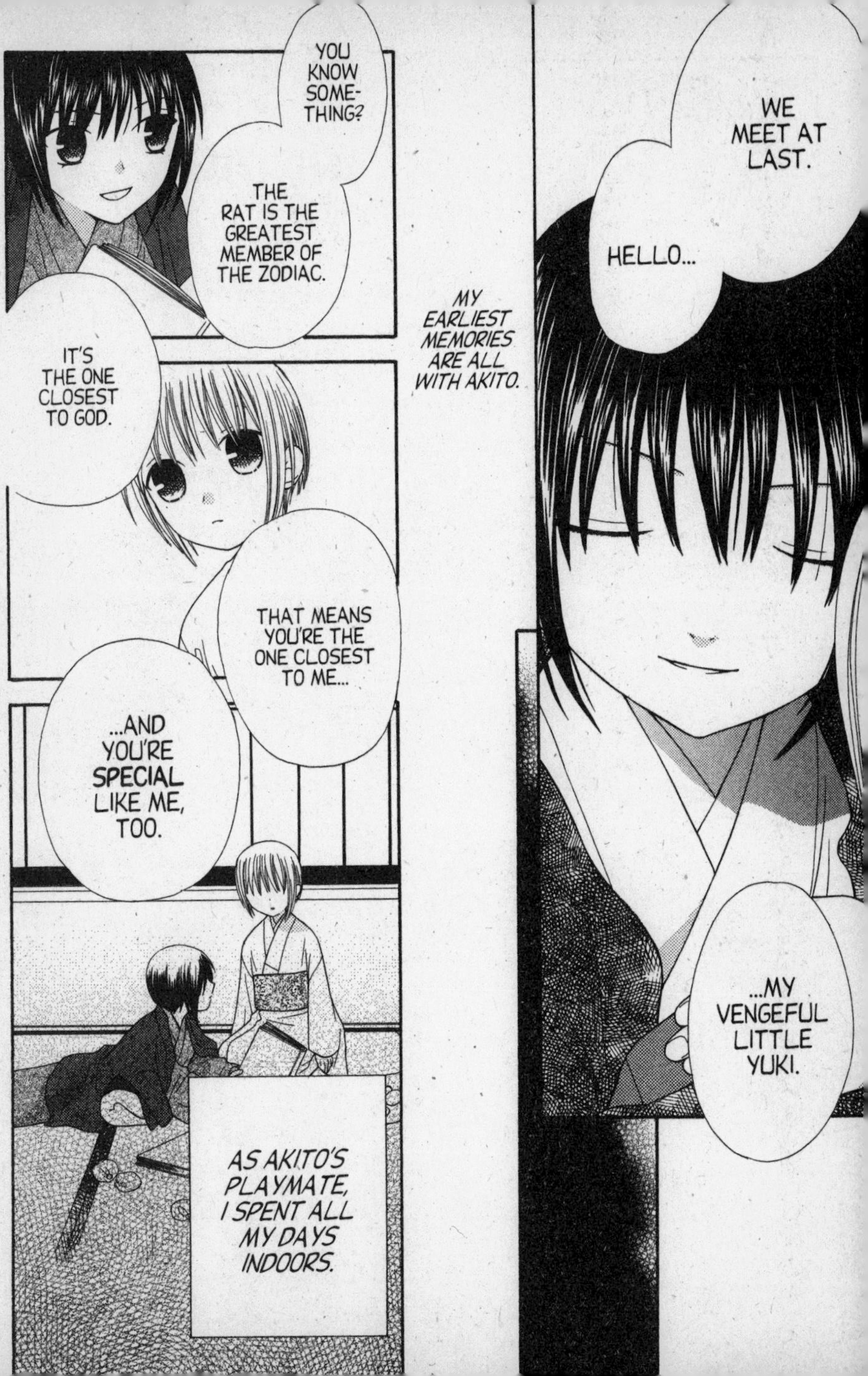
WE MEET AT LAST.
HELLO...
...MY VENGEFUL LITTLE YUKI.
MY EARLIEST MEMORIES ARE ALL WITH AKITO.
YOU KNOW SOME-THING?
THE RAT IS THE GREATEST MEMBER OF THE ZODIAC.
IT'S THE ONE CLOSEST TO GOD.
THAT MEANS YOU'RE THE ONE CLOSEST TO ME...
...AND YOU'RE SPECIAL LIKE ME, TOO.
AS AKITO'S PLAYMATE, I SPENT ALL MY DAYS INDOORS.

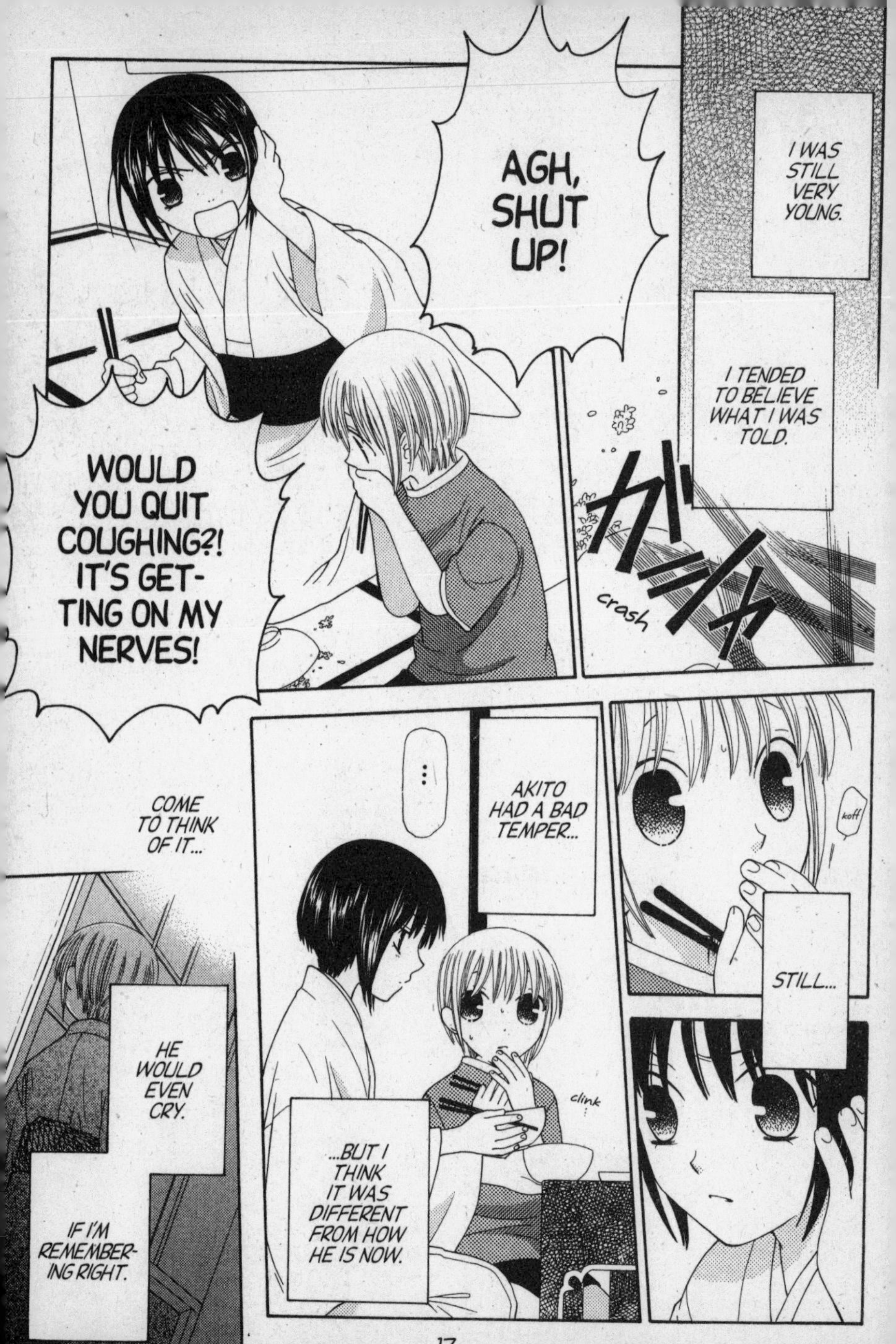
I WAS STILL VERY YOUNG.
I TENDED TO BELIEVE WHAT I WAS TOLD.
ガシャ
crash
AGH, SHUT UP!
WOULD YOU QUIT COUGHING?! IT'S GETTING ON MY NERVES!
koff
STILL...
...
AKITO HAD A BAD TEMPER...
clink
...BUT I THINK IT WAS DIFFERENT FROM HOW HE IS NOW.
COME TO THINK OF IT...
HE WOULD EVEN CRY.
IF I'M REMEMBERING RIGHT.

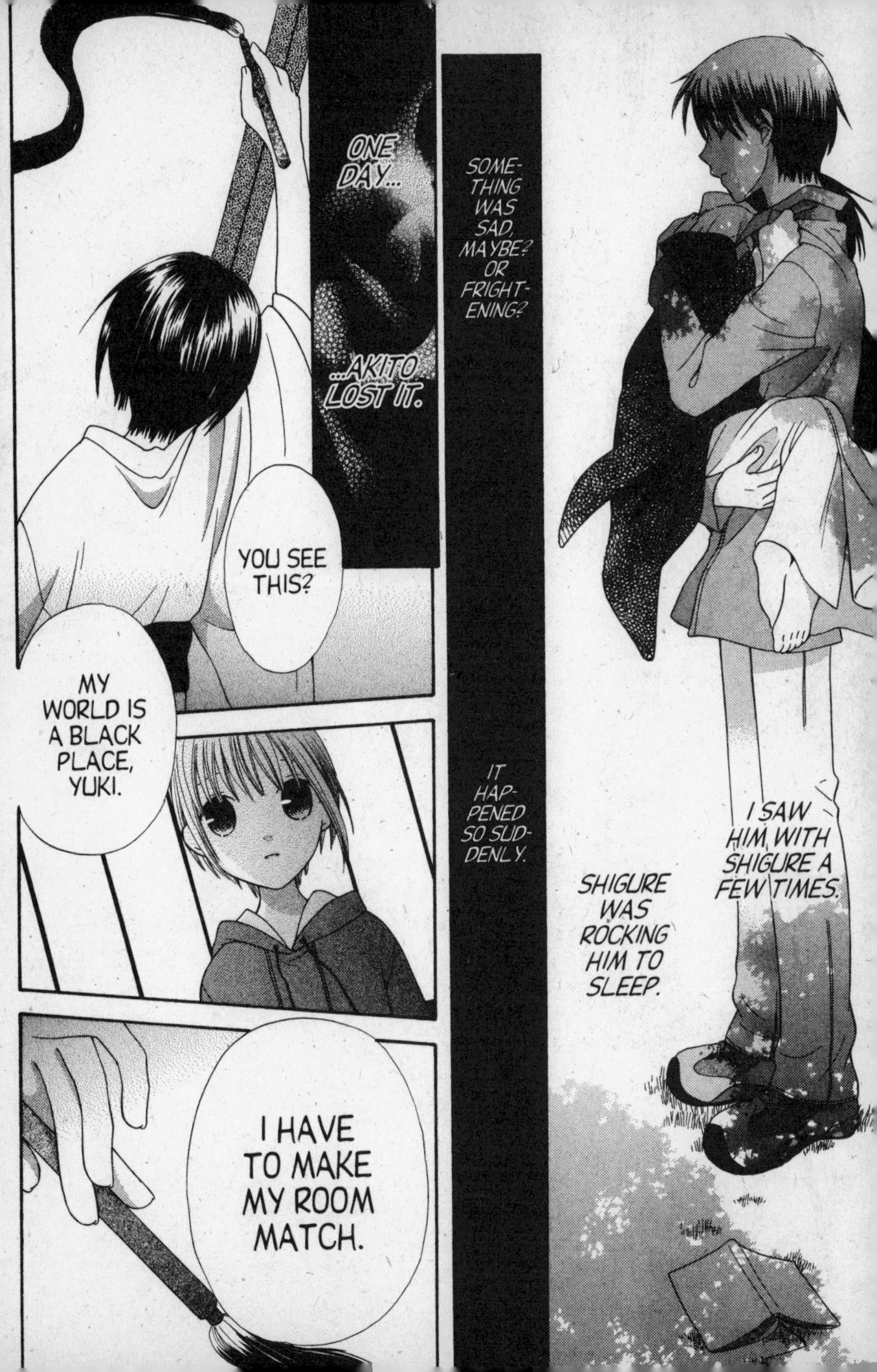
I SAW HIM WITH SHIGURE A FEW TIMES.
SHIGURE WAS ROCKING HIM TO SLEEP.
SOME-THING WAS SAD, MAYBE? OR FRIGHT-ENING?
IT HAP-PENED SO SUD-DENLY.
ONE DAY...
...AKITO LOST IT.
YOU SEE THIS?
MY WORLD IS A BLACK PLACE, YUKI.
I HAVE TO MAKE MY ROOM MATCH.

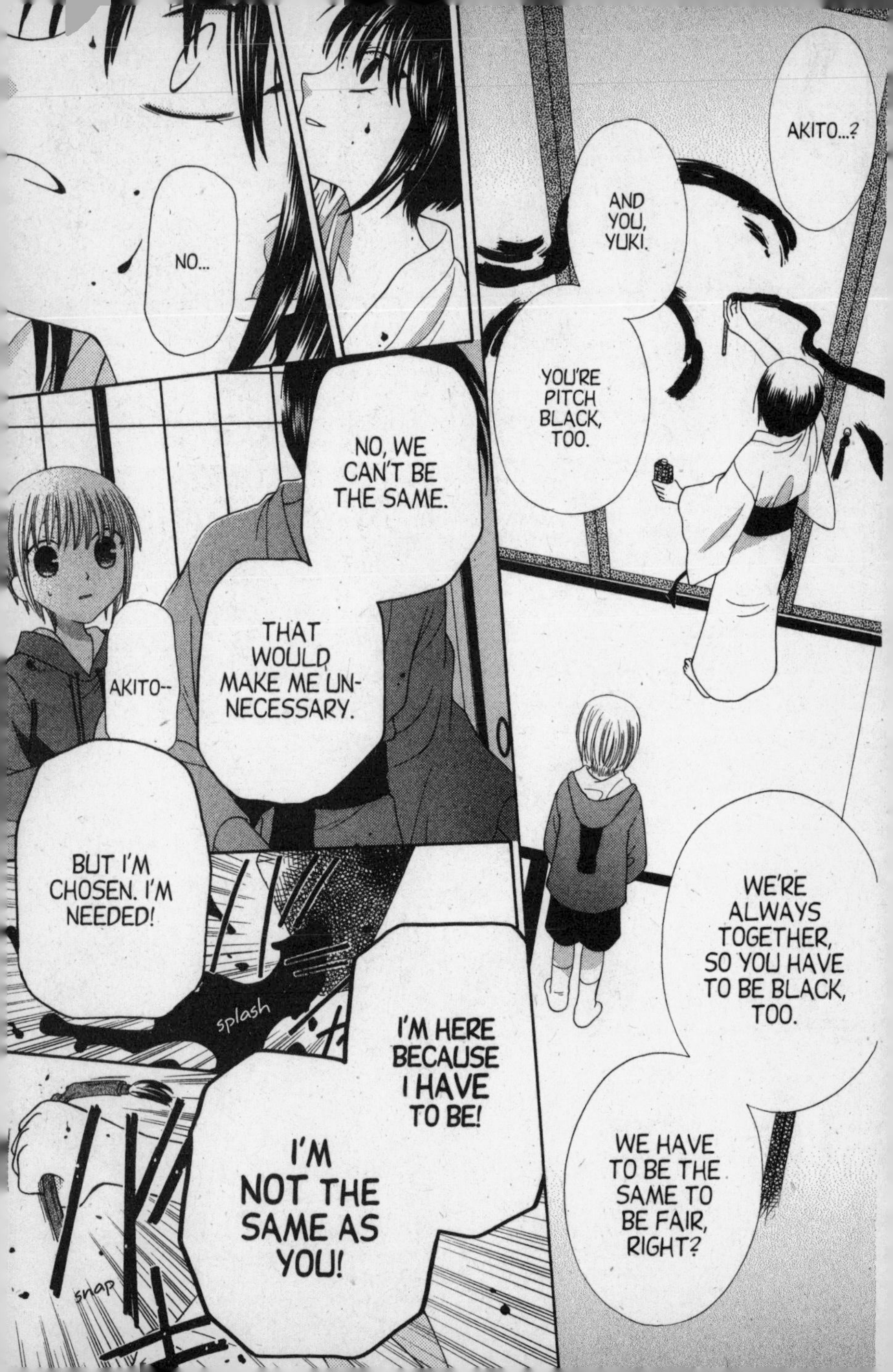
AKITO...?
AND YOU, YUKI.
YOU'RE PITCH BLACK, TOO.
WE'RE ALWAYS TOGETHER, SO YOU HAVE TO BE BLACK, TOO.
WE HAVE TO BE THE SAME TO BE FAIR, RIGHT?
NO...
NO, WE CAN'T BE THE SAME.
THAT WOULD MAKE ME UN-NECESSARY.
AKITO--
BUT I'M CHOSEN. I'M NEEDED!
splash
I'M HERE BECAUSE I HAVE TO BE!
I'M NOT THE SAME AS YOU!
snap

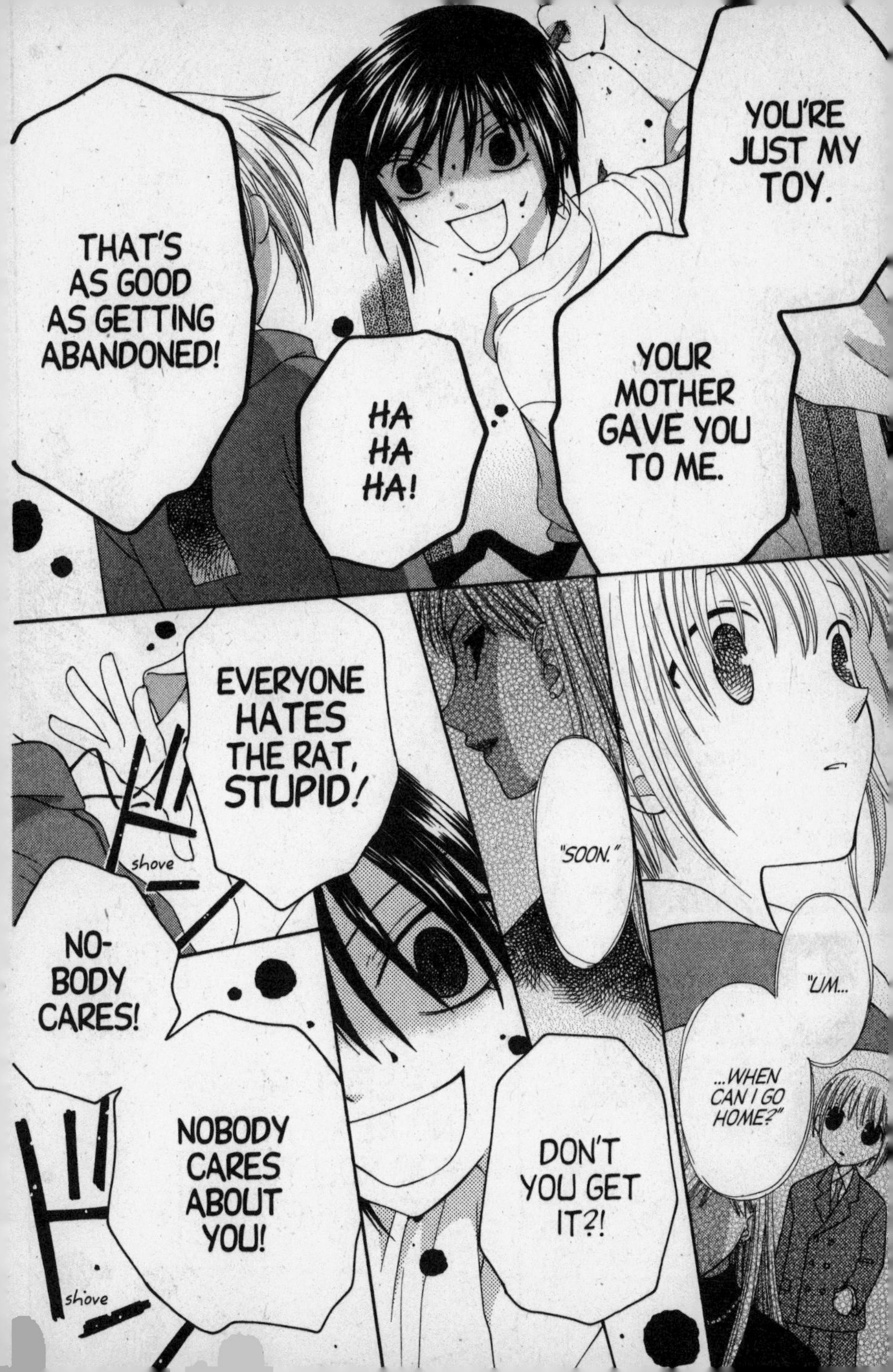
YOU'RE JUST MY TOY.
YOUR MOTHER GAVE YOU TO ME.
HA HA HA!
THAT'S AS GOOD AS GETTING ABANDONED!
"UM...
...WHEN CAN I GO HOME?"
"SOON."
EVERYONE HATES THE RAT, STUPID!
shove
NO-BODY CARES!
DON'T YOU GET IT?!
NOBODY CARES ABOUT YOU!
shove

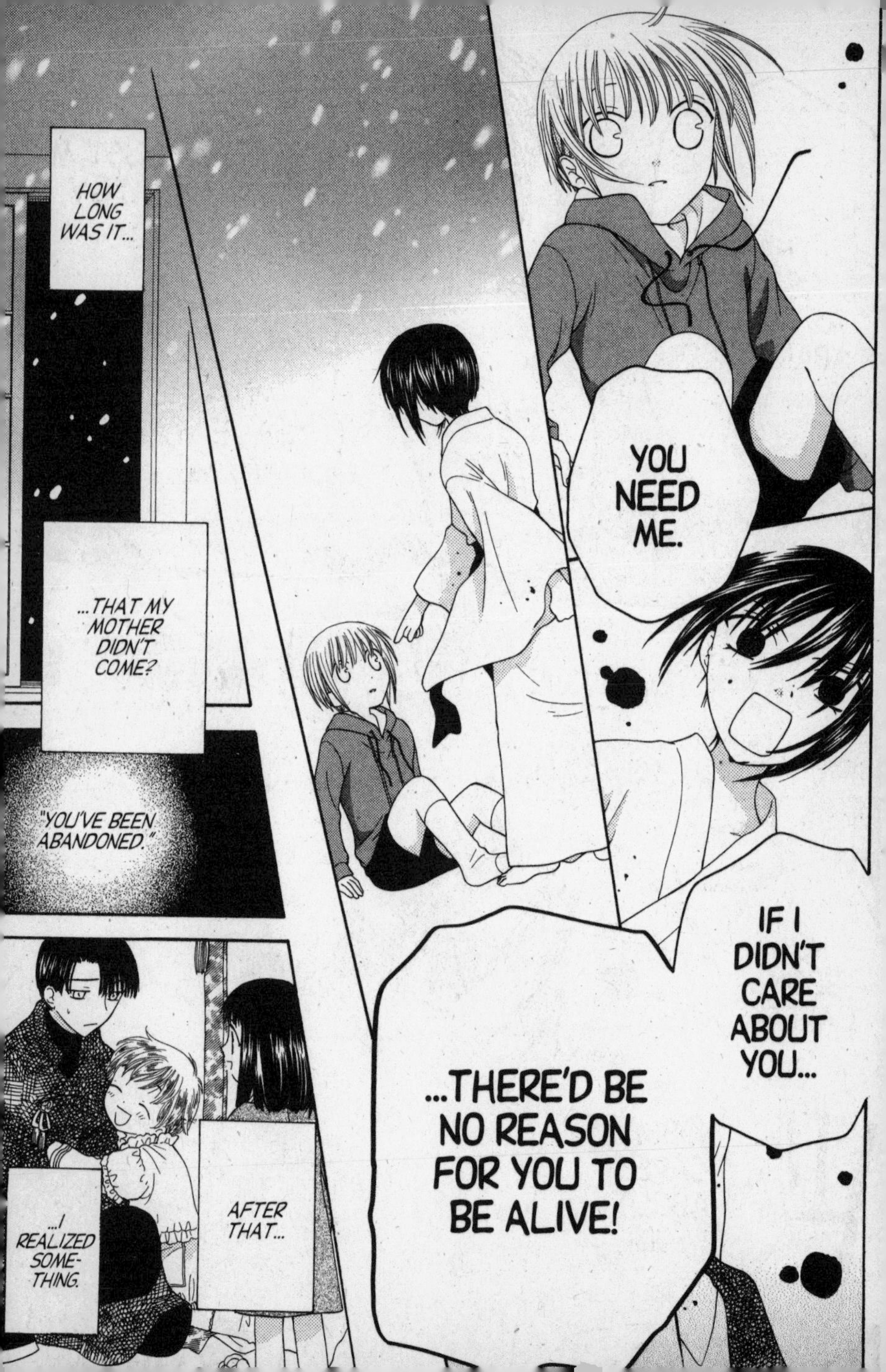
YOU NEED ME.
IF I DIDN'T CARE ABOUT YOU...
...THERE'D BE NO REASON FOR YOU TO BE ALIVE!
HOW LONG WAS IT...
...THAT MY MOTHER DIDN'T COME?
"YOU'VE BEEN ABANDONED."
AFTER THAT...
...I REALIZED SOME-THING.

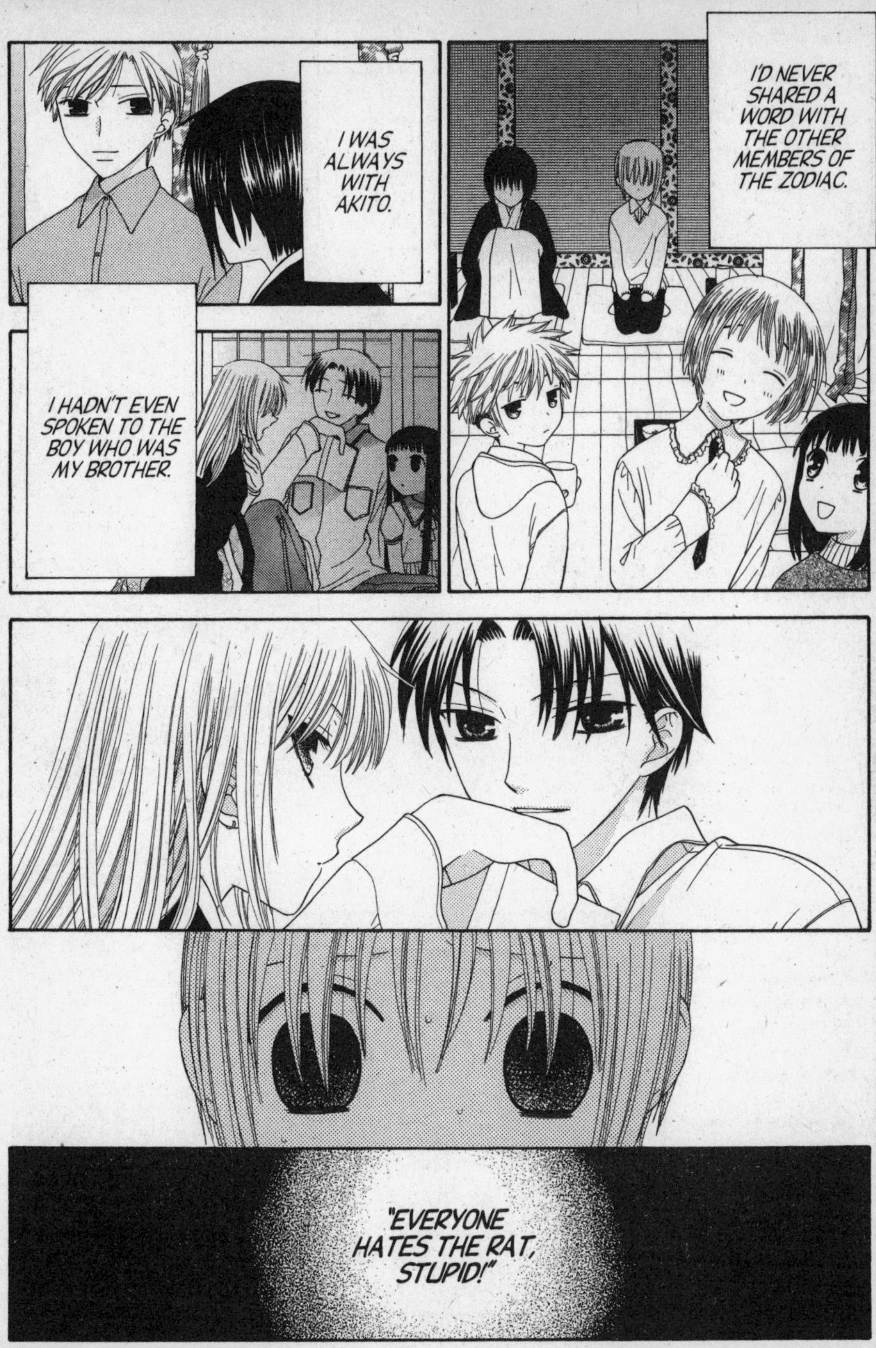
I'D NEVER SHARED A WORD WITH THE OTHER MEMBERS OF THE ZODIAC.
I WAS ALWAYS WITH AKITO.
I HADN'T EVEN SPOKEN TO THE BOY WHO WAS MY BROTHER.
"EVERYONE HATES THE RAT, STUPID!"

Fruits Basket 15

Nice to meet you! I'm Takaya, and this is Volume 15.

...That's right, folks--we're all the way to Volume 15.

The cover is Akkii this time around. I think various aspects of Akkii's background--or true nature, maybe? circumstances, perhaps?--have been revealed by now in *Hana to Yume* magazine. (Finally.)

For those of you who only read this series in book format, you still have a little while before you can read all that--but I won't give any spoilers in these columns, so not to worry. Having Akito on the cover of the book that talks about Yuki's past... it's another aftereffect of their unbreakable bond, I guess. Sorry, Yun-chan. I didn't do that on purpose.

Anyway, please enjoy Volume 15.

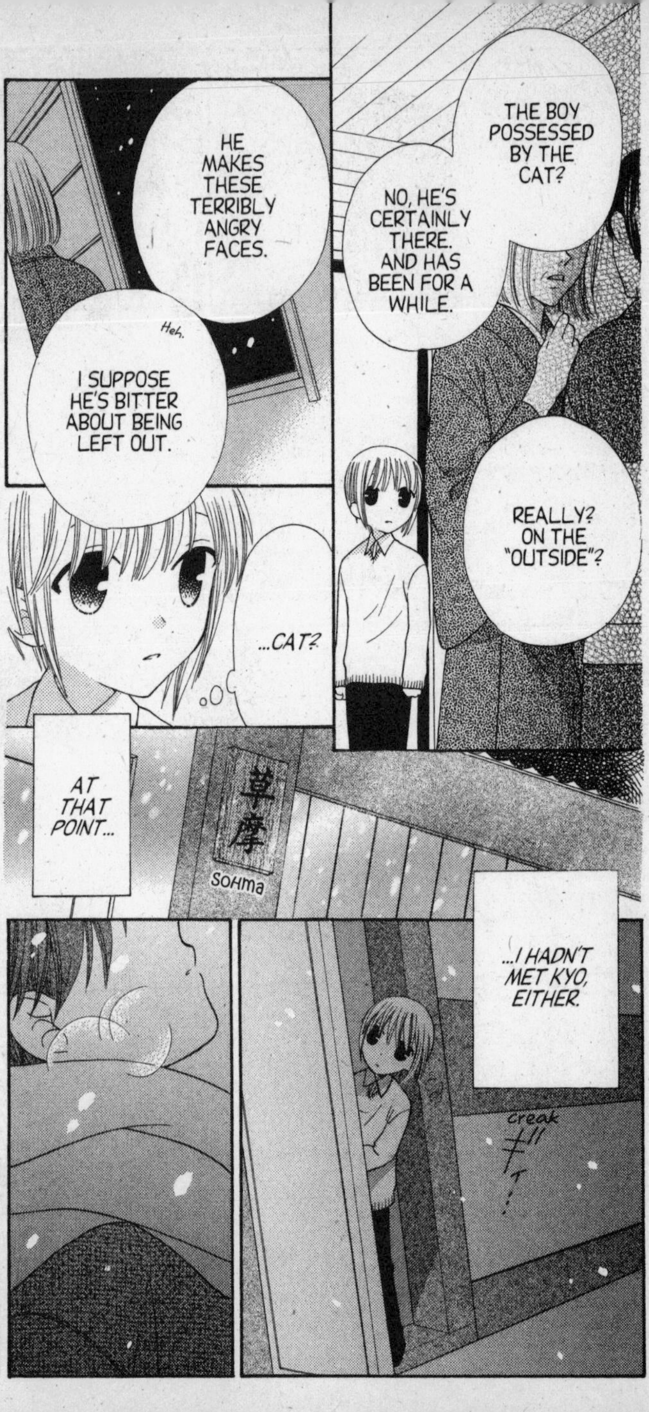
THE BOY POSSESSED BY THE CAT?
NO, HE'S CERTAINLY THERE. AND HAS BEEN FOR A WHILE.
REALLY? ON THE "OUTSIDE"?
HE MAKES THESE TERRIBLY ANGRY FACES.
Heh.
I SUPPOSE HE'S BITTER ABOUT BEING LEFT OUT.
...CAT?
AT THAT POINT...
草摩
SOHMA
...I HADN'T MET KYO, EITHER.
creak

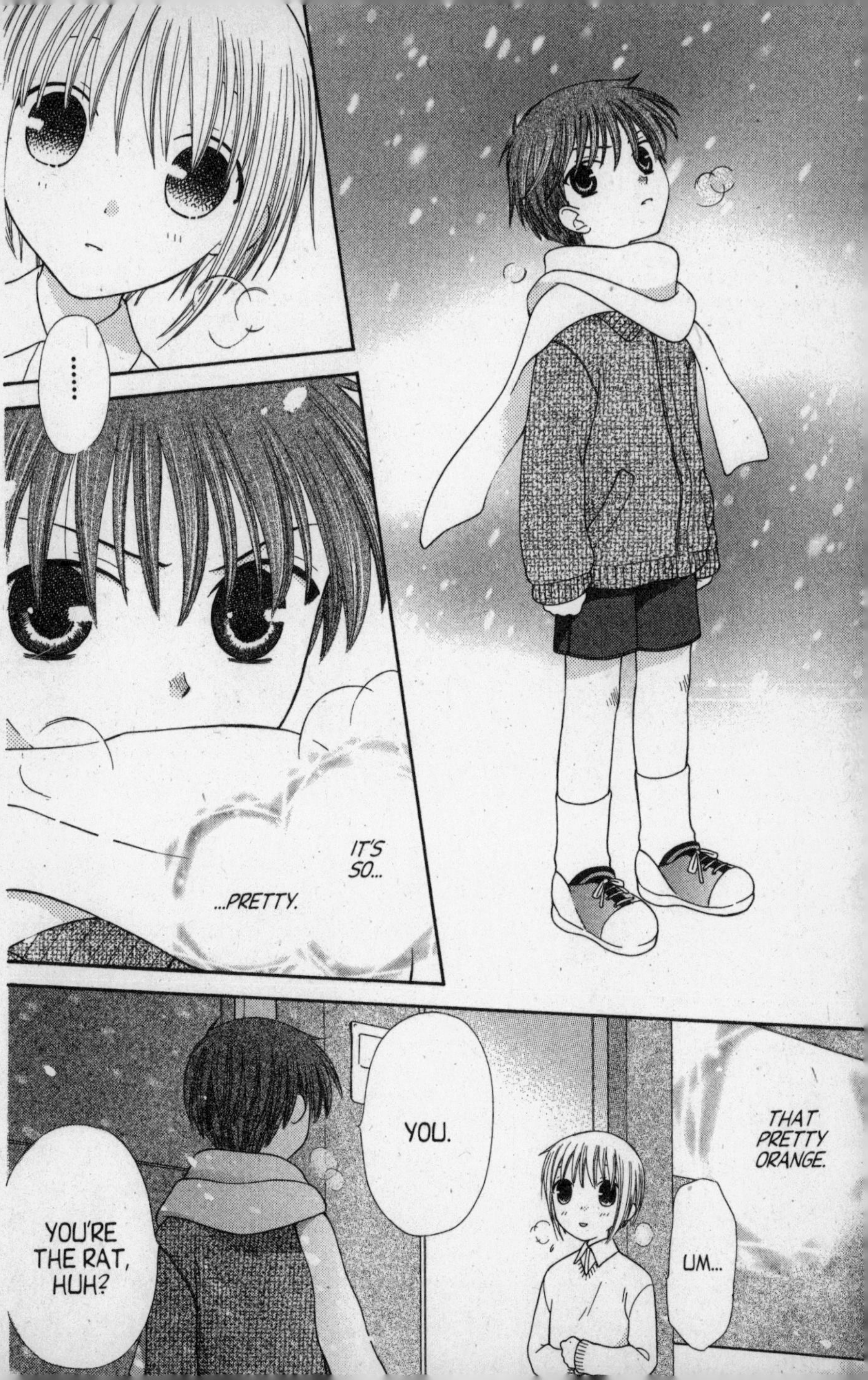
......
IT'S SO...
...PRETTY.
THAT PRETTY ORANGE.
UM...
YOU.
YOU'RE THE RAT, HUH?

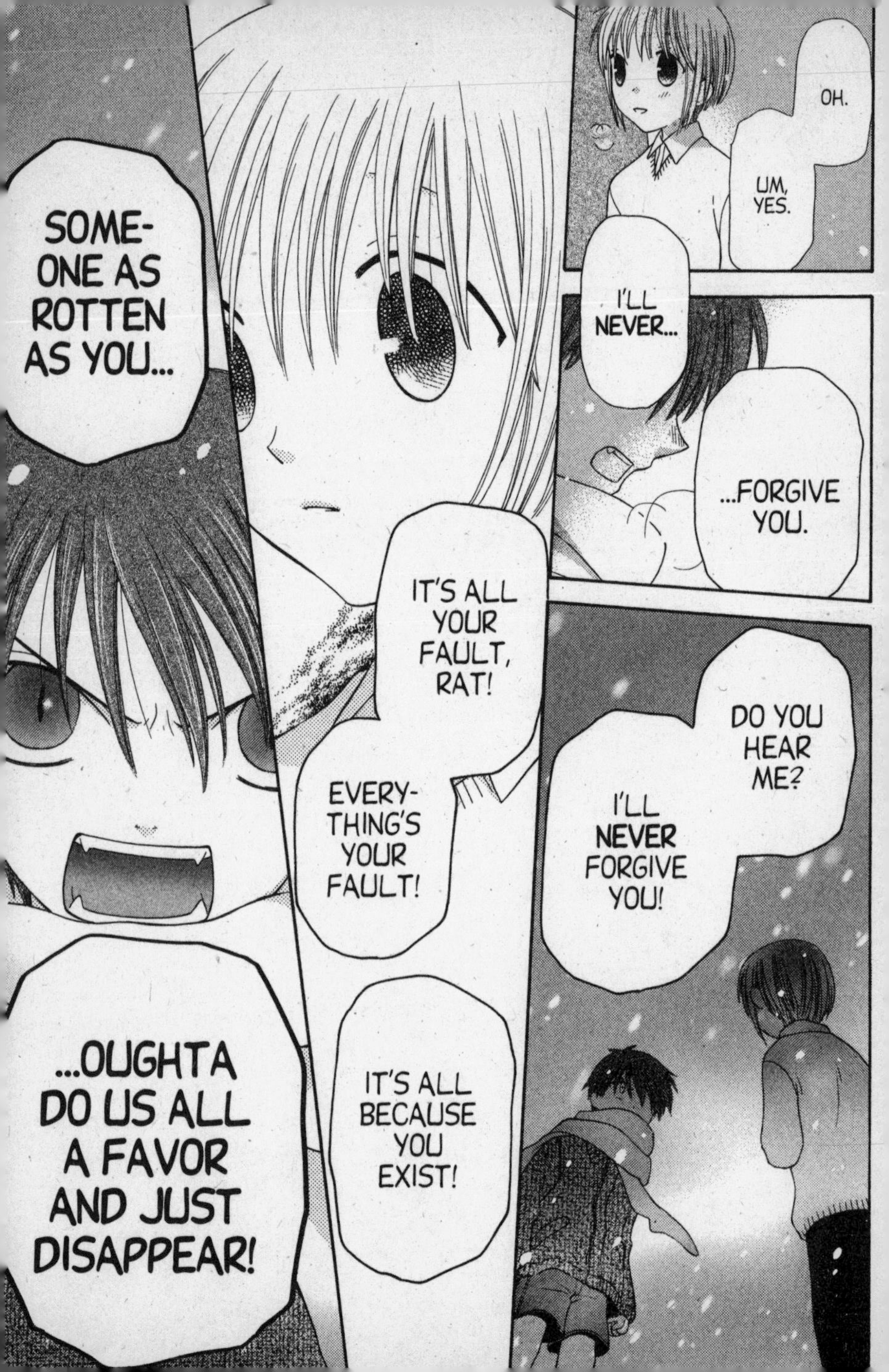
OH.
UM, YES.
I'LL NEVER...
...FORGIVE YOU.
DO YOU HEAR ME?
I'LL NEVER FORGIVE YOU!
IT'S ALL YOUR FAULT, RAT!
EVERYTHING'S YOUR FAULT!
IT'S ALL BECAUSE YOU EXIST!
SOMEONE AS ROTTEN AS YOU...
...OUGHTA DO US ALL A FAVOR AND JUST DISAPPEAR!

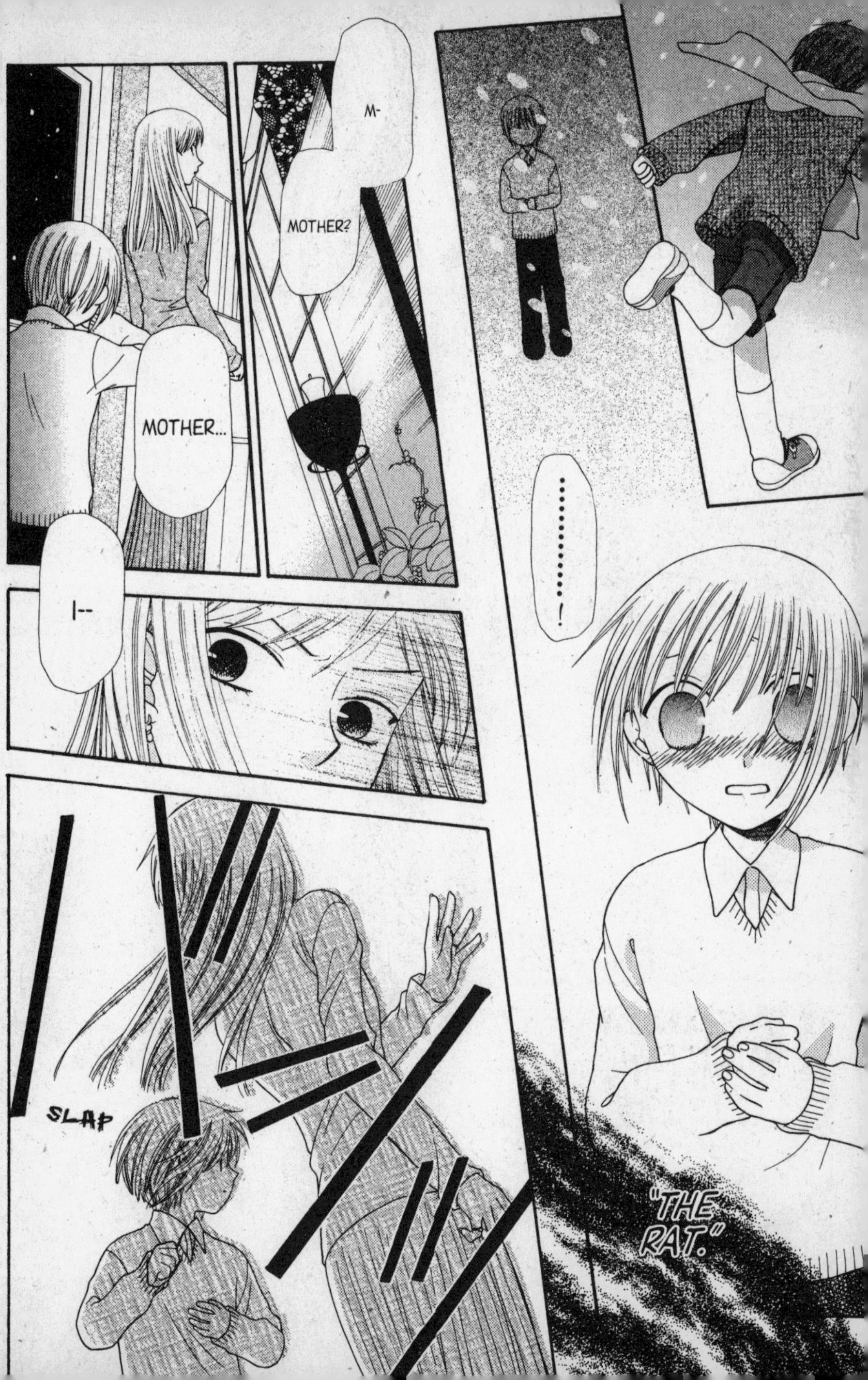

......!
"THE RAT."
M-
MOTHER?
MOTHER...
I--
SLAP

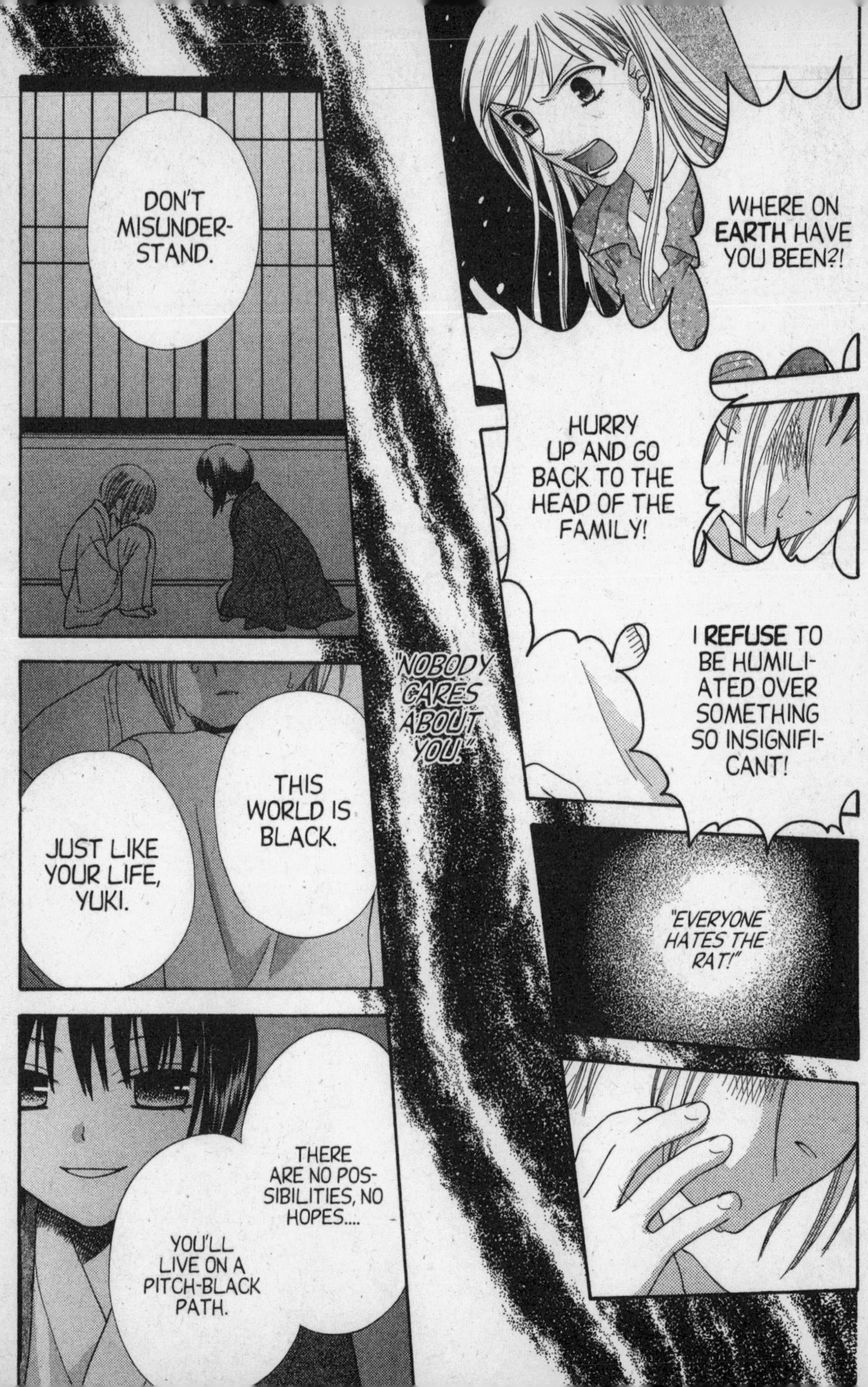
WHERE ON **EARTH** HAVE YOU BEEN?!
HURRY UP AND GO BACK TO THE HEAD OF THE FAMILY!
I **REFUSE** TO BE HUMILIATED OVER SOMETHING SO INSIGNIFICANT!
"EVERYONE HATES THE RAT!"
"NOBODY CARES ABOUT YOU."
DON'T MISUNDERSTAND.
THIS WORLD IS BLACK.
JUST LIKE YOUR LIFE, YUKI.
THERE ARE NO POSSIBILITIES, NO HOPES....
YOU'LL LIVE ON A PITCH-BLACK PATH.

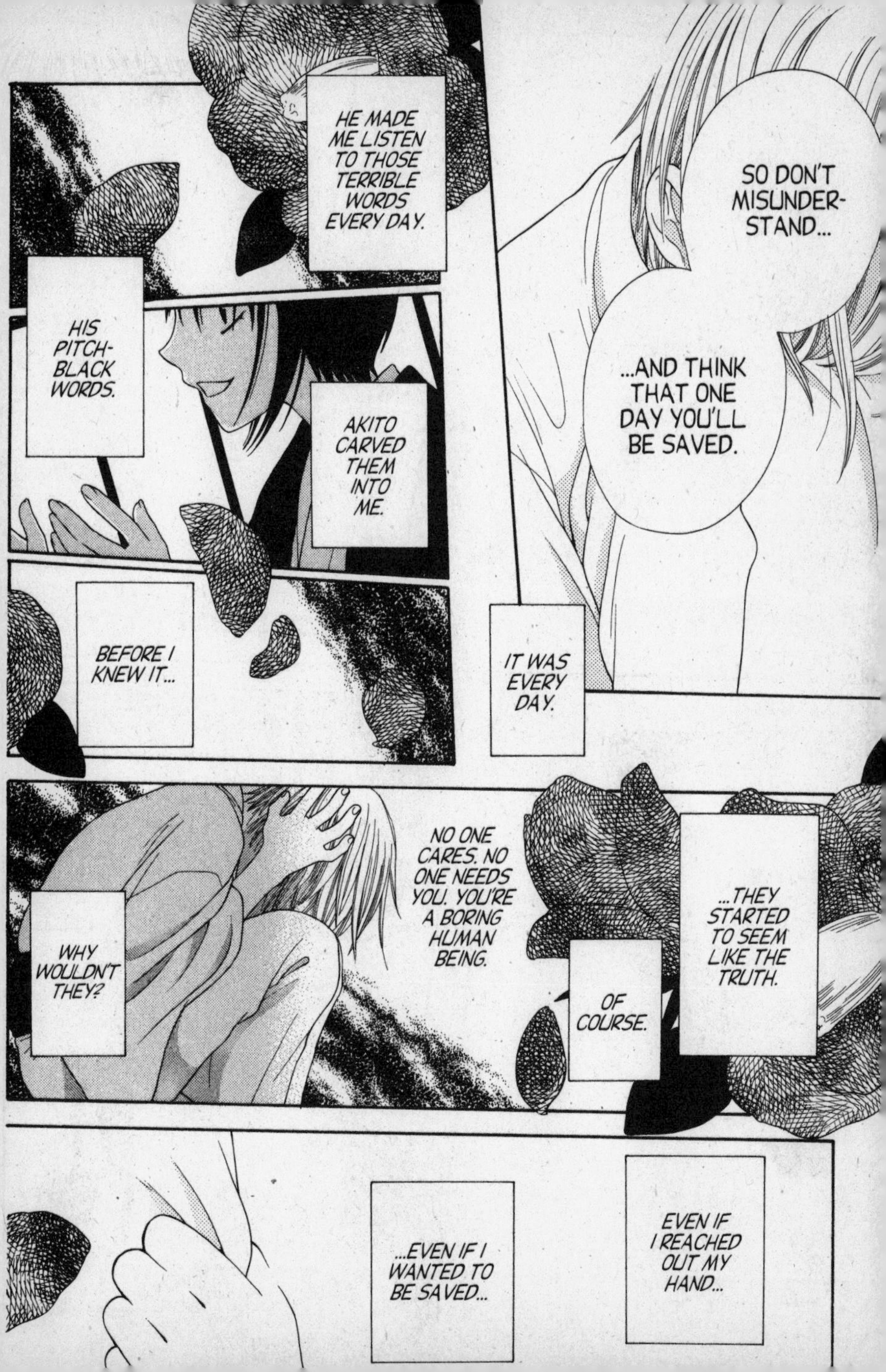
SO DON'T MISUNDERSTAND...
...AND THINK THAT ONE DAY YOU'LL BE SAVED.
IT WAS EVERY DAY.
HE MADE ME LISTEN TO THOSE TERRIBLE WORDS EVERY DAY.
HIS PITCH-BLACK WORDS.
AKITO CARVED THEM INTO ME.
BEFORE I KNEW IT...
...THEY STARTED TO SEEM LIKE THE TRUTH.
OF COURSE.
NO ONE CARES. NO ONE NEEDS YOU. YOU'RE A BORING HUMAN BEING.
WHY WOULDN'T THEY?
EVEN IF I REACHED OUT MY HAND...
...EVEN IF I WANTED TO BE SAVED...

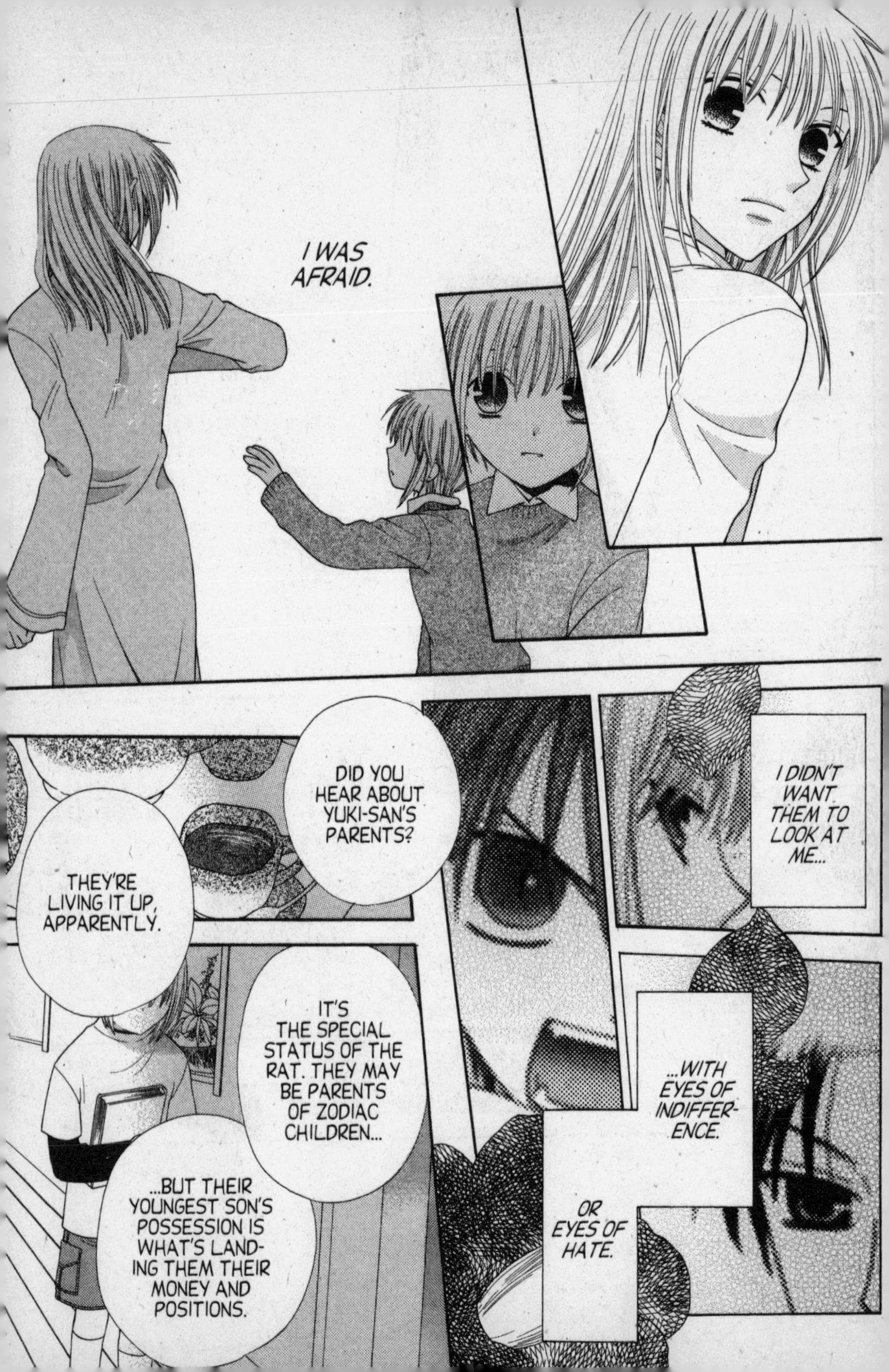
I WAS AFRAID.
I DIDN'T WANT THEM TO LOOK AT ME...
...WITH EYES OF INDIFFERENCE.
OR EYES OF HATE.
DID YOU HEAR ABOUT YUKI-SAN'S PARENTS?
THEY'RE LIVING IT UP, APPARENTLY.
IT'S THE SPECIAL STATUS OF THE RAT. THEY MAY BE PARENTS OF ZODIAC CHILDREN...
...BUT THEIR YOUNGEST SON'S POSSESSION IS WHAT'S LANDING THEM THEIR MONEY AND POSITIONS.

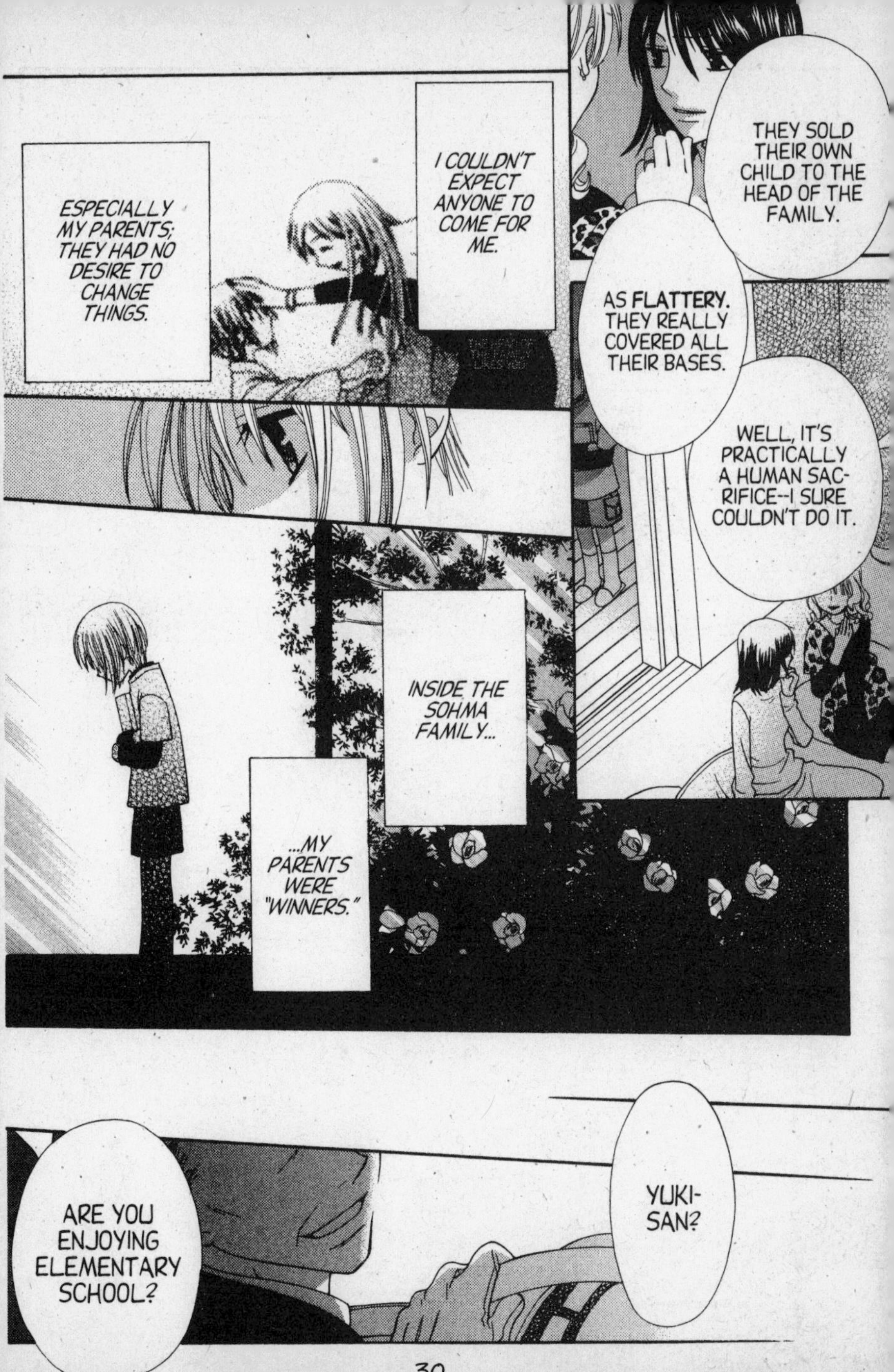
THEY SOLD THEIR OWN CHILD TO THE HEAD OF THE FAMILY.
AS **FLATTERY.** THEY REALLY COVERED ALL THEIR BASES.
WELL, IT'S PRACTICALLY A HUMAN SACRIFICE--I SURE COULDN'T DO IT.
I COULDN'T EXPECT ANYONE TO COME FOR ME.
ESPECIALLY MY PARENTS; THEY HAD NO DESIRE TO CHANGE THINGS.
INSIDE THE SOHMA FAMILY...
...MY PARENTS WERE "WINNERS."
YUKI-SAN?
ARE YOU ENJOYING ELEMENTARY SCHOOL?

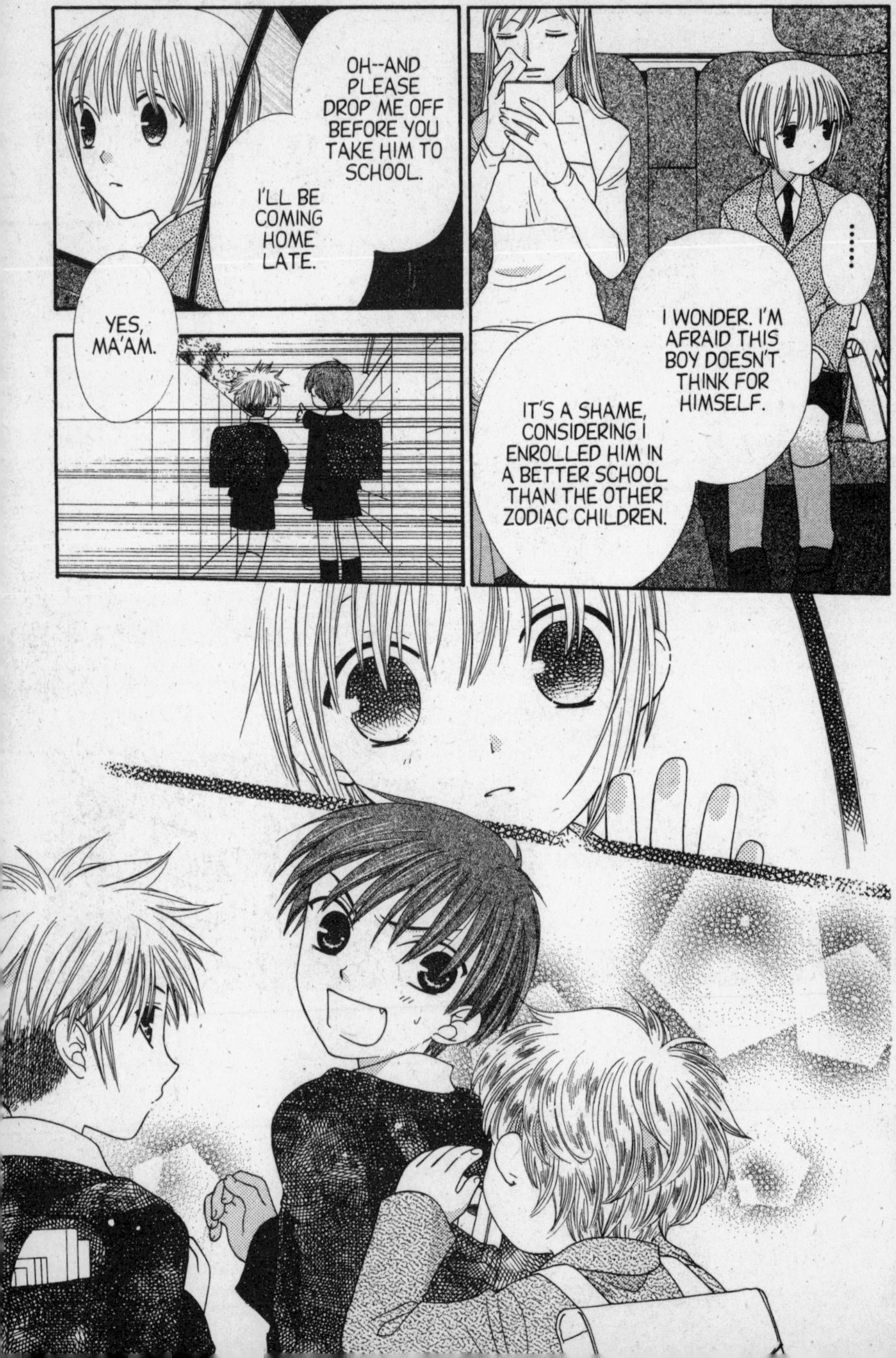
......
I WONDER. I'M AFRAID THIS BOY DOESN'T THINK FOR HIMSELF.
IT'S A SHAME, CONSIDERING I ENROLLED HIM IN A BETTER SCHOOL THAN THE OTHER ZODIAC CHILDREN.
OH--AND PLEASE DROP ME OFF BEFORE YOU TAKE HIM TO SCHOOL.
I'LL BE COMING HOME LATE.
YES, MA'AM.

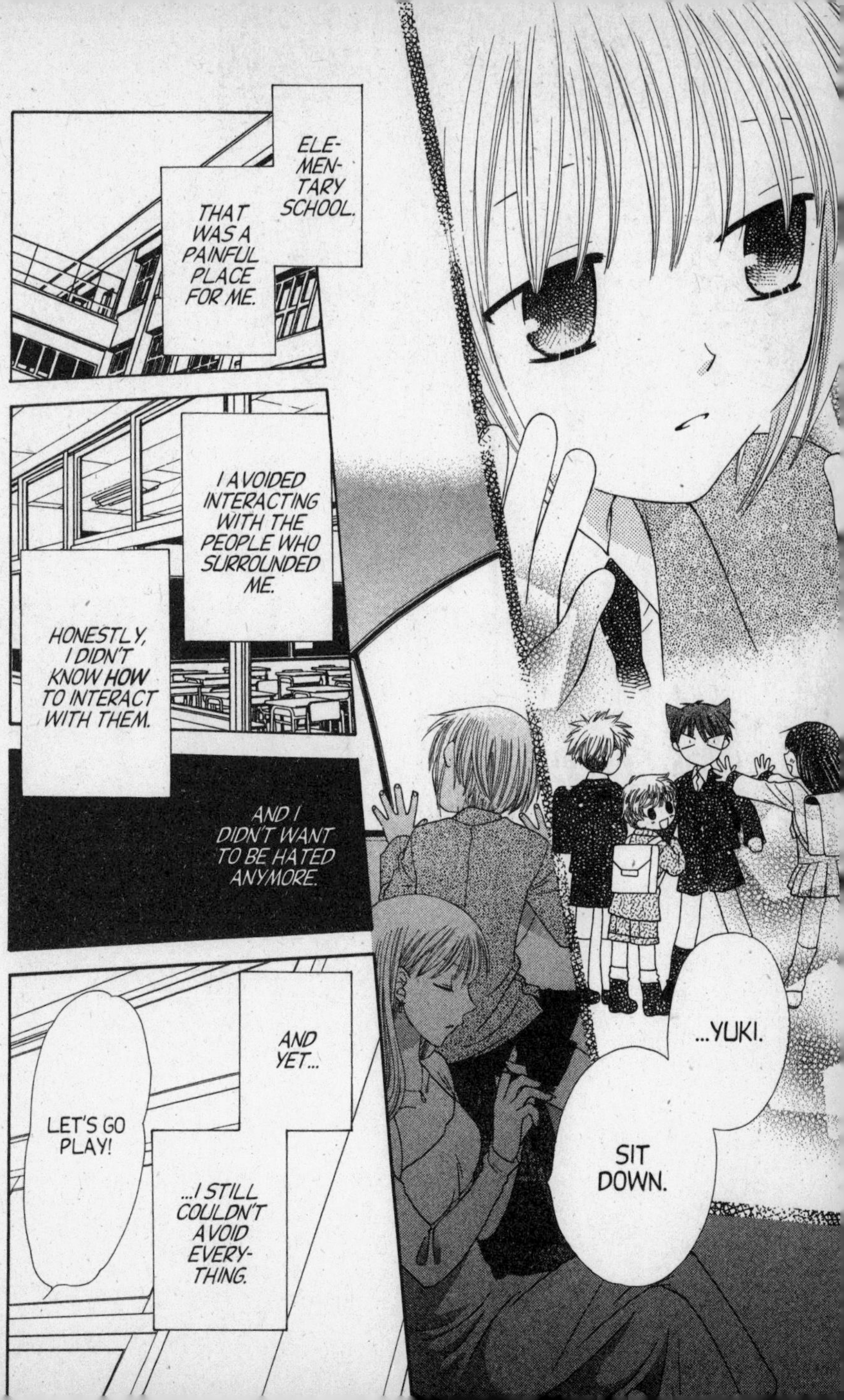
ELEMENTARY SCHOOL.
THAT WAS A PAINFUL PLACE FOR ME.
I AVOIDED INTERACTING WITH THE PEOPLE WHO SURROUNDED ME.
HONESTLY, I DIDN'T KNOW HOW TO INTERACT WITH THEM.
AND I DIDN'T WANT TO BE HATED ANYMORE.
AND YET...
LET'S GO PLAY!
...I STILL COULDN'T AVOID EVERYTHING.
...YUKI.
SIT DOWN.

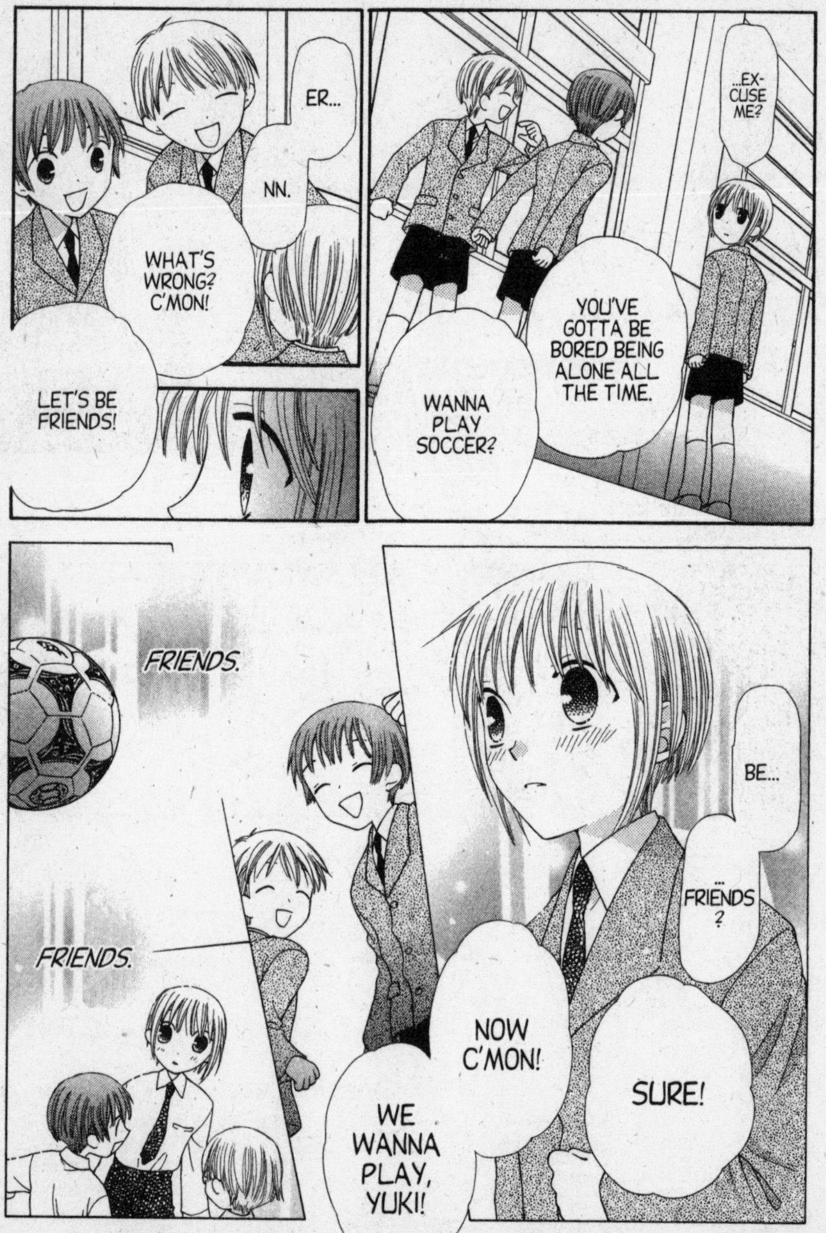
...EX-CUSE ME?
YOU'VE GOTTA BE BORED BEING ALONE ALL THE TIME.
WANNA PLAY SOCCER?
ER...
NN.
WHAT'S WRONG? C'MON!
LET'S BE FRIENDS!
BE...
...FRIENDS?
SURE!
NOW C'MON!
WE WANNA PLAY, YUKI!
FRIENDS.
FRIENDS.

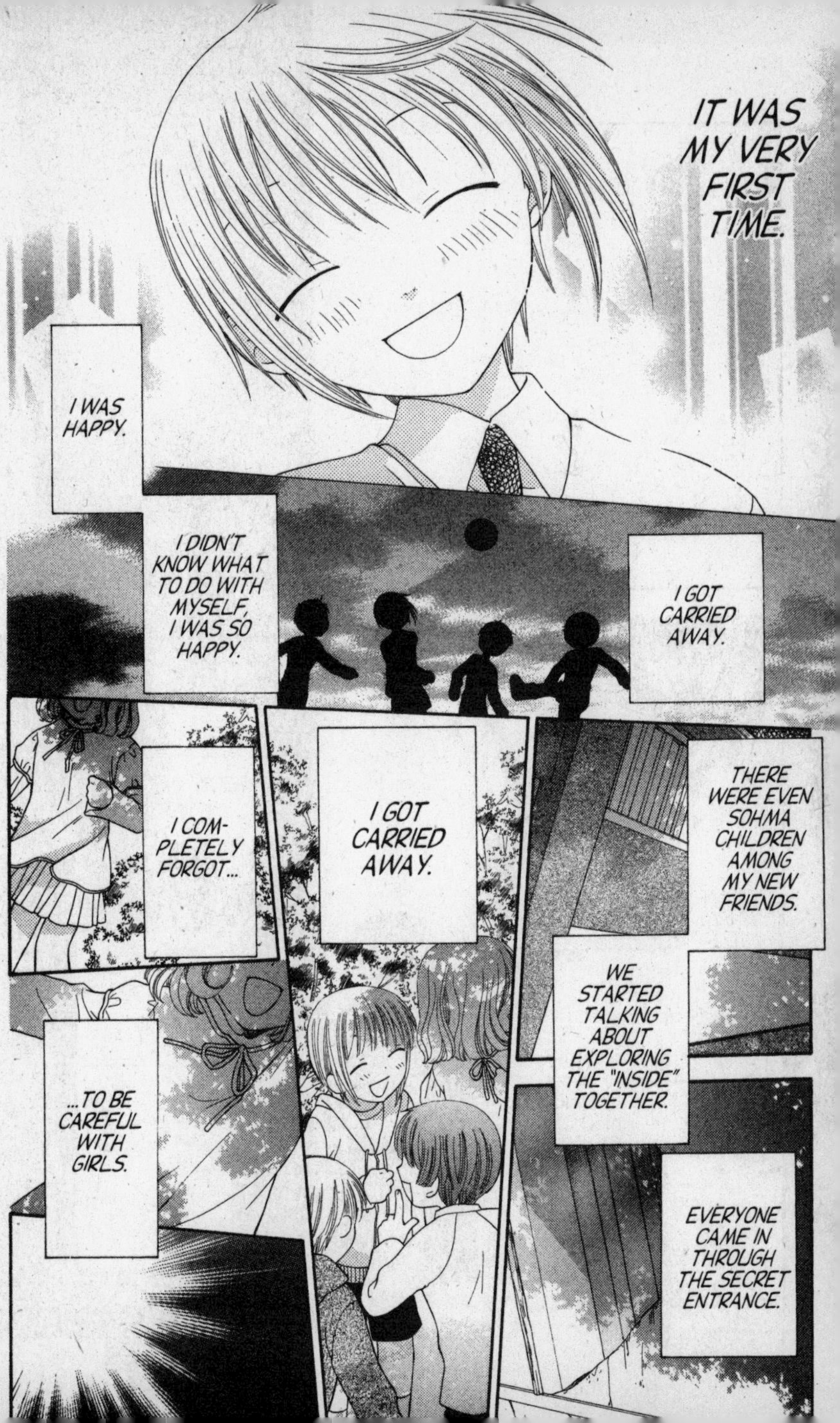
IT WAS MY VERY FIRST TIME.
I WAS HAPPY.
I DIDN'T KNOW WHAT TO DO WITH MYSELF, I WAS SO HAPPY.
I GOT CARRIED AWAY.
THERE WERE EVEN SOHMA CHILDREN AMONG MY NEW FRIENDS.
WE STARTED TALKING ABOUT EXPLORING THE "INSIDE" TOGETHER.
EVERYONE CAME IN THROUGH THE SECRET ENTRANCE.
I GOT CARRIED AWAY.
I COM-PLETELY FORGOT...
...TO BE CAREFUL WITH GIRLS.

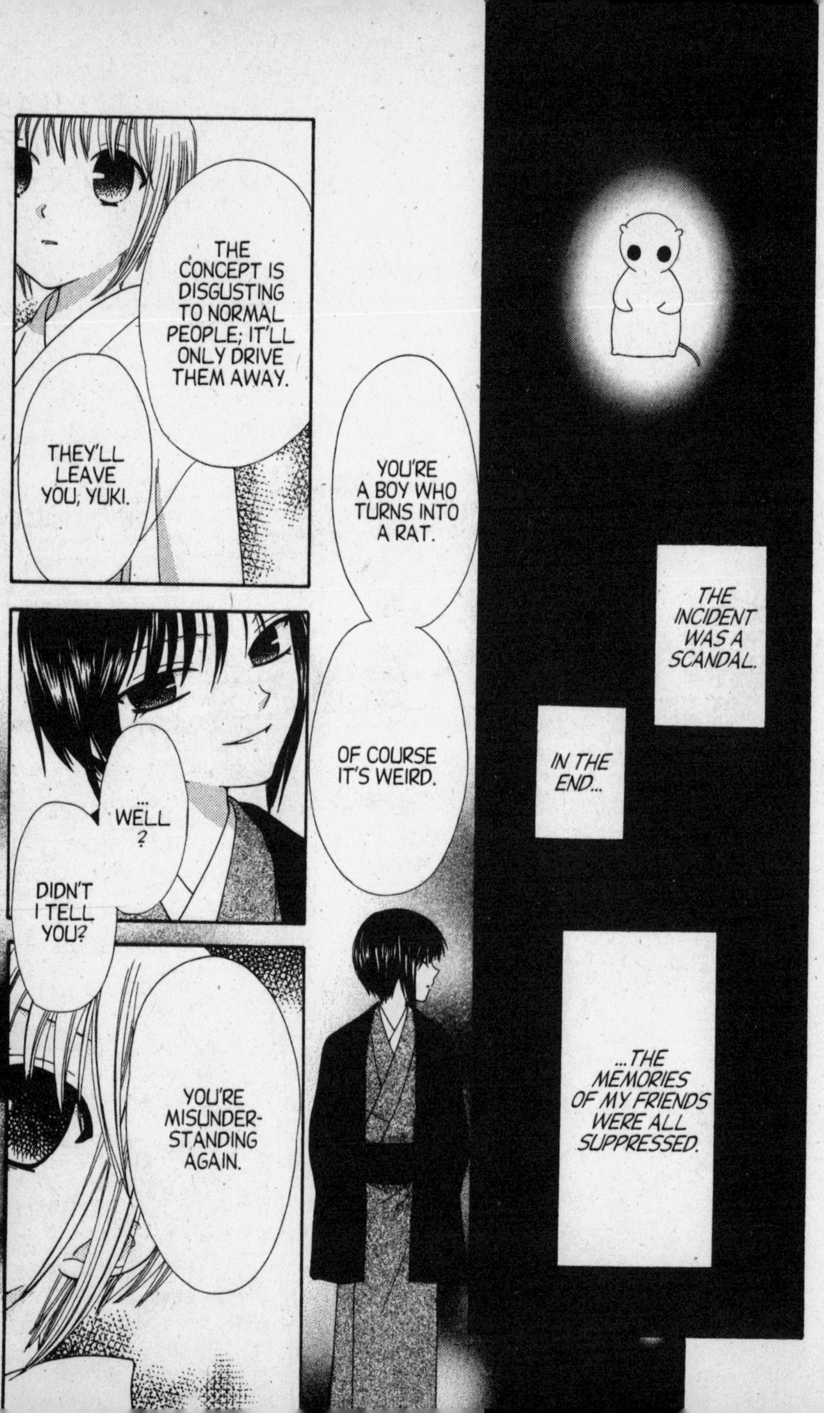
THE INCIDENT WAS A SCANDAL.
IN THE END...
...THE MEMORIES OF MY FRIENDS WERE ALL SUPPRESSED.
YOU'RE A BOY WHO TURNS INTO A RAT.
OF COURSE IT'S WEIRD.
THE CONCEPT IS DISGUSTING TO NORMAL PEOPLE; IT'LL ONLY DRIVE THEM AWAY.
THEY'LL LEAVE YOU, YUKI.
...WELL?
DIDN'T I TELL YOU?
YOU'RE MISUNDER-STANDING AGAIN.

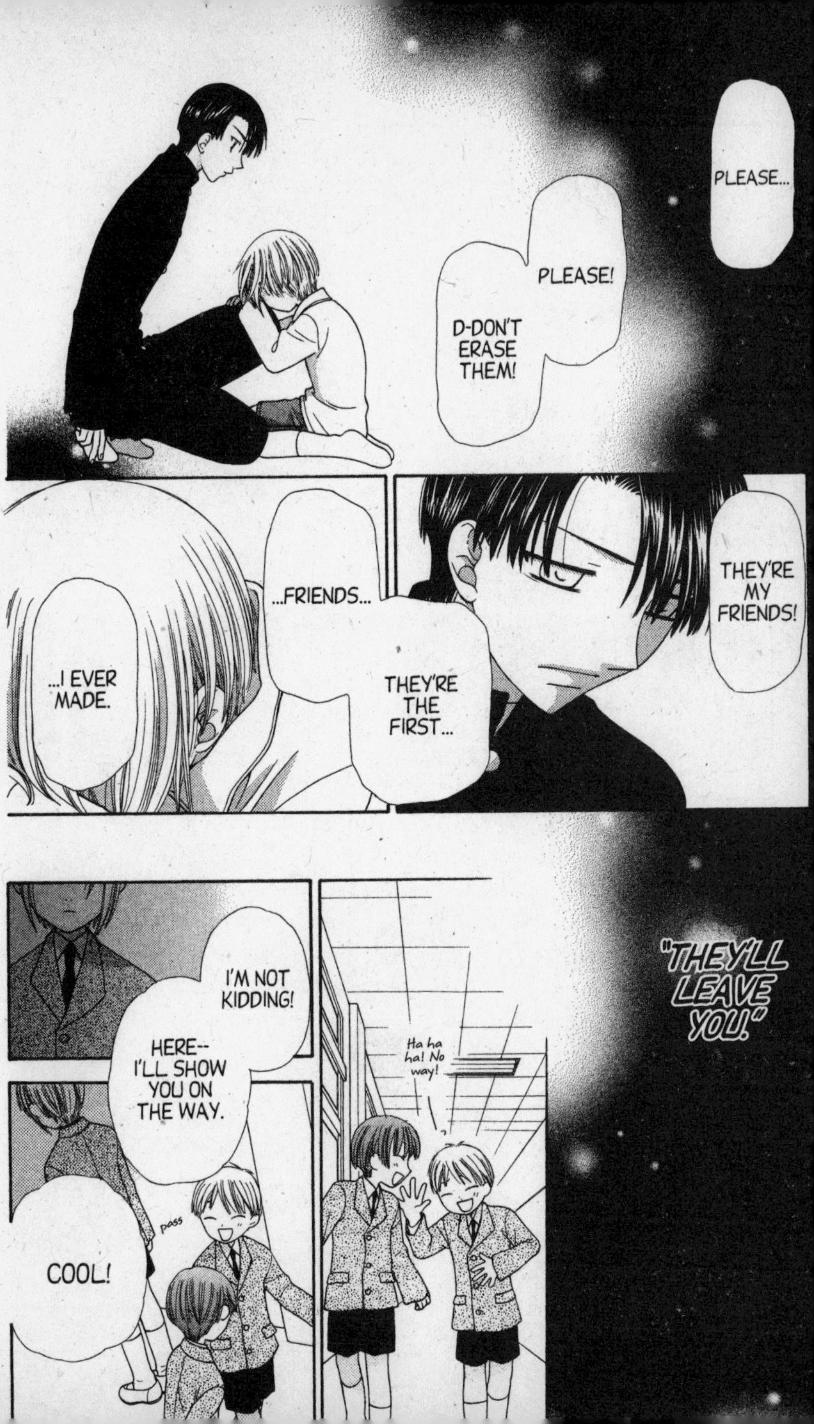
PLEASE...
PLEASE!
D-DON'T ERASE THEM!
THEY'RE MY FRIENDS!
THEY'RE THE FIRST...
...FRIENDS...
...I EVER MADE.
"THEY'LL LEAVE YOU."
Ha ha ha! No way!
I'M NOT KIDDING!
HERE-- I'LL SHOW YOU ON THE WAY.
pass
COOL!

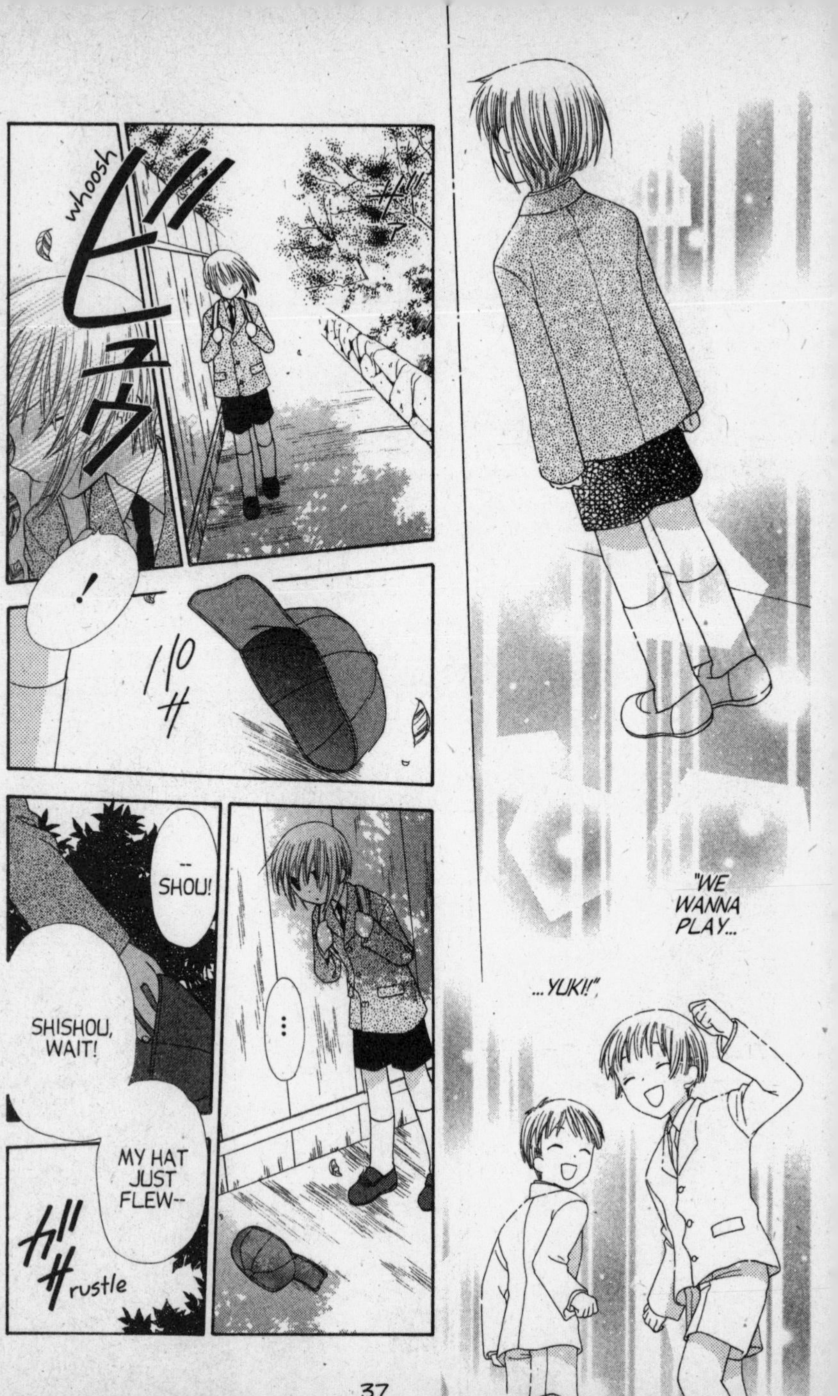
"WE WANNA PLAY...
...YUKI!"
whoosh
!
--SHOU!
...
SHISHOU, WAIT!
MY HAT JUST FLEW--
rustle

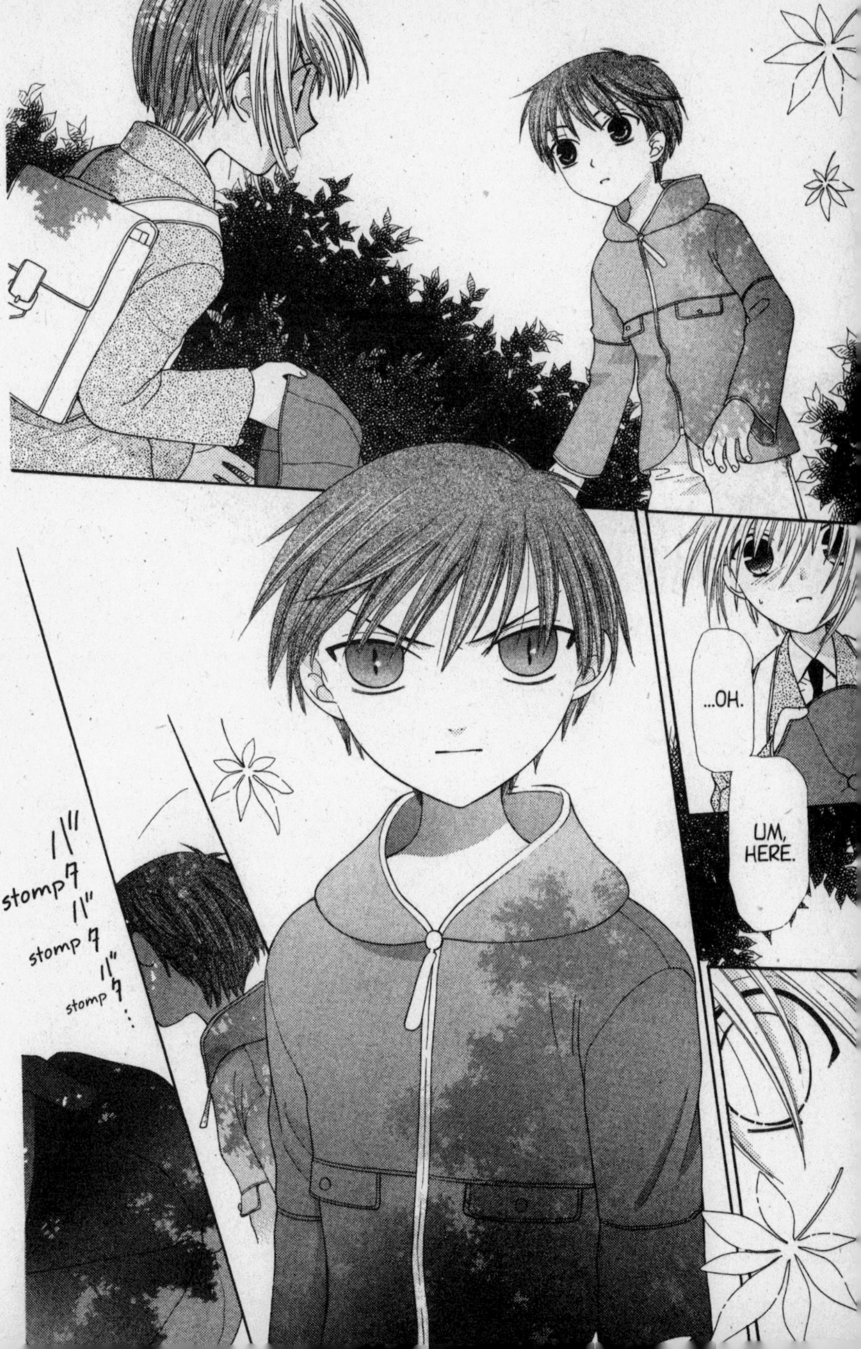
...OH.
UM, HERE.
バ stomp
バ stomp
バ stomp...

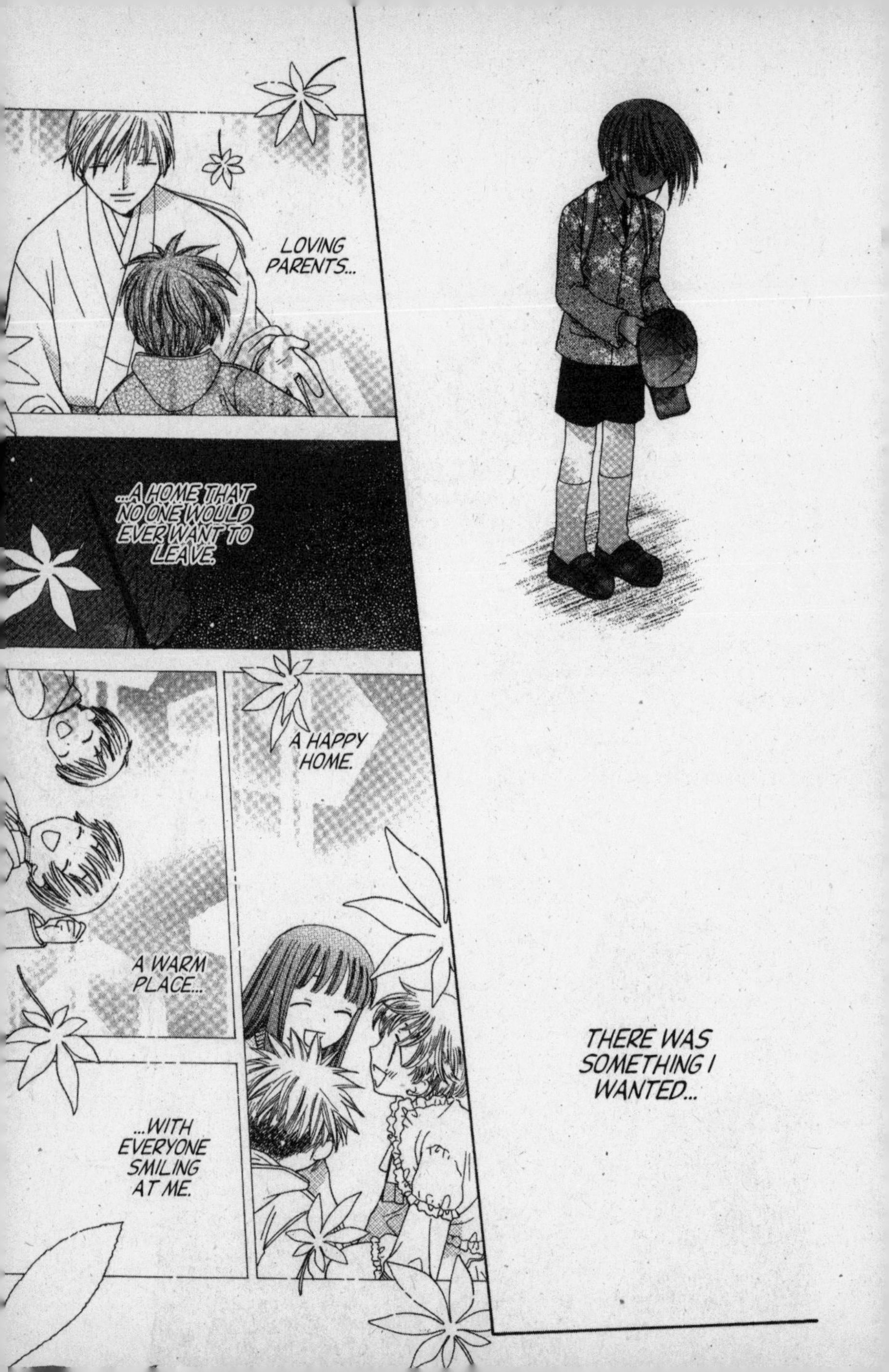
THERE WAS SOMETHING I WANTED...
LOVING PARENTS...
...A HOME THAT NO ONE WOULD EVER WANT TO LEAVE.
A HAPPY HOME.
A WARM PLACE...
...WITH EVERYONE SMILING AT ME.

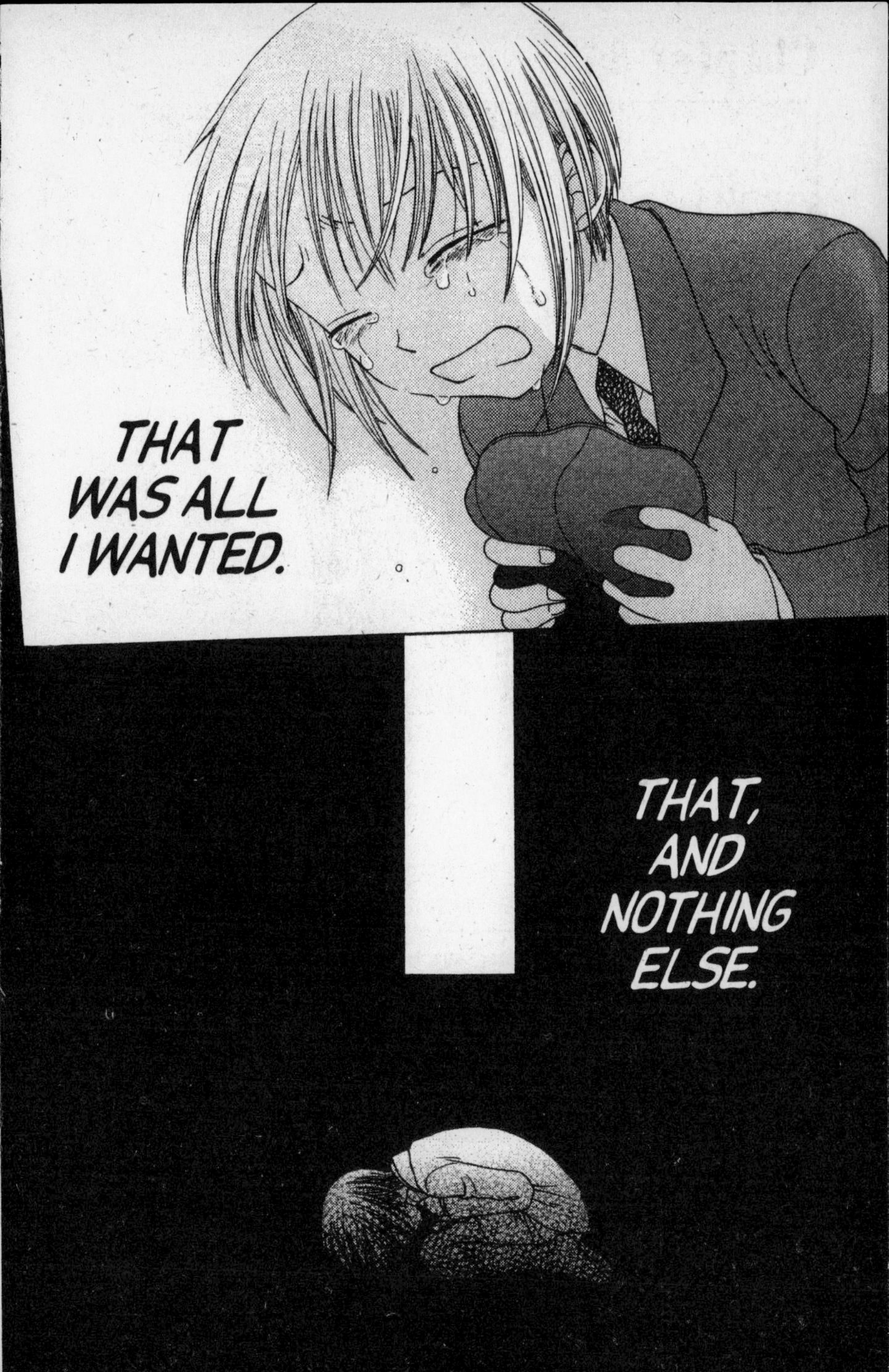
THAT WAS ALL I WANTED.
THAT, AND NOTHING ELSE.

Chapter 85

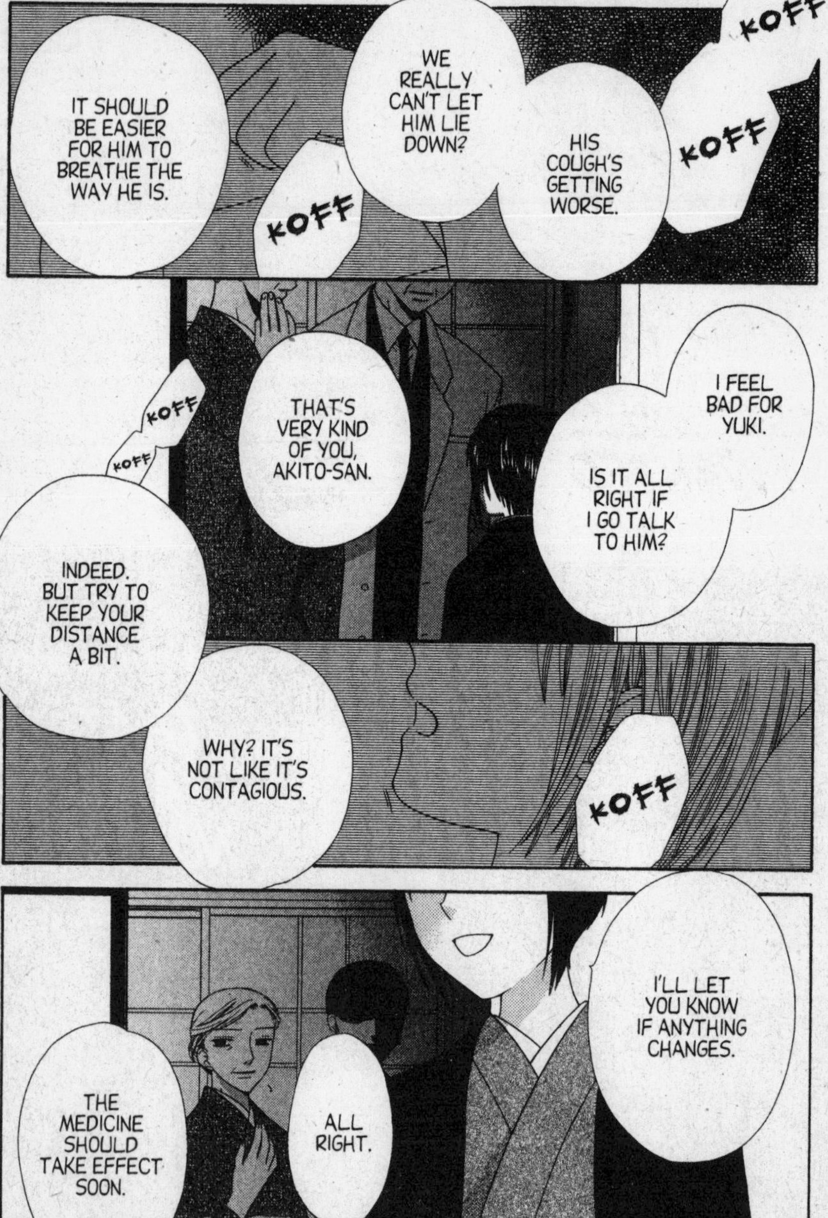

KOFF
KOFF
HIS COUGH'S GETTING WORSE.
WE REALLY CAN'T LET HIM LIE DOWN?
KOFF
IT SHOULD BE EASIER FOR HIM TO BREATHE THE WAY HE IS.
I FEEL BAD FOR YUKI.
IS IT ALL RIGHT IF I GO TALK TO HIM?
THAT'S VERY KIND OF YOU, AKITO-SAN.
KOFF
KOFF
INDEED. BUT TRY TO KEEP YOUR DISTANCE A BIT.
KOFF
WHY? IT'S NOT LIKE IT'S CONTAGIOUS.
I'LL LET YOU KNOW IF ANYTHING CHANGES.
ALL RIGHT.
THE MEDICINE SHOULD TAKE EFFECT SOON.

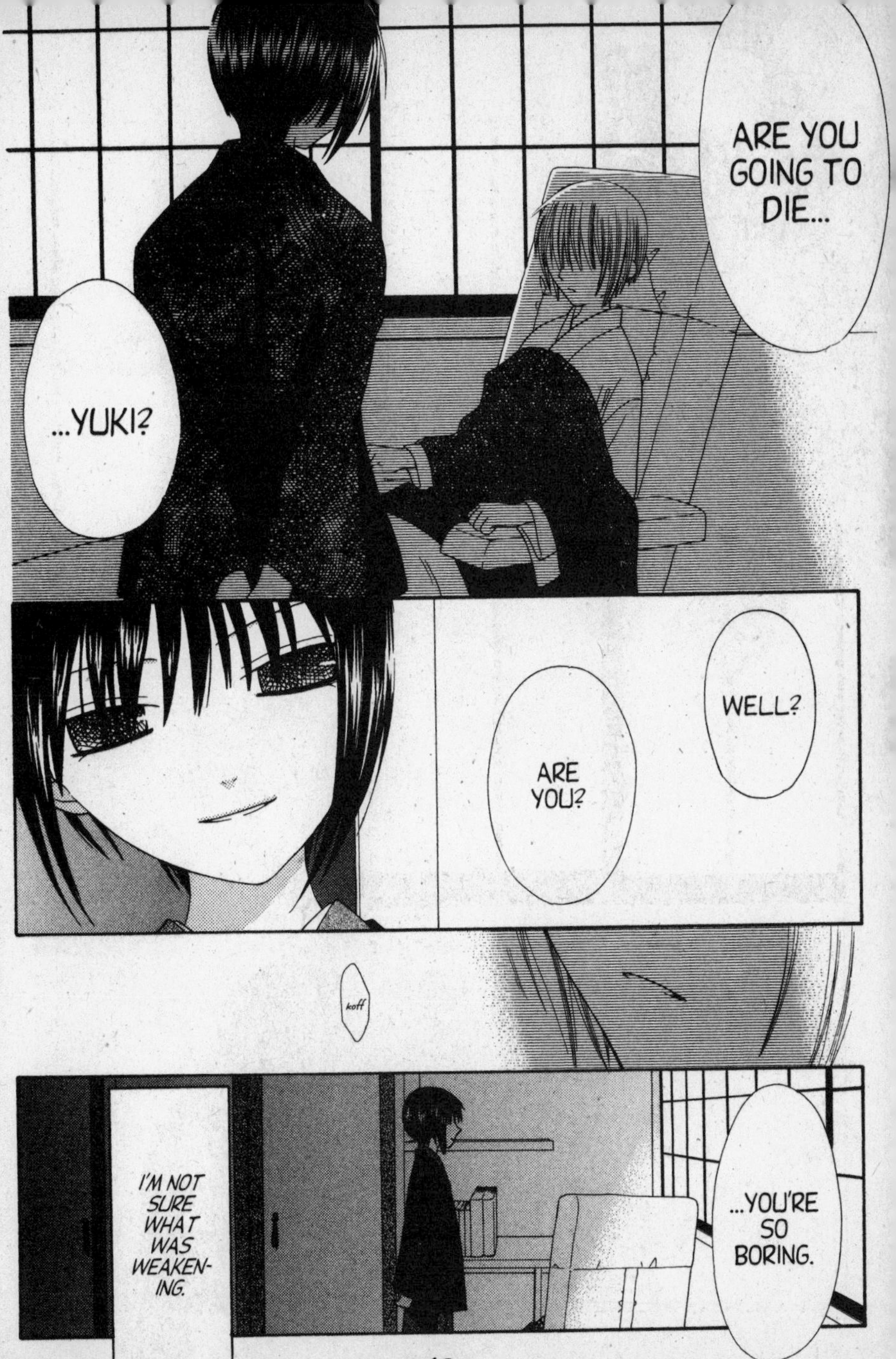
ARE YOU GOING TO DIE...
...YUKI?
WELL?
ARE YOU?
koff
...YOU'RE SO BORING.
I'M NOT SURE WHAT WAS WEAKEN-ING.

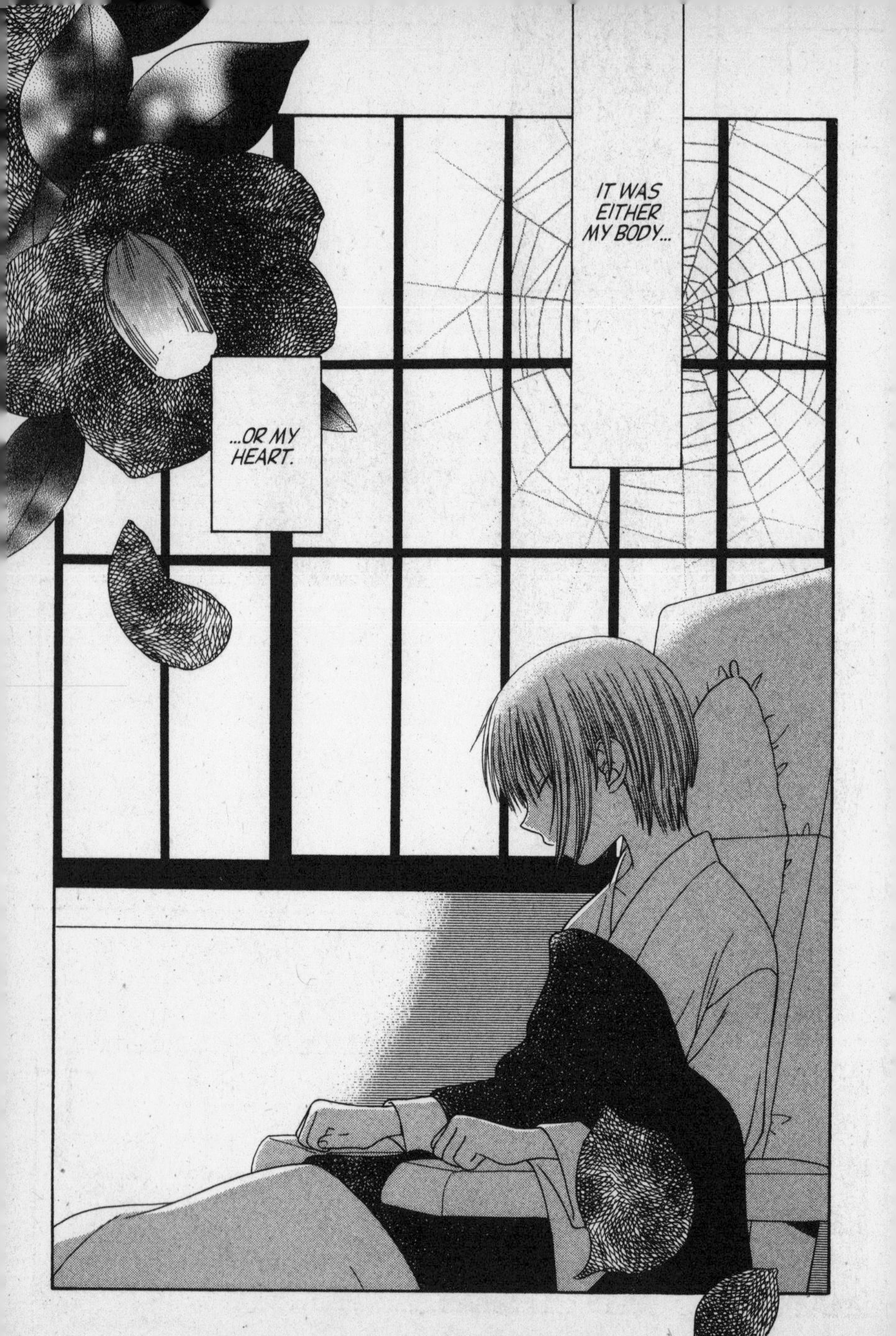
IT WAS EITHER MY BODY...
...OR MY HEART.

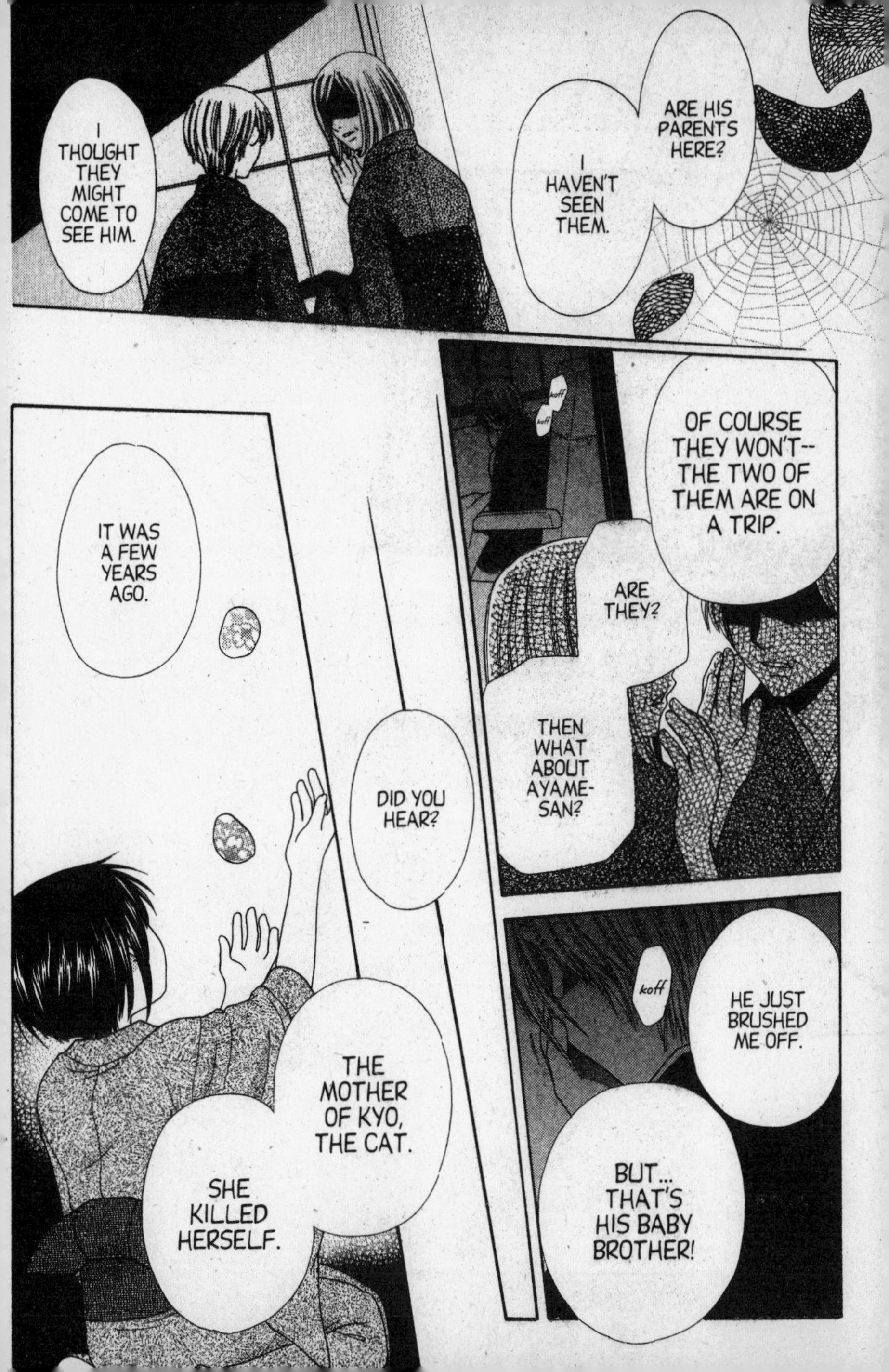
ARE HIS PARENTS HERE?
I HAVEN'T SEEN THEM.
I THOUGHT THEY MIGHT COME TO SEE HIM.
koff
koff
OF COURSE THEY WON'T-- THE TWO OF THEM ARE ON A TRIP.
ARE THEY?
THEN WHAT ABOUT AYAME-SAN?
koff
HE JUST BRUSHED ME OFF.
BUT... THAT'S HIS BABY BROTHER!
IT WAS A FEW YEARS AGO.
DID YOU HEAR?
THE MOTHER OF KYO, THE CAT.
SHE KILLED HERSELF.

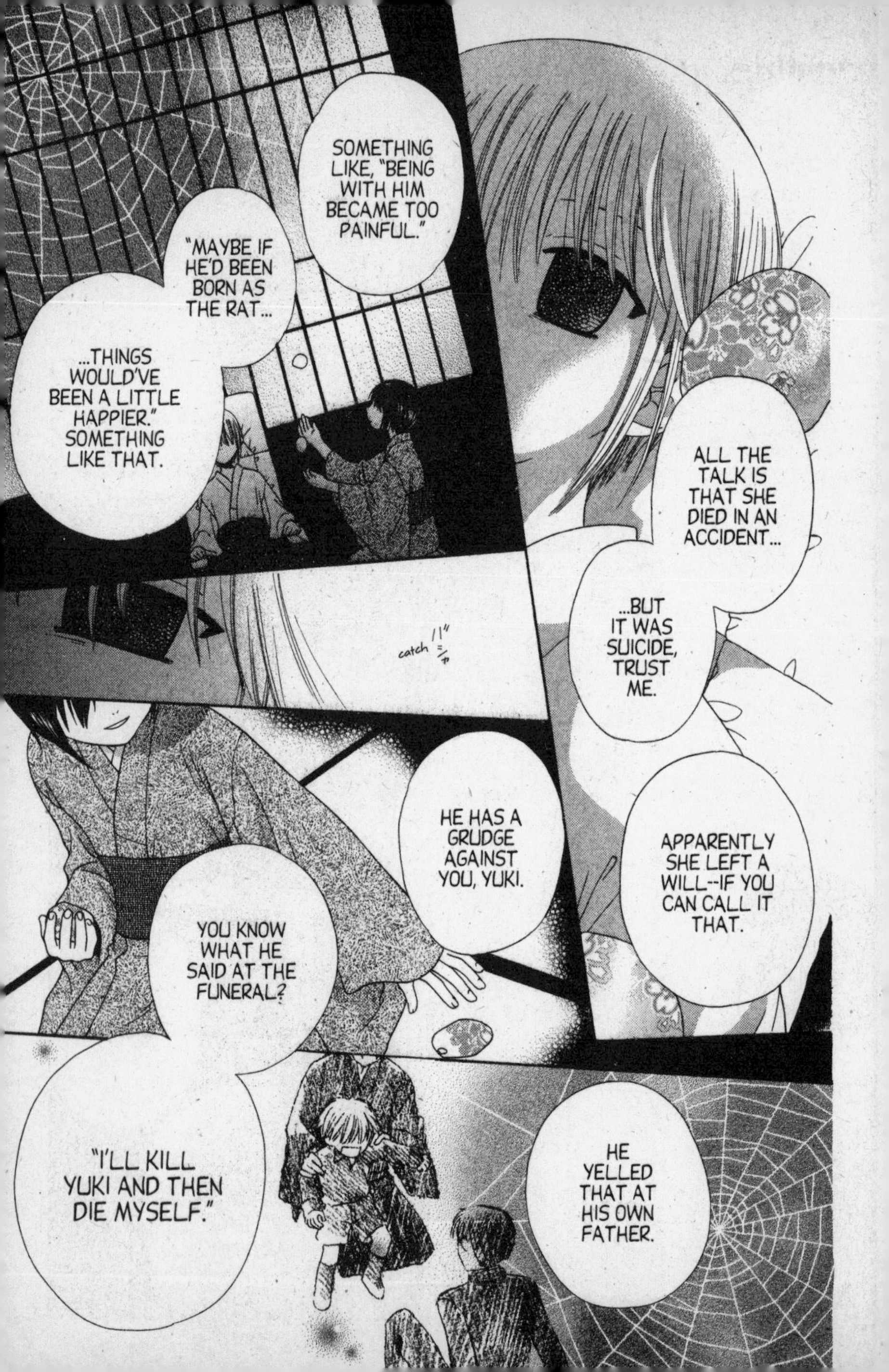
ALL THE TALK IS THAT SHE DIED IN AN ACCIDENT...
...BUT IT WAS SUICIDE, TRUST ME.
APPARENTLY SHE LEFT A WILL--IF YOU CAN CALL IT THAT.
SOMETHING LIKE, "BEING WITH HIM BECAME TOO PAINFUL."
"MAYBE IF HE'D BEEN BORN AS THE RAT...
...THINGS WOULD'VE BEEN A LITTLE HAPPIER." SOMETHING LIKE THAT.
catch
HE HAS A GRUDGE AGAINST YOU, YUKI.
YOU KNOW WHAT HE SAID AT THE FUNERAL?
HE YELLED THAT AT HIS OWN FATHER.
"I'LL KILL YUKI AND THEN DIE MYSELF."

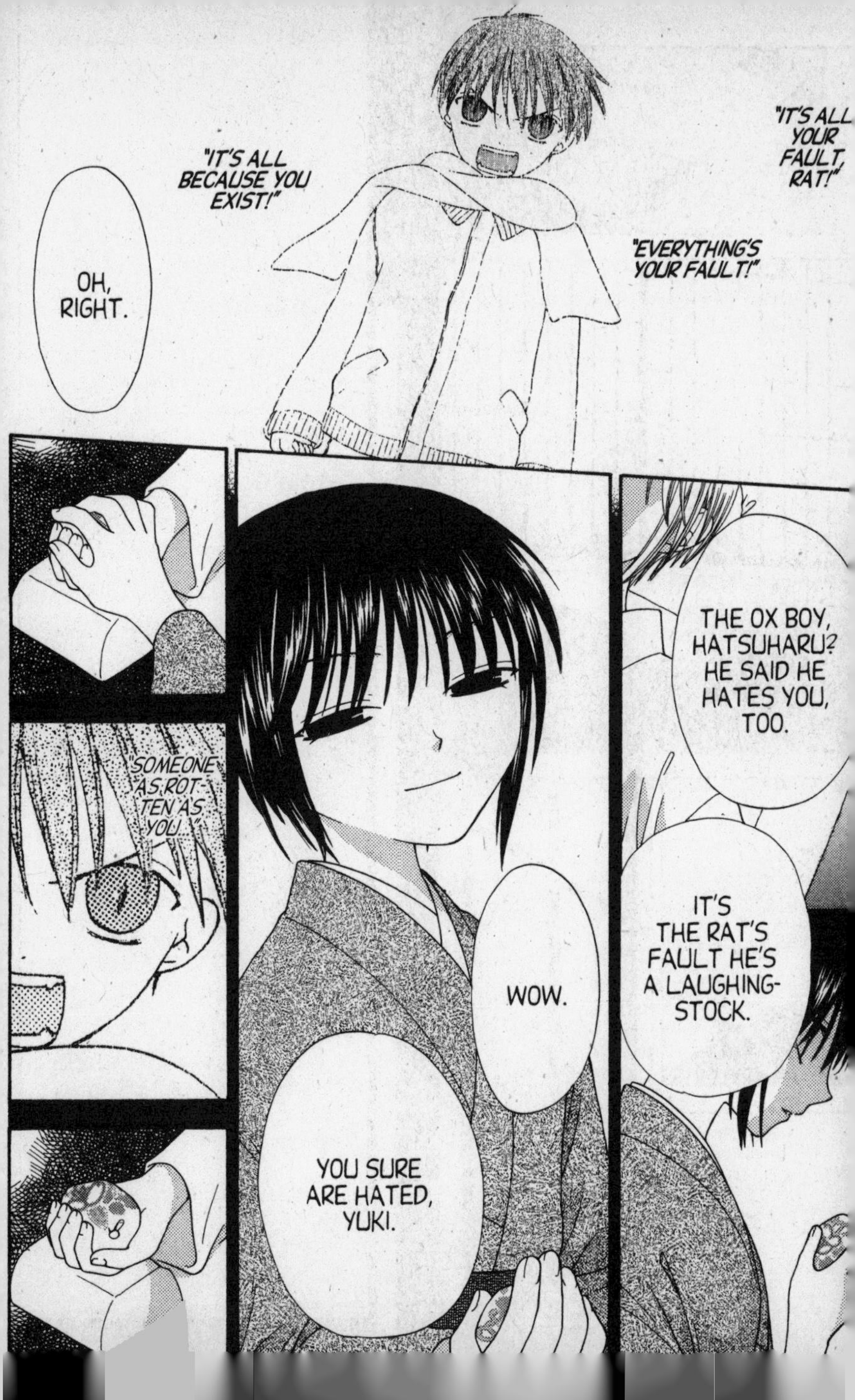
"IT'S ALL YOUR FAULT, RAT!"
"EVERYTHING'S YOUR FAULT!"
"IT'S ALL BECAUSE YOU EXIST!"
OH, RIGHT.
THE OX BOY, HATSUHARU? HE SAID HE HATES YOU, TOO.
IT'S THE RAT'S FAULT HE'S A LAUGHING-STOCK.
WOW.
YOU SURE ARE HATED, YUKI.
SOMEONE AS ROT-TEN AS YOU..."

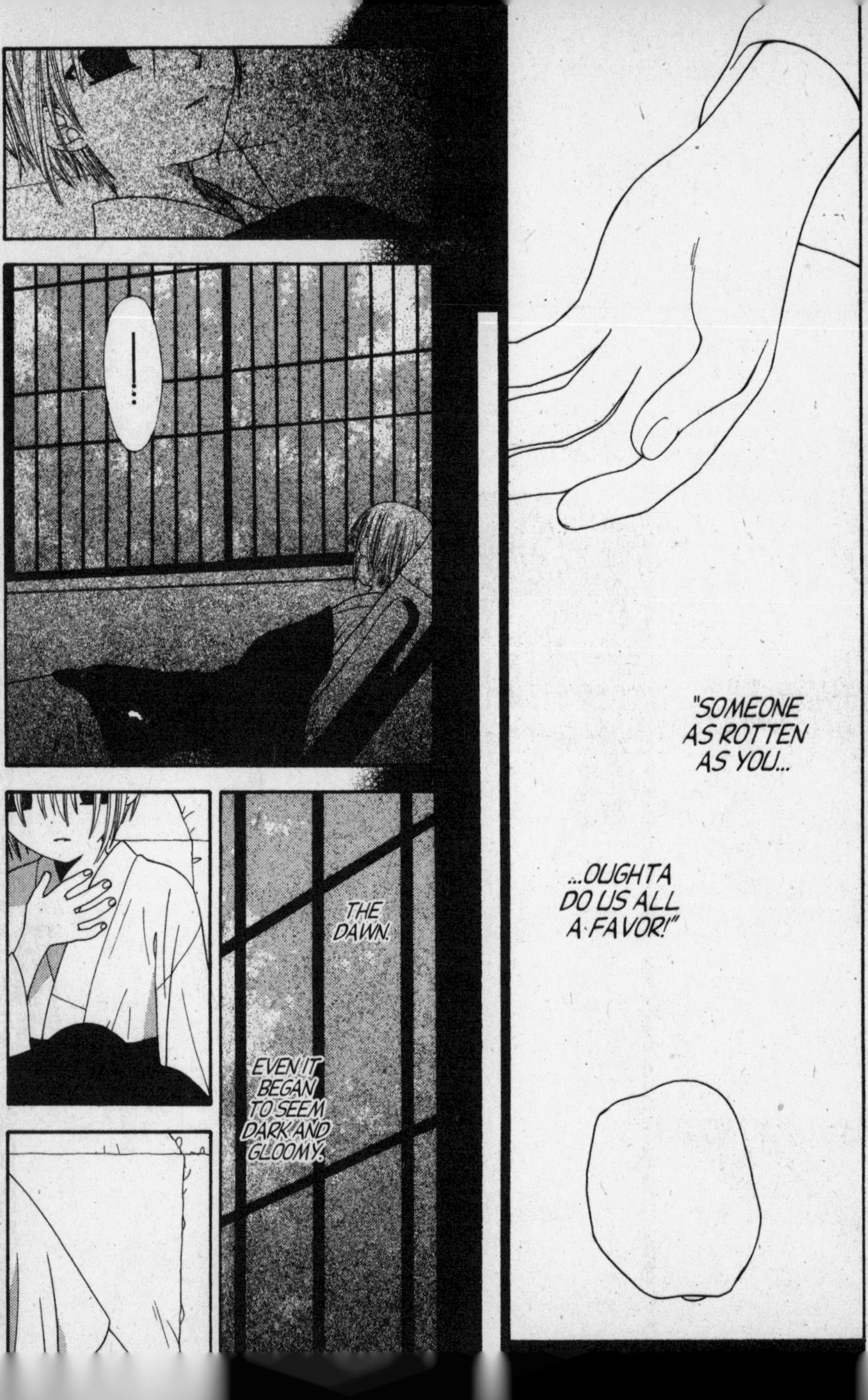
"SOMEONE AS ROTTEN AS YOU...
...OUGHTA DO US ALL A FAVOR!"
!...
THE DAWN.
EVEN IT BEGAN TO SEEM DARK AND GLOOMY.

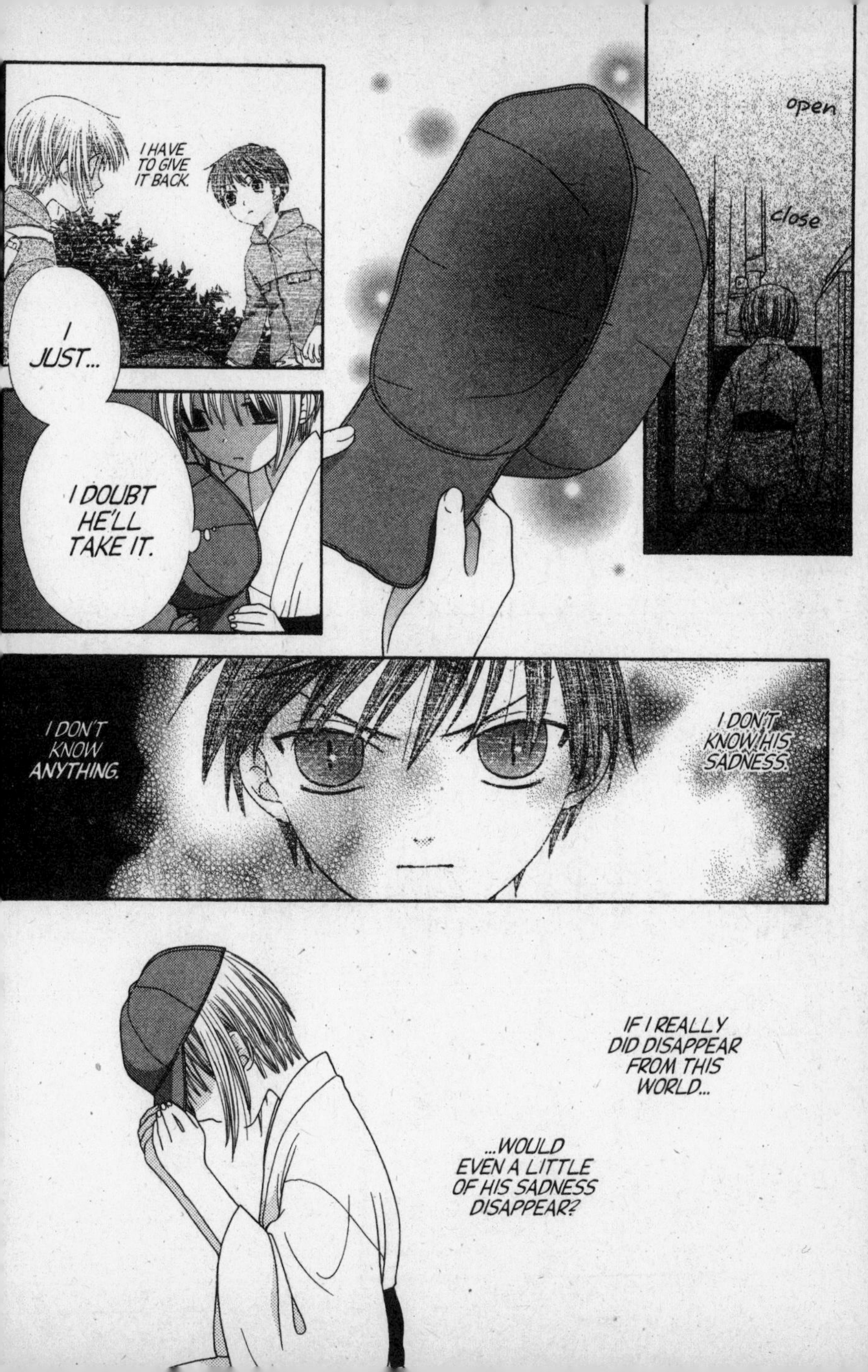
open
close
I HAVE TO GIVE IT BACK.
I JUST...
I DOUBT HE'LL TAKE IT.
I DON'T KNOW HIS SADNESS.
I DON'T KNOW ANYTHING.
IF I REALLY DID DISAPPEAR FROM THIS WORLD...
...WOULD EVEN A LITTLE OF HIS SADNESS DISAPPEAR?

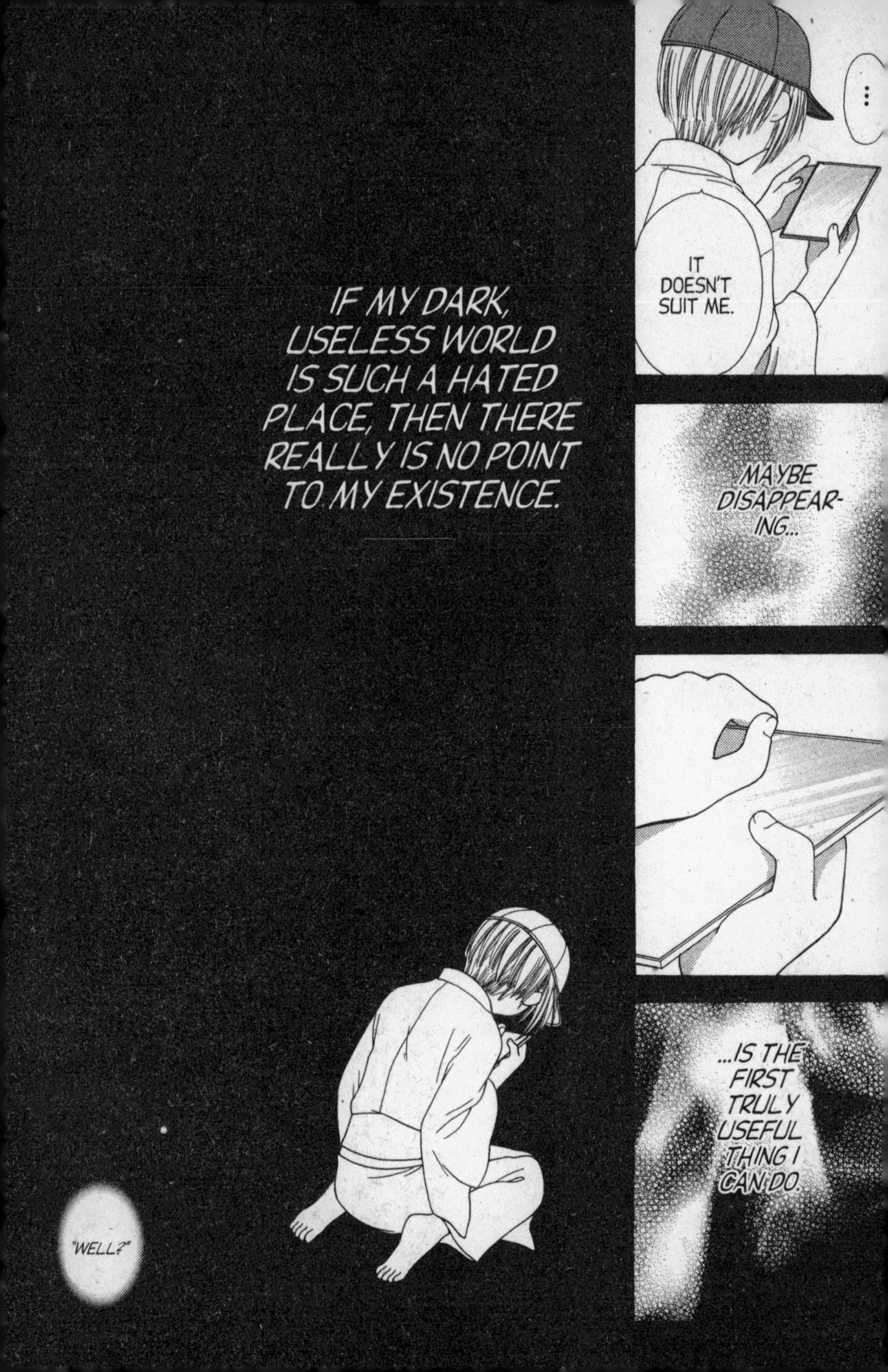
...
IT DOESN'T SUIT ME.
MAYBE DISAPPEAR-ING...
...IS THE FIRST TRULY USEFUL THING I CAN DO.
IF MY DARK, USELESS WORLD IS SUCH A HATED PLACE, THEN THERE REALLY IS NO POINT TO MY EXISTENCE.
"WELL?"

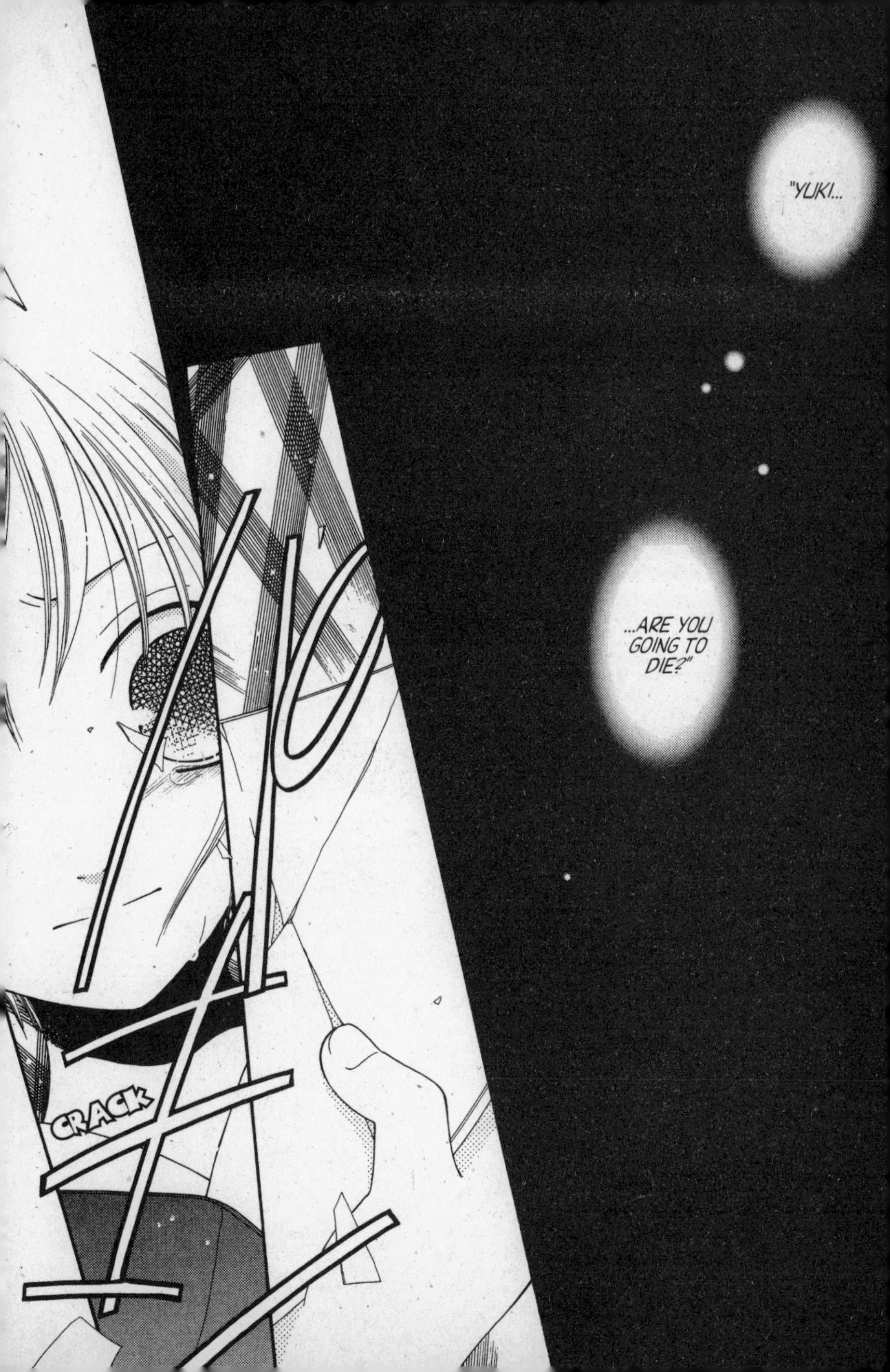
"YUKI...
...ARE YOU GOING TO DIE?"
CRACK

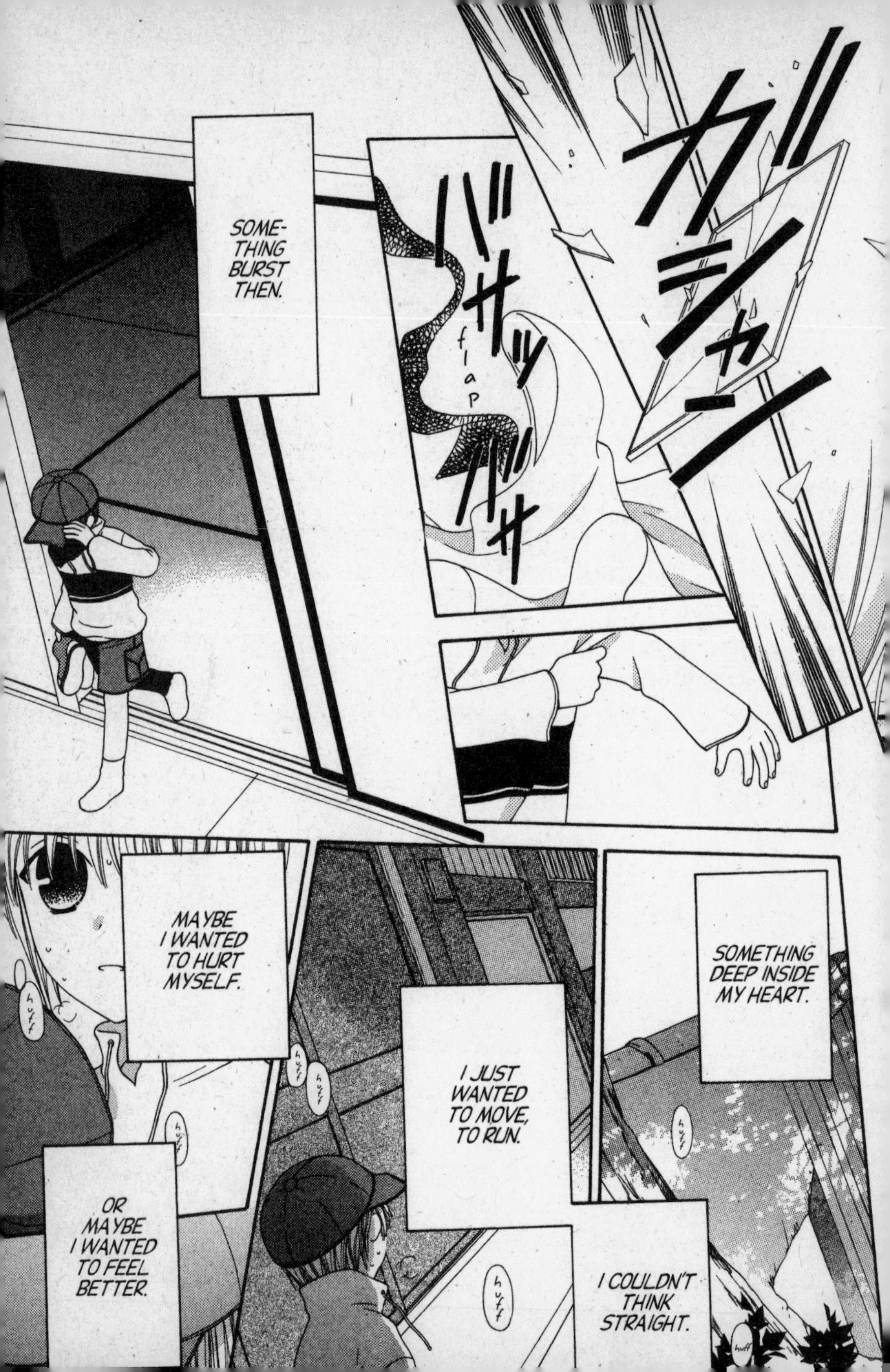
ガシャーン
バサッ
flap
バサ
SOMETHING BURST THEN.
SOMETHING DEEP INSIDE MY HEART.
huff
I COULDN'T THINK STRAIGHT.
huff
I JUST WANTED TO MOVE, TO RUN.
huff
huff
huff
MAYBE I WANTED TO HURT MYSELF.
huff
huff
OR MAYBE I WANTED TO FEEL BETTER.

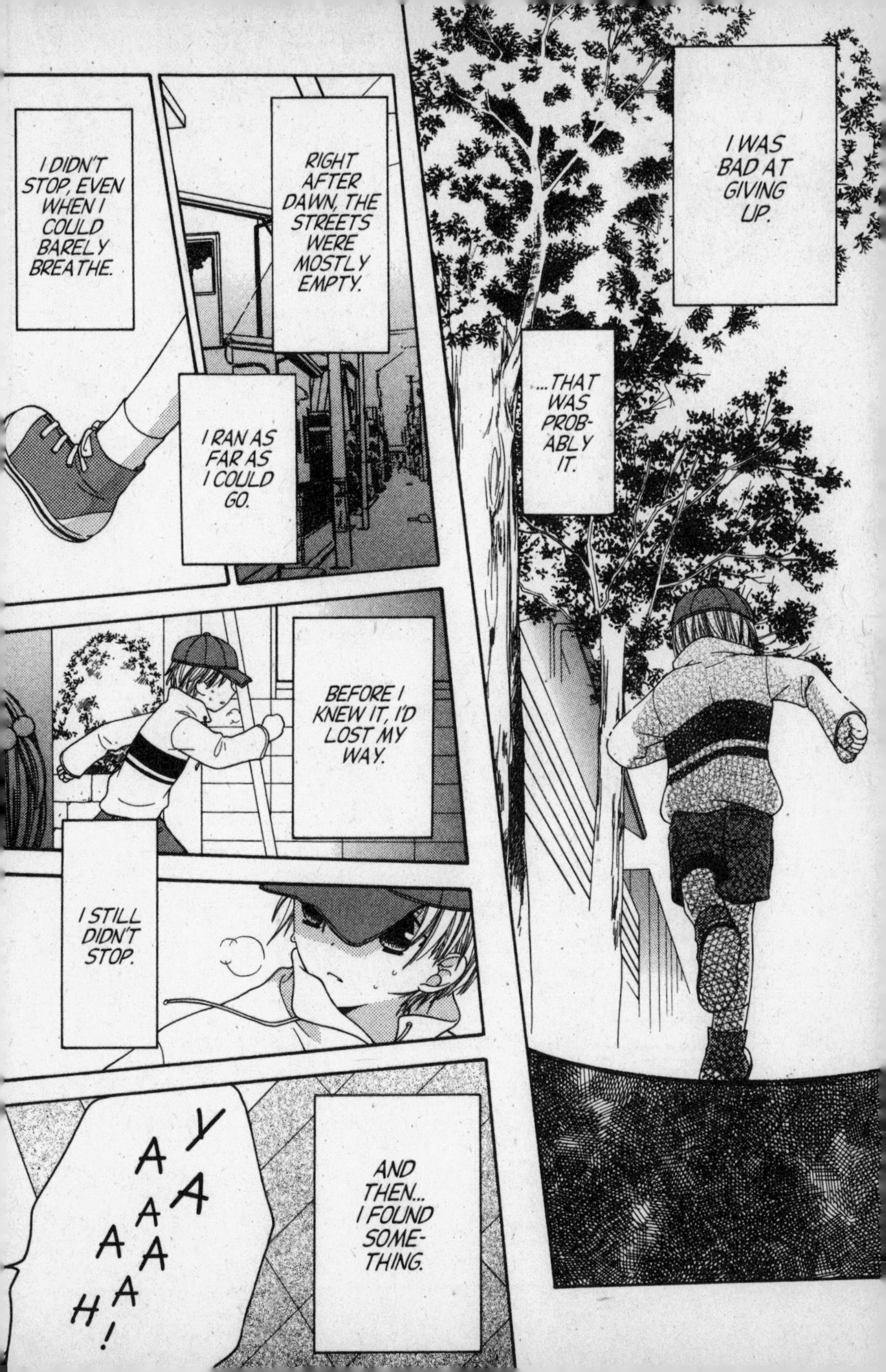
I WAS BAD AT GIVING UP.
...THAT WAS PROBABLY IT.
RIGHT AFTER DAWN, THE STREETS WERE MOSTLY EMPTY.
I RAN AS FAR AS I COULD GO.
I DIDN'T STOP, EVEN WHEN I COULD BARELY BREATHE.
BEFORE I KNEW IT, I'D LOST MY WAY.
I STILL DIDN'T STOP.
AND THEN... I FOUND SOMETHING.
YAAAAAAH!

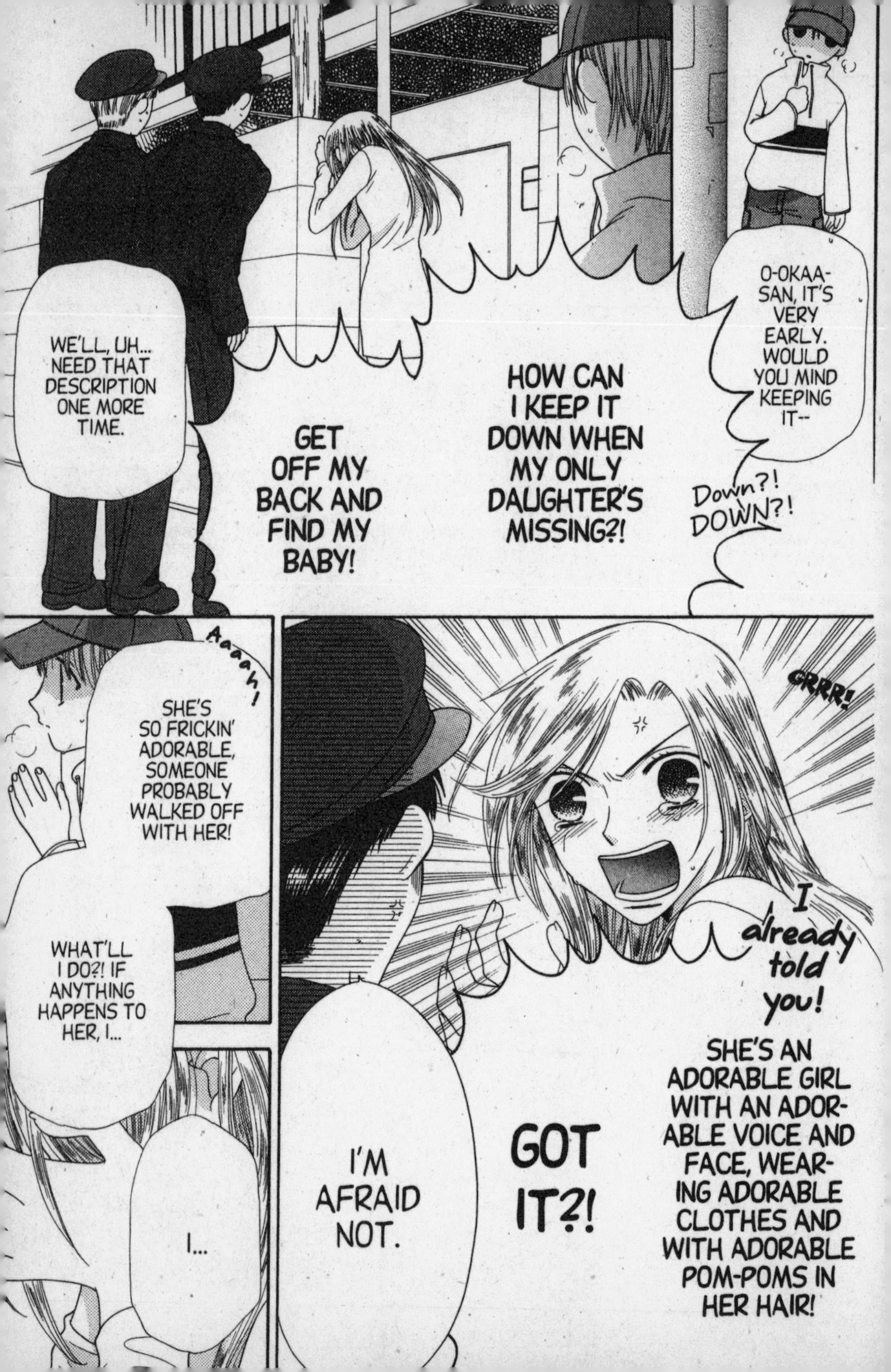
O-OKAA-SAN, IT'S VERY EARLY. WOULD YOU MIND KEEPING IT--
Down?! DOWN?!
HOW CAN I KEEP IT DOWN WHEN MY ONLY DAUGHTER'S MISSING?!
GET OFF MY BACK AND FIND MY BABY!
WE'LL, UH... NEED THAT DESCRIPTION ONE MORE TIME.
GRRR!
I already told you!
SHE'S AN ADORABLE GIRL WITH AN ADOR-ABLE VOICE AND FACE, WEAR-ING ADORABLE CLOTHES AND WITH ADORABLE POM-POMS IN HER HAIR!
GOT IT?!
I'M AFRAID NOT.
Aaaah!
SHE'S SO FRICKIN' ADORABLE, SOMEONE PROBABLY WALKED OFF WITH HER!
WHAT'LL I DO?! IF ANYTHING HAPPENS TO HER, I...
I...

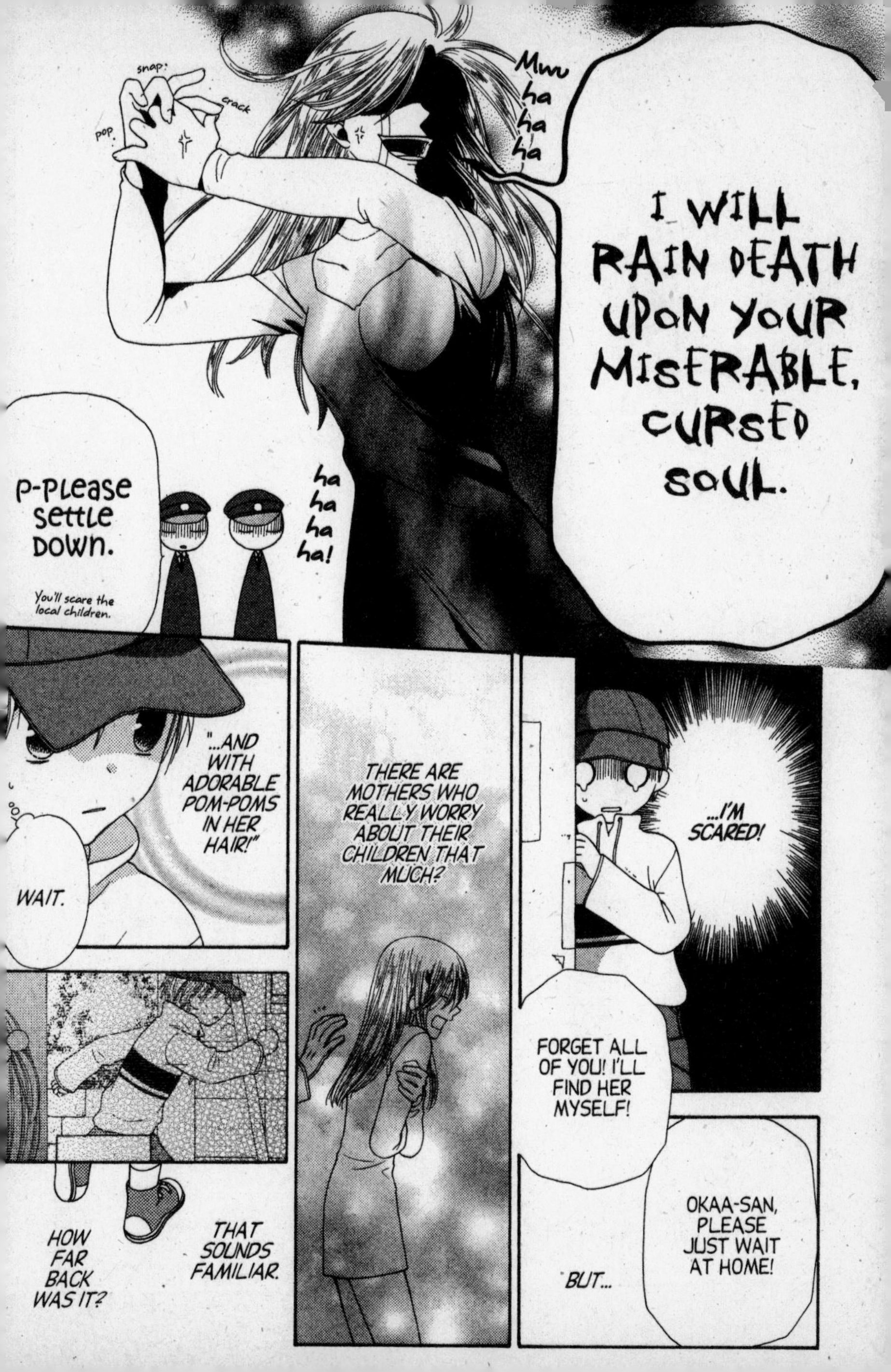
Mwu ha ha ha
I WILL RAIN DEATH UPON YOUR MISERABLE, CURSED SOUL.
snap.
crack
pop.
ha ha ha ha!
P-PLEASE SETTLE DOWN.
You'll scare the local children.
...I'M SCARED!
FORGET ALL OF YOU! I'LL FIND HER MYSELF!
OKAA-SAN, PLEASE JUST WAIT AT HOME!
BUT...
THERE ARE MOTHERS WHO REALLY WORRY ABOUT THEIR CHILDREN THAT MUCH?
"...AND WITH ADORABLE POM-POMS IN HER HAIR!"
WAIT.
THAT SOUNDS FAMILIAR.
HOW FAR BACK WAS IT?

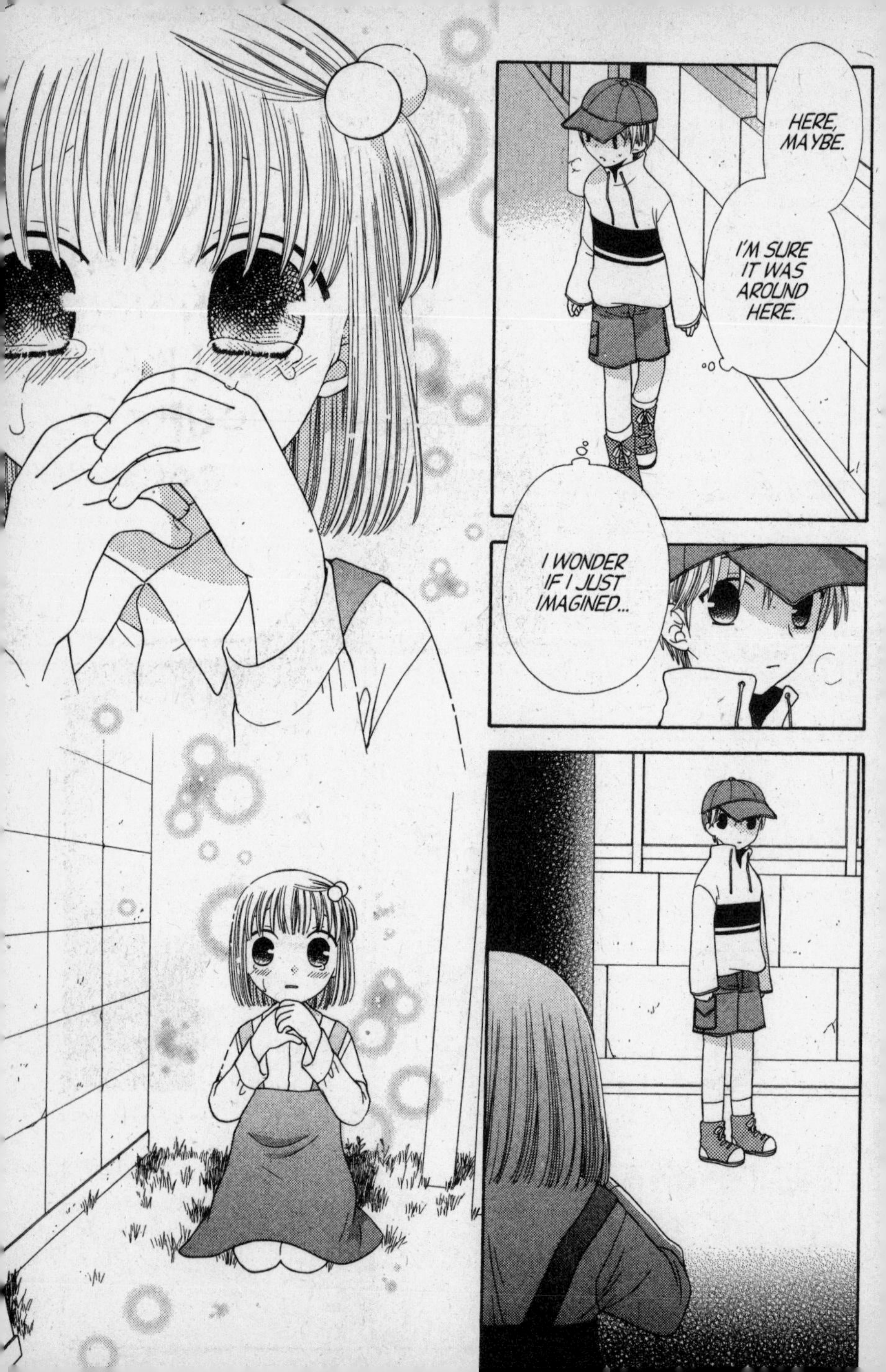
HERE, MAYBE.
I'M SURE IT WAS AROUND HERE.
I WONDER IF I JUST IMAGINED...

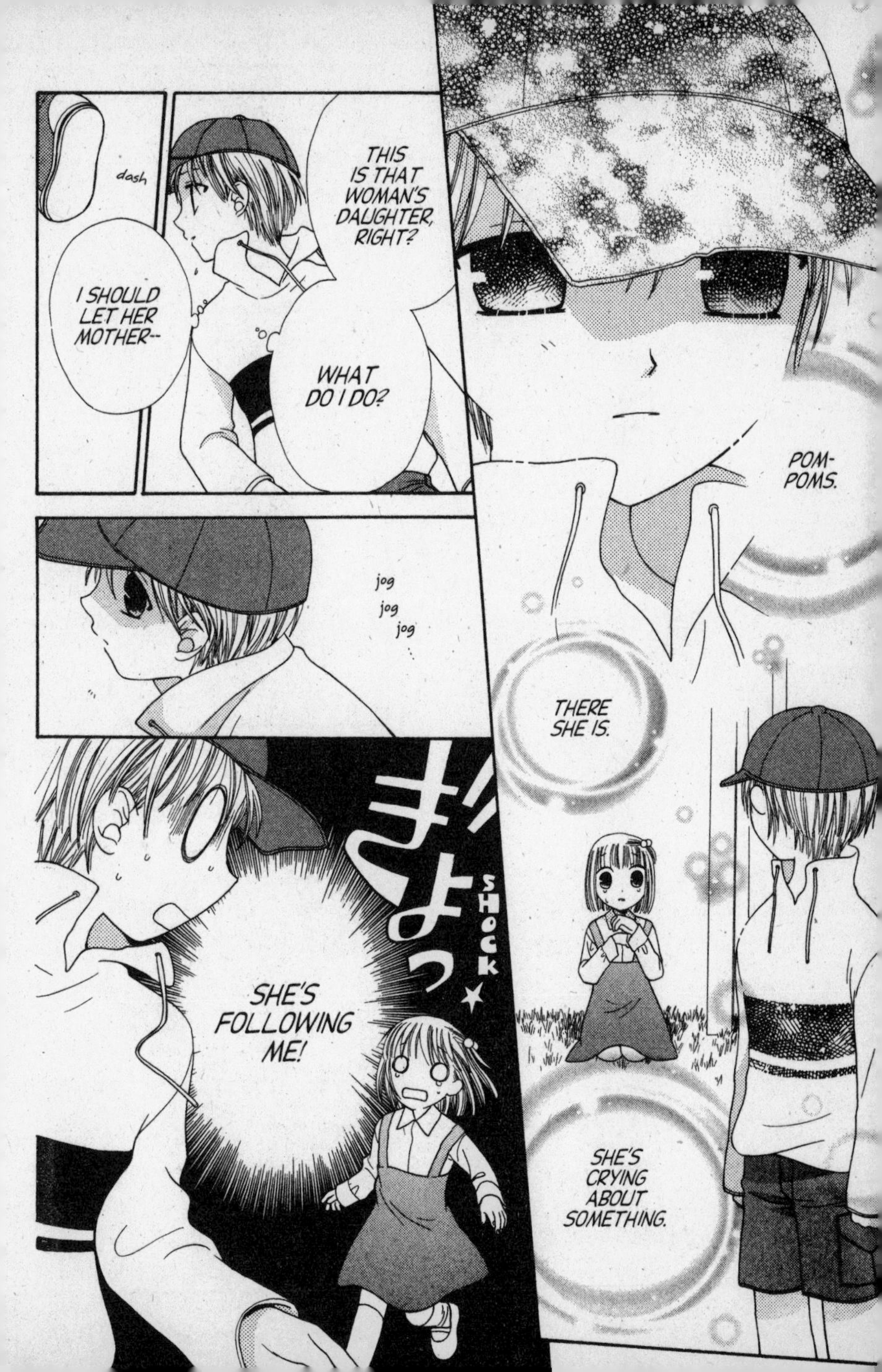
POM-POMS.
THERE SHE IS.
SHE'S CRYING ABOUT SOMETHING.
THIS IS THAT WOMAN'S DAUGHTER, RIGHT?
WHAT DO I DO?
I SHOULD LET HER MOTHER--
dash
jog jog jog
ぎょっ
SHOCK
SHE'S FOLLOWING ME!

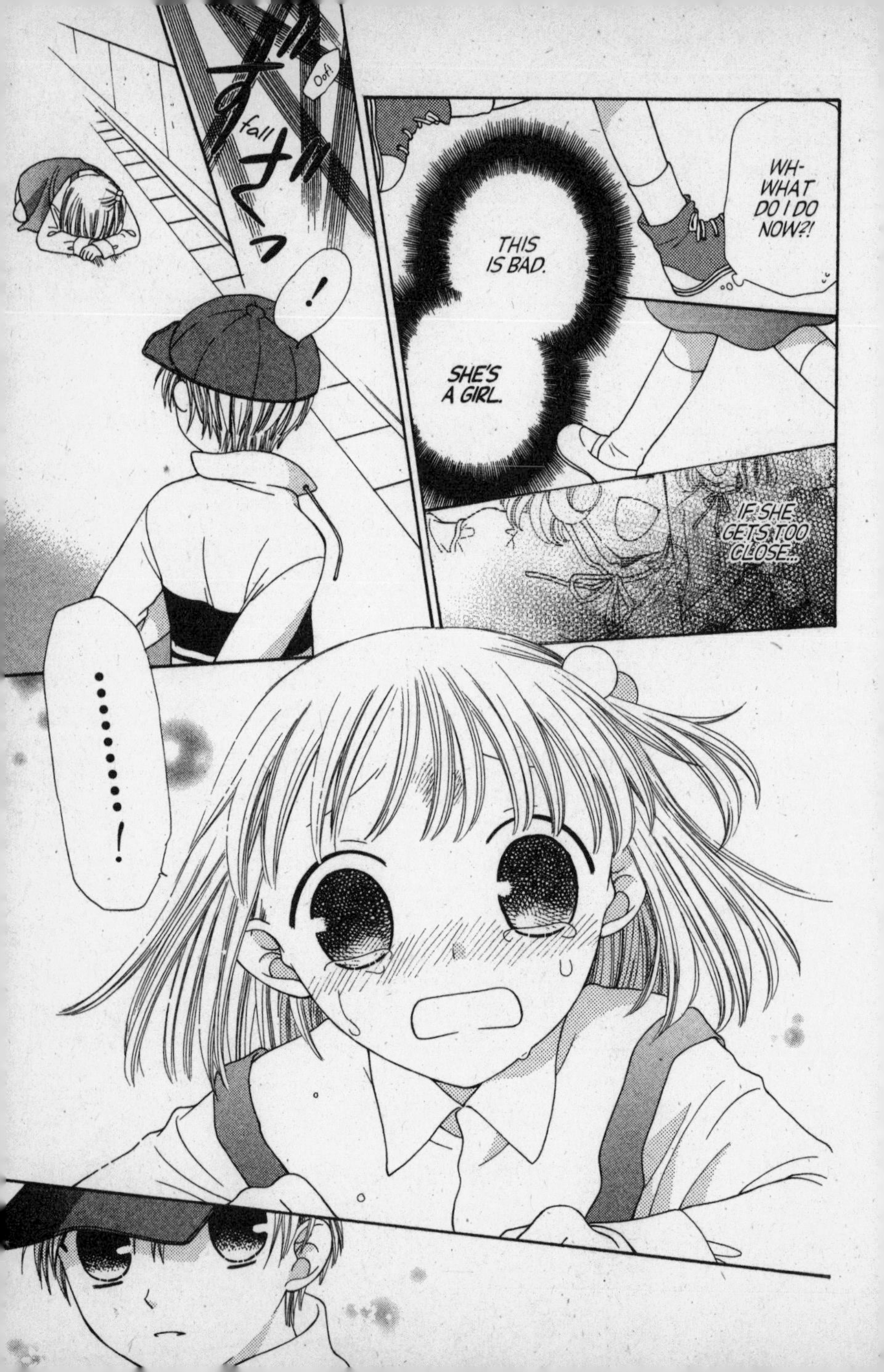
WH- WHAT DO I DO NOW?!
THIS IS BAD.
SHE'S A GIRL.
IF SHE GETS TOO CLOSE...
Oof!
fall
!
......!

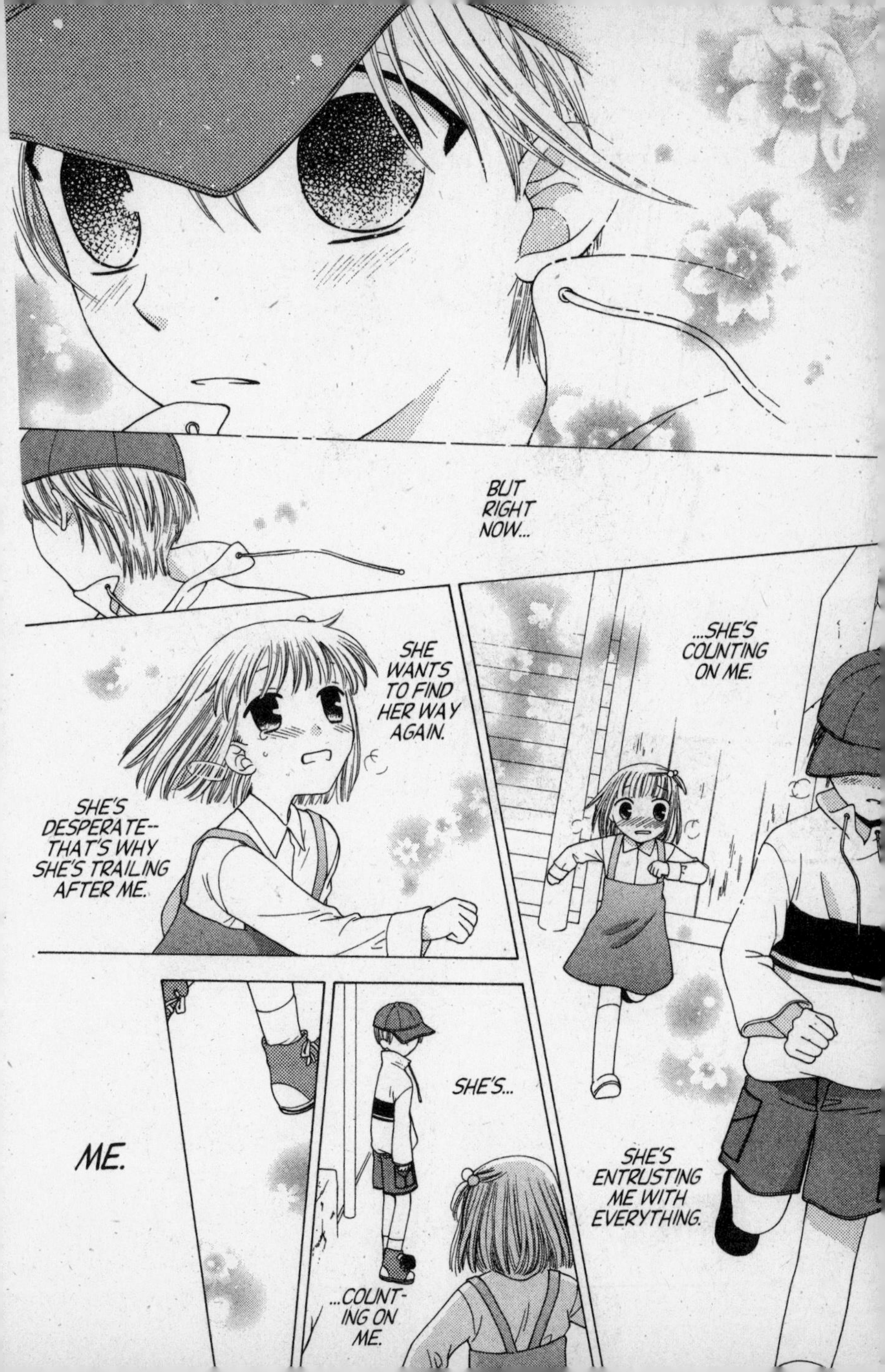
BUT RIGHT NOW...
...SHE'S COUNTING ON ME.
SHE'S ENTRUSTING ME WITH EVERYTHING.
SHE WANTS TO FIND HER WAY AGAIN.
SHE'S DESPERATE-- THAT'S WHY SHE'S TRAILING AFTER ME.
SHE'S...
...COUNT-ING ON ME.
ME.

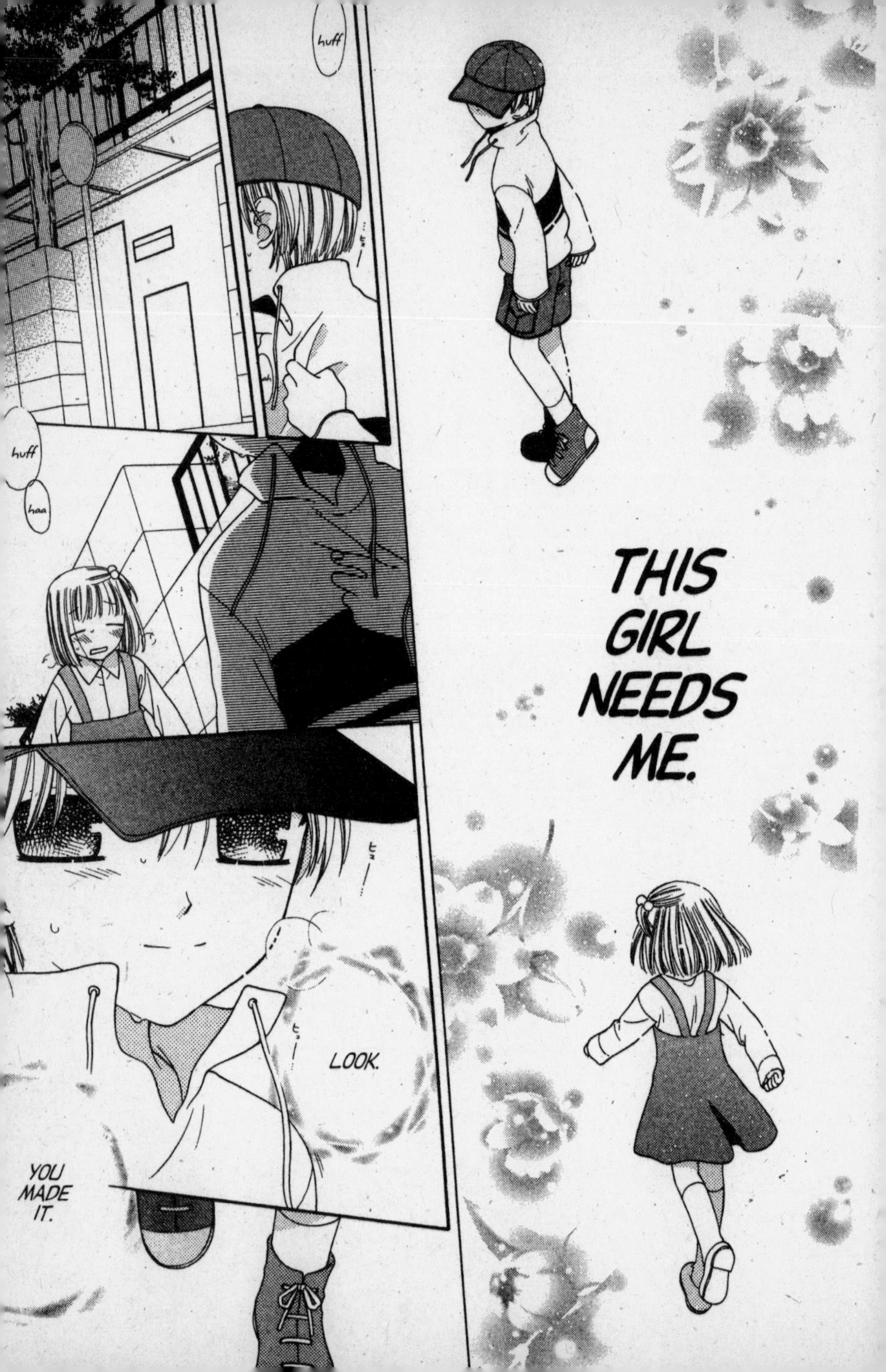
THIS GIRL NEEDS ME.
huff
huff
haa
LOOK.
YOU MADE IT.

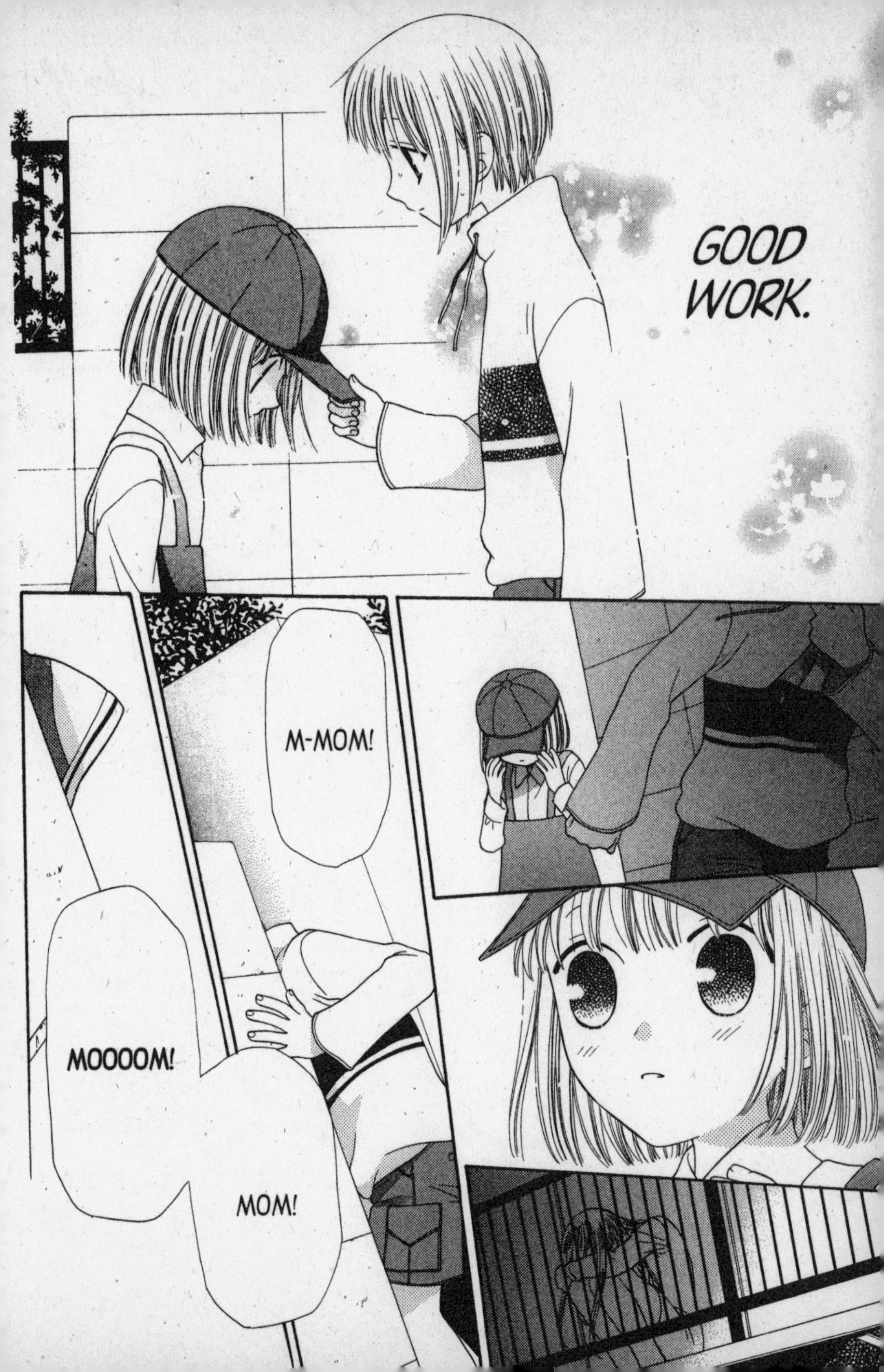
GOOD WORK.
M-MOM!
MOOOOM!
MOM!

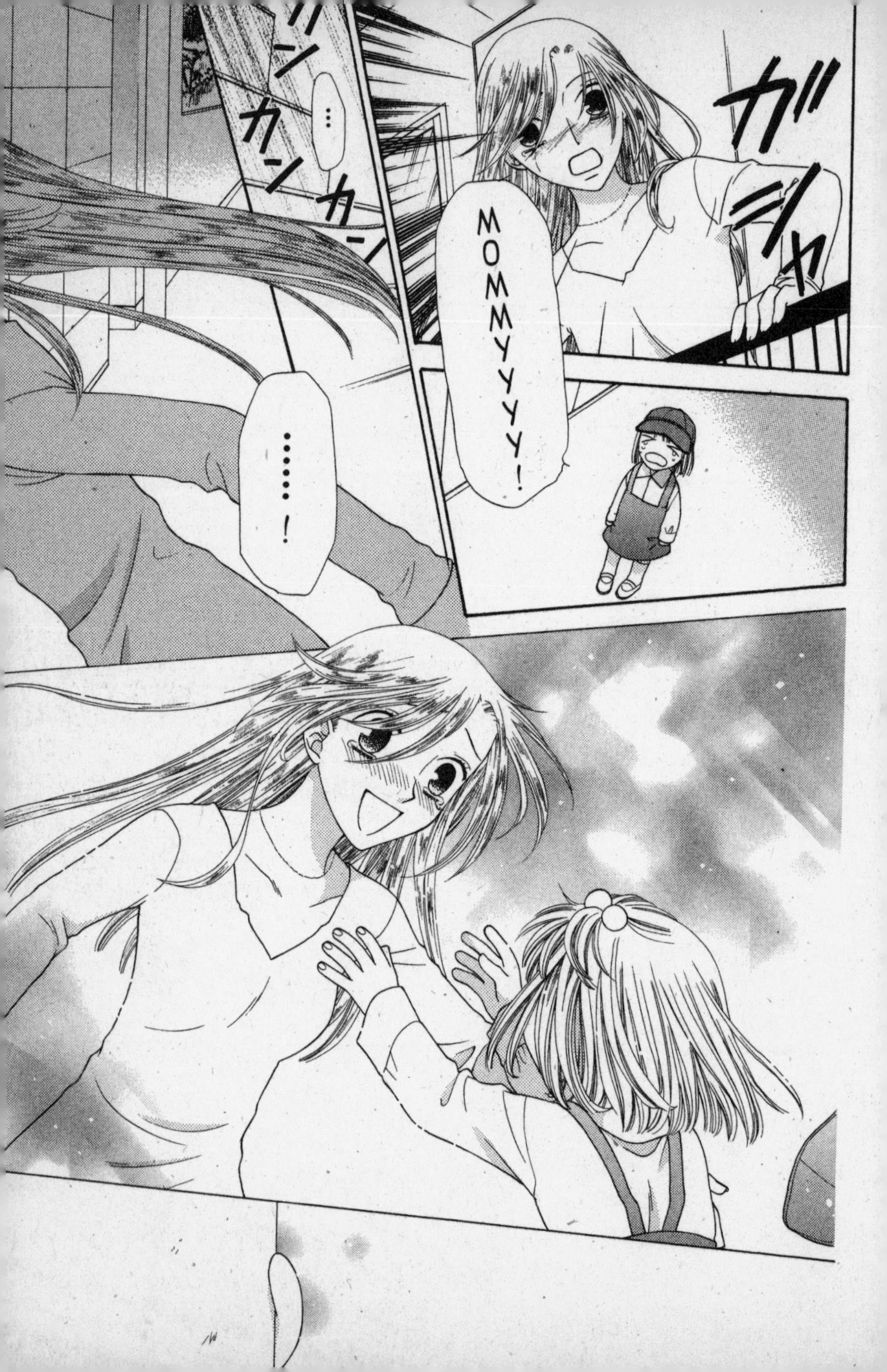
ガシャ
MOMMYYYYY!
…
カンカン
……!

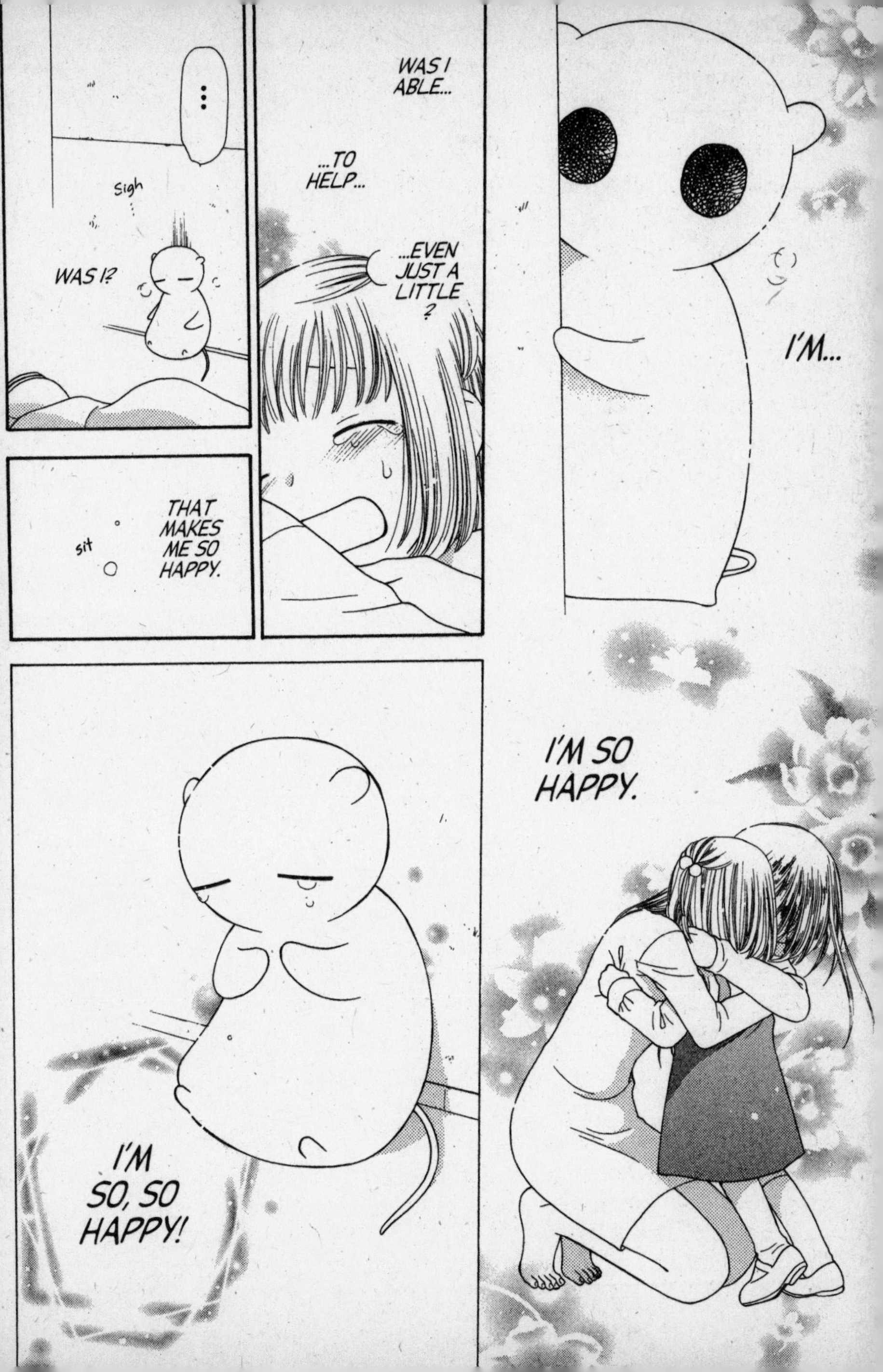
I'M...
WAS I ABLE...
...TO HELP...
...EVEN JUST A LITTLE?
...
Sigh
WAS I?
sit
THAT MAKES ME SO HAPPY.
I'M SO HAPPY.
I'M SO, SO HAPPY!

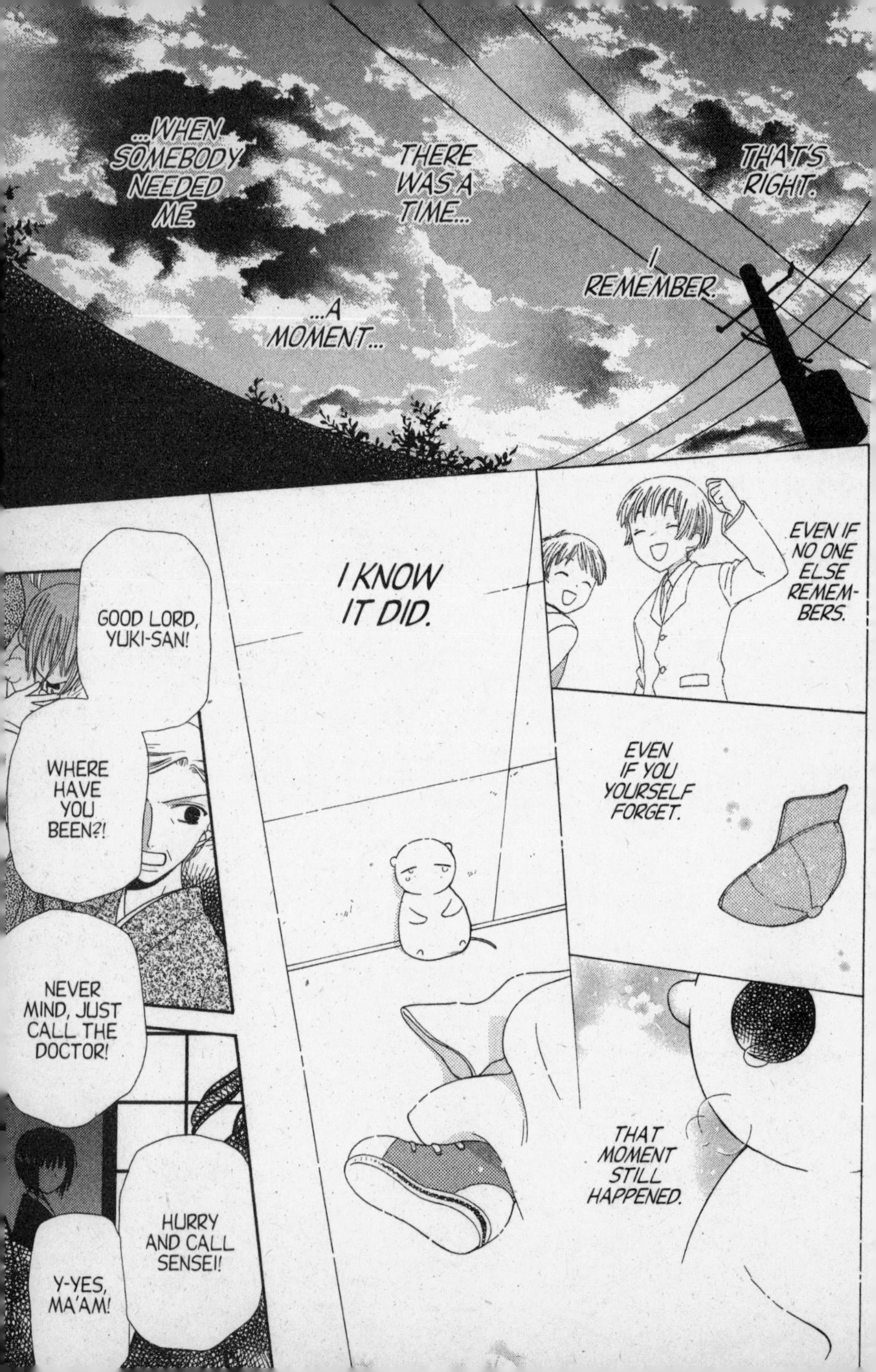
THAT'S RIGHT.
I REMEMBER.
THERE WAS A TIME...
...A MOMENT...
...WHEN SOMEBODY NEEDED ME.
EVEN IF NO ONE ELSE REMEM-BERS.
EVEN IF YOU YOURSELF FORGET.
THAT MOMENT STILL HAPPENED.
I KNOW IT DID.
GOOD LORD, YUKI-SAN!
WHERE HAVE YOU BEEN?!
NEVER MIND, JUST CALL THE DOCTOR!
HURRY AND CALL SENSEI!
Y-YES, MA'AM!

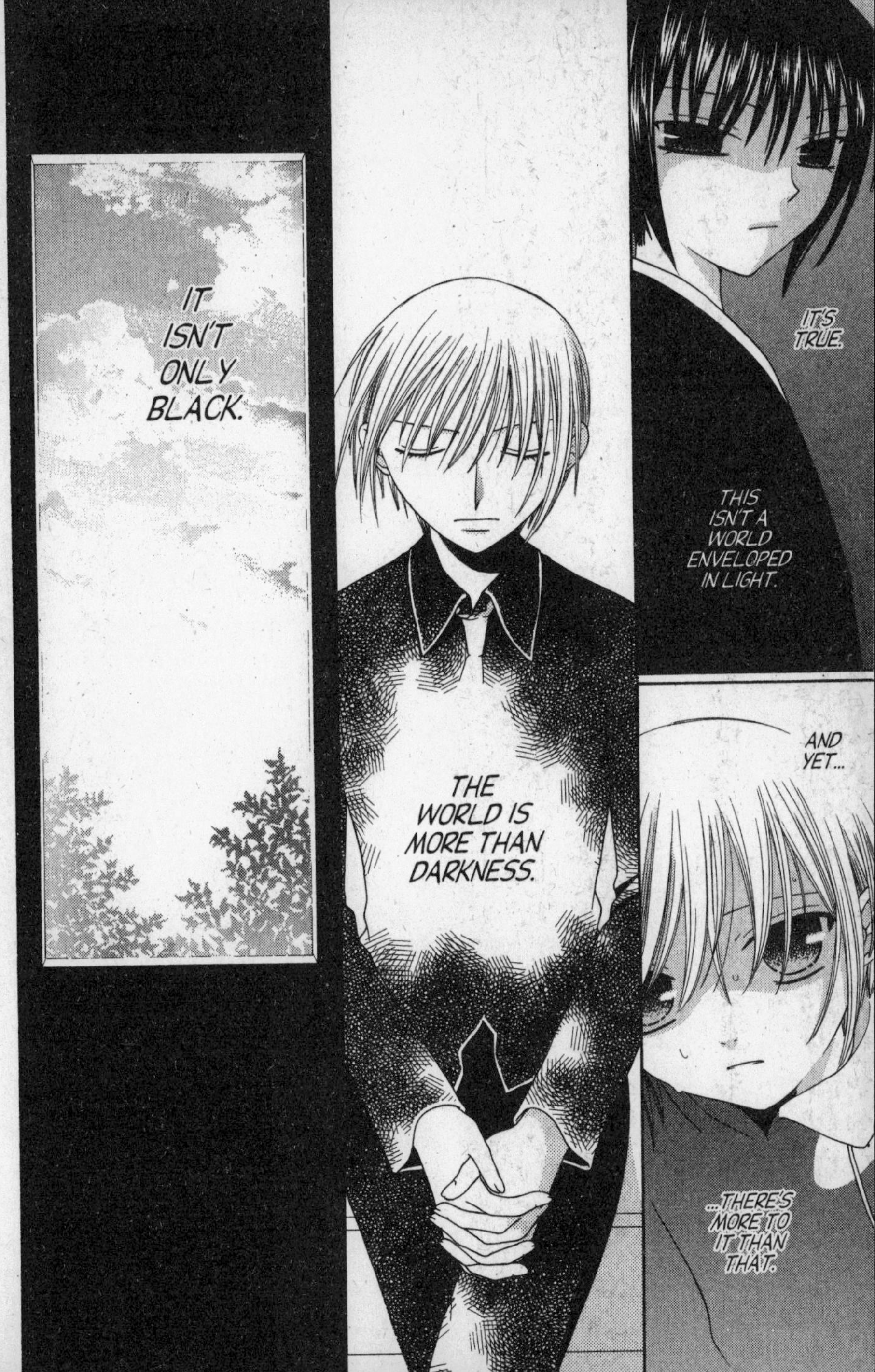
IT'S TRUE.
THIS ISN'T A WORLD ENVELOPED IN LIGHT.
AND YET...
...THERE'S MORE TO IT THAN THAT.
THE WORLD IS MORE THAN DARKNESS.
IT ISN'T ONLY BLACK.

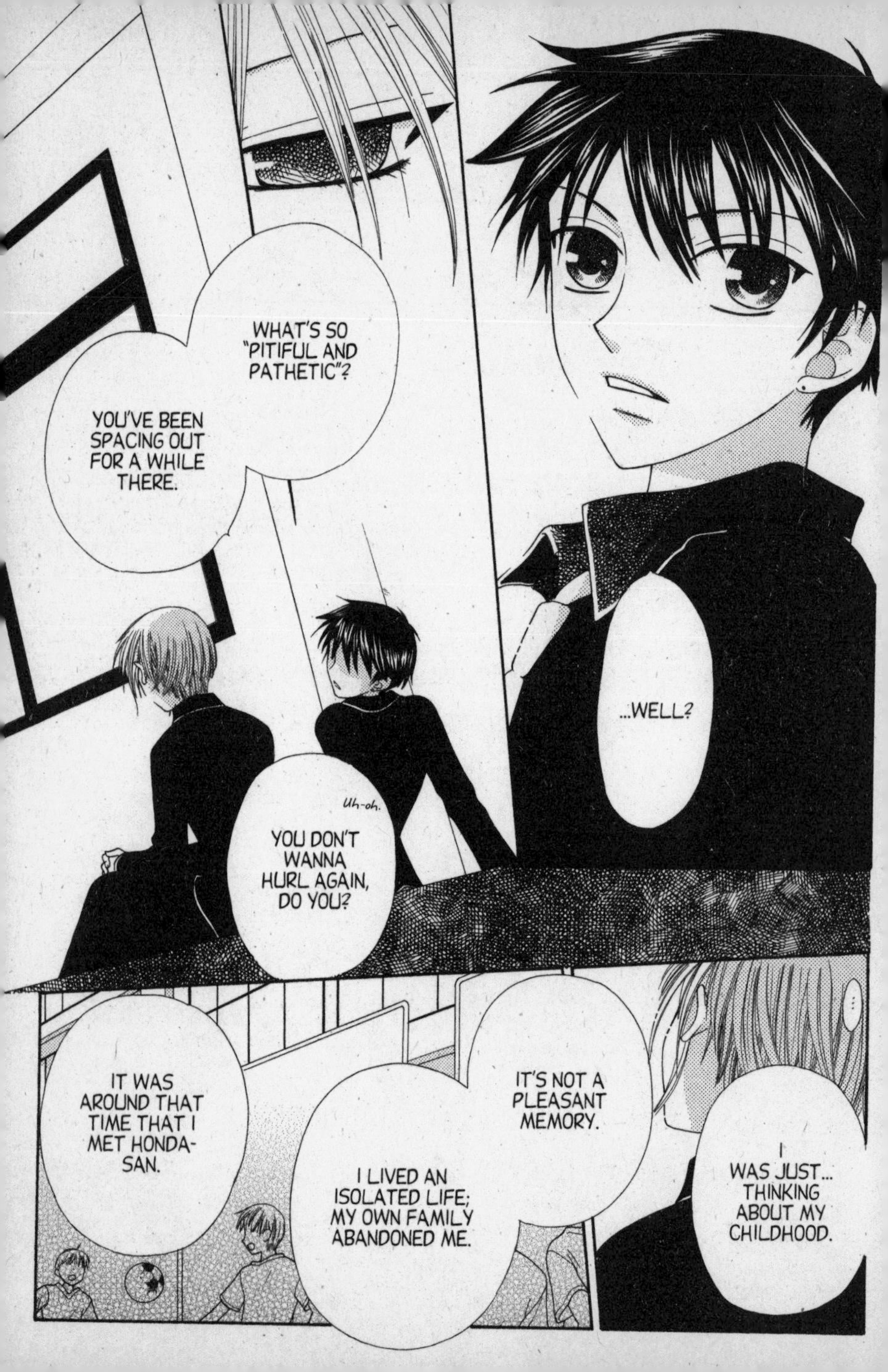
WHAT'S SO "PITIFUL AND PATHETIC"?
YOU'VE BEEN SPACING OUT FOR A WHILE THERE.
...WELL?
Uh-oh.
YOU DON'T WANNA HURL AGAIN, DO YOU?
...
I WAS JUST... THINKING ABOUT MY CHILDHOOD.
IT'S NOT A PLEASANT MEMORY.
I LIVED AN ISOLATED LIFE; MY OWN FAMILY ABANDONED ME.
IT WAS AROUND THAT TIME THAT I MET HONDA-SAN.

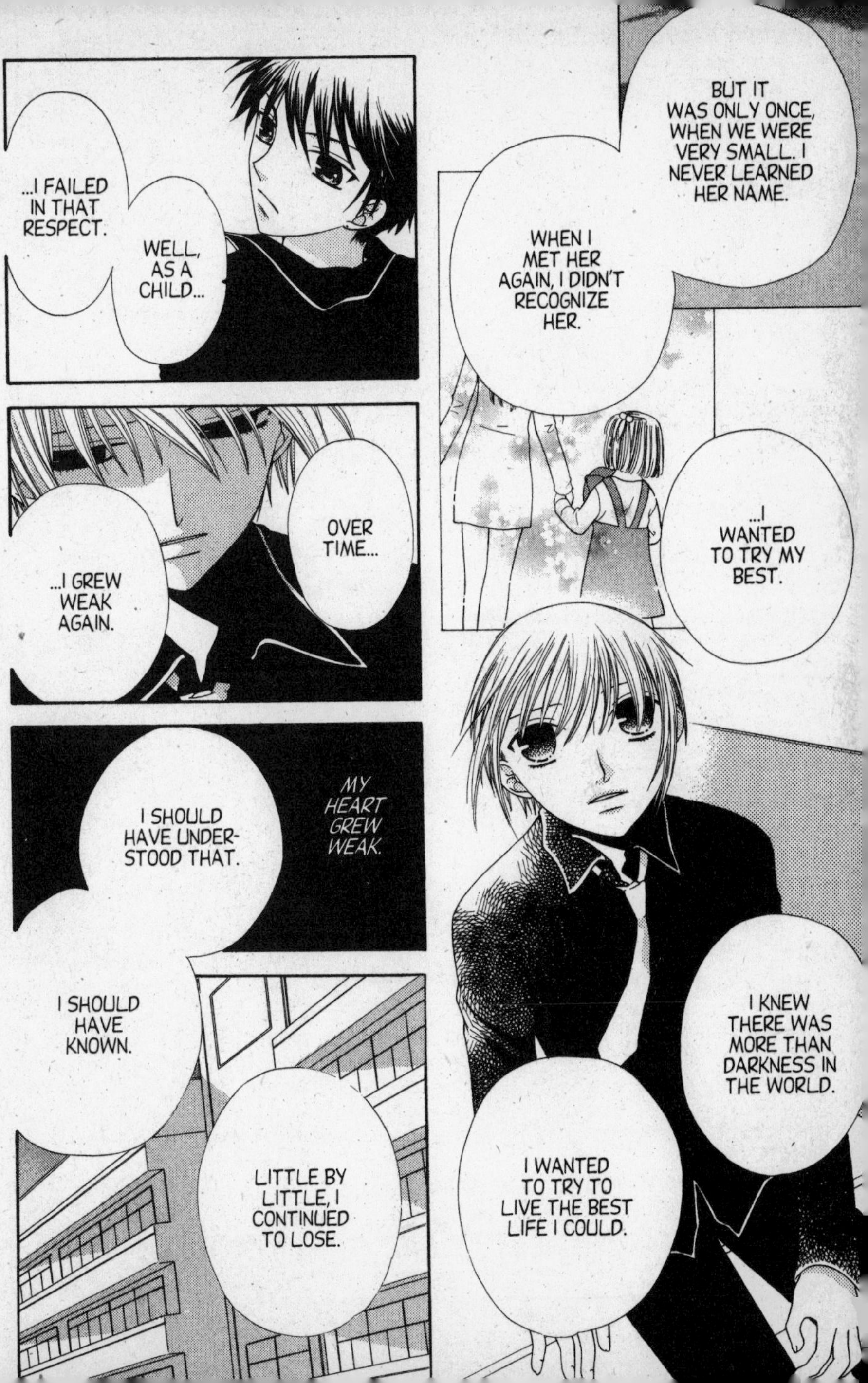
BUT IT WAS ONLY ONCE, WHEN WE WERE VERY SMALL. I NEVER LEARNED HER NAME.
WHEN I MET HER AGAIN, I DIDN'T RECOGNIZE HER.
...I WANTED TO TRY MY BEST.
I KNEW THERE WAS MORE THAN DARKNESS IN THE WORLD.
I WANTED TO TRY TO LIVE THE BEST LIFE I COULD.
WELL, AS A CHILD...
...I FAILED IN THAT RESPECT.
OVER TIME...
...I GREW WEAK AGAIN.
MY HEART GREW WEAK.
I SHOULD HAVE UNDER-STOOD THAT.
I SHOULD HAVE KNOWN.
LITTLE BY LITTLE, I CONTINUED TO LOSE.

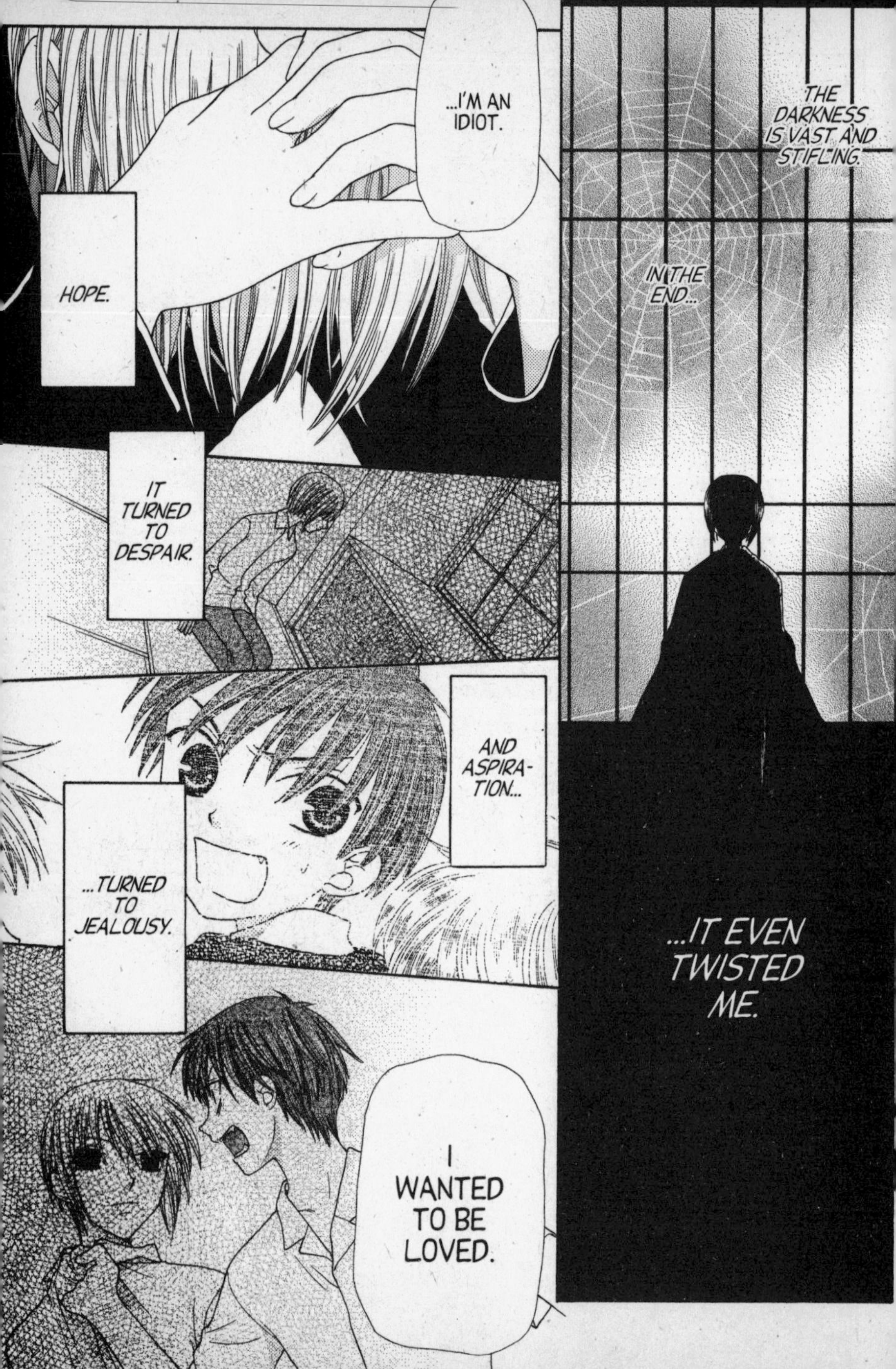
THE DARKNESS IS VAST AND STIFLING.
IN THE END...
...IT EVEN TWISTED ME.
...I'M AN IDIOT.
HOPE.
IT TURNED TO DESPAIR.
AND ASPIRATION...
...TURNED TO JEALOUSY.
I WANTED TO BE LOVED.

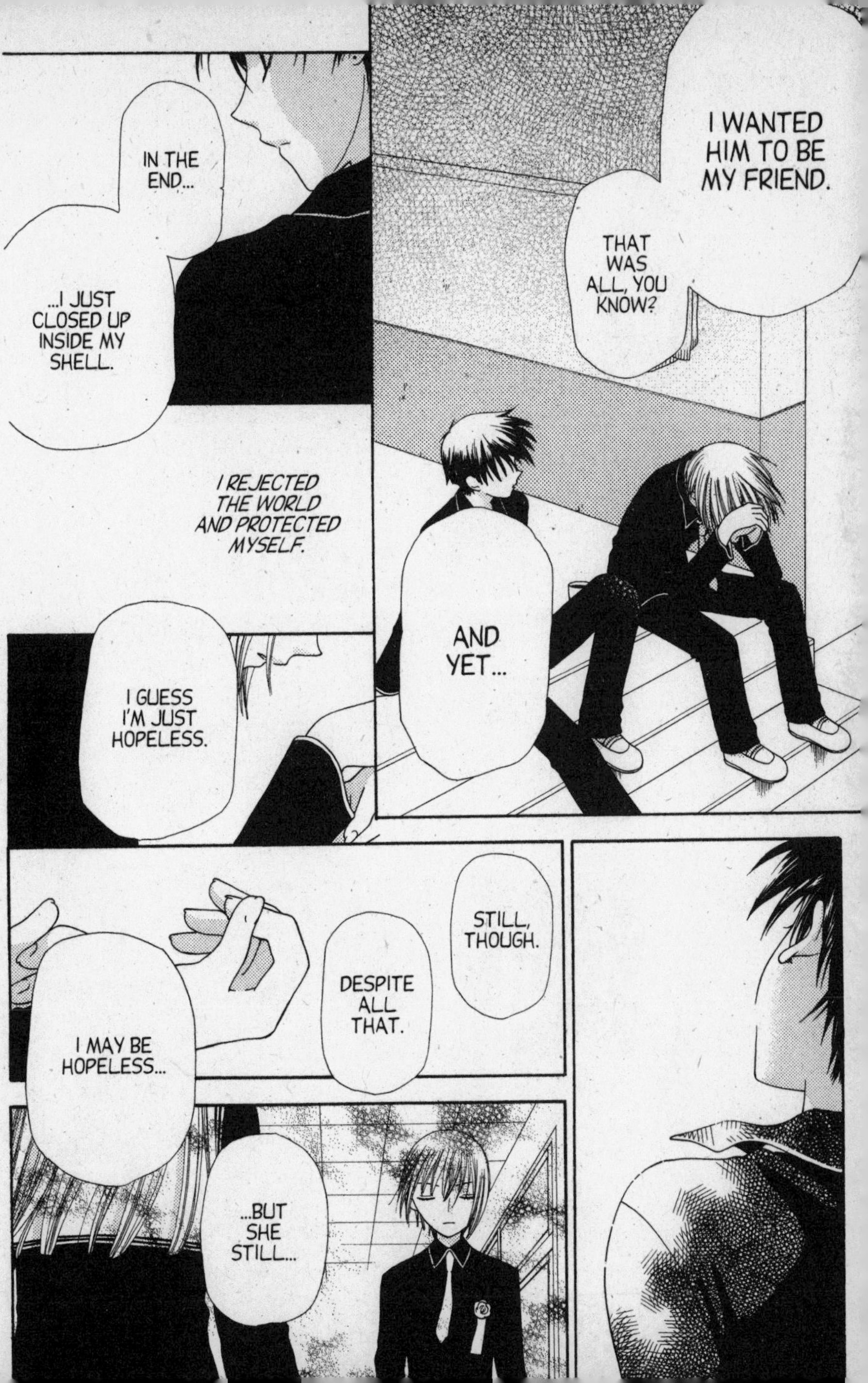
I WANTED HIM TO BE MY FRIEND.
THAT WAS ALL, YOU KNOW?
AND YET...
IN THE END...
...I JUST CLOSED UP INSIDE MY SHELL.
I REJECTED THE WORLD AND PROTECTED MYSELF.
I GUESS I'M JUST HOPELESS.
STILL, THOUGH.
DESPITE ALL THAT.
I MAY BE HOPELESS...
...BUT SHE STILL...

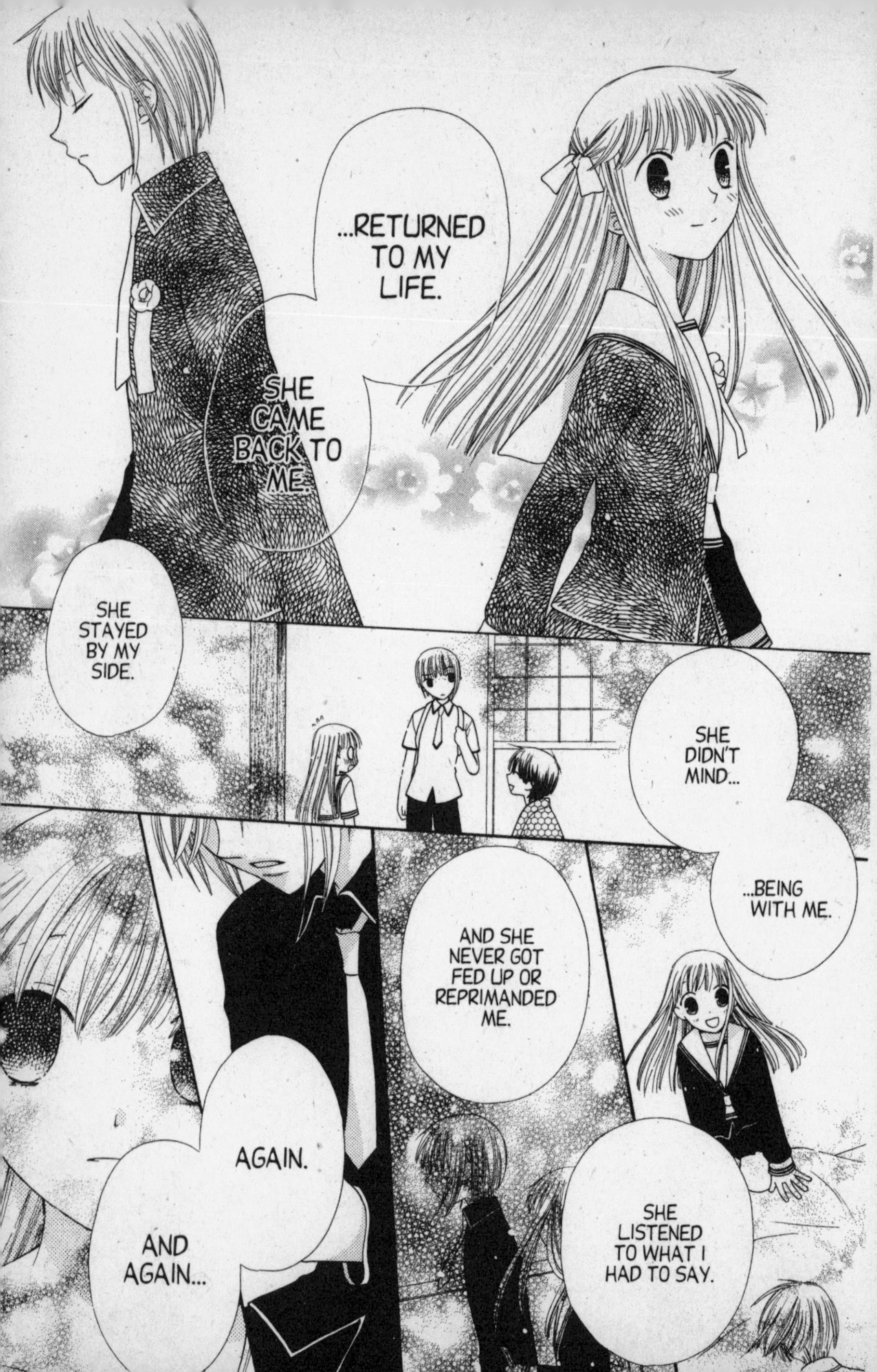
...RETURNED TO MY LIFE.
SHE CAME BACK TO ME.
SHE STAYED BY MY SIDE.
SHE DIDN'T MIND...
...BEING WITH ME.
SHE LISTENED TO WHAT I HAD TO SAY.
AND SHE NEVER GOT FED UP OR REPRIMANDED ME.
AGAIN.
AND AGAIN...

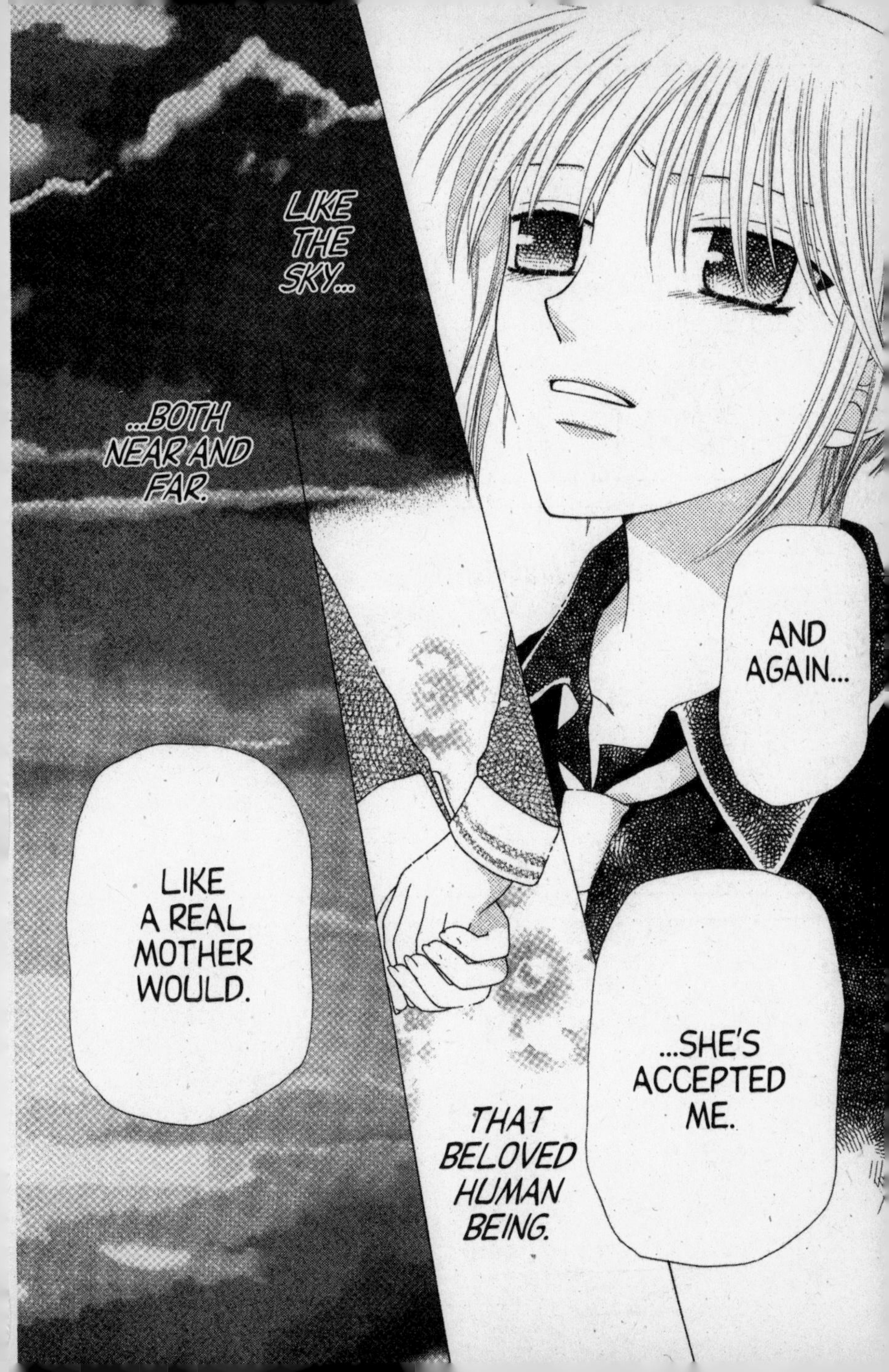
AND AGAIN...
...SHE'S ACCEPTED ME.
THAT BELOVED HUMAN BEING.
LIKE THE SKY...
...BOTH NEAR AND FAR.
LIKE A REAL MOTHER WOULD.

Chapter 86

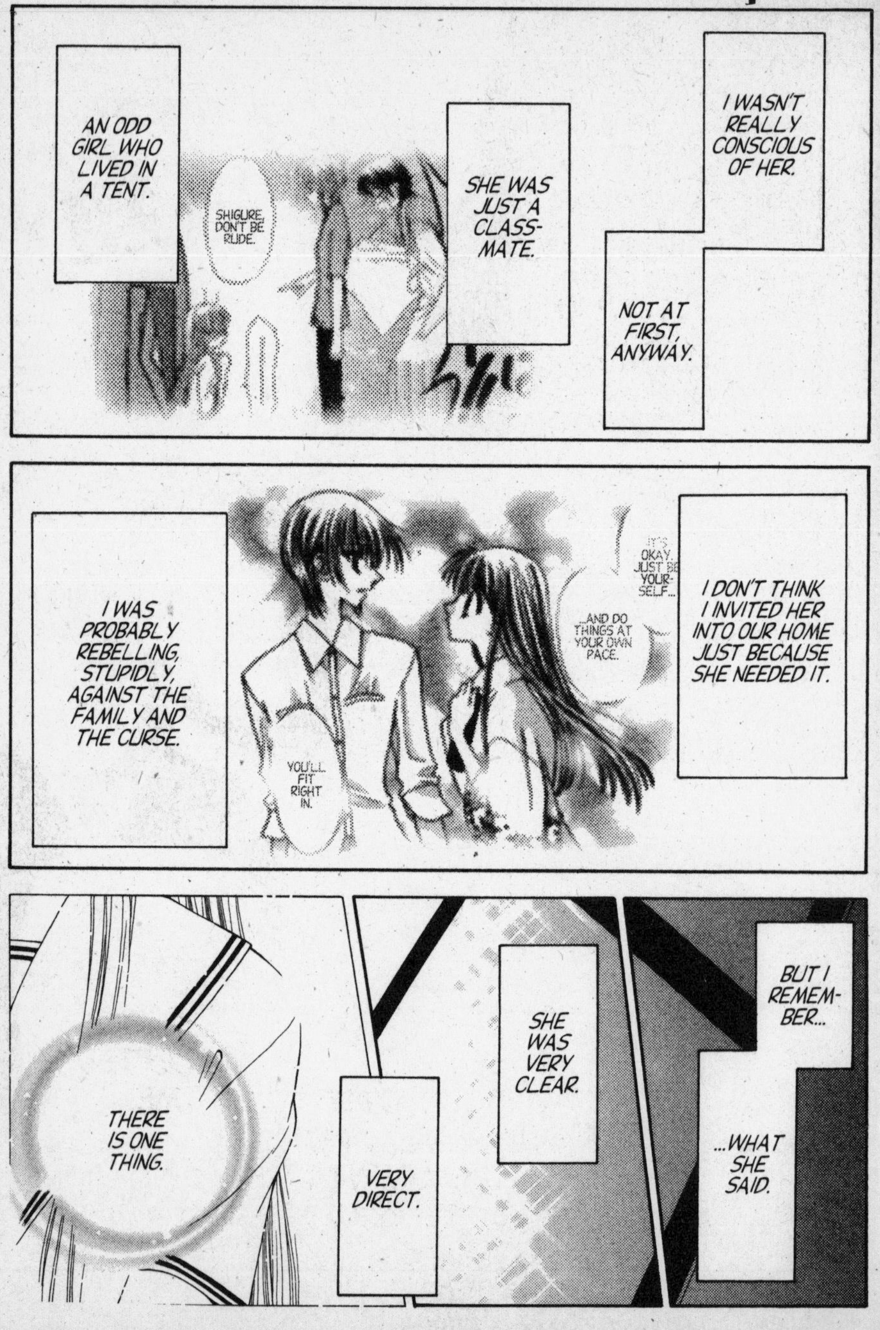
I WASN'T REALLY CONSCIOUS OF HER.
NOT AT FIRST, ANYWAY.
SHE WAS JUST A CLASS-MATE.
SHIGURE, DON'T BE RUDE.
AN ODD GIRL WHO LIVED IN A TENT.
I DON'T THINK I INVITED HER INTO OUR HOME JUST BECAUSE SHE NEEDED IT.
IT'S OKAY. JUST BE YOUR-SELF...
...AND DO THINGS AT YOUR OWN PACE.
YOU'LL FIT RIGHT IN.
I WAS PROBABLY REBELLING, STUPIDLY, AGAINST THE FAMILY AND THE CURSE.
BUT I REMEM-BER...
...WHAT SHE SAID.
SHE WAS VERY CLEAR.
VERY DIRECT.
THERE IS ONE THING.

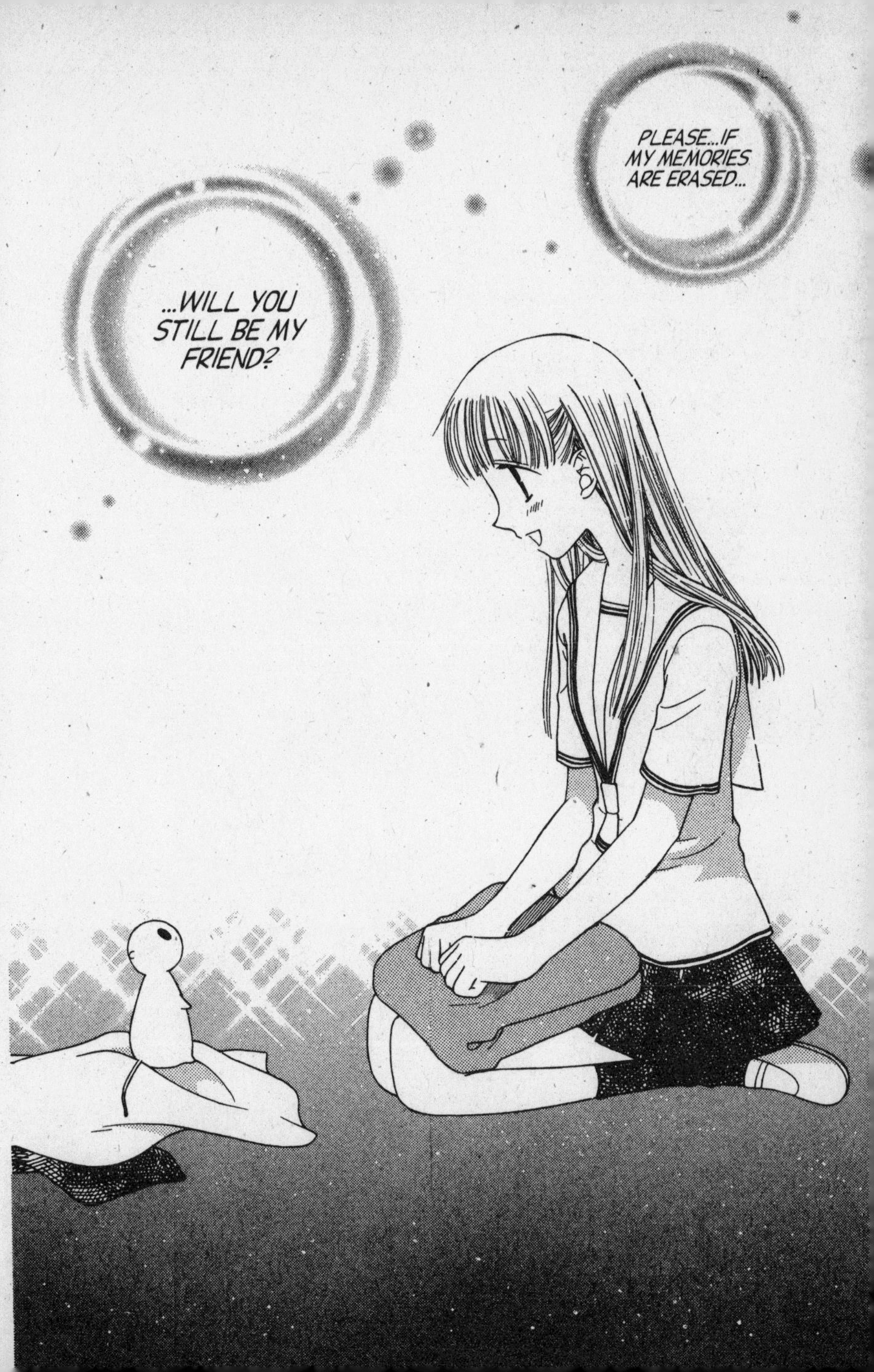
PLEASE...IF MY MEMORIES ARE ERASED...
...WILL YOU STILL BE MY FRIEND?

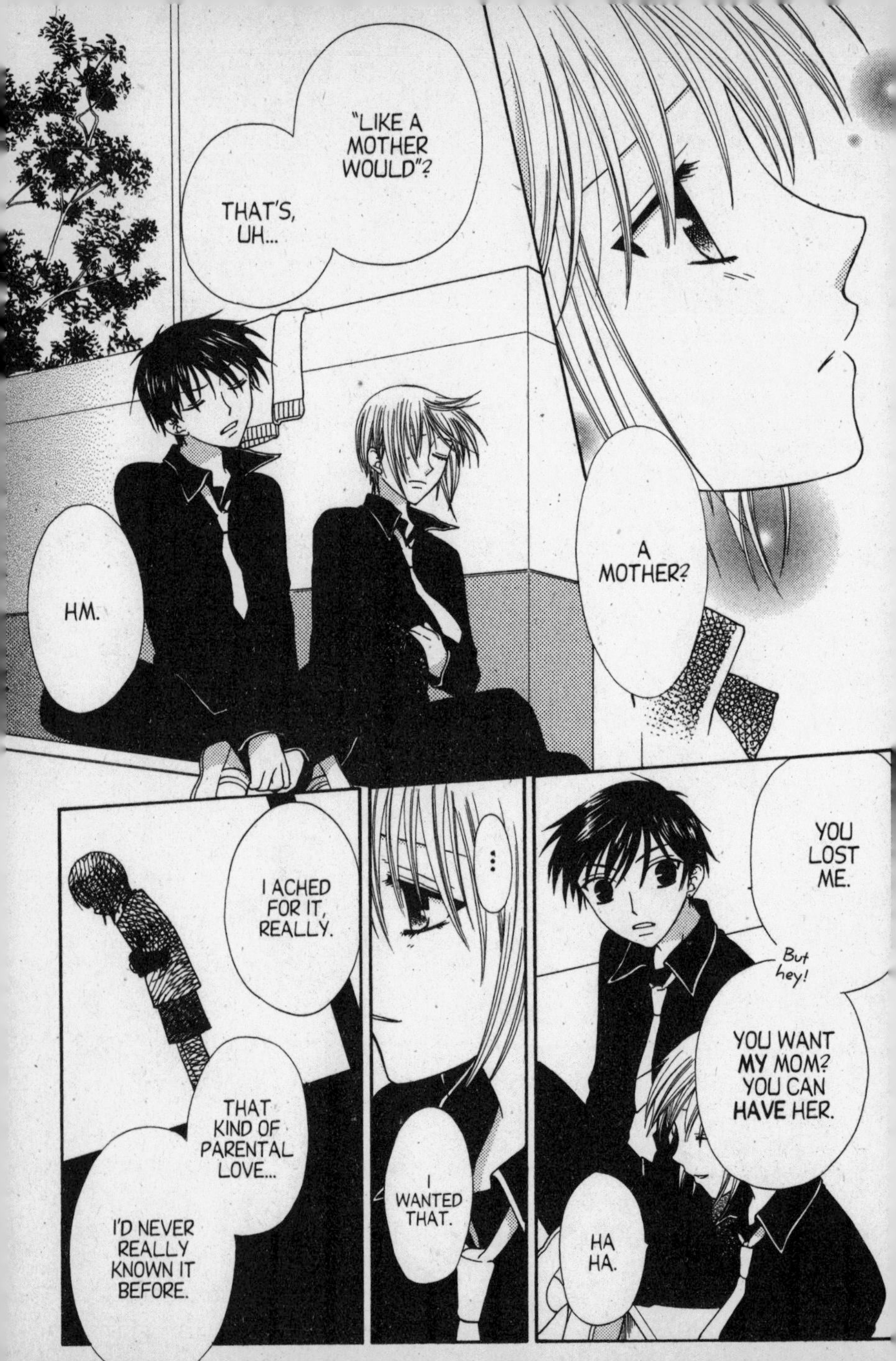
A MOTHER?
"LIKE A MOTHER WOULD"?
THAT'S, UH...
HM.
YOU LOST ME.
But hey!
YOU WANT MY MOM? YOU CAN HAVE HER.
HA HA.
...
I WANTED THAT.
I ACHED FOR IT, REALLY.
THAT KIND OF PARENTAL LOVE...
I'D NEVER REALLY KNOWN IT BEFORE.

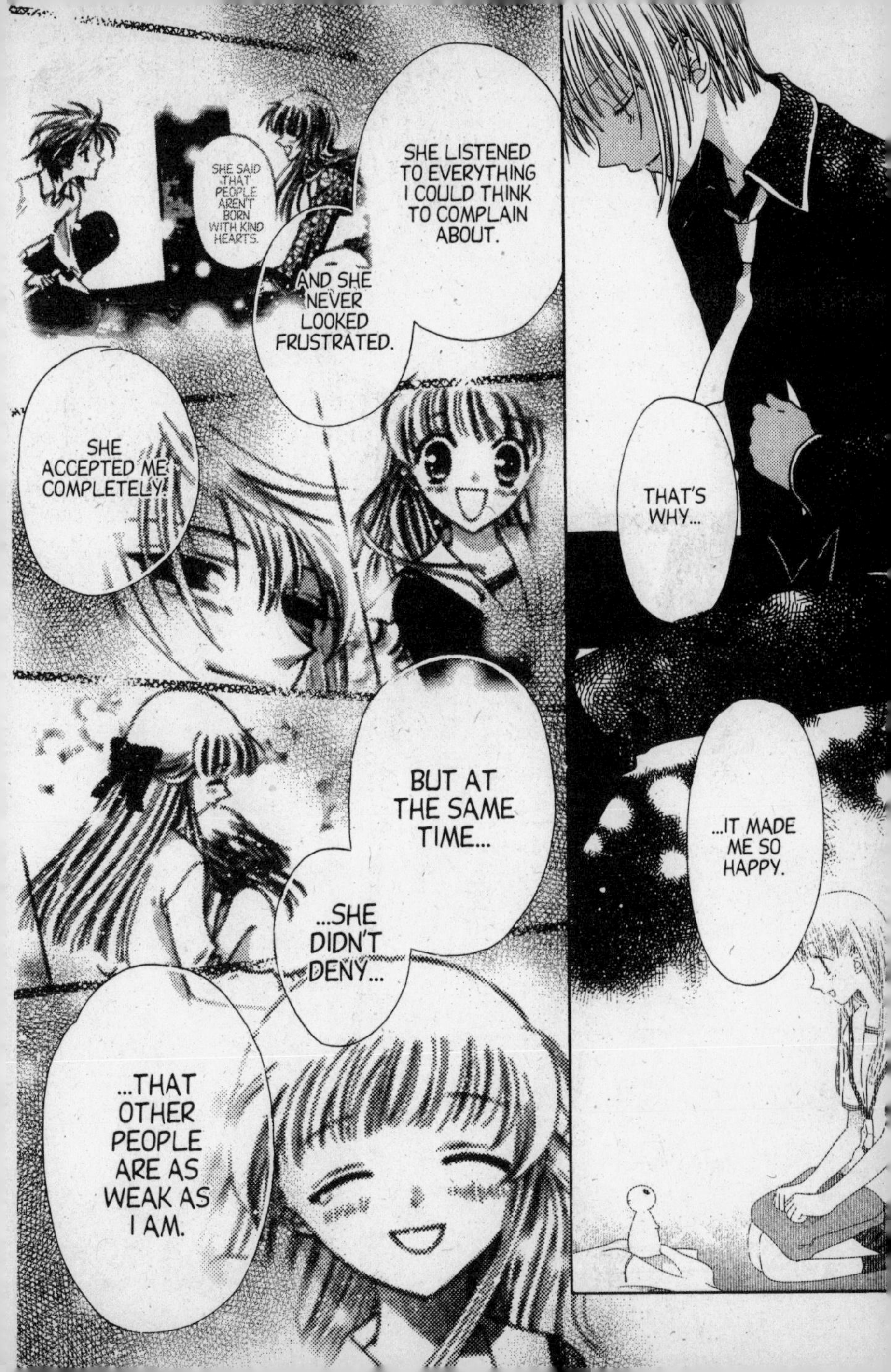
SHE LISTENED TO EVERYTHING I COULD THINK TO COMPLAIN ABOUT.
SHE SAID THAT PEOPLE AREN'T BORN WITH KIND HEARTS.
AND SHE NEVER LOOKED FRUSTRATED.
SHE ACCEPTED ME COMPLETELY.
BUT AT THE SAME TIME...
...SHE DIDN'T DENY...
...THAT OTHER PEOPLE ARE AS WEAK AS I AM.
THAT'S WHY...
...IT MADE ME SO HAPPY.

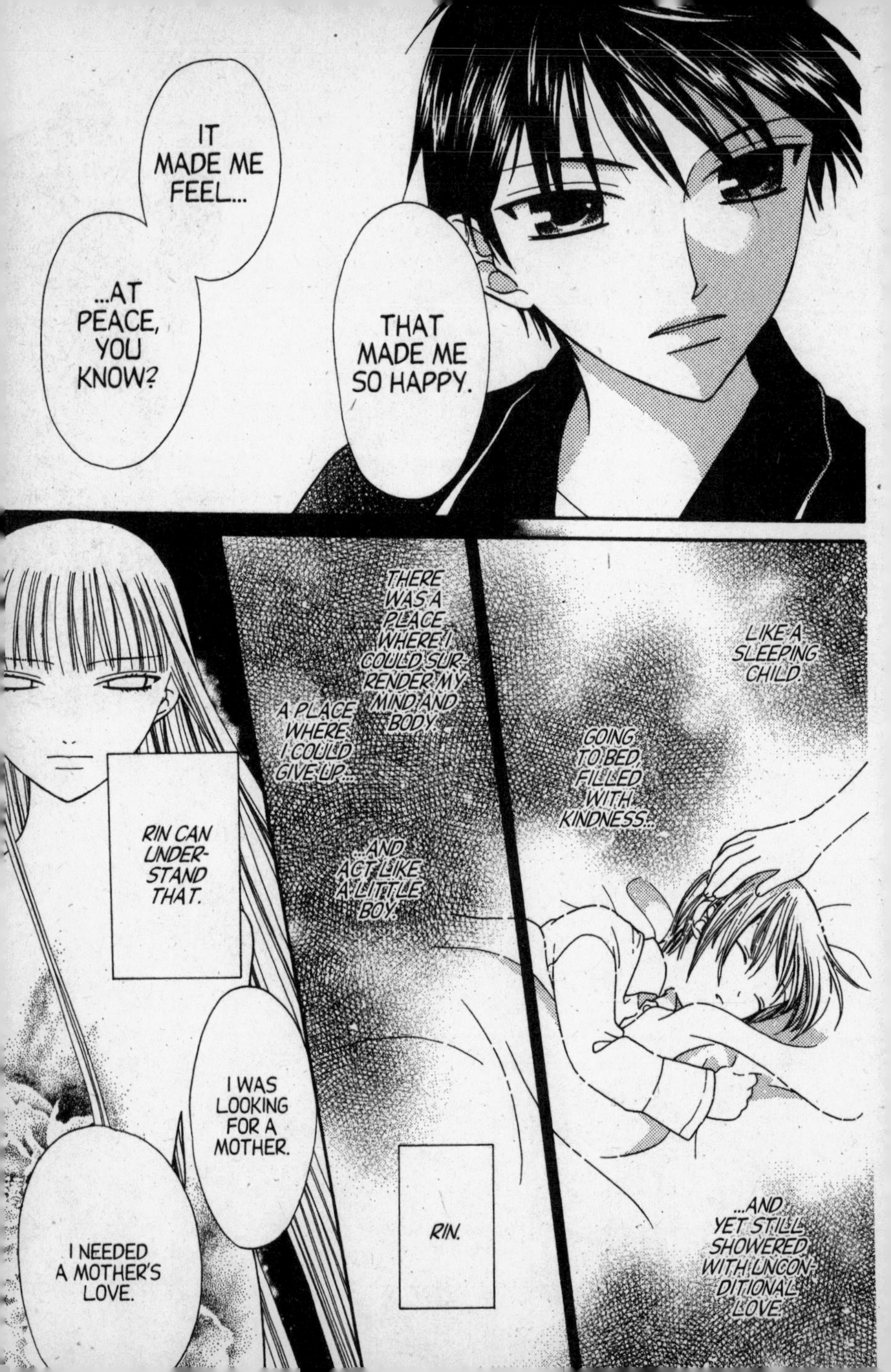
THAT MADE ME SO HAPPY.
IT MADE ME FEEL...
...AT PEACE, YOU KNOW?
LIKE A SLEEPING CHILD.
GOING TO BED, FILLED WITH KINDNESS...
...AND YET STILL SHOWERED WITH UNCON-DITIONAL LOVE.
THERE WAS A PLACE WHERE I COULD SUR-RENDER MY MIND AND BODY.
A PLACE WHERE I COULD GIVE UP...
...AND ACT LIKE A LITTLE BOY.
RIN.
RIN CAN UNDER-STAND THAT.
I WAS LOOKING FOR A MOTHER.
I NEEDED A MOTHER'S LOVE.

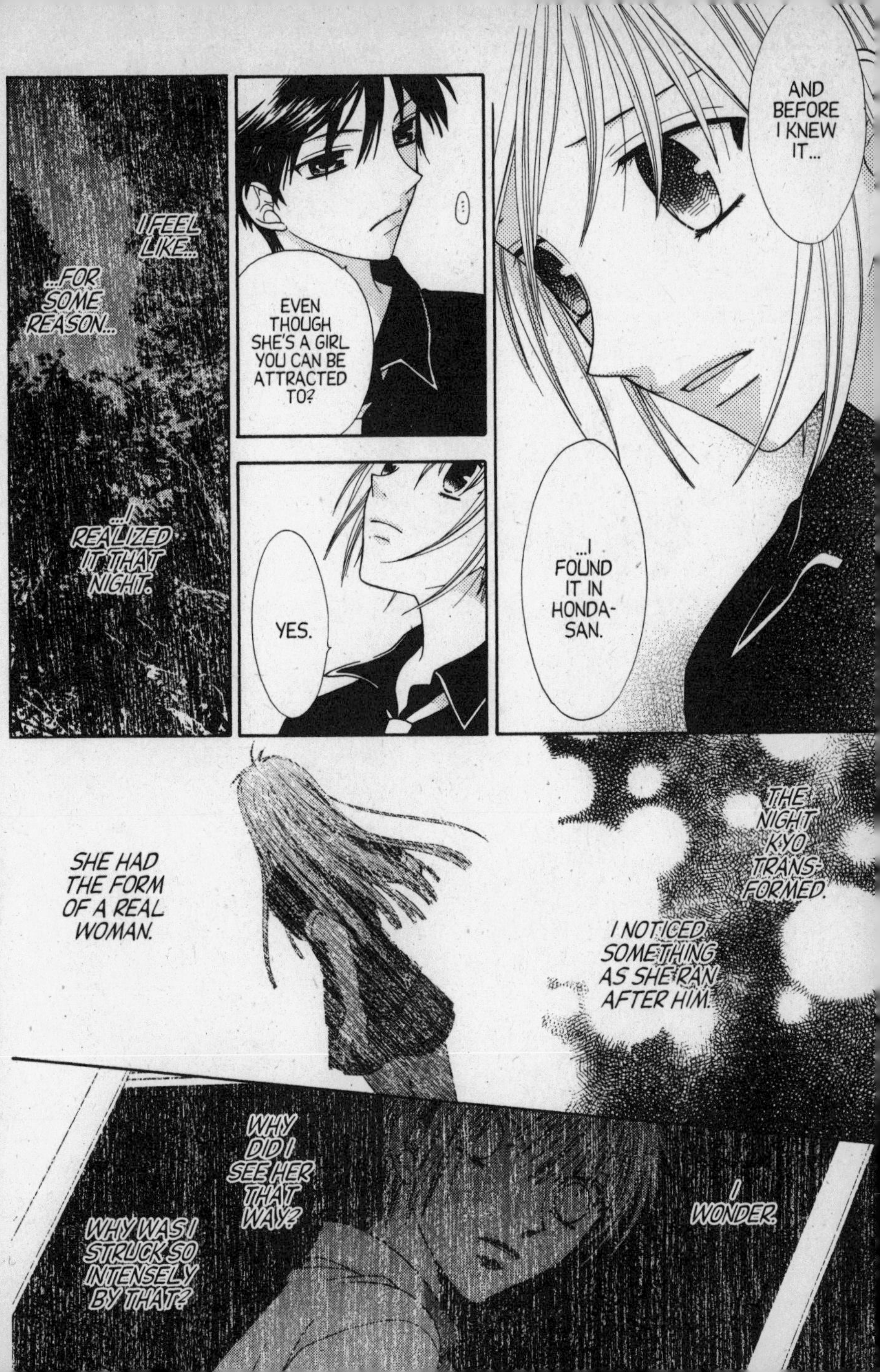
AND BEFORE I KNEW IT...
...I FOUND IT IN HONDA-SAN.
...
EVEN THOUGH SHE'S A GIRL YOU CAN BE ATTRACTED TO?
YES.
I FEEL LIKE...
...FOR SOME REASON...
...I REALIZED IT THAT NIGHT.
THE NIGHT KYO TRANS-FORMED.
I NOTICED SOMETHING AS SHE RAN AFTER HIM.
SHE HAD THE FORM OF A REAL WOMAN.
I WONDER.
WHY DID I SEE HER THAT WAY?
WHY WAS I STRUCK SO INTENSELY BY THAT?

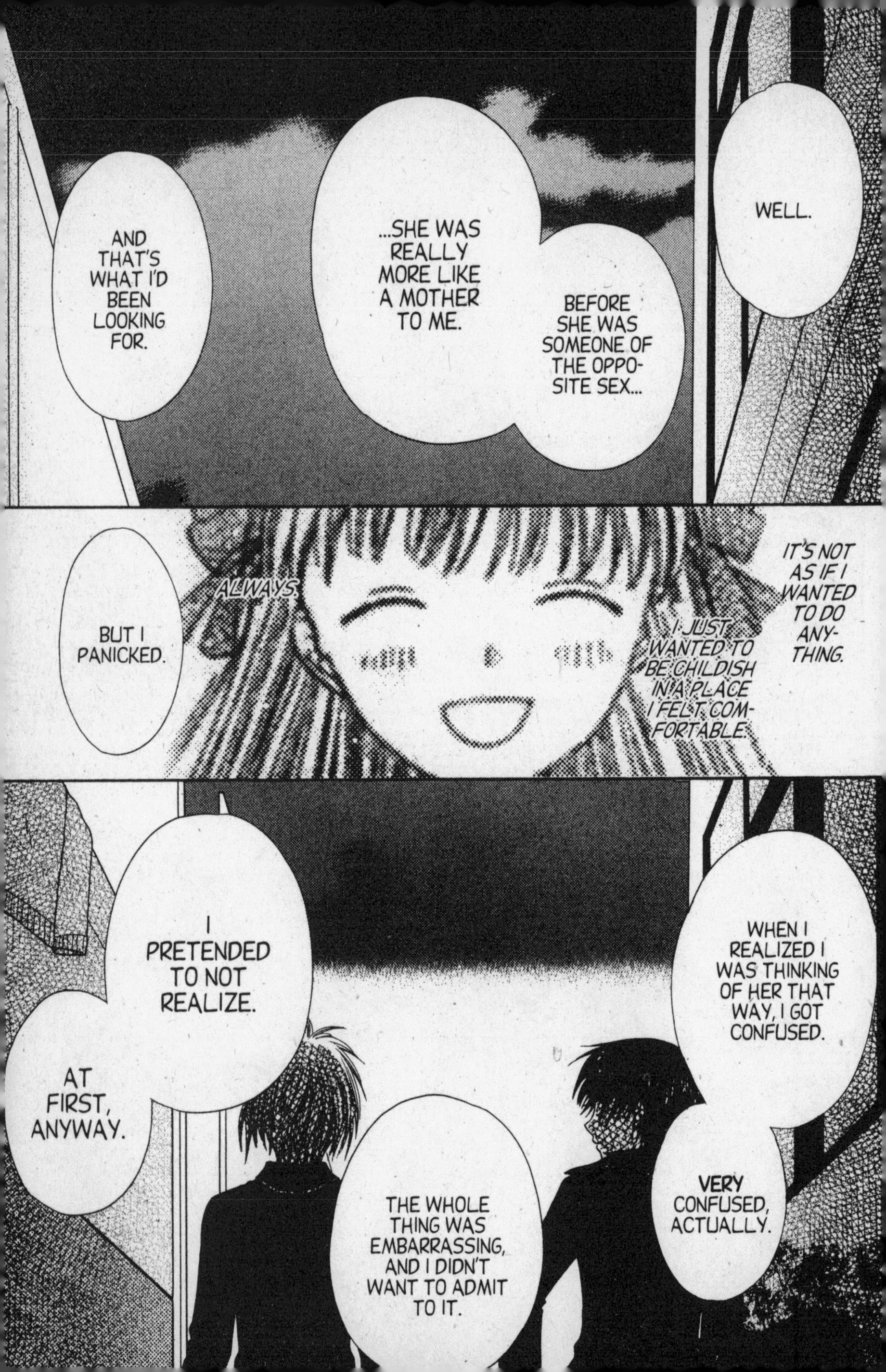
WELL.
BEFORE SHE WAS SOMEONE OF THE OPPOSITE SEX...
...SHE WAS REALLY MORE LIKE A MOTHER TO ME.
AND THAT'S WHAT I'D BEEN LOOKING FOR.
IT'S NOT AS IF I WANTED TO DO ANYTHING.
I JUST WANTED TO BE CHILDISH IN A PLACE I FELT COMFORTABLE.
ALWAYS.
BUT I PANICKED.
WHEN I REALIZED I WAS THINKING OF HER THAT WAY, I GOT CONFUSED.
VERY CONFUSED, ACTUALLY.
THE WHOLE THING WAS EMBARRASSING, AND I DIDN'T WANT TO ADMIT TO IT.
I PRETENDED TO NOT REALIZE.
AT FIRST, ANYWAY.

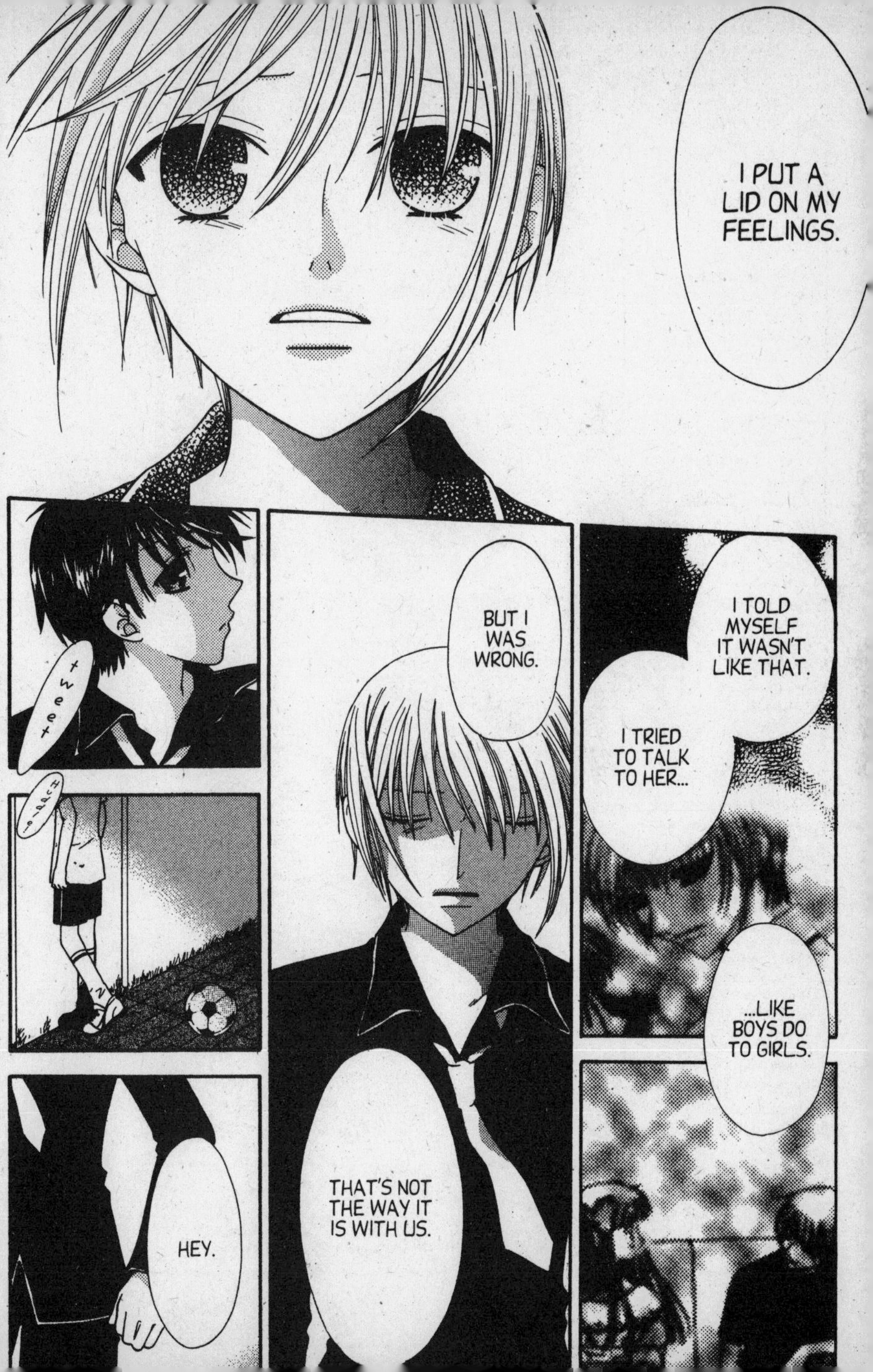
I PUT A LID ON MY FEELINGS.
I TOLD MYSELF IT WASN'T LIKE THAT.
I TRIED TO TALK TO HER...
...LIKE BOYS DO TO GIRLS.
BUT I WAS WRONG.
THAT'S NOT THE WAY IT IS WITH US.
tweet
HEY.

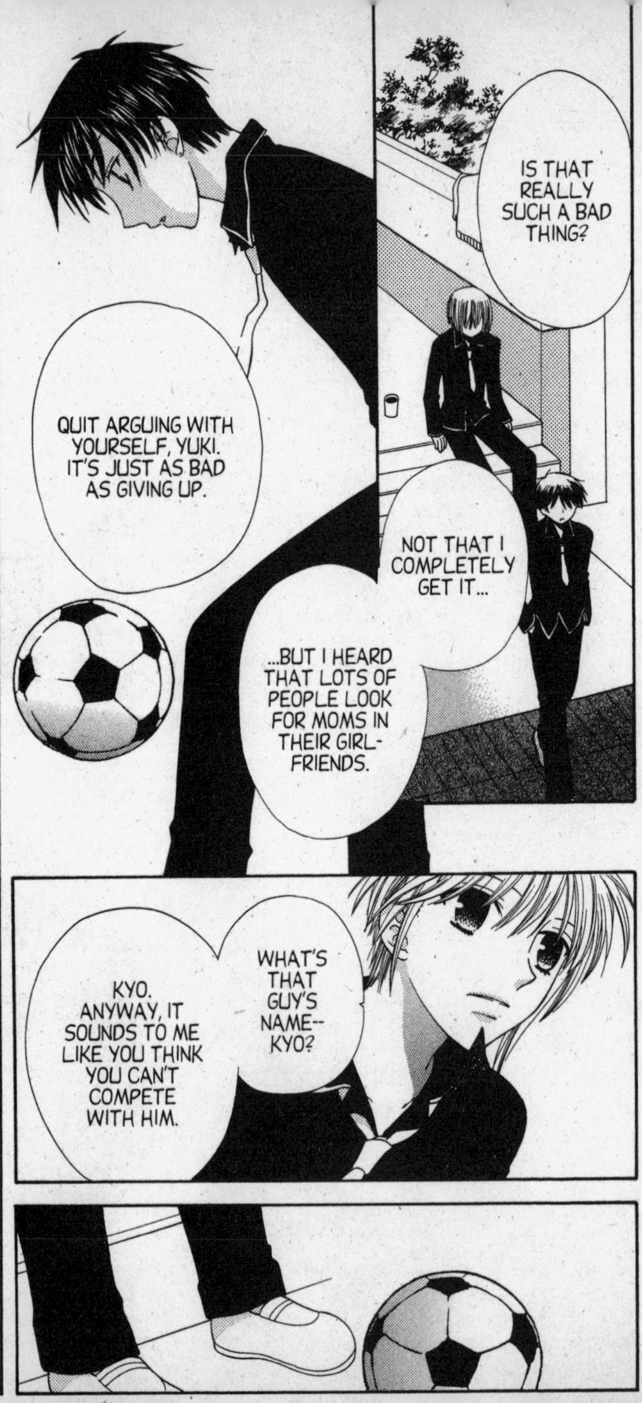
IS THAT REALLY SUCH A BAD THING?
NOT THAT I COMPLETELY GET IT...
...BUT I HEARD THAT LOTS OF PEOPLE LOOK FOR MOMS IN THEIR GIRL-FRIENDS.
QUIT ARGUING WITH YOURSELF, YUKI. IT'S JUST AS BAD AS GIVING UP.
WHAT'S THAT GUY'S NAME--KYO?
KYO. ANYWAY, IT SOUNDS TO ME LIKE YOU THINK YOU CAN'T COMPETE WITH HIM.

Slowly.

Now I'm going to revive all the chat of the Furuba characters. I wonder if I should talk about main characters, too? Even the lead characters have pieces of their back stories the manga can't cover. I think I'll write carefully about them and center on those things. And so, without daring to comment on whether or not I should bother writing things that aren't in the manga, here you go... (I'm losing material.)

We'll begin with he who is often known as the best marriage material of the cast:

Hatori.

Hatori was once part of a family of three, with his father (who died of an illness when he was in high school) and his mother (who died of an illness when he was in elementary school).

By the way, the doctor who appears in the first scene of Chapter 85 is Hatori's father. (You can't tell.)

They were very strict parents. It wasn't a particularly warm home.

←

To be continued...

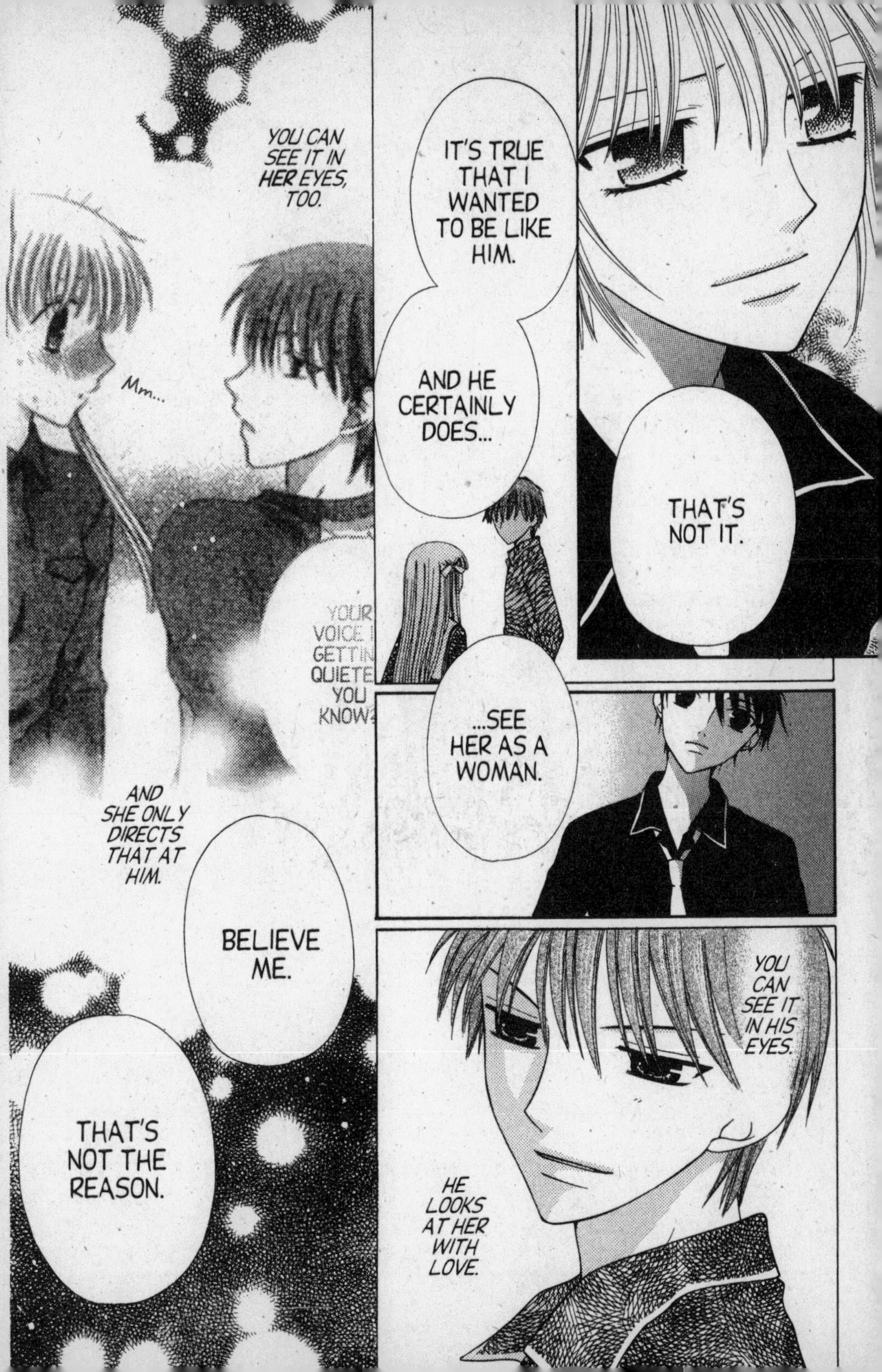

THAT'S NOT IT.
IT'S TRUE THAT I WANTED TO BE LIKE HIM.
AND HE CERTAINLY DOES...
...SEE HER AS A WOMAN.
YOU CAN SEE IT IN HIS EYES.
HE LOOKS AT HER WITH LOVE.
YOU CAN SEE IT IN HER EYES, TOO.
Mm...
YOUR VOICE I GETTIN QUIETE YOU KNOW?
AND SHE ONLY DIRECTS THAT AT HIM.
BELIEVE ME.
THAT'S NOT THE REASON.

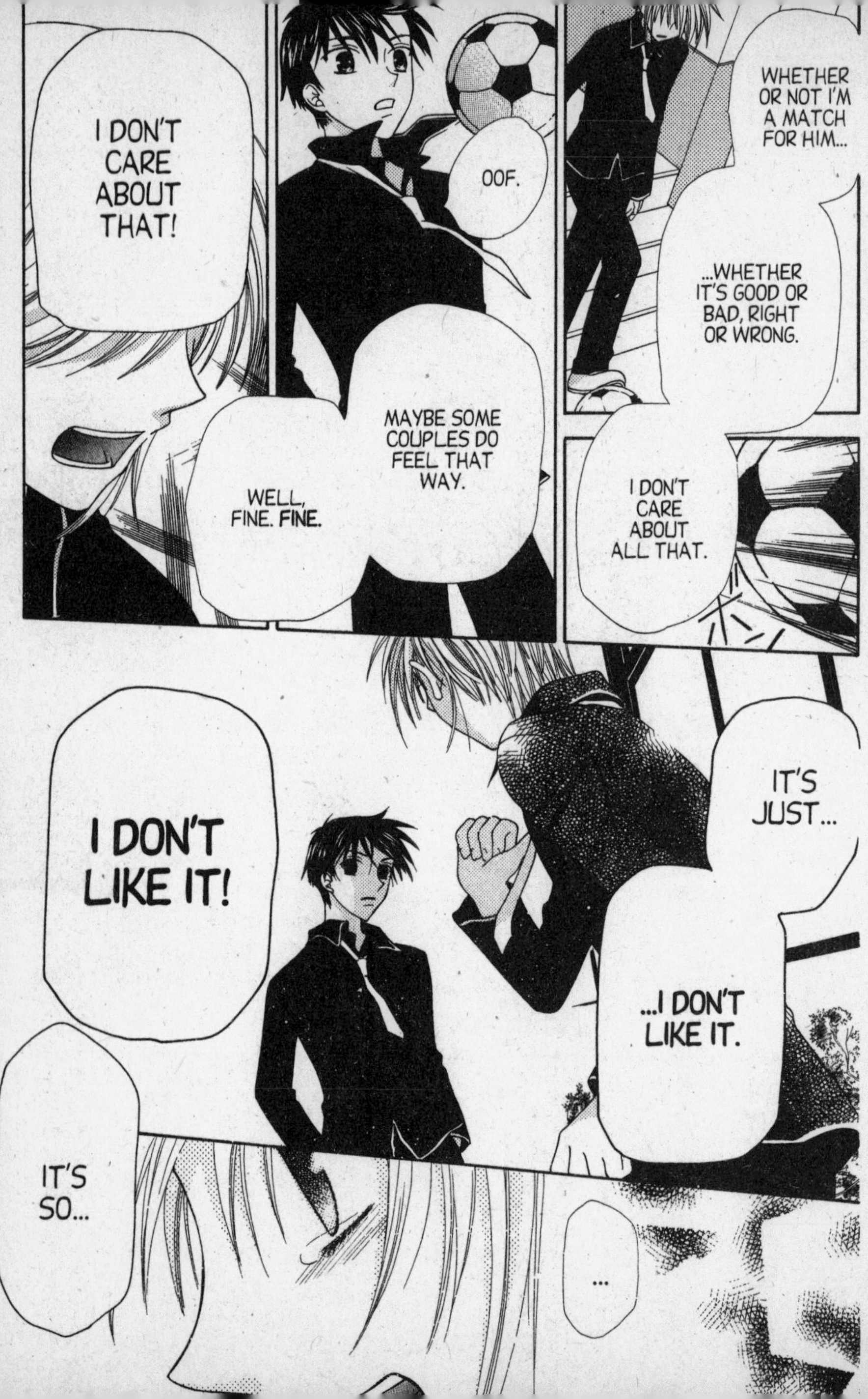
WHETHER OR NOT I'M A MATCH FOR HIM...
...WHETHER IT'S GOOD OR BAD, RIGHT OR WRONG.
I DON'T CARE ABOUT ALL THAT.
OOF.
MAYBE SOME COUPLES DO FEEL THAT WAY.
WELL, FINE. FINE.
I DON'T CARE ABOUT THAT!
IT'S JUST...
...I DON'T LIKE IT.
I DON'T LIKE IT!
...
IT'S SO...

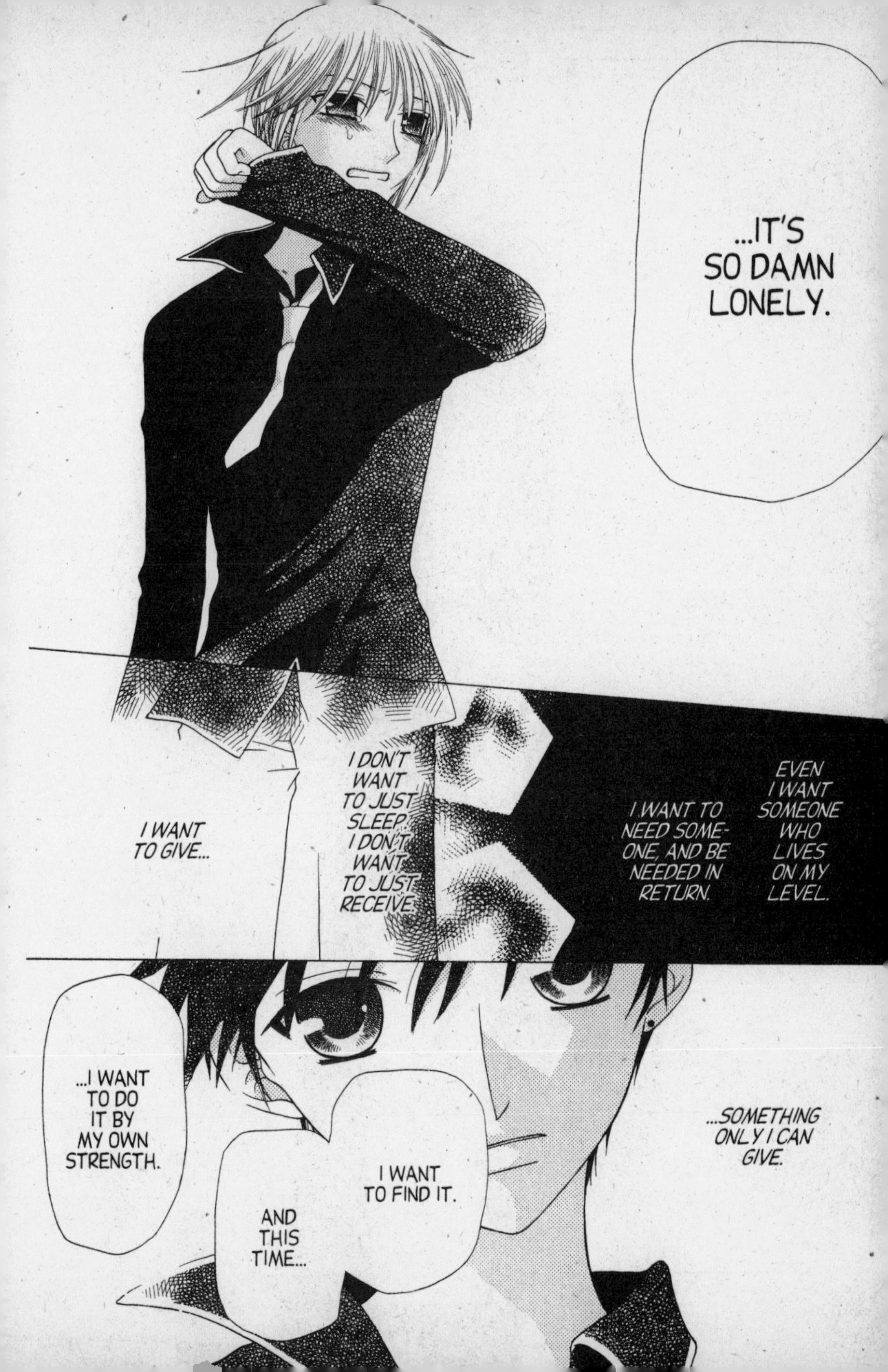
...IT'S SO DAMN LONELY.
EVEN I WANT SOMEONE WHO LIVES ON MY LEVEL.
I WANT TO NEED SOME-ONE, AND BE NEEDED IN RETURN.
I DON'T WANT TO JUST SLEEP. I DON'T WANT TO JUST RECEIVE.
I WANT TO GIVE...
...SOMETHING ONLY I CAN GIVE.
I WANT TO FIND IT.
AND THIS TIME...
...I WANT TO DO IT BY MY OWN STRENGTH.

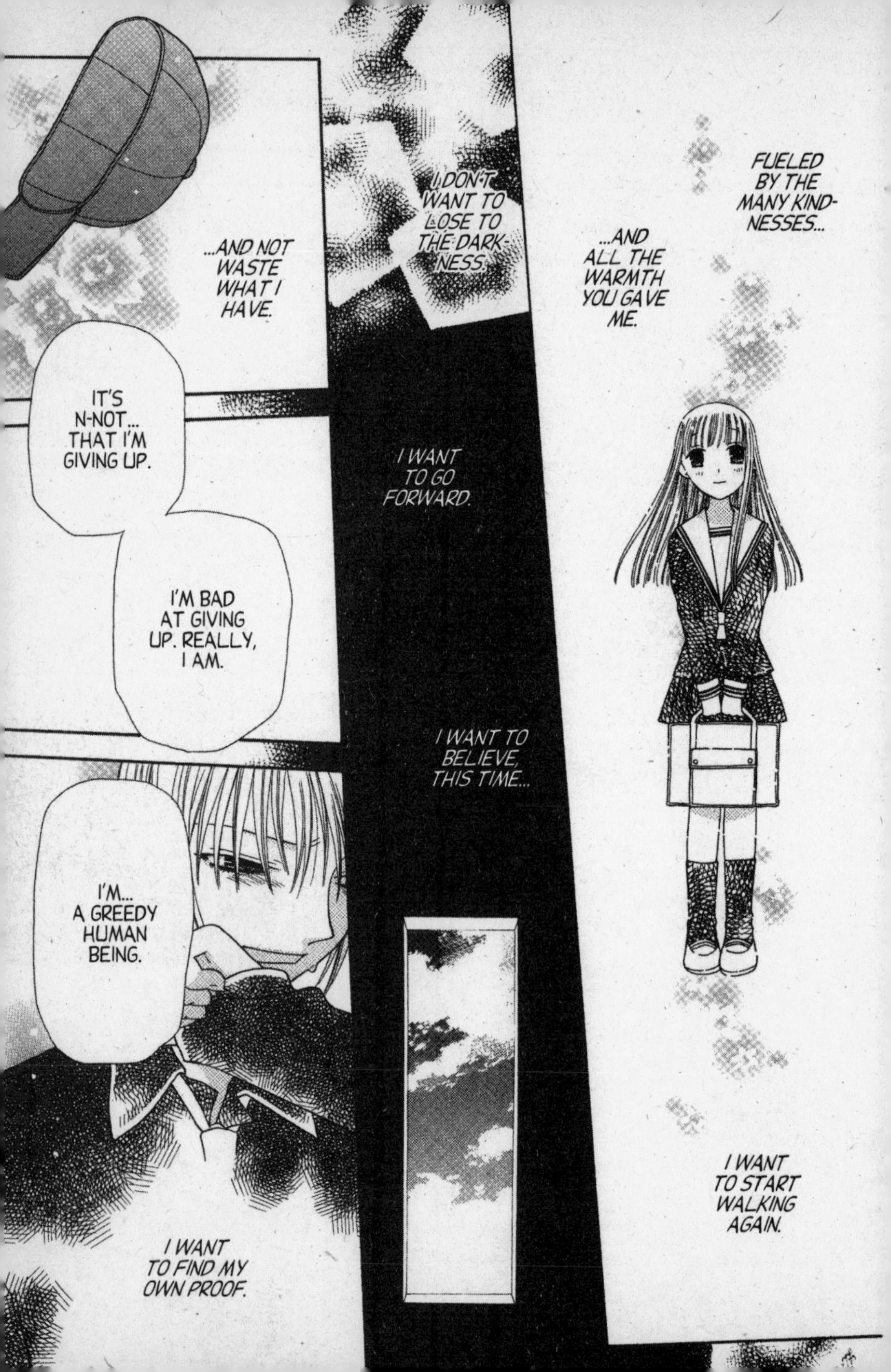
FUELED BY THE MANY KINDNESSES...
...AND ALL THE WARMTH YOU GAVE ME.
I WANT TO START WALKING AGAIN.
I DON'T WANT TO LOSE TO THE DARKNESS.
I WANT TO GO FORWARD.
I WANT TO BELIEVE, THIS TIME...
...AND NOT WASTE WHAT I HAVE.
IT'S N-NOT... THAT I'M GIVING UP.
I'M BAD AT GIVING UP. REALLY, I AM.
I'M... A GREEDY HUMAN BEING.
I WANT TO FIND MY OWN PROOF.

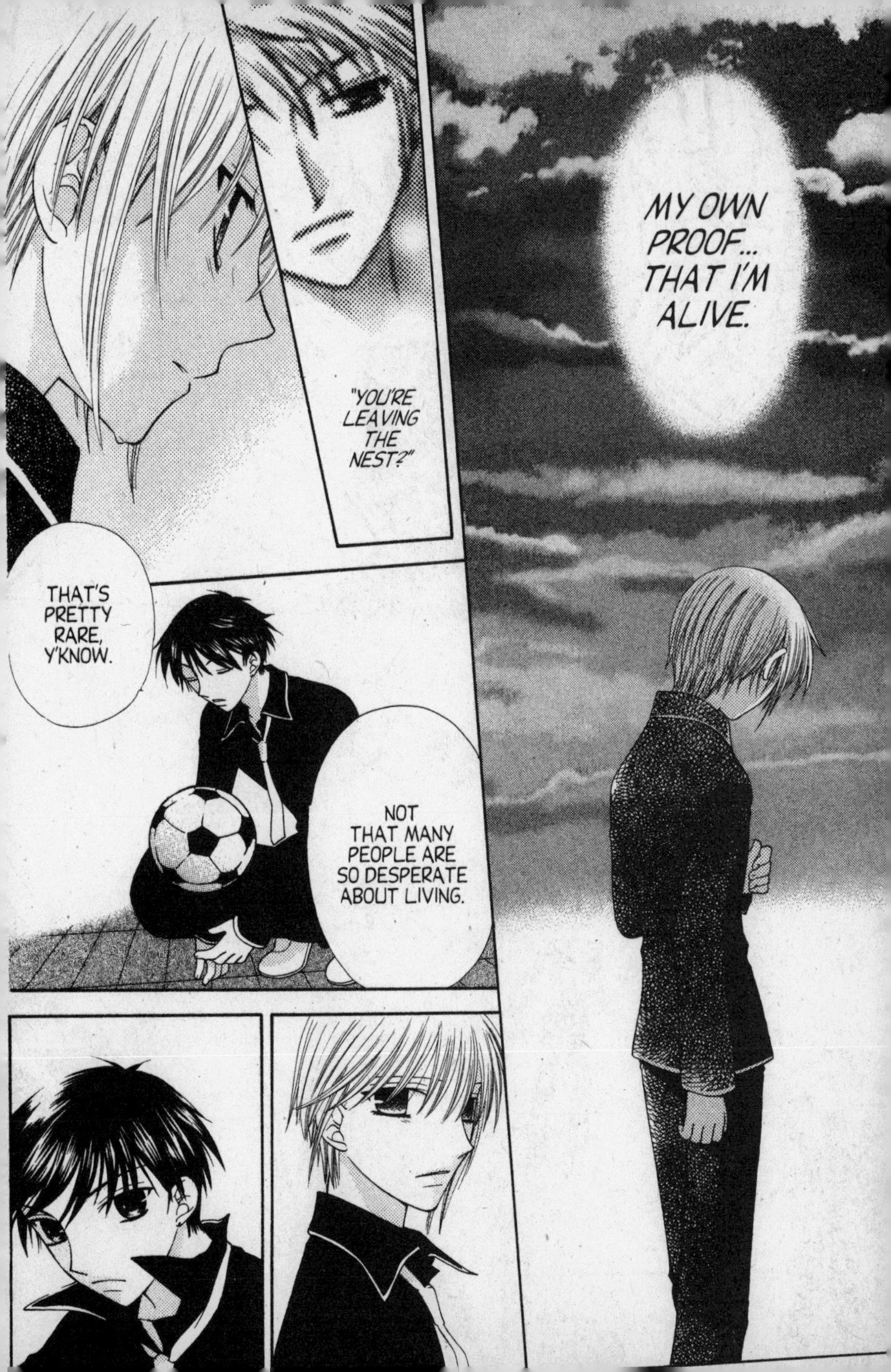
MY OWN PROOF... THAT I'M ALIVE.
"YOU'RE LEAVING THE NEST?"
THAT'S PRETTY RARE, Y'KNOW.
NOT THAT MANY PEOPLE ARE SO DESPERATE ABOUT LIVING.

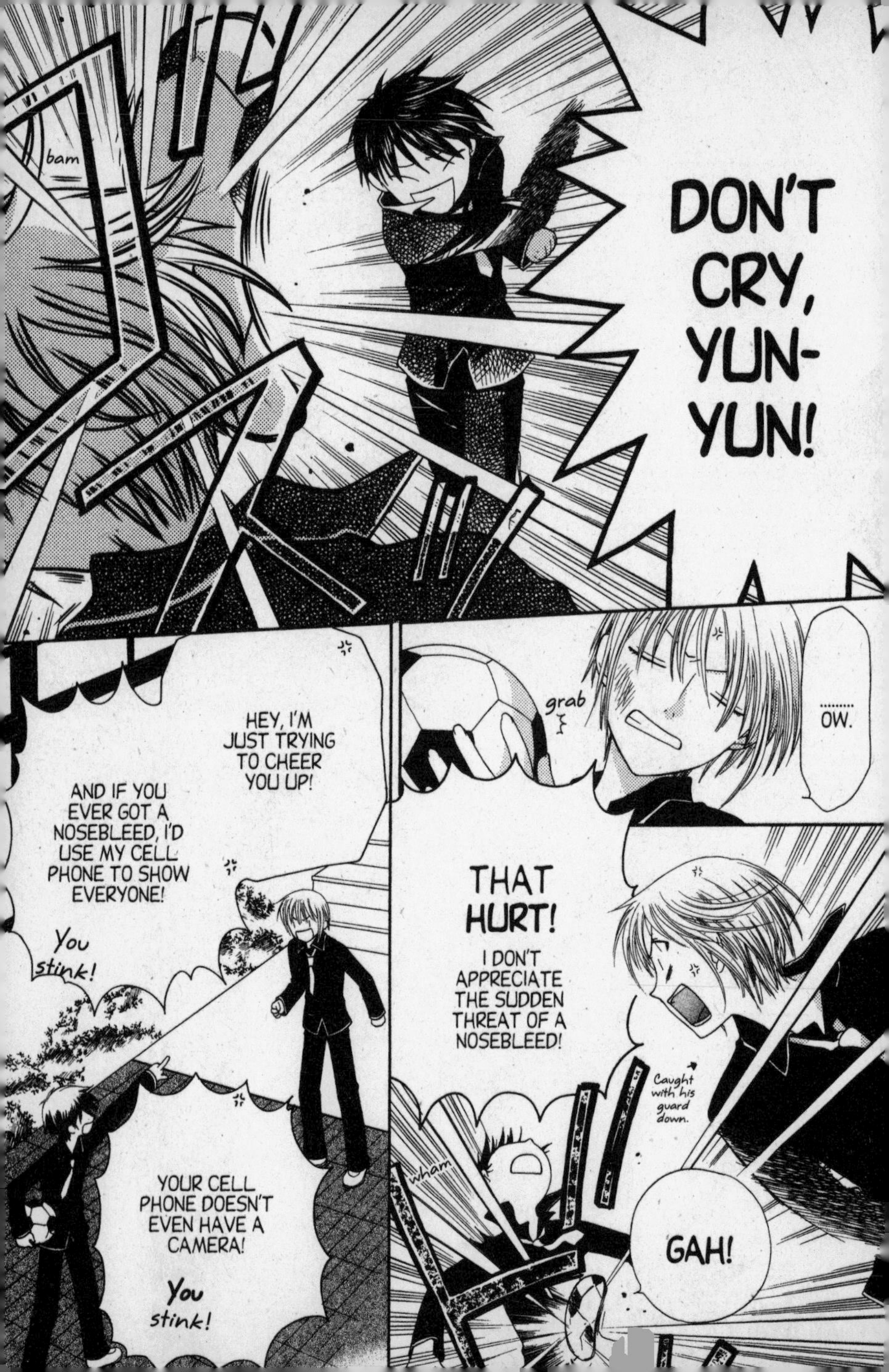
bam
DON'T CRY, YUN-YUN!
.... OW.
grab
THAT HURT!
I DON'T APPRECIATE THE SUDDEN THREAT OF A NOSEBLEED!
Caught with his guard down.
wham
GAH!
HEY, I'M JUST TRYING TO CHEER YOU UP!
AND IF YOU EVER GOT A NOSEBLEED, I'D USE MY CELL PHONE TO SHOW EVERYONE!
You stink!
YOUR CELL PHONE DOESN'T EVEN HAVE A CAMERA!
You stink!

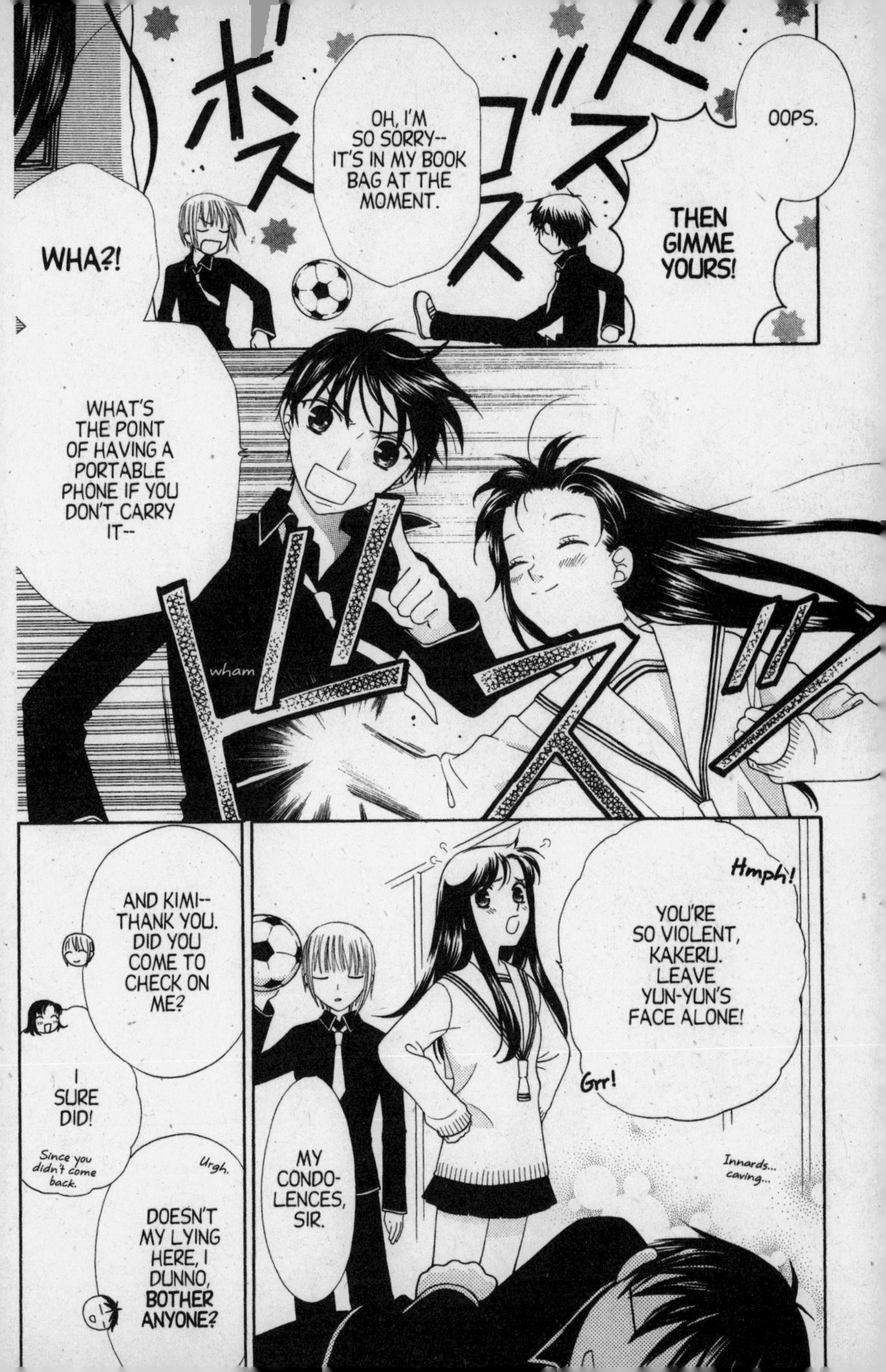
OOPS.
THEN GIMME YOURS!
ドス
ゴス
ボス
OH, I'M SO SORRY-- IT'S IN MY BOOK BAG AT THE MOMENT.
WHA?!
WHAT'S THE POINT OF HAVING A PORTABLE PHONE IF YOU DON'T CARRY IT--
wham
Hmph!
YOU'RE SO VIOLENT, KAKERU. LEAVE YUN-YUN'S FACE ALONE!
Grr!
Innards... caving...
MY CONDOLENCES, SIR.
AND KIMI-- THANK YOU. DID YOU COME TO CHECK ON ME?
I SURE DID!
Since you didn't come back.
Urgh.
DOESN'T MY LYING HERE, I DUNNO, BOTHER ANYONE?

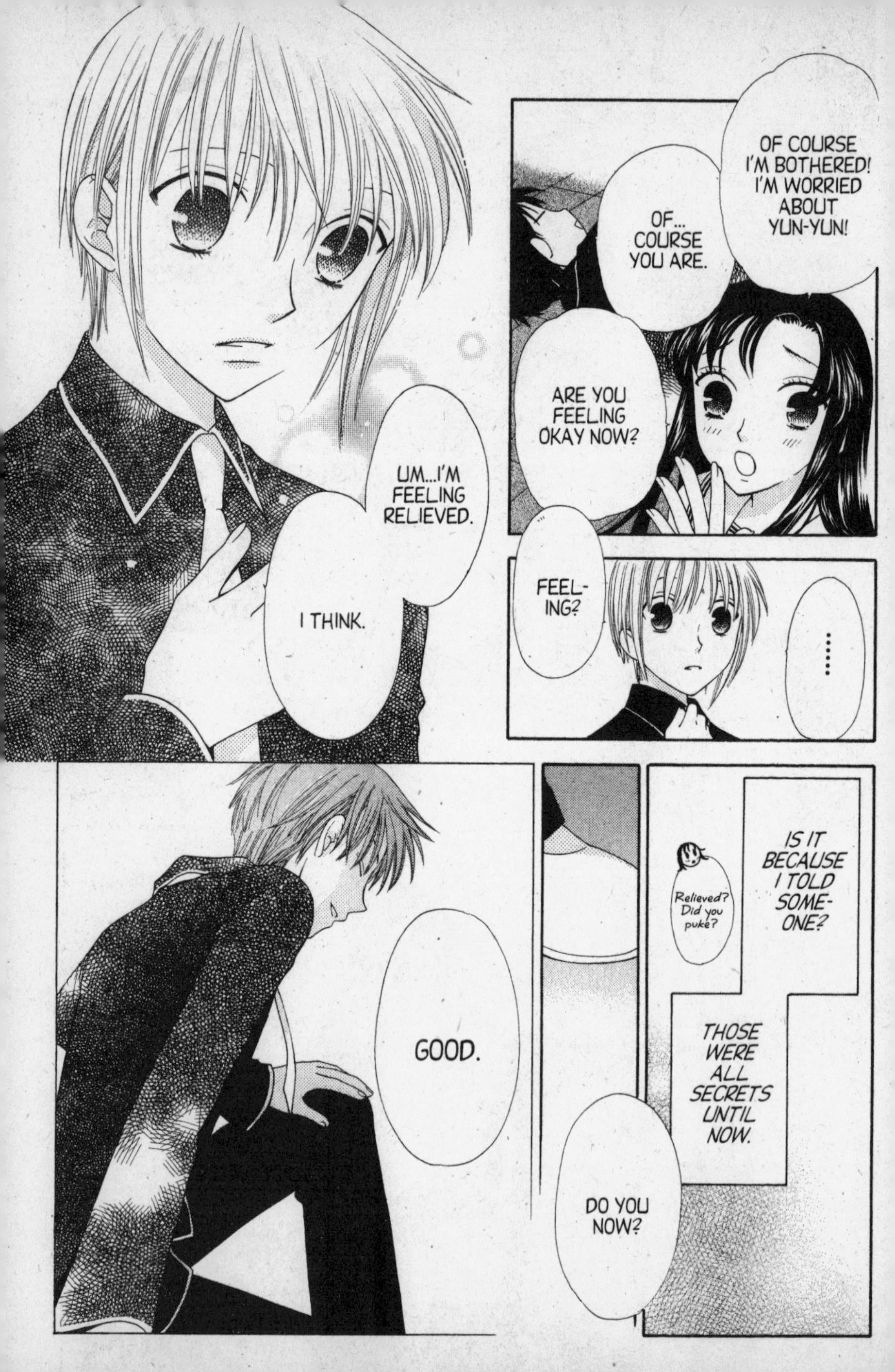
OF COURSE I'M BOTHERED! I'M WORRIED ABOUT YUN-YUN!
OF... COURSE YOU ARE.
ARE YOU FEELING OKAY NOW?
......
FEEL-ING?
UM...I'M FEELING RELIEVED.
I THINK.
IS IT BECAUSE I TOLD SOME-ONE?
Relieved? Did you puke?
THOSE WERE ALL SECRETS UNTIL NOW.
DO YOU NOW?
GOOD.

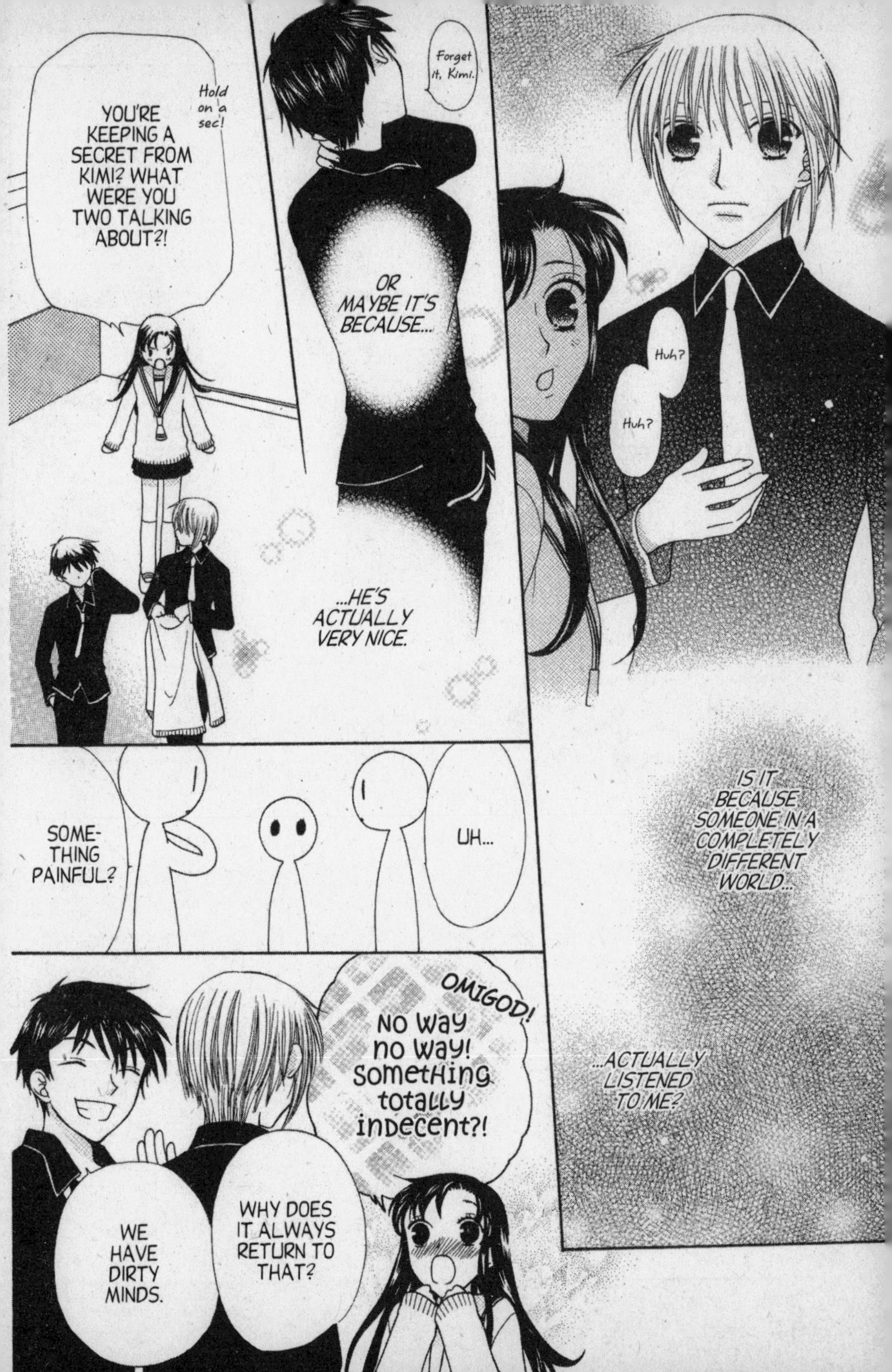

Huh?
Huh?
IS IT BECAUSE SOMEONE IN A COMPLETELY DIFFERENT WORLD...
...ACTUALLY LISTENED TO ME?
Forget it, Kimi.
OR MAYBE IT'S BECAUSE...
...HE'S ACTUALLY VERY NICE.
Hold on a sec!
YOU'RE KEEPING A SECRET FROM KIMI? WHAT WERE YOU TWO TALKING ABOUT?!
UH...
SOME-THING PAINFUL?
OMIGOD!
No way no way! Something totally indecent?!
WHY DOES IT ALWAYS RETURN TO THAT?
WE HAVE DIRTY MINDS.

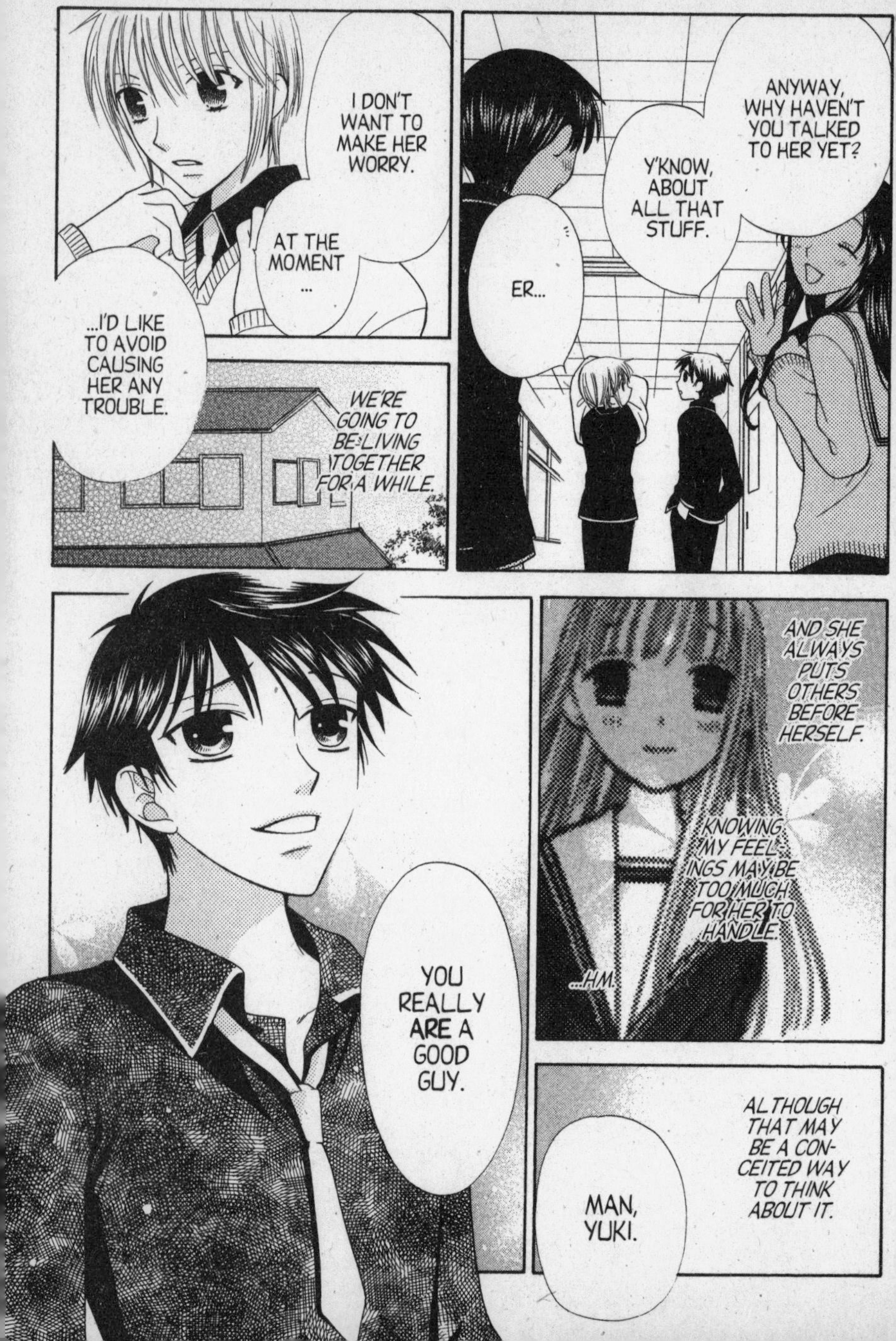
ANYWAY, WHY HAVEN'T YOU TALKED TO HER YET?
Y'KNOW, ABOUT ALL THAT STUFF.
ER...
I DON'T WANT TO MAKE HER WORRY.
AT THE MOMENT ...
...I'D LIKE TO AVOID CAUSING HER ANY TROUBLE.
WE'RE GOING TO BE LIVING TOGETHER FOR A WHILE.
AND SHE ALWAYS PUTS OTHERS BEFORE HERSELF.
KNOWING MY FEELINGS MAY BE TOO MUCH FOR HER TO HANDLE.
...HM.
ALTHOUGH THAT MAY BE A CONCEITED WAY TO THINK ABOUT IT.
MAN, YUKI.
YOU REALLY ARE A GOOD GUY.

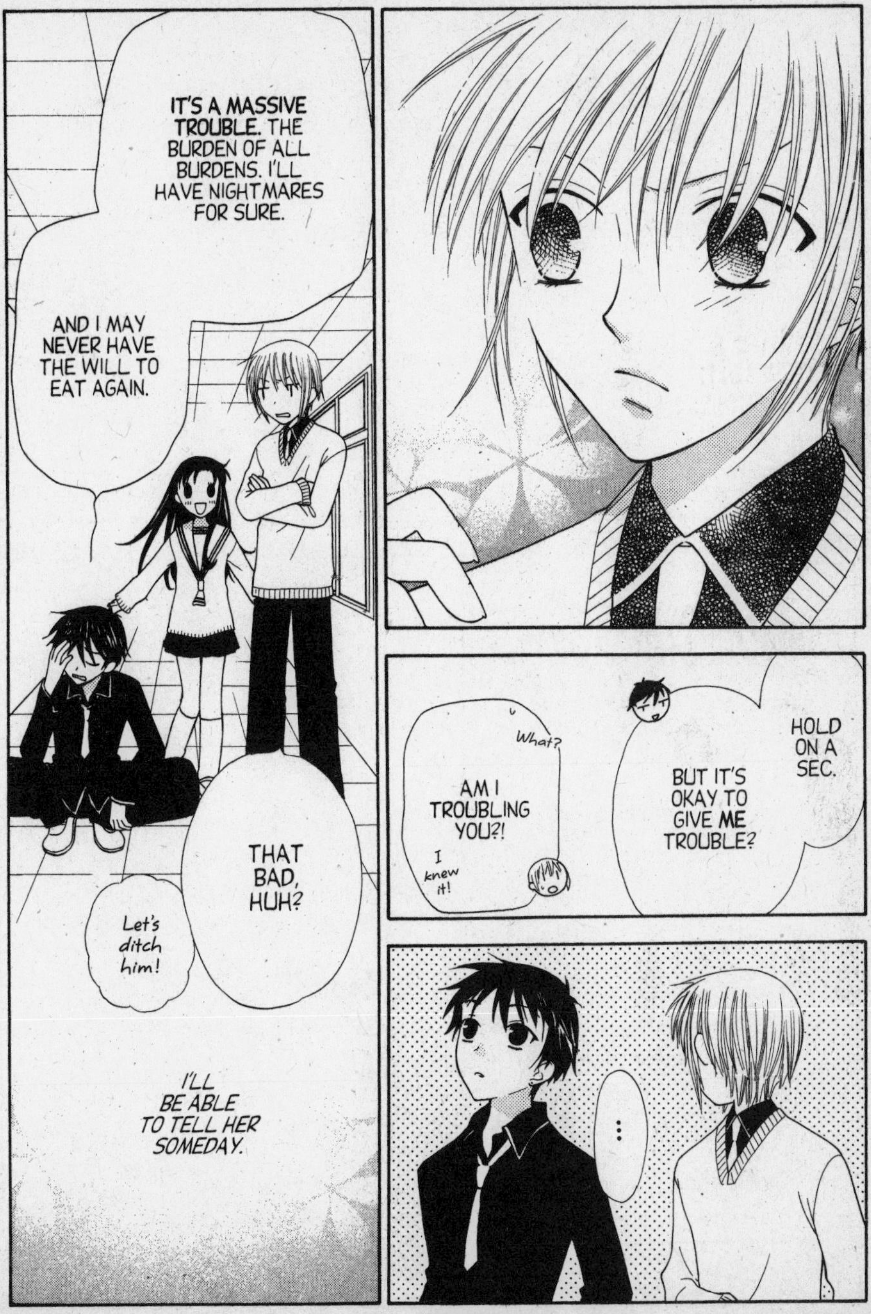
HOLD ON A SEC.
BUT IT'S OKAY TO GIVE ME TROUBLE?
What?
AM I TROUBLING YOU?!
I knew it!
...
IT'S A MASSIVE TROUBLE. THE BURDEN OF ALL BURDENS. I'LL HAVE NIGHTMARES FOR SURE.
AND I MAY NEVER HAVE THE WILL TO EAT AGAIN.
THAT BAD, HUH?
Let's ditch him!
I'LL BE ABLE TO TELL HER SOMEDAY.

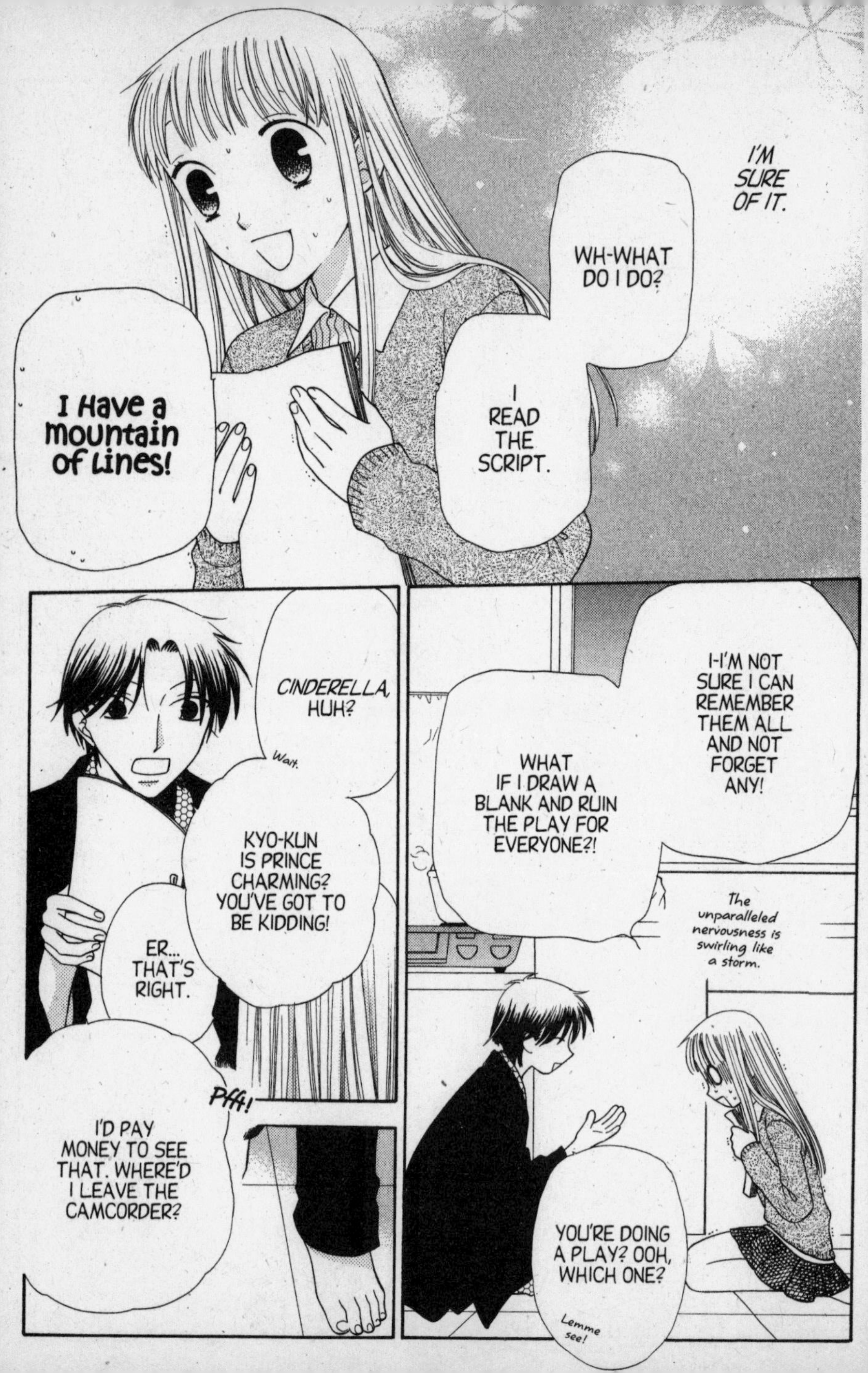
I'M SURE OF IT.
WH-WHAT DO I DO?
I READ THE SCRIPT.
I Have a mountain of Lines!
I-I'M NOT SURE I CAN REMEMBER THEM ALL AND NOT FORGET ANY!
WHAT IF I DRAW A BLANK AND RUIN THE PLAY FOR EVERYONE?!
The unparalleled nervousness is swirling like a storm.
YOU'RE DOING A PLAY? OOH, WHICH ONE?
Lemme see!
CINDERELLA, HUH?
Wait.
KYO-KUN IS PRINCE CHARMING? YOU'VE GOT TO BE KIDDING!
ER... THAT'S RIGHT.
Pfft!
I'D PAY MONEY TO SEE THAT. WHERE'D I LEAVE THE CAMCORDER?

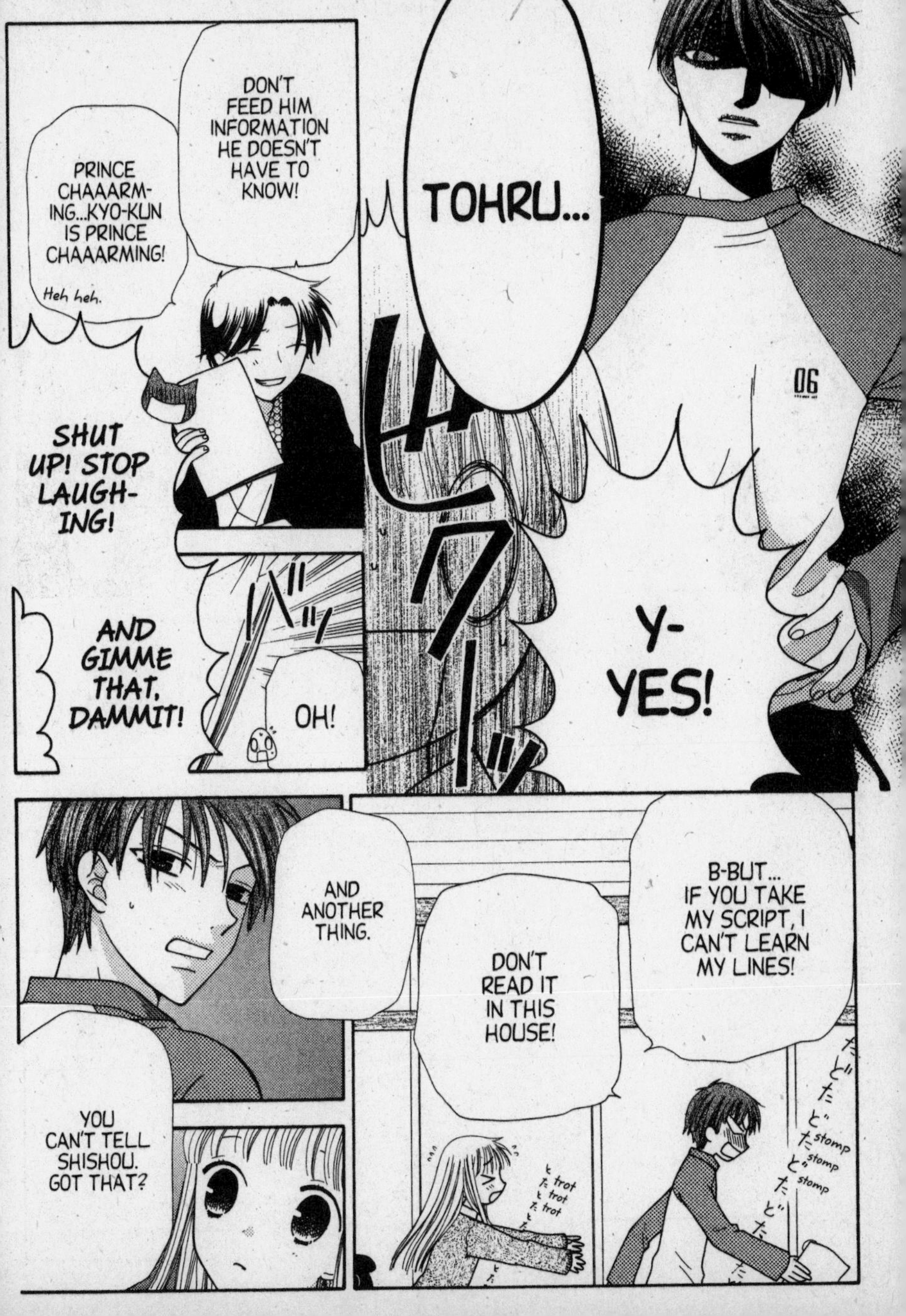
TOHRU...
Y-YES!
DON'T FEED HIM INFORMATION HE DOESN'T HAVE TO KNOW!
PRINCE CHAAARMING...KYO-KUN IS PRINCE CHAAARMING!
Heh heh.
SHUT UP! STOP LAUGHING!
OH!
AND GIMME THAT, DAMMIT!
B-BUT... IF YOU TAKE MY SCRIPT, I CAN'T LEARN MY LINES!
DON'T READ IT IN THIS HOUSE!
stomp stomp stomp
trot trot trot
AND ANOTHER THING.
YOU CAN'T TELL SHISHOU. GOT THAT?

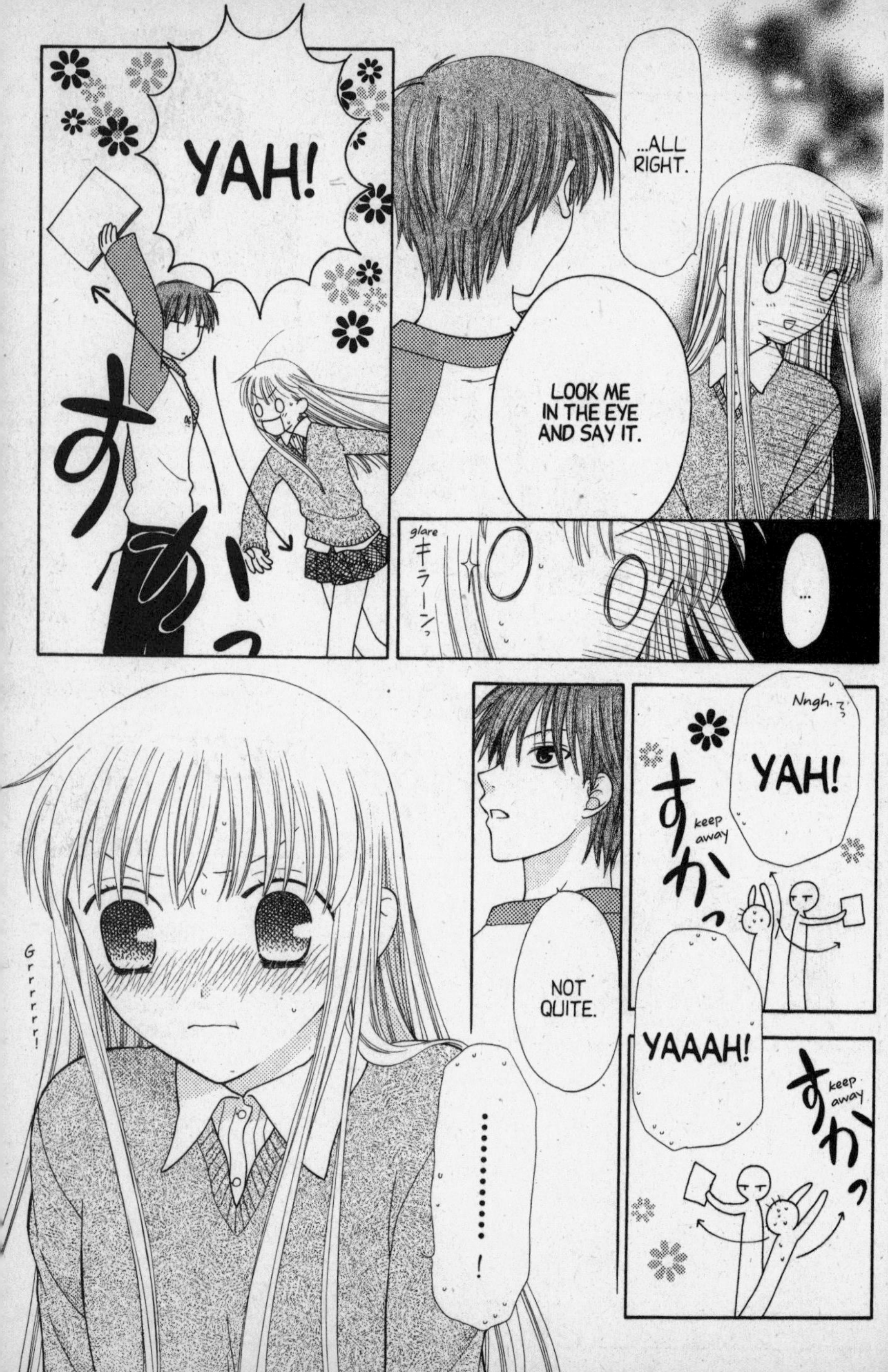
...ALL RIGHT.
LOOK ME IN THE EYE AND SAY IT.
glare
キラーン
...
YAH!
すかっ
Nngh.
YAH!
すかっ
keep away
YAAAH!
すかっ
keep away
NOT QUITE.
Grrrrrr!
.........!

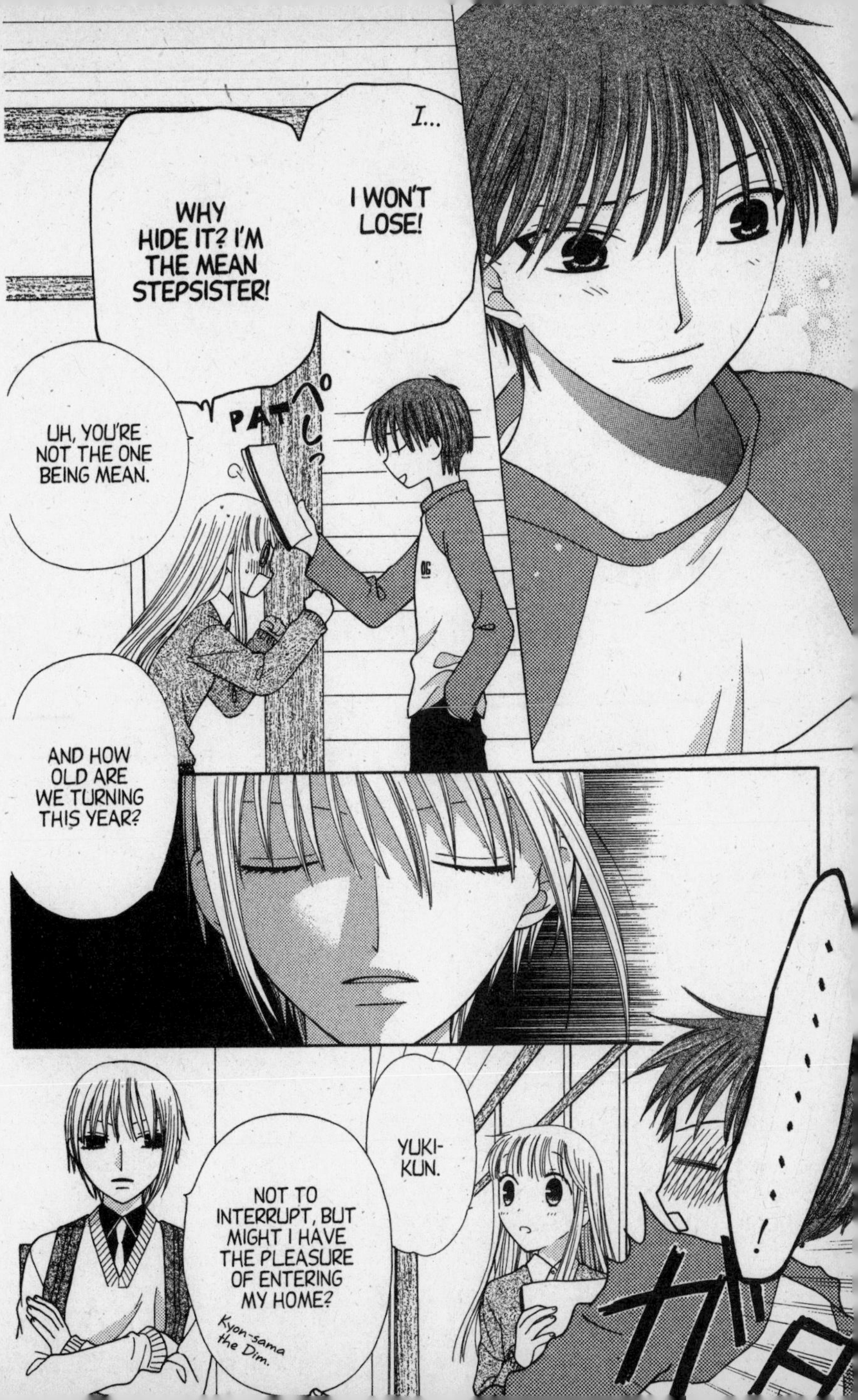
I...
I WON'T LOSE!
WHY HIDE IT? I'M THE MEAN STEPSISTER!
PAT
UH, YOU'RE NOT THE ONE BEING MEAN.
AND HOW OLD ARE WE TURNING THIS YEAR?
YUKI-KUN.
NOT TO INTERRUPT, BUT MIGHT I HAVE THE PLEASURE OF ENTERING MY HOME?
Kyon-sama the Dim.

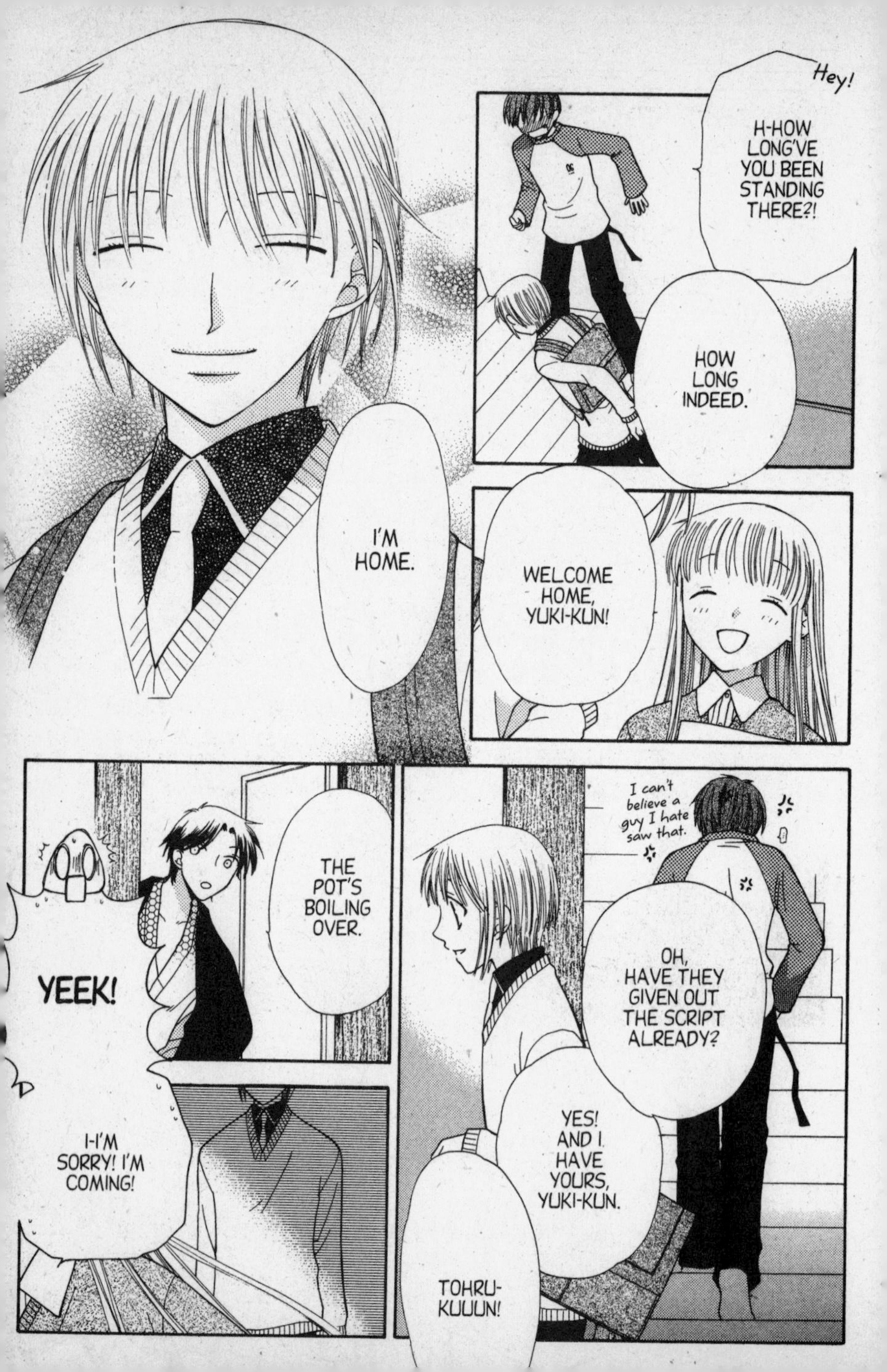
Hey!
H-HOW LONG'VE YOU BEEN STANDING THERE?!
HOW LONG INDEED.
WELCOME HOME, YUKI-KUN!
I'M HOME.
I can't believe a guy I hate saw that.
OH, HAVE THEY GIVEN OUT THE SCRIPT ALREADY?
YES! AND I HAVE YOURS, YUKI-KUN.
TOHRU-KUUUN!
THE POT'S BOILING OVER.
YEEK!
I-I'M SORRY! I'M COMING!

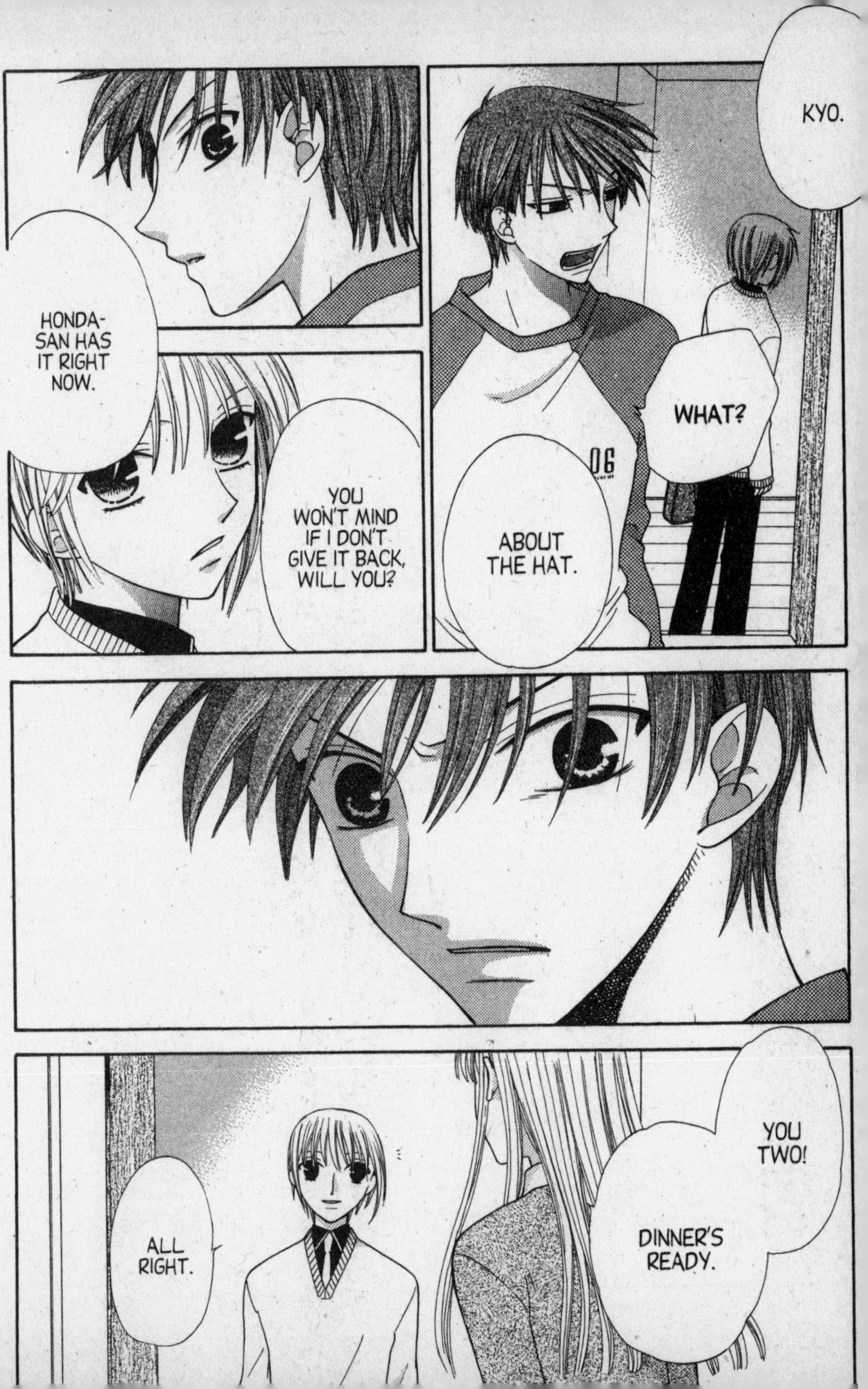
KYO.
WHAT?
ABOUT THE HAT.
HONDA-SAN HAS IT RIGHT NOW.
YOU WON'T MIND IF I DON'T GIVE IT BACK, WILL YOU?
YOU TWO!
DINNER'S READY.
ALL RIGHT.

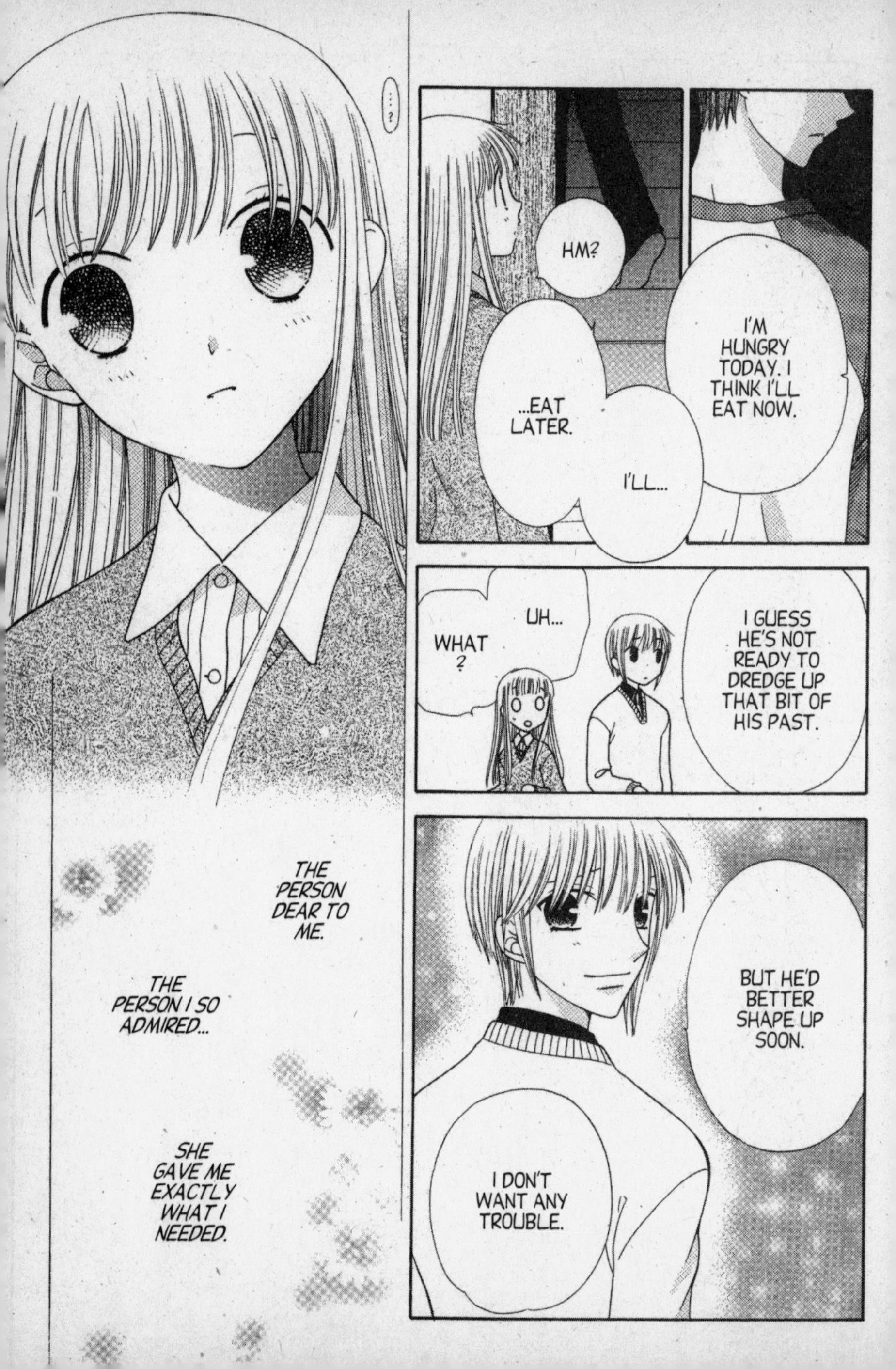
I'M HUNGRY TODAY. I THINK I'LL EAT NOW.
I'LL...
...EAT LATER.
HM?
I GUESS HE'S NOT READY TO DREDGE UP THAT BIT OF HIS PAST.
UH...
WHAT?
BUT HE'D BETTER SHAPE UP SOON.
I DON'T WANT ANY TROUBLE.
...?
THE PERSON DEAR TO ME.
THE PERSON I SO ADMIRED...
SHE GAVE ME EXACTLY WHAT I NEEDED.

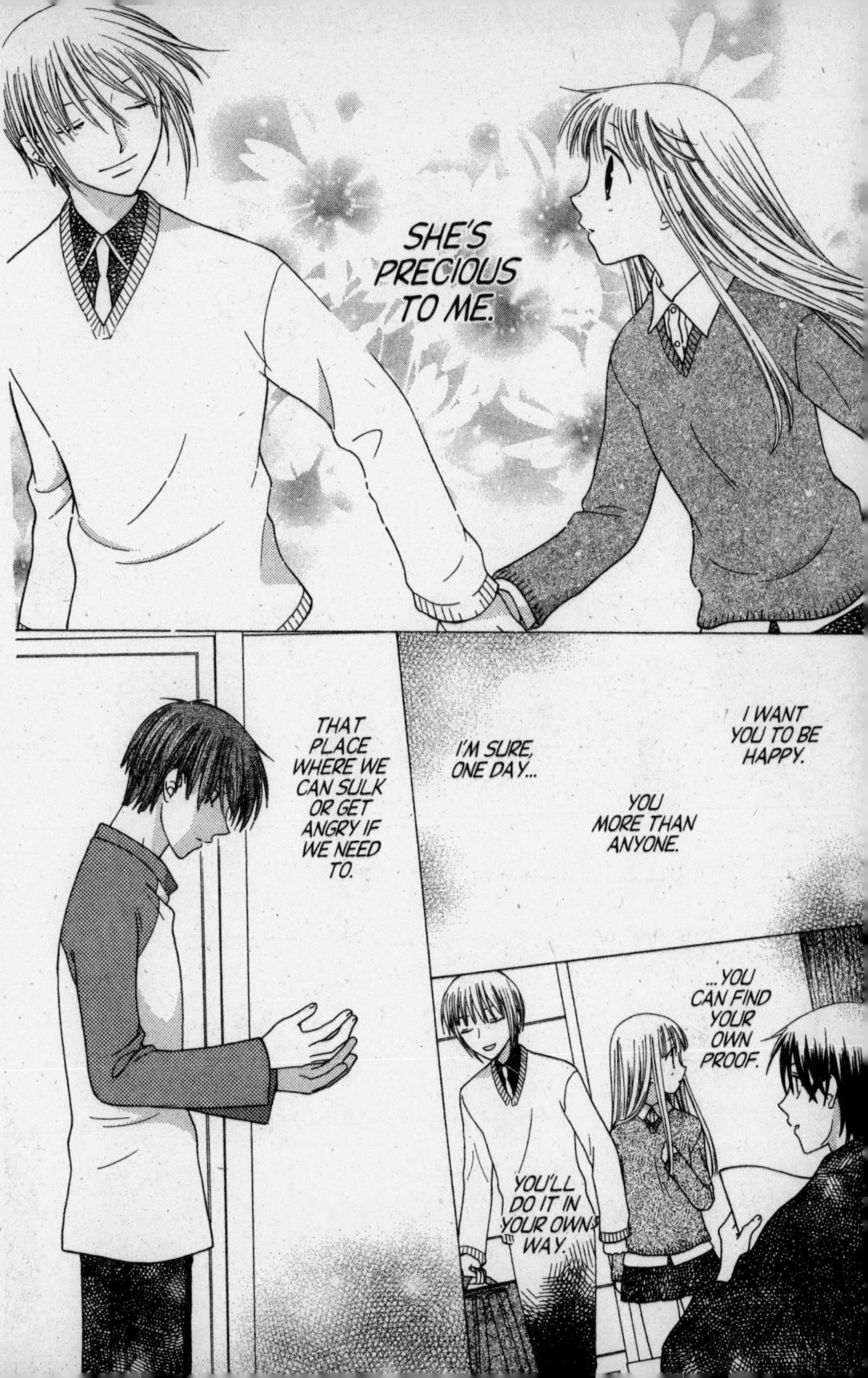
SHE'S PRECIOUS TO ME.
I WANT YOU TO BE HAPPY.
YOU MORE THAN ANYONE.
I'M SURE, ONE DAY...
...YOU CAN FIND YOUR OWN PROOF.
YOU'LL DO IT IN YOUR OWN WAY.
THAT PLACE WHERE WE CAN SULK OR GET ANGRY IF WE NEED TO.

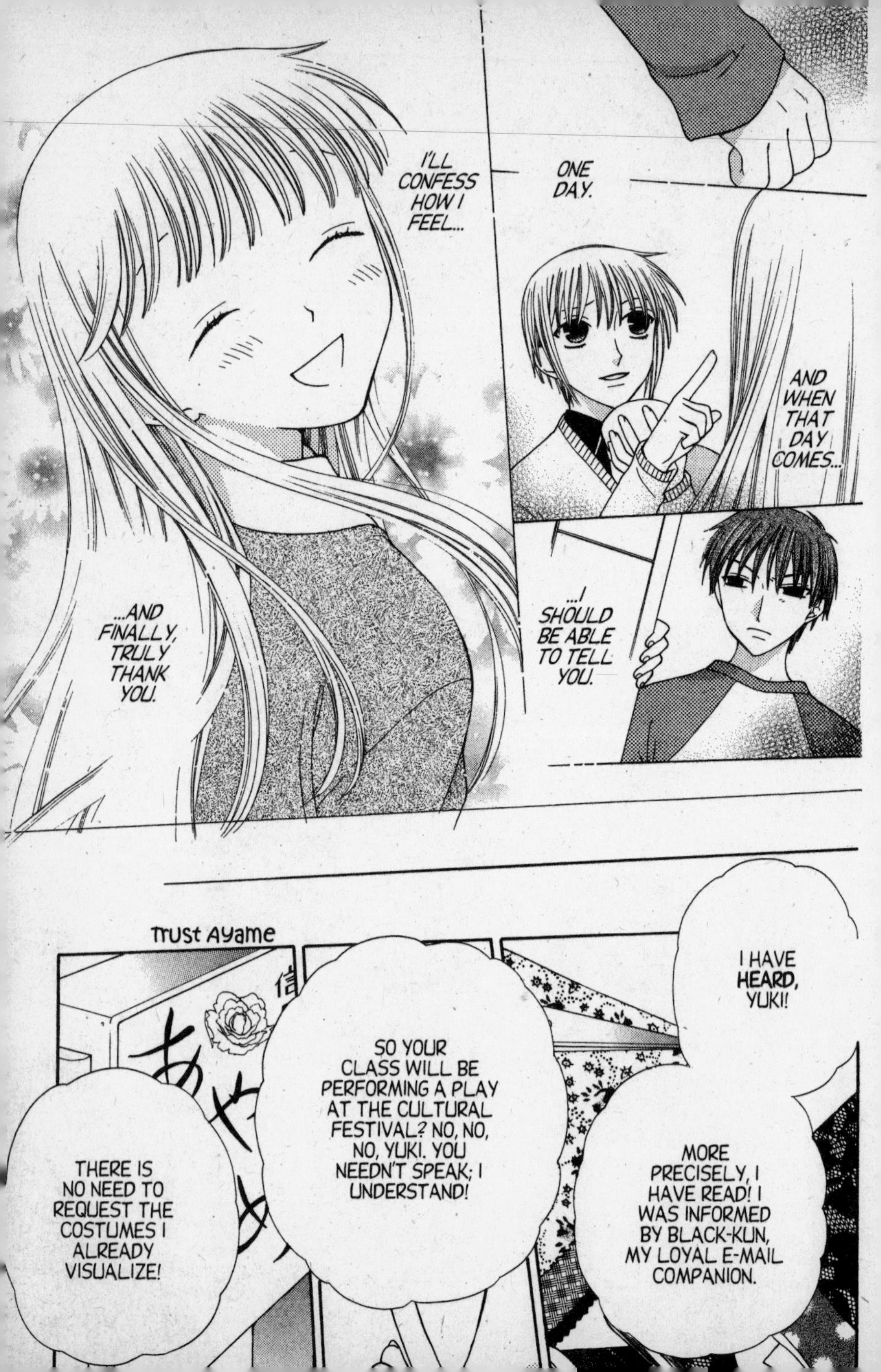
ONE DAY.
AND WHEN THAT DAY COMES...
...I SHOULD BE ABLE TO TELL YOU.
I'LL CONFESS HOW I FEEL...
...AND FINALLY, TRULY THANK YOU.
Trust Ayame
I HAVE HEARD, YUKI!
MORE PRECISELY, I HAVE READ! I WAS INFORMED BY BLACK-KUN, MY LOYAL E-MAIL COMPANION.
SO YOUR CLASS WILL BE PERFORMING A PLAY AT THE CULTURAL FESTIVAL? NO, NO, NO, YUKI. YOU NEEDN'T SPEAK; I UNDERSTAND!
THERE IS NO NEED TO REQUEST THE COSTUMES I ALREADY VISUALIZE!

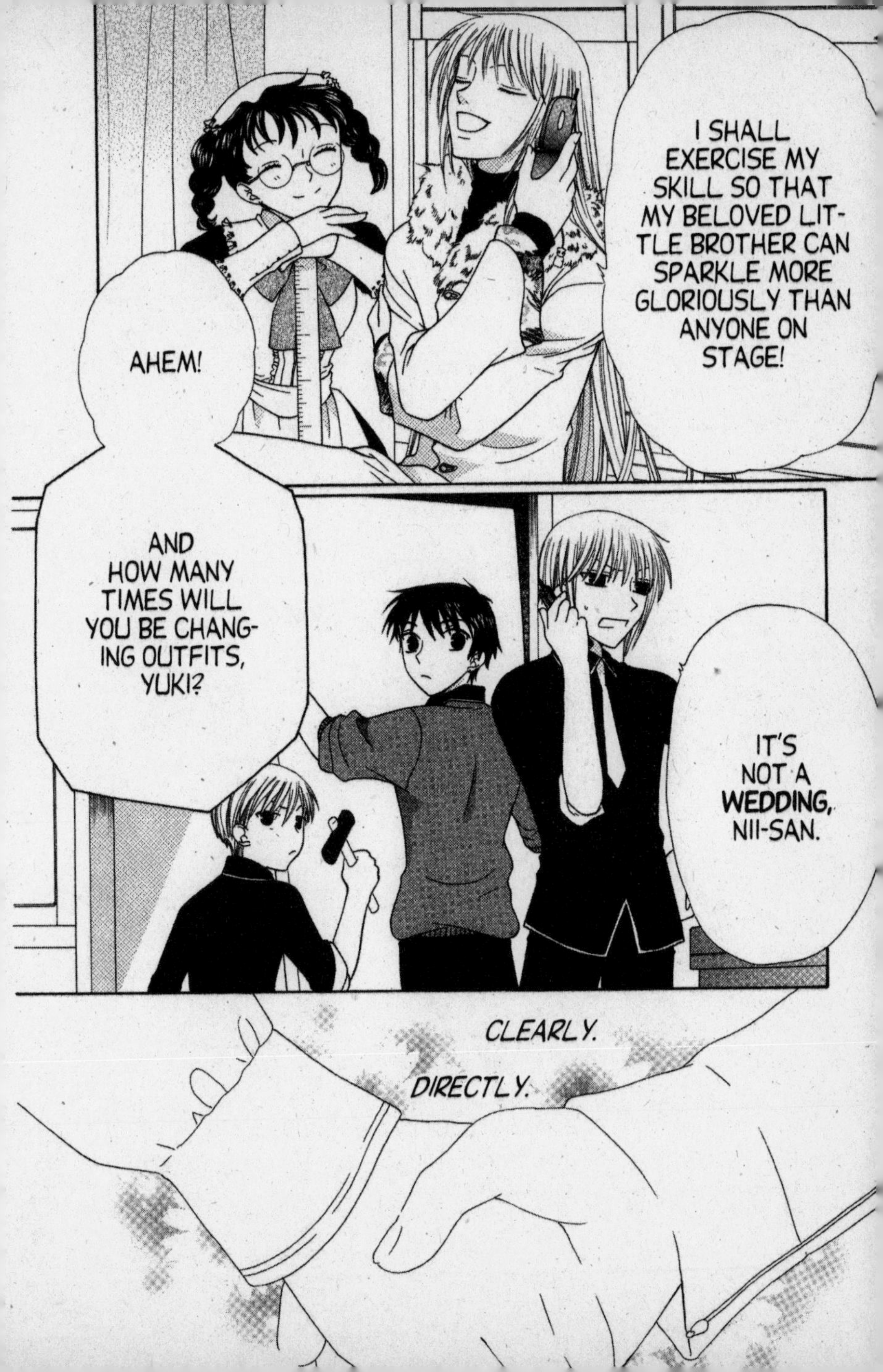
I SHALL EXERCISE MY SKILL SO THAT MY BELOVED LIT-TLE BROTHER CAN SPARKLE MORE GLORIOUSLY THAN ANYONE ON STAGE!
AHEM!
AND HOW MANY TIMES WILL YOU BE CHANG-ING OUTFITS, YUKI?
IT'S NOT A **WEDDING,** NII-SAN.
CLEARLY.
DIRECTLY.

Filler Sketch

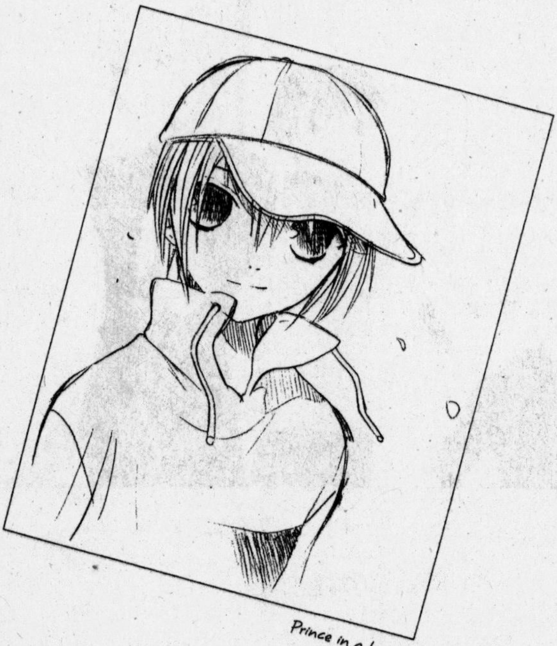

Prince in a hat.

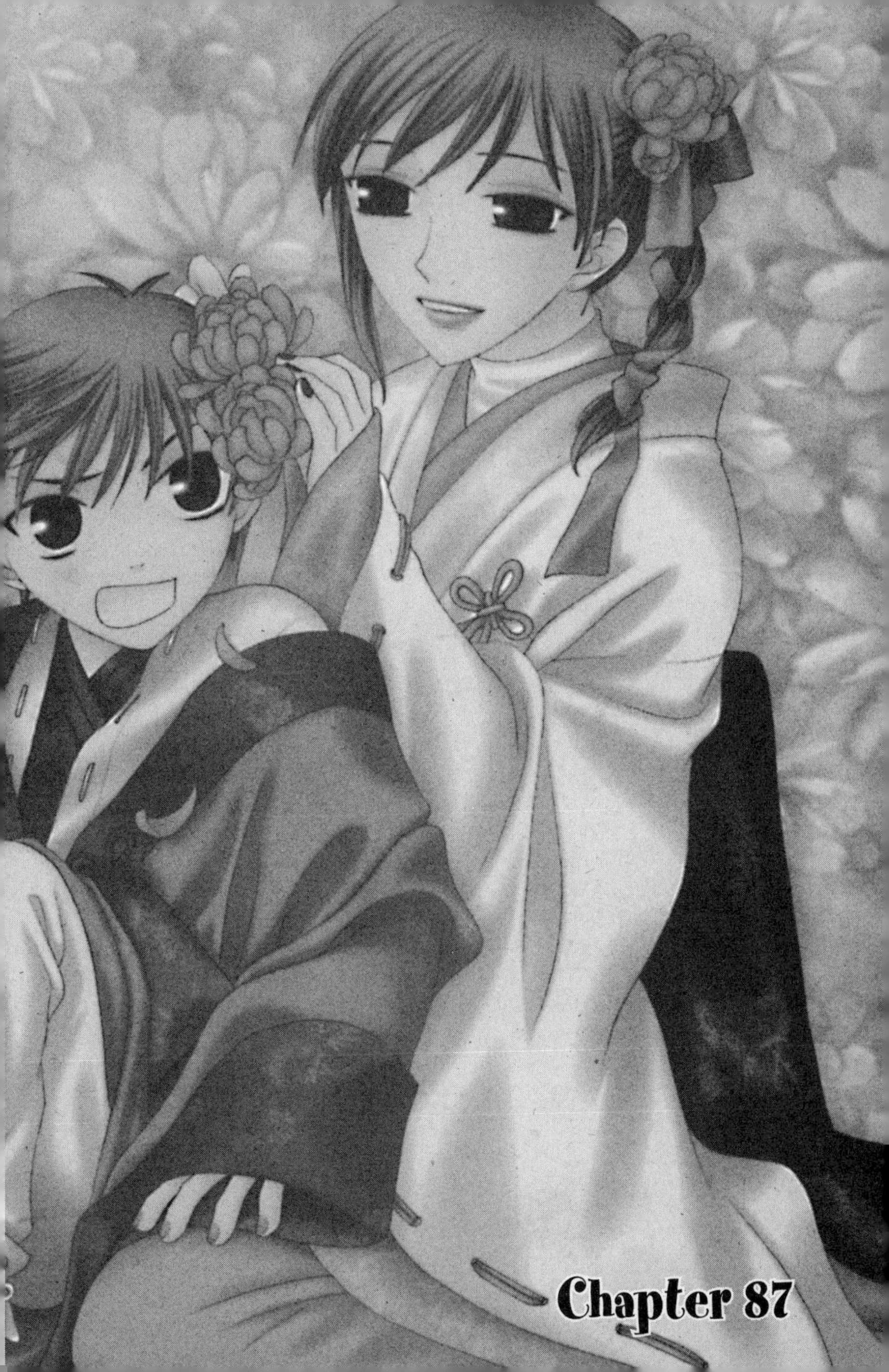

Chapter 87

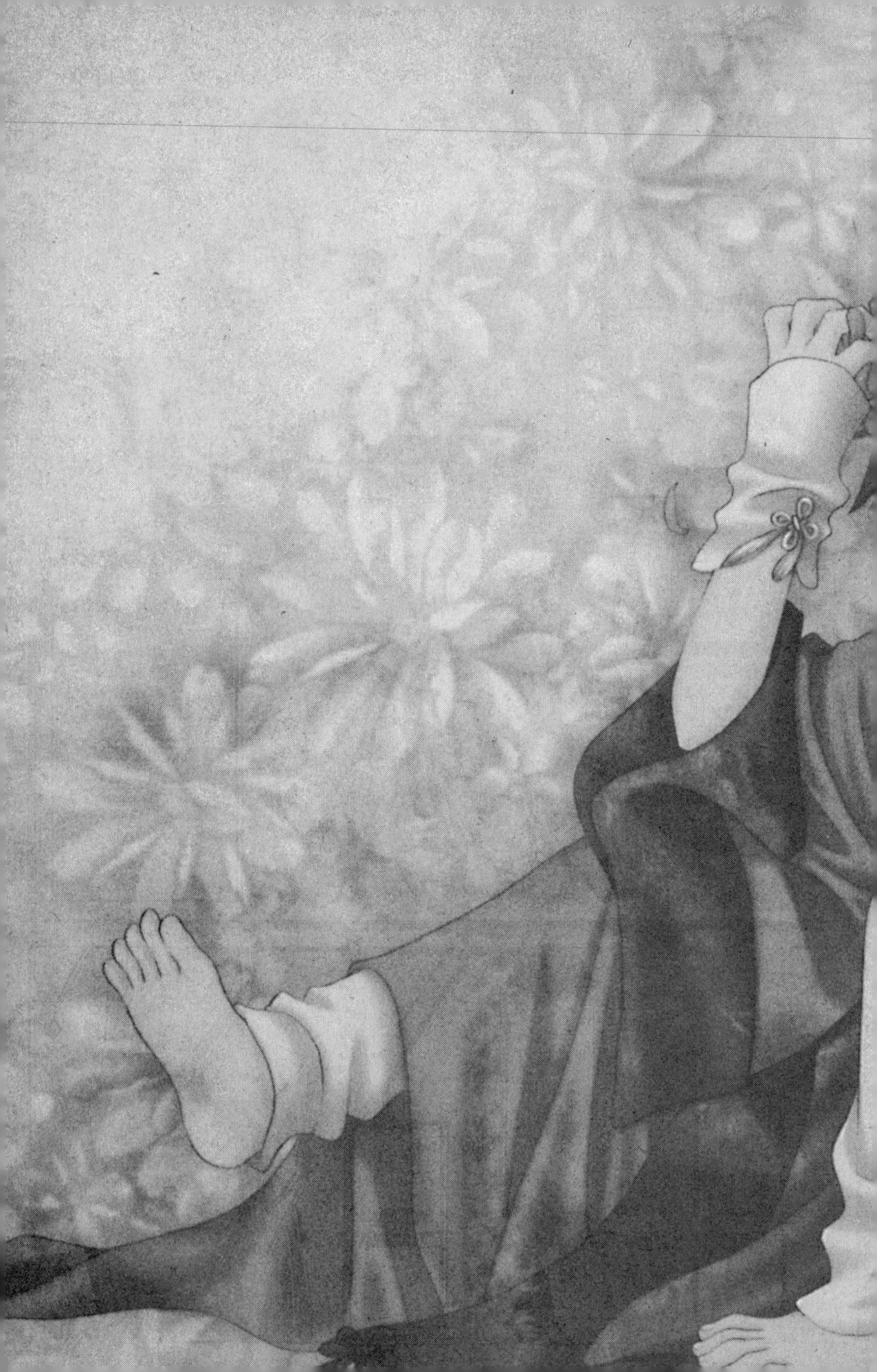

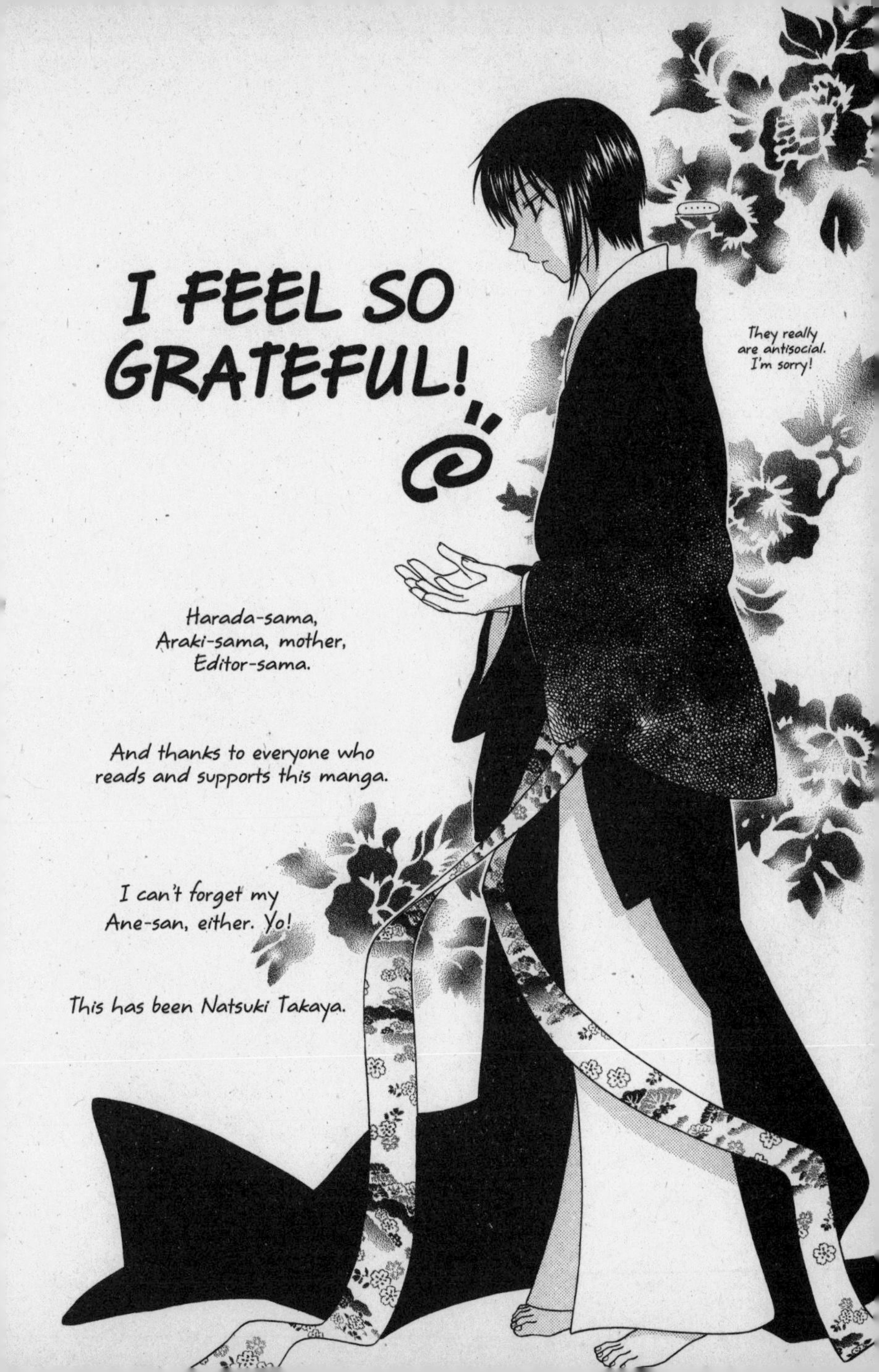
I FEEL SO GRATEFUL!
They really are antisocial. I'm sorry!
Harada-sama, Araki-sama, mother, Editor-sama.
And thanks to everyone who reads and supports this manga.
I can't forget my Ane-san, either. Yo!
This has been Natsuki Takaya.

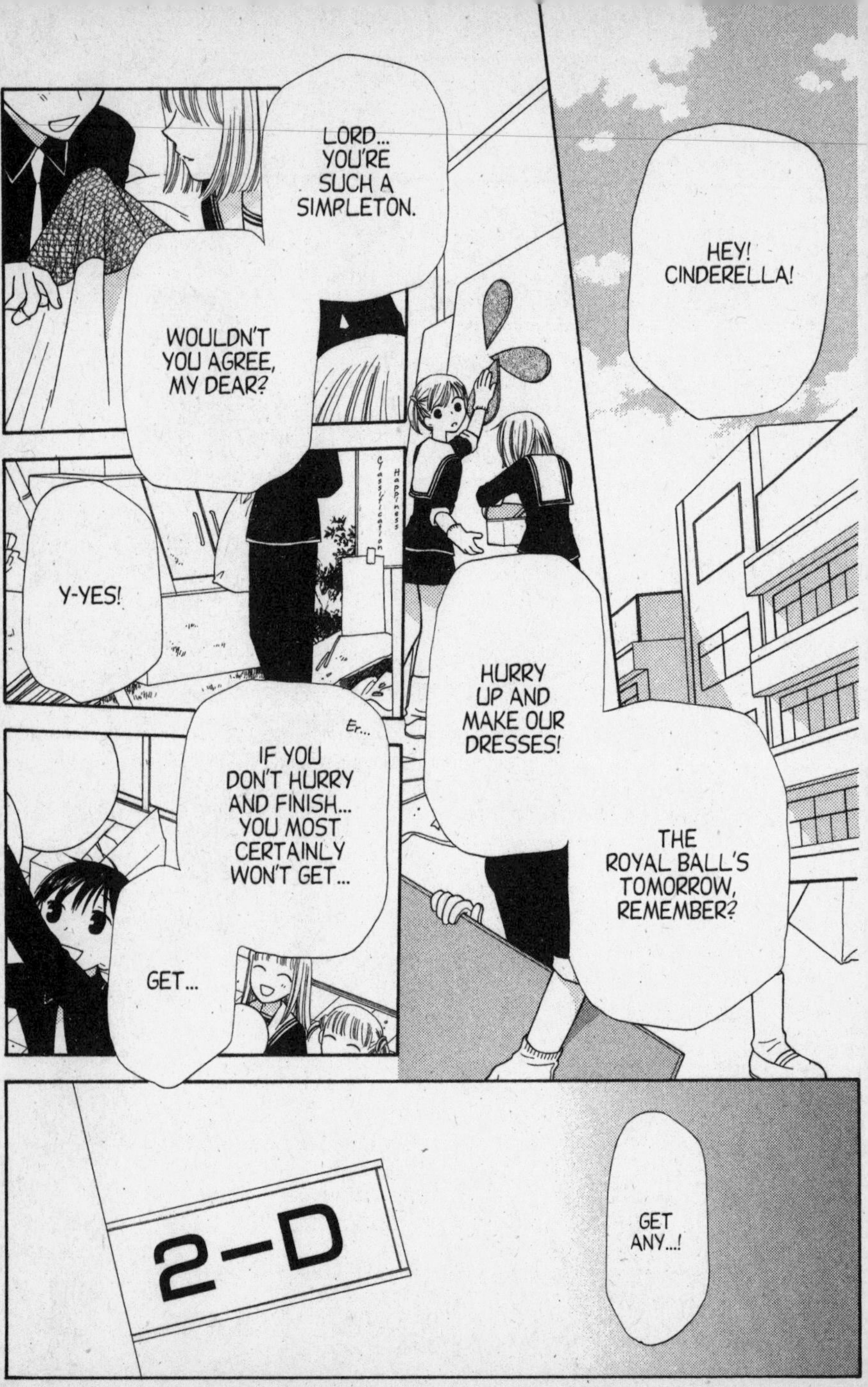
HEY! CINDERELLA!
HURRY UP AND MAKE OUR DRESSES!
THE ROYAL BALL'S TOMORROW, REMEMBER?
LORD... YOU'RE SUCH A SIMPLETON.
WOULDN'T YOU AGREE, MY DEAR?
Y-YES!
Er...
IF YOU DON'T HURRY AND FINISH... YOU MOST CERTAINLY WON'T GET...
GET...
2-D
GET ANY...!

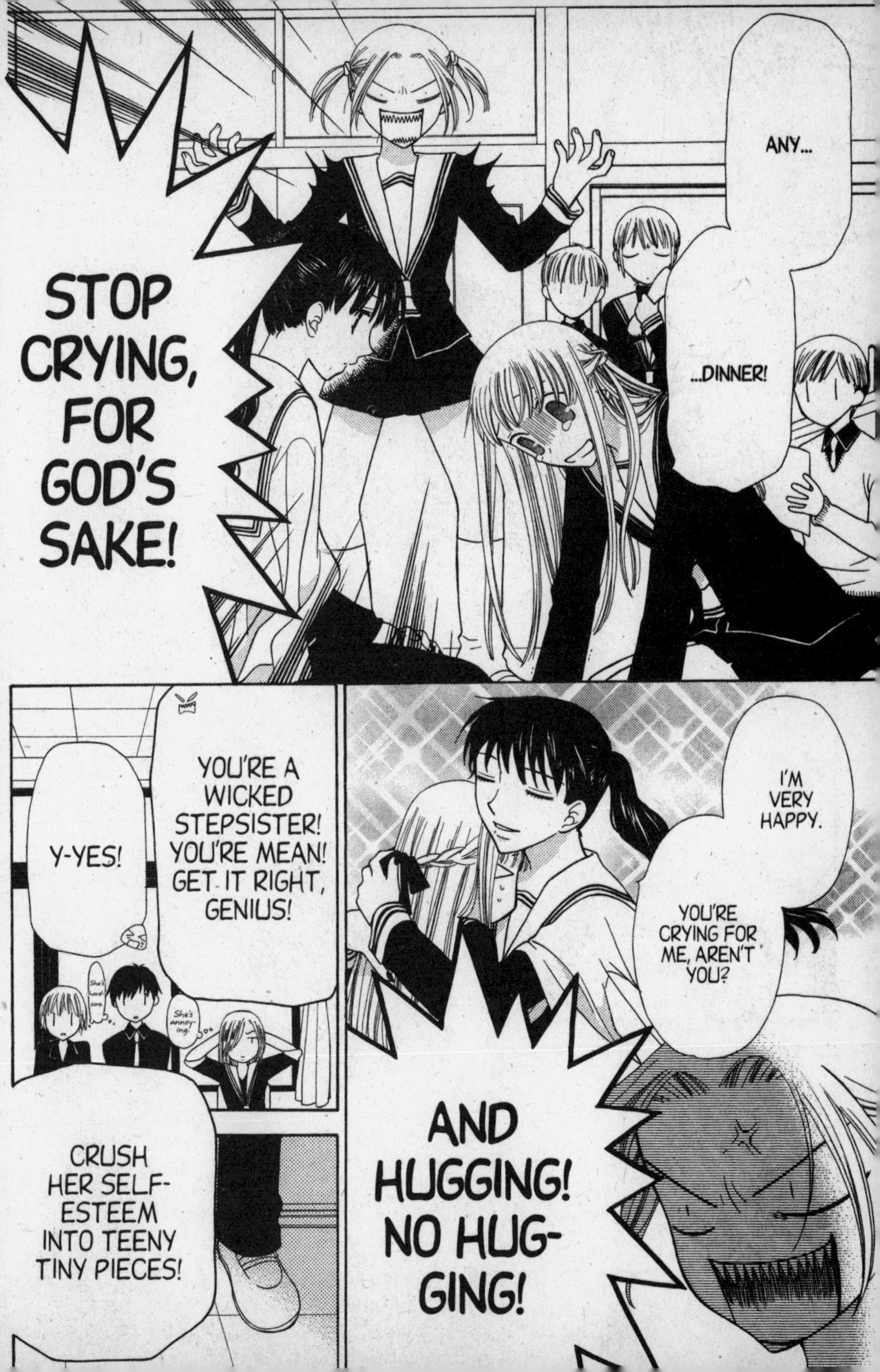
ANY...
...DINNER!
STOP CRYING, FOR GOD'S SAKE!
I'M VERY HAPPY.
YOU'RE CRYING FOR ME, AREN'T YOU?
AND HUGGING! NO HUG-GING!
YOU'RE A WICKED STEPSISTER! YOU'RE MEAN! GET IT RIGHT, GENIUS!
Y-YES!
She's hard-core.
She's annoy-ing.
CRUSH HER SELF-ESTEEM INTO TEENY TINY PIECES!

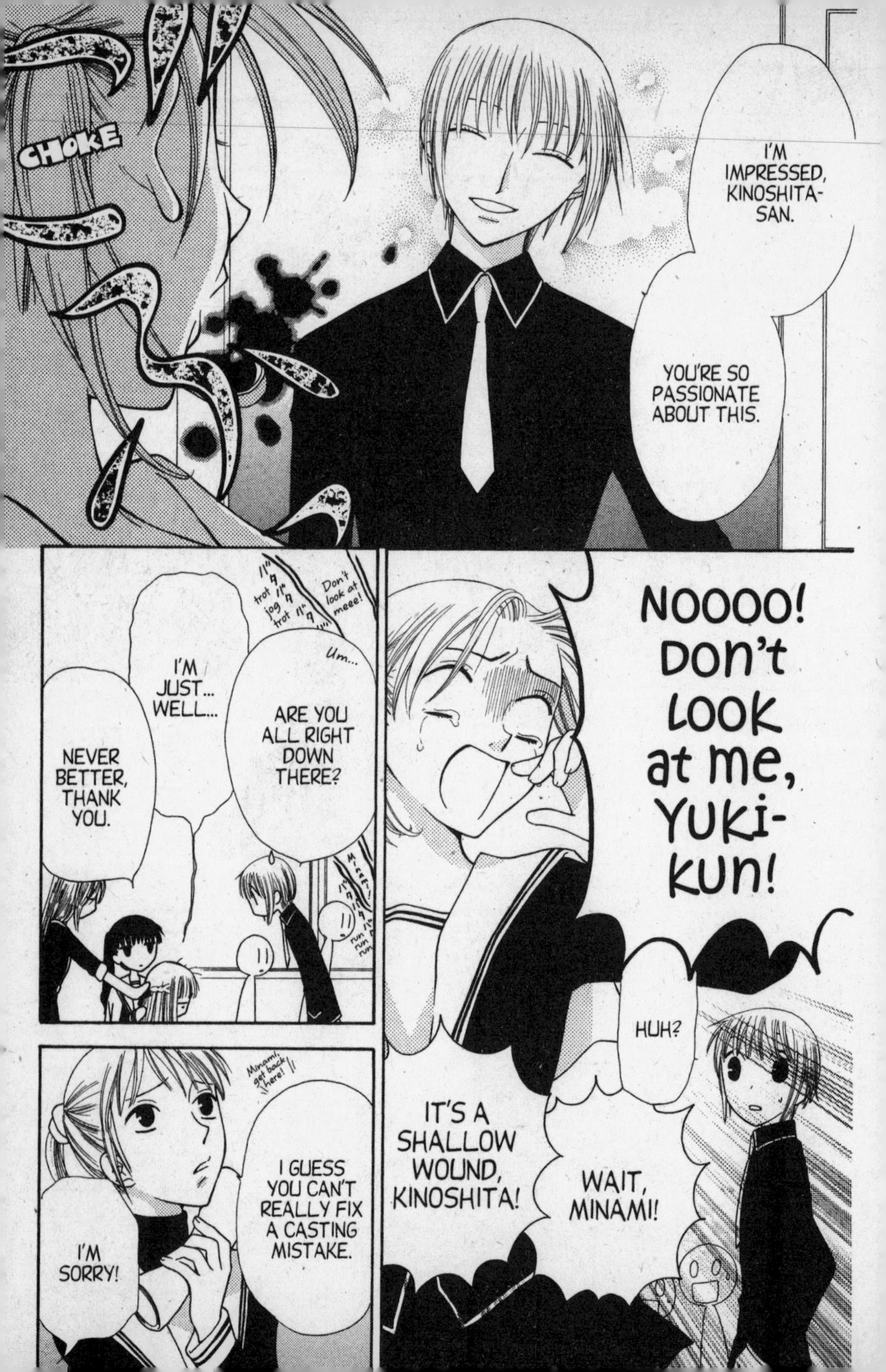
I'M IMPRESSED, KINOSHITA-SAN.
YOU'RE SO PASSIONATE ABOUT THIS.
CHOKE
NOOOO! Don't LOOK at me, YUKI-KUN!
HUH?
WAIT, MINAMI!
IT'S A SHALLOW WOUND, KINOSHITA!
Don't look at meee!
trot jog trot
Um...
ARE YOU ALL RIGHT DOWN THERE?
I'M JUST... WELL...
NEVER BETTER, THANK YOU.
Minami, get back here!
I GUESS YOU CAN'T REALLY FIX A CASTING MISTAKE.
I'M SORRY!

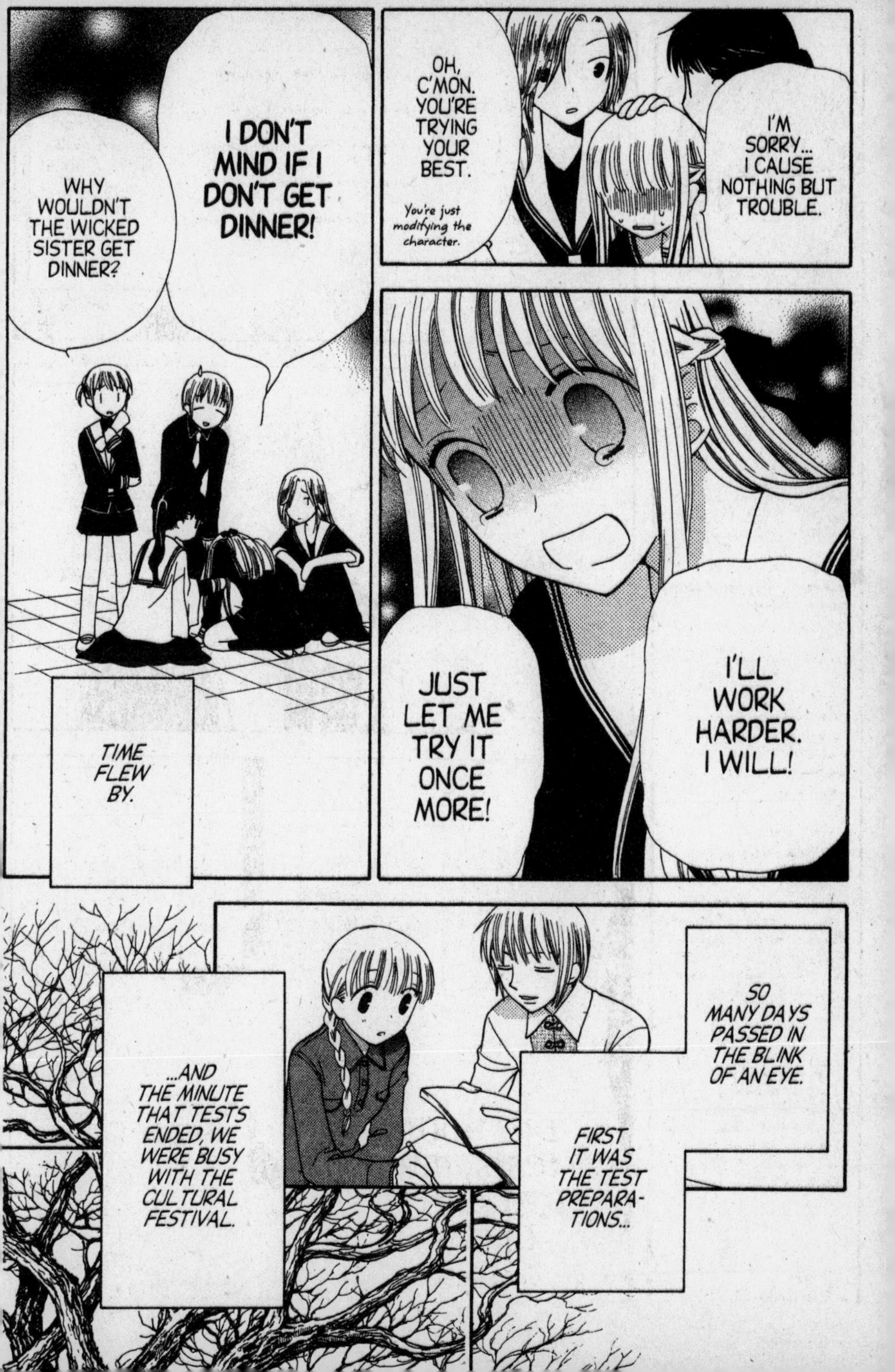
I'M SORRY... I CAUSE NOTHING BUT TROUBLE.
OH, C'MON. YOU'RE TRYING YOUR BEST.
You're just modifying the character.
I'LL WORK HARDER. I WILL!
JUST LET ME TRY IT ONCE MORE!
I DON'T MIND IF I DON'T GET DINNER!
WHY WOULDN'T THE WICKED SISTER GET DINNER?
TIME FLEW BY.
SO MANY DAYS PASSED IN THE BLINK OF AN EYE.
FIRST IT WAS THE TEST PREPARATIONS...
...AND THE MINUTE THAT TESTS ENDED, WE WERE BUSY WITH THE CULTURAL FESTIVAL.

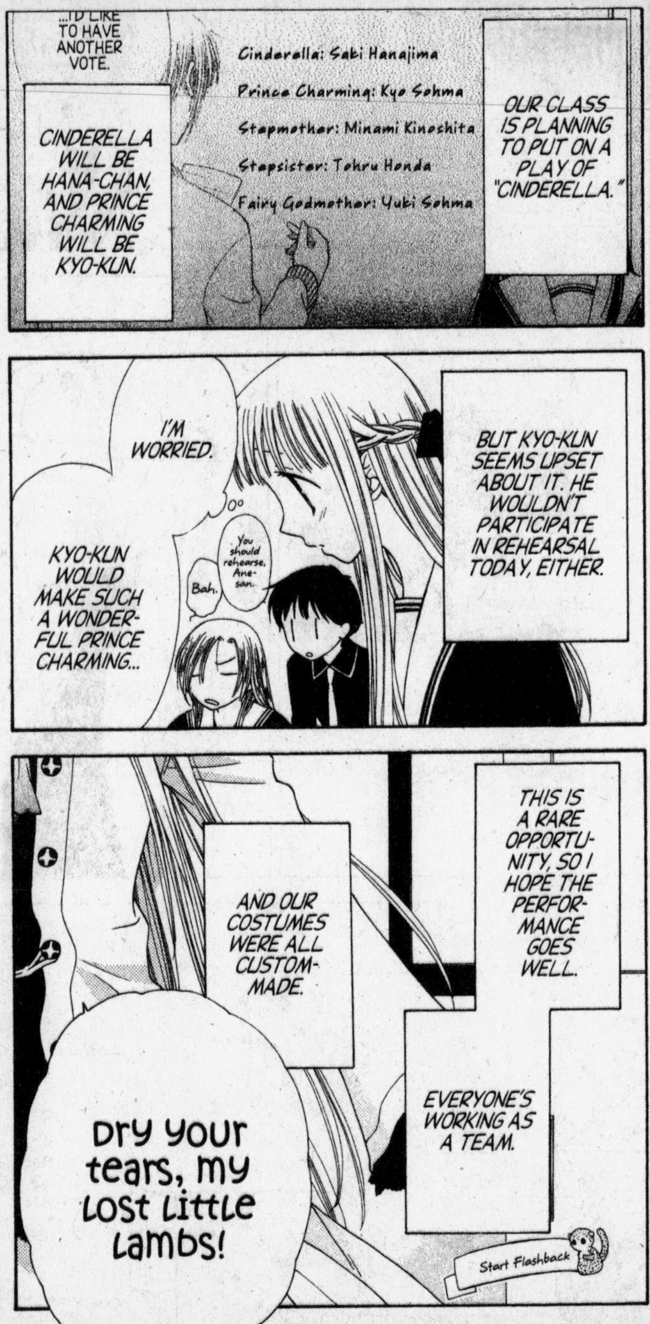
OUR CLASS IS PLANNING TO PUT ON A PLAY OF "CINDERELLA."
Cinderella: Saki Hanajima
Prince Charming: Kyo Sohma
Stepmother: Minami Kinoshita
Stepsister: Tohru Honda
Fairy Godmother: Yuki Sohma
CINDERELLA WILL BE HANA-CHAN, AND PRINCE CHARMING WILL BE KYO-KUN.
...I'D LIKE TO HAVE ANOTHER VOTE.
BUT KYO-KUN SEEMS UPSET ABOUT IT. HE WOULDN'T PARTICIPATE IN REHEARSAL TODAY, EITHER.
I'M WORRIED.
KYO-KUN WOULD MAKE SUCH A WONDERFUL PRINCE CHARMING...
You should rehearse, Ane-san.
Bah.
THIS IS A RARE OPPORTUNITY, SO I HOPE THE PERFORMANCE GOES WELL.
AND OUR COSTUMES WERE ALL CUSTOM-MADE.
EVERYONE'S WORKING AS A TEAM.
Dry your tears, my lost little lambs!
Start Flashback

Continuation →

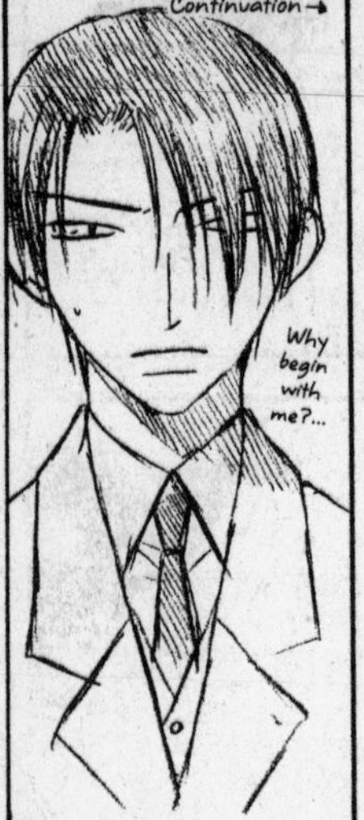
Why begin with me?...

The memory-suppression technique was passed down from his father.

It's similar to hypnosis, really.

Hatori doesn't specifically have to be the one who suppresses memories, but his family is the one that hands down the technique.

He enjoys smoking and can hold his liquor.

He's lazy in some respects. When he undresses, for example, he tends to leave his clothes lying around.

When he was in high school, he was fairly popular with the students from the girls' school next door. All three of the Mabudachi Trio were popular in that regard.

← To be continued

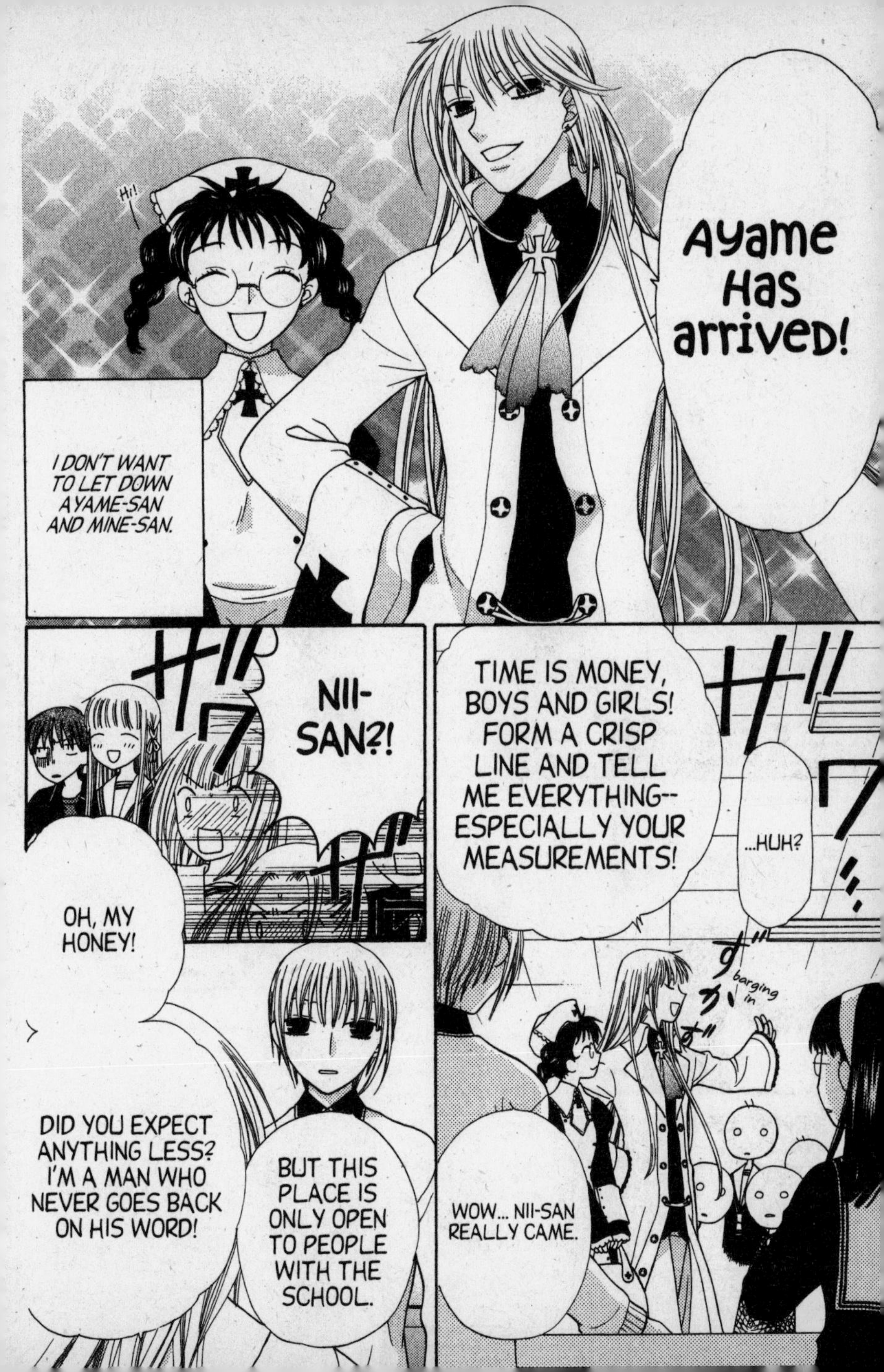
Ayame Has arrived!
I DON'T WANT TO LET DOWN AYAME-SAN AND MINE-SAN.
TIME IS MONEY, BOYS AND GIRLS! FORM A CRISP LINE AND TELL ME EVERYTHING-- ESPECIALLY YOUR MEASUREMENTS!
...HUH?
barging in
WOW... NII-SAN REALLY CAME.
NII-SAN?!
OH, MY HONEY!
BUT THIS PLACE IS ONLY OPEN TO PEOPLE WITH THE SCHOOL.
DID YOU EXPECT ANYTHING LESS? I'M A MAN WHO NEVER GOES BACK ON HIS WORD!

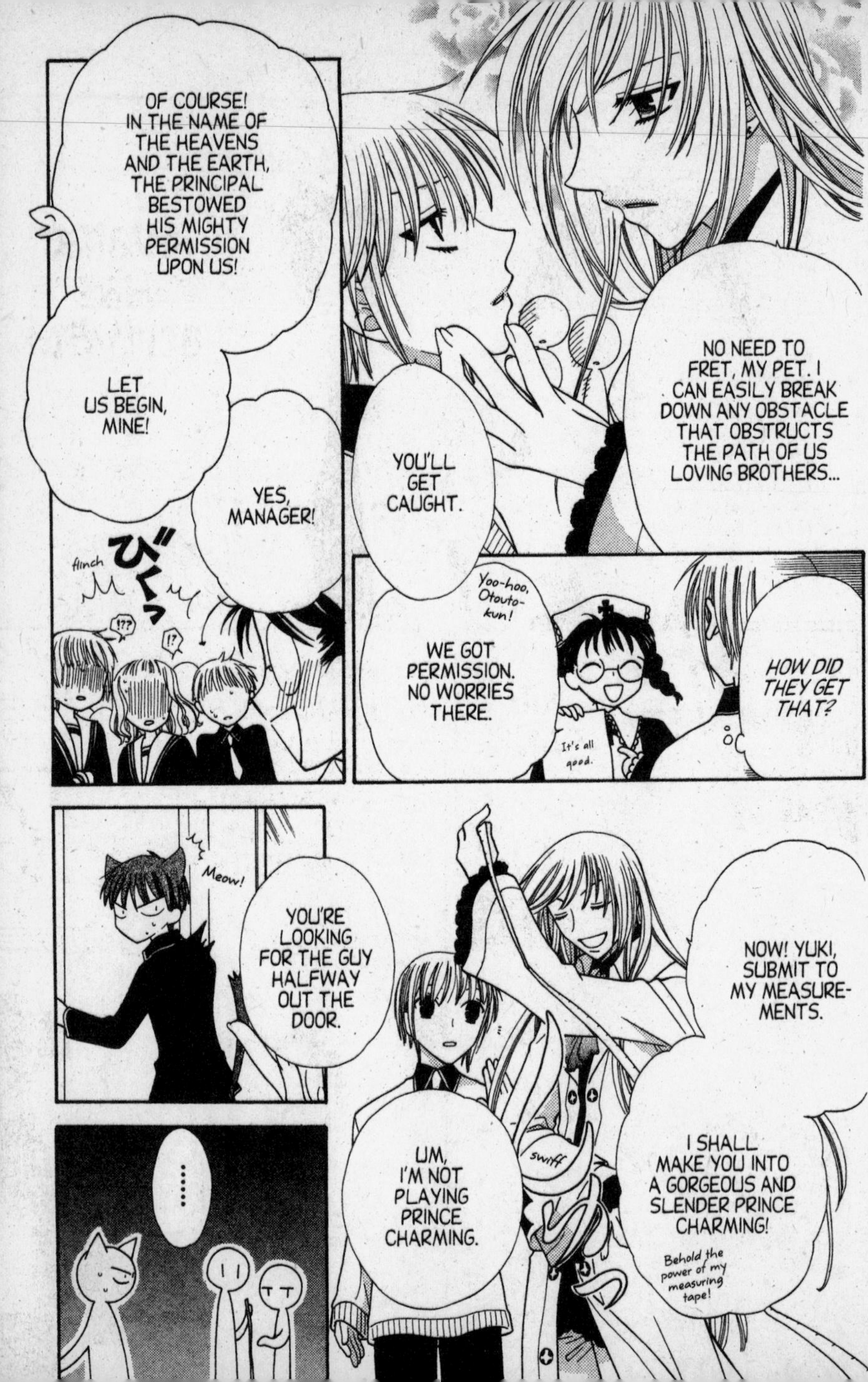
NO NEED TO FRET, MY PET. I CAN EASILY BREAK DOWN ANY OBSTACLE THAT OBSTRUCTS THE PATH OF US LOVING BROTHERS...
YOU'LL GET CAUGHT.
HOW DID THEY GET THAT?
Yoo-hoo, Otouto-kun!
WE GOT PERMISSION. NO WORRIES THERE.
It's all good.
OF COURSE! IN THE NAME OF THE HEAVENS AND THE EARTH, THE PRINCIPAL BESTOWED HIS MIGHTY PERMISSION UPON US!
LET US BEGIN, MINE!
YES, MANAGER!
びくっ
flinch
!??
!?
NOW! YUKI, SUBMIT TO MY MEASUREMENTS.
I SHALL MAKE YOU INTO A GORGEOUS AND SLENDER PRINCE CHARMING!
Behold the power of my measuring tape!
swiff
UM, I'M NOT PLAYING PRINCE CHARMING.
Meow!
YOU'RE LOOKING FOR THE GUY HALFWAY OUT THE DOOR.
......

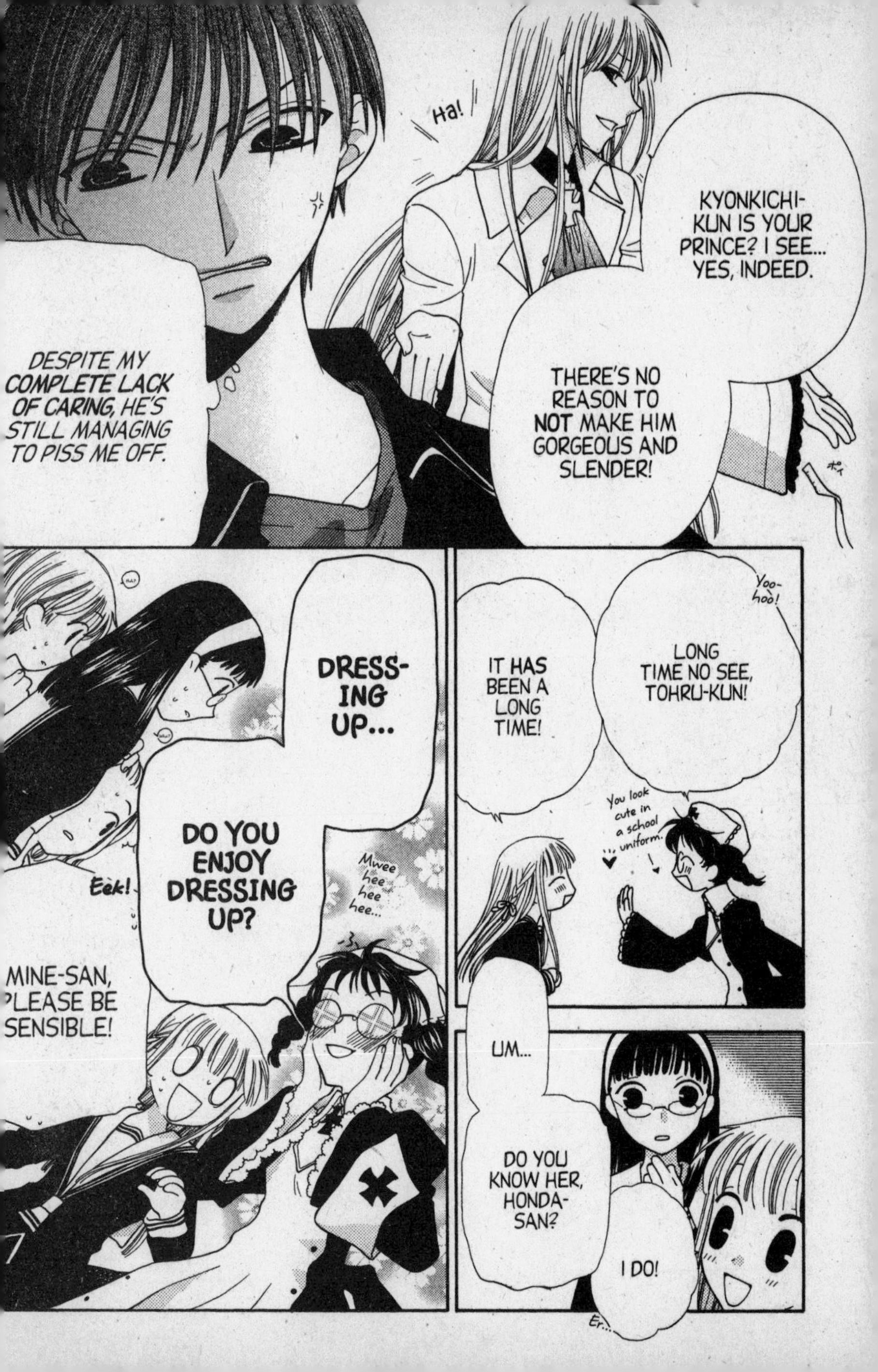
Ha!
KYONKICHI-KUN IS YOUR PRINCE? I SEE... YES, INDEED.
THERE'S NO REASON TO NOT MAKE HIM GORGEOUS AND SLENDER!
DESPITE MY COMPLETE LACK OF CARING, HE'S STILL MANAGING TO PISS ME OFF.
Yoo-hoo!
LONG TIME NO SEE, TOHRU-KUN!
IT HAS BEEN A LONG TIME!
You look cute in a school uniform.
UM...
DO YOU KNOW HER, HONDA-SAN?
I DO!
Er...
DRESS-ING UP...
DO YOU ENJOY DRESSING UP?
Mwee hee hee hee...
Eek!
MINE-SAN, PLEASE BE SENSIBLE!

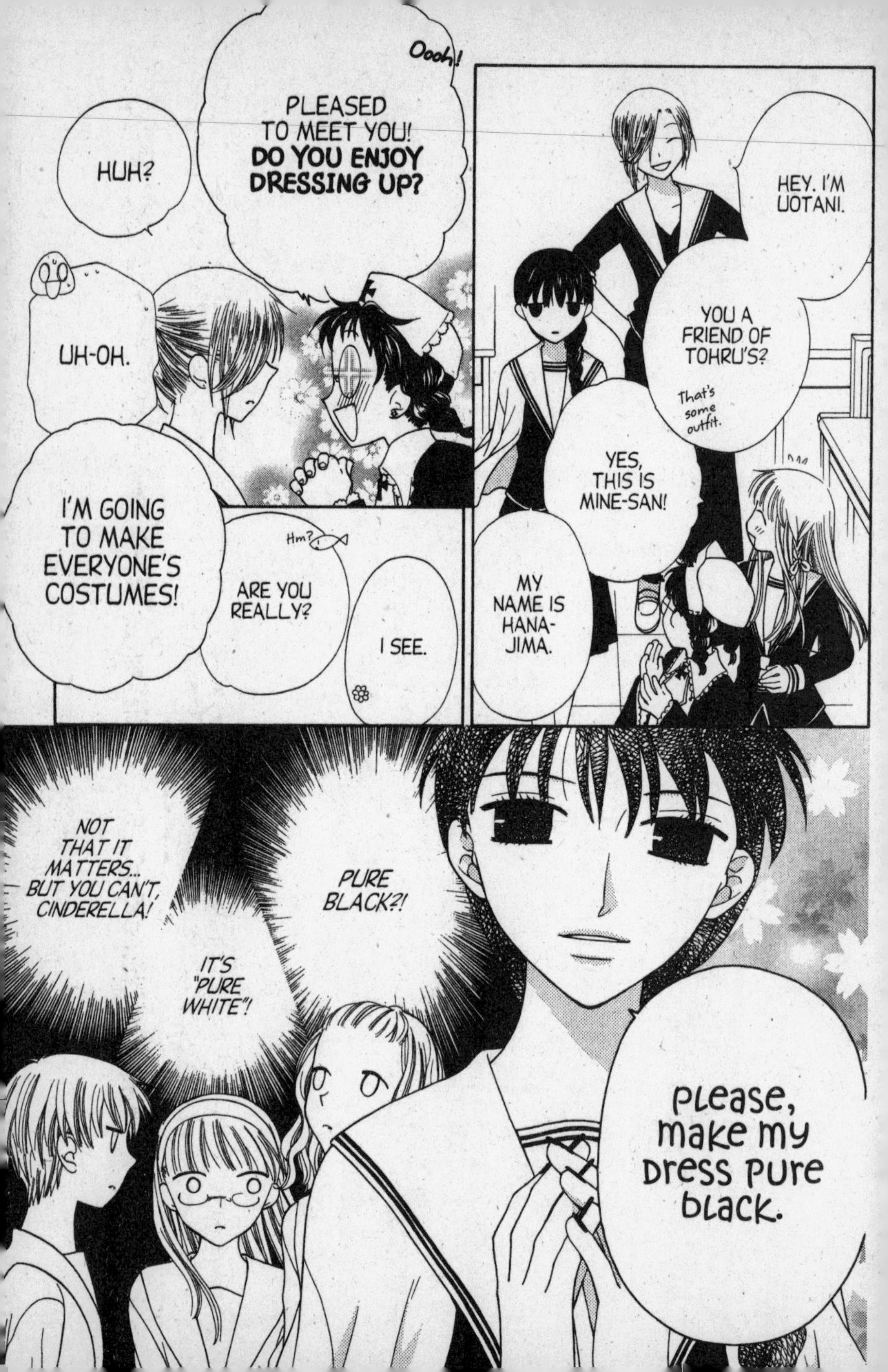
HEY. I'M UOTANI.
YOU A FRIEND OF TOHRU'S?
That's some outfit.
YES, THIS IS MINE-SAN!
MY NAME IS HANA-JIMA.
Oooh!
PLEASED TO MEET YOU! **DO YOU ENJOY DRESSING UP?**
HUH?
UH-OH.
I'M GOING TO MAKE EVERYONE'S COSTUMES!
Hm?
ARE YOU REALLY?
I SEE.
Please, make my dress pure black.
PURE BLACK?!
IT'S "PURE WHITE"!
NOT THAT IT MATTERS... BUT YOU CAN'T, CINDERELLA!

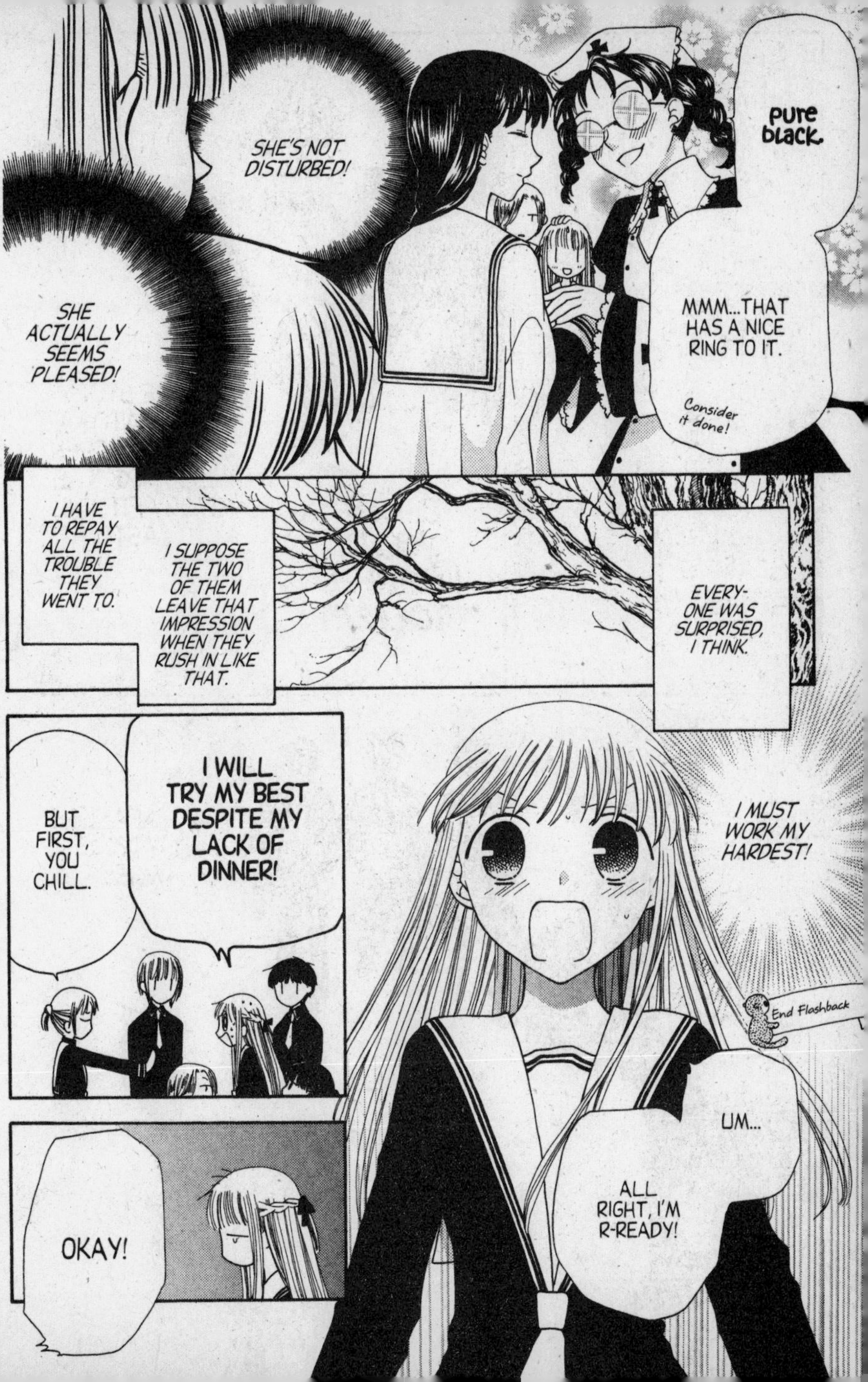
Pure black.
MMM...THAT HAS A NICE RING TO IT.
Consider it done!
SHE'S NOT DISTURBED!
SHE ACTUALLY SEEMS PLEASED!
EVERY-ONE WAS SURPRISED, I THINK.
I SUPPOSE THE TWO OF THEM LEAVE THAT IMPRESSION WHEN THEY RUSH IN LIKE THAT.
I HAVE TO REPAY ALL THE TROUBLE THEY WENT TO.
I MUST WORK MY HARDEST!
End Flashback
UM...
ALL RIGHT, I'M R-READY!
I WILL TRY MY BEST DESPITE MY LACK OF DINNER!
BUT FIRST, YOU CHILL.
OKAY!

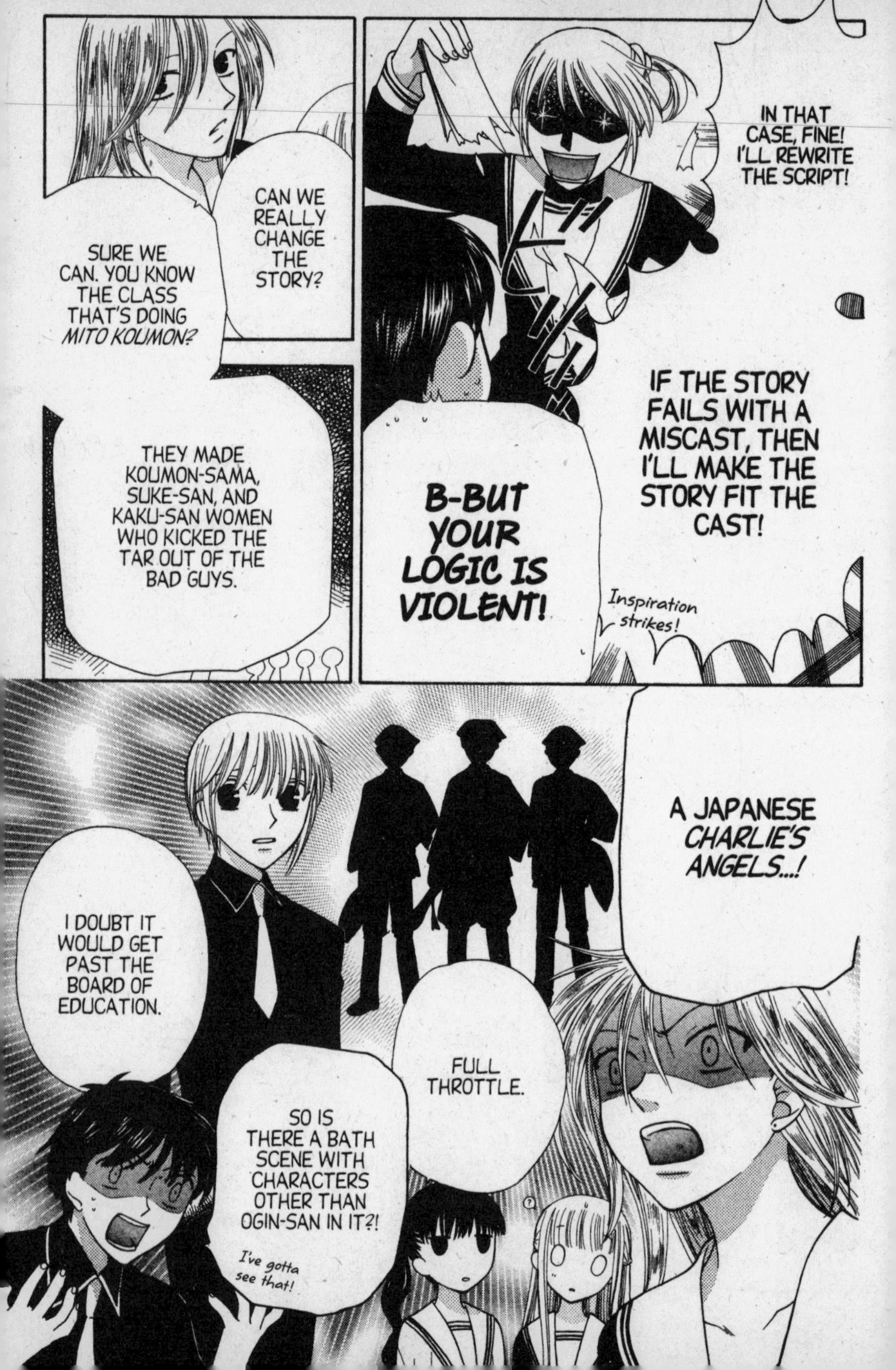

IN THAT CASE, FINE! I'LL REWRITE THE SCRIPT!
IF THE STORY FAILS WITH A MISCAST, THEN I'LL MAKE THE STORY FIT THE CAST!
B-BUT YOUR LOGIC IS VIOLENT!
Inspiration strikes!
CAN WE REALLY CHANGE THE STORY?
SURE WE CAN. YOU KNOW THE CLASS THAT'S DOING *MITO KOUMON*?
THEY MADE KOUMON-SAMA, SUKE-SAN, AND KAKU-SAN WOMEN WHO KICKED THE TAR OUT OF THE BAD GUYS.
A JAPANESE *CHARLIE'S ANGELS*...!
FULL THROTTLE.
I DOUBT IT WOULD GET PAST THE BOARD OF EDUCATION.
SO IS THERE A BATH SCENE WITH CHARACTERS OTHER THAN OGIN-SAN IN IT?!
I've gotta see that!

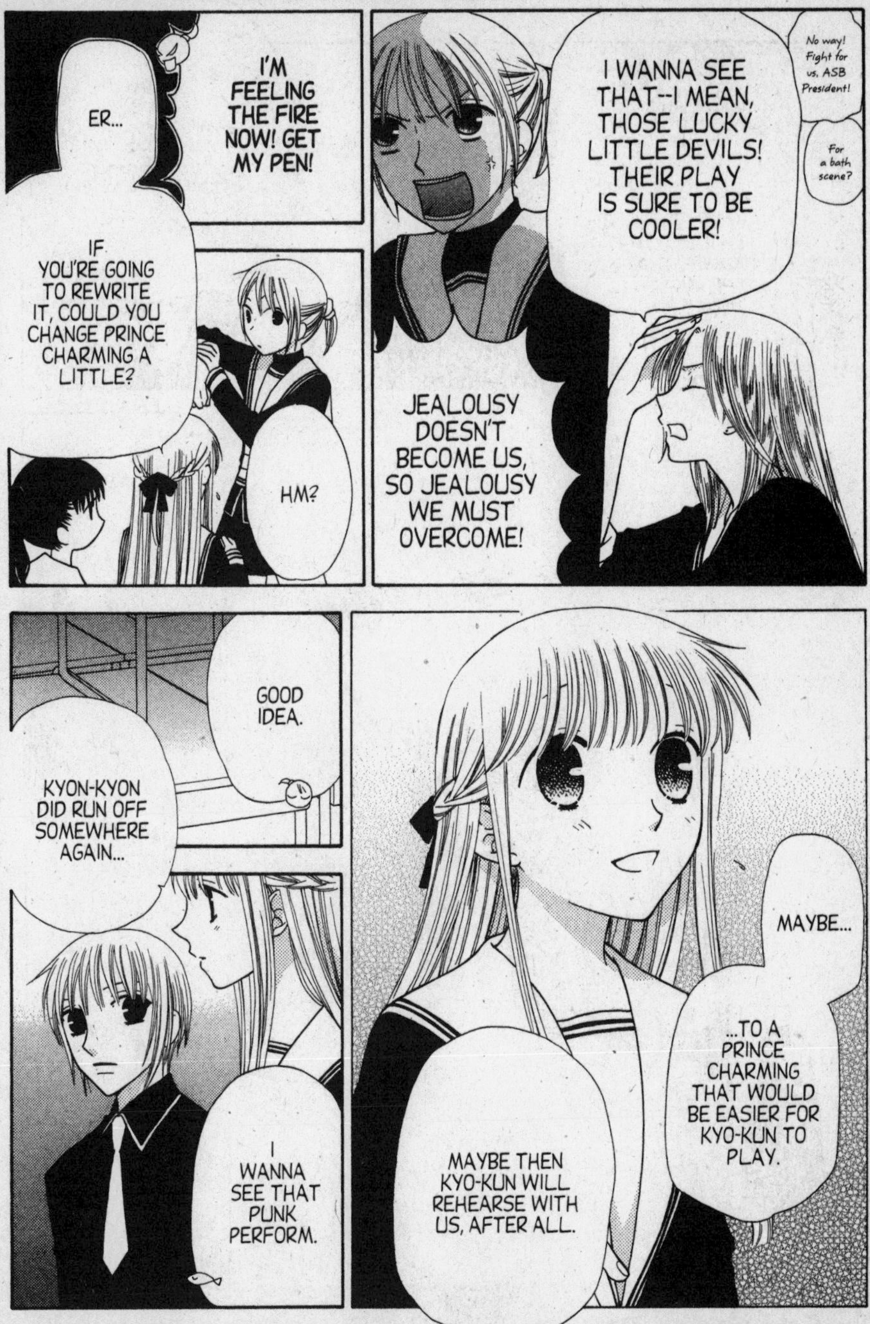
I WANNA SEE THAT--I MEAN, THOSE LUCKY LITTLE DEVILS! THEIR PLAY IS SURE TO BE COOLER!
No way! Fight for us, ASB President!
For a bath scene?
JEALOUSY DOESN'T BECOME US, SO JEALOUSY WE MUST OVERCOME!
I'M FEELING THE FIRE NOW! GET MY PEN!
ER...
IF YOU'RE GOING TO REWRITE IT, COULD YOU CHANGE PRINCE CHARMING A LITTLE?
HM?
MAYBE...
...TO A PRINCE CHARMING THAT WOULD BE EASIER FOR KYO-KUN TO PLAY.
MAYBE THEN KYO-KUN WILL REHEARSE WITH US, AFTER ALL.
GOOD IDEA.
KYON-KYON DID RUN OFF SOMEWHERE AGAIN...
I WANNA SEE THAT PUNK PERFORM.

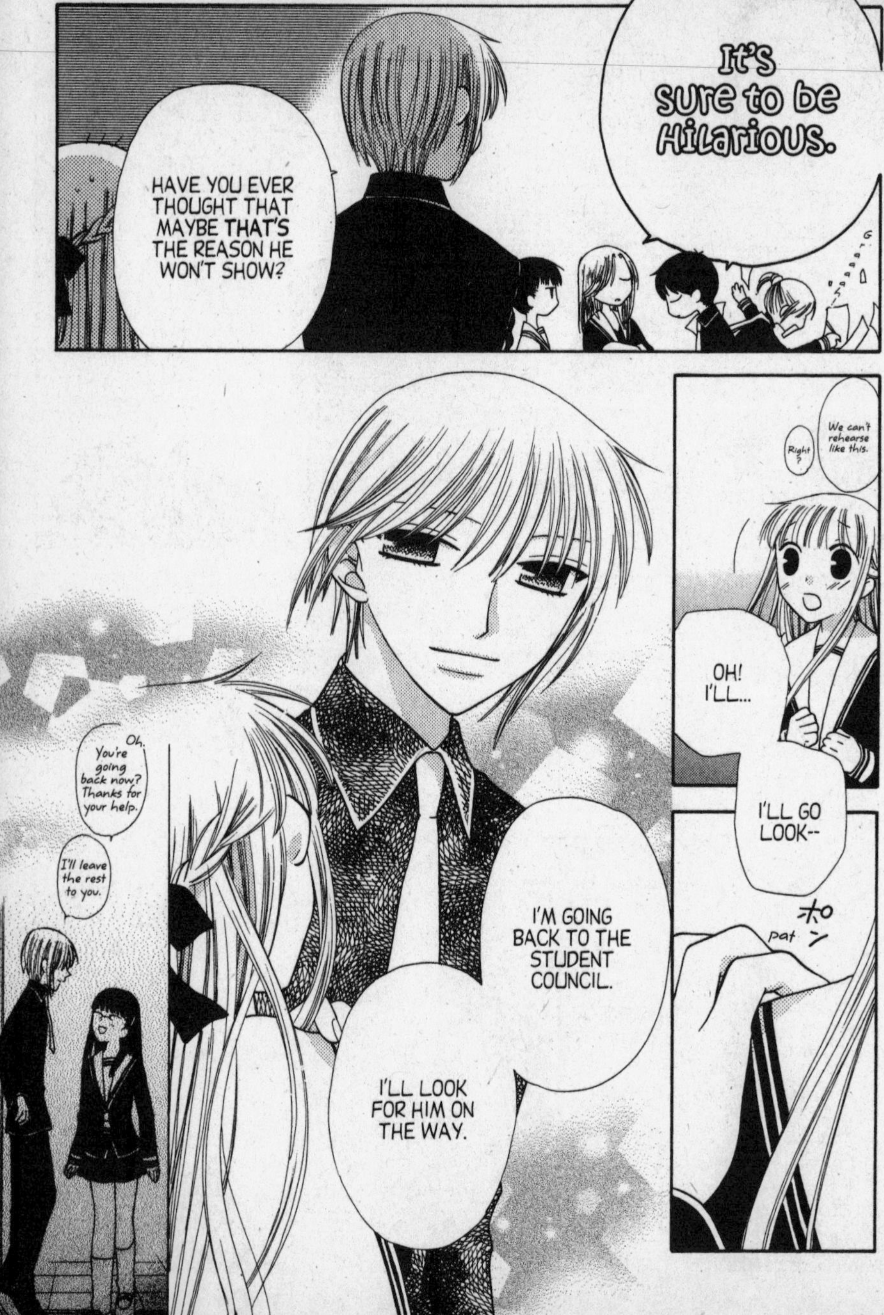
It's sure to be Hilarious.
HAVE YOU EVER THOUGHT THAT MAYBE THAT'S THE REASON HE WON'T SHOW?
We can't rehearse like this.
Right?
OH! I'LL...
I'LL GO LOOK--
pat
I'M GOING BACK TO THE STUDENT COUNCIL.
I'LL LOOK FOR HIM ON THE WAY.
Oh. You're going back now? Thanks for your help.
I'll leave the rest to you.

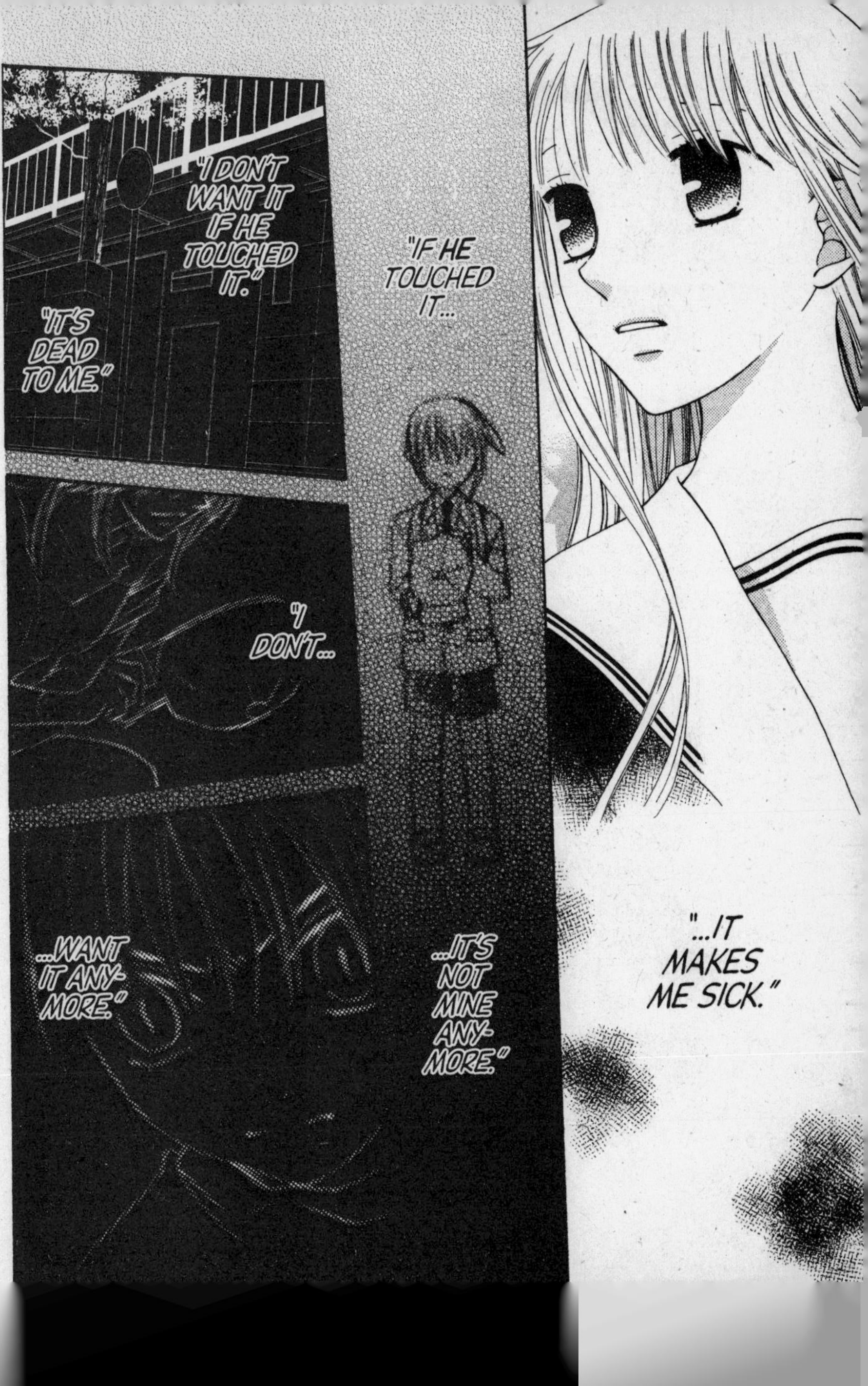
"...IT MAKES ME SICK."
"IF HE TOUCHED IT...
...IT'S NOT MINE ANYMORE."
"I DON'T WANT IT IF HE TOUCHED IT."
"IT'S DEAD TO ME."
"I DON'T...
...WANT IT ANYMORE."

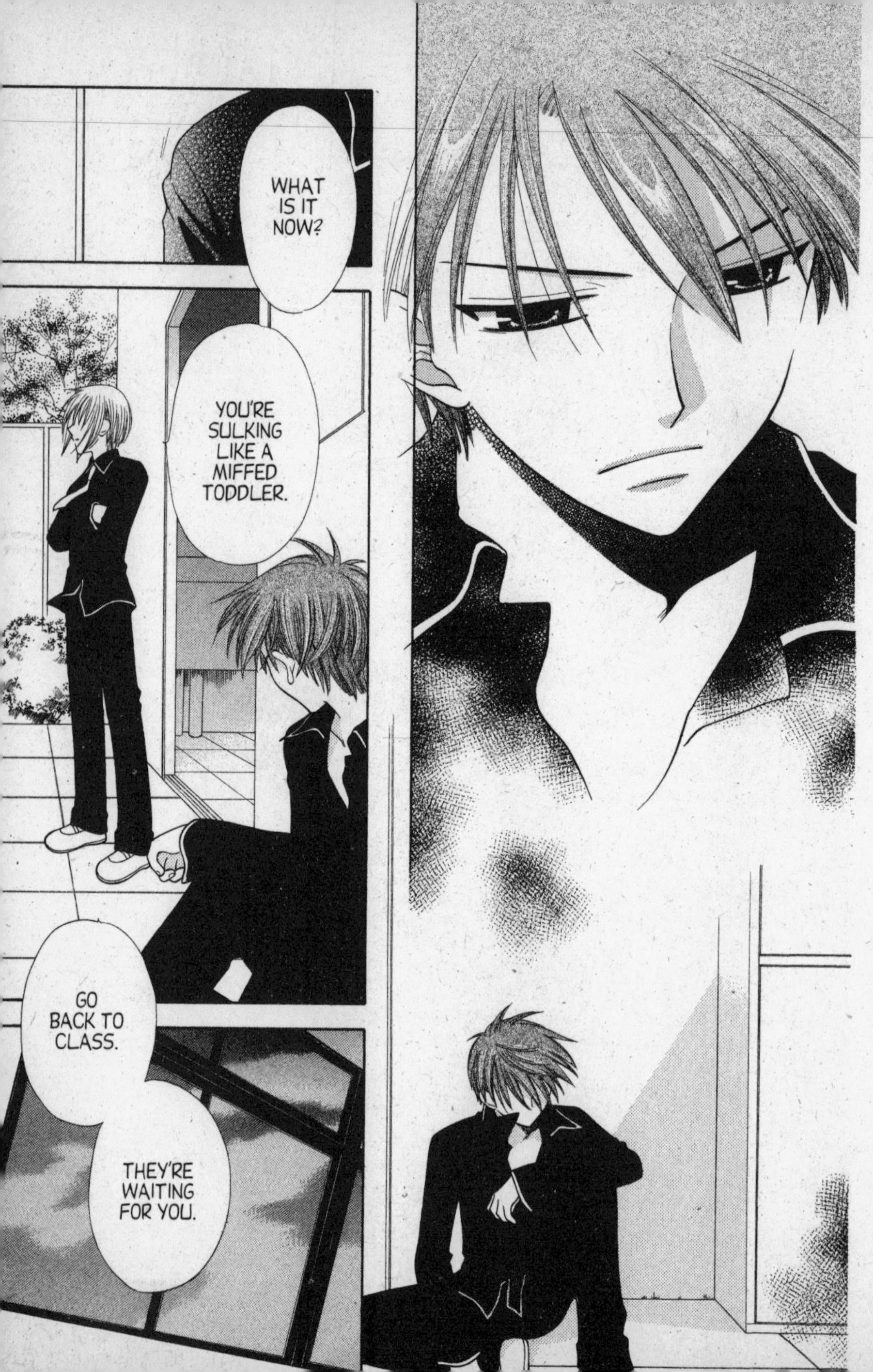
WHAT IS IT NOW?
YOU'RE SULKING LIKE A MIFFED TODDLER.
GO BACK TO CLASS.
THEY'RE WAITING FOR YOU.

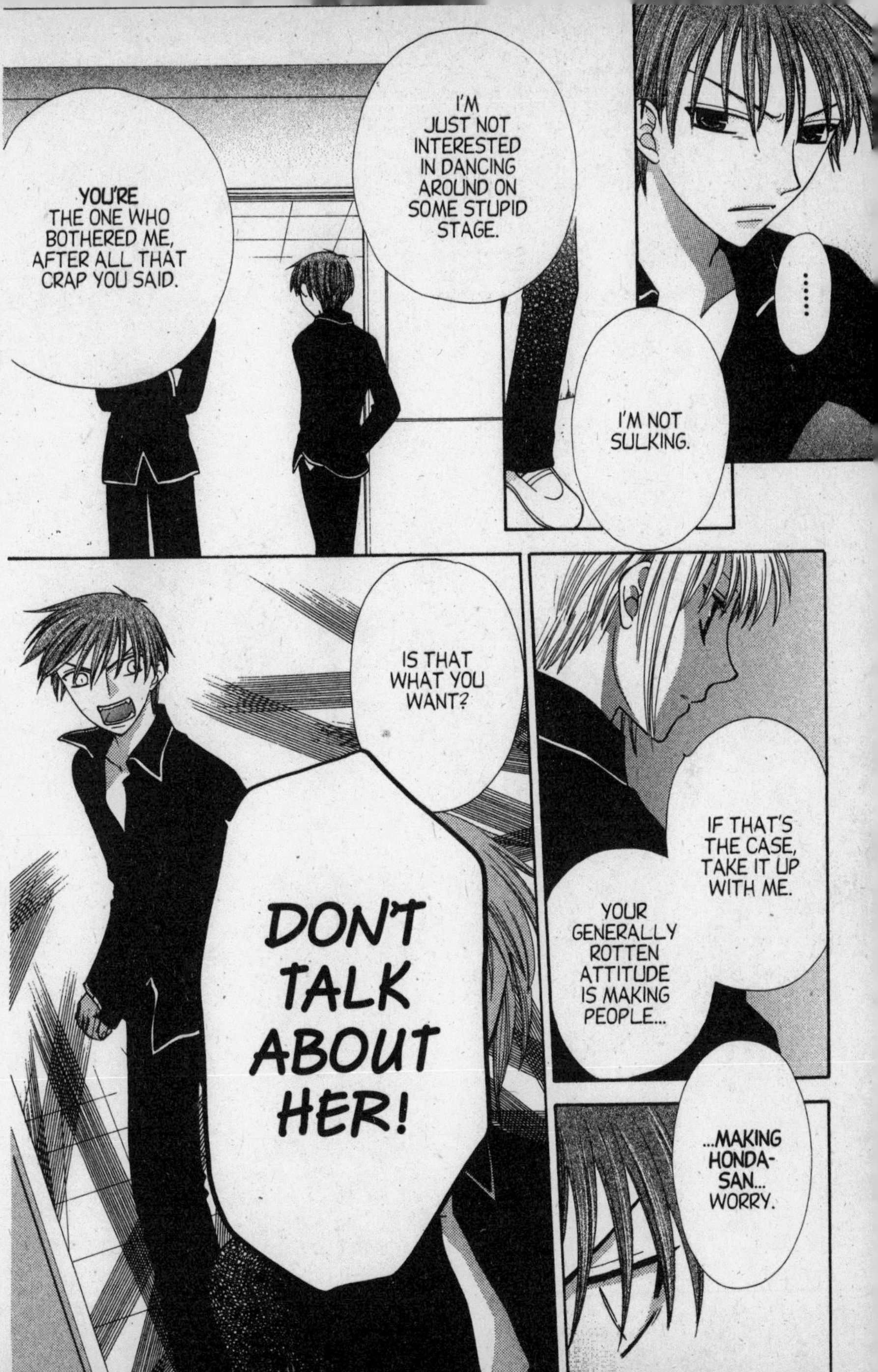
......
I'M NOT SULKING.
I'M JUST NOT INTERESTED IN DANCING AROUND ON SOME STUPID STAGE.
YOU'RE THE ONE WHO BOTHERED ME, AFTER ALL THAT CRAP YOU SAID.
IF THAT'S THE CASE, TAKE IT UP WITH ME.
YOUR GENERALLY ROTTEN ATTITUDE IS MAKING PEOPLE...
...MAKING HONDA-SAN... WORRY.
IS THAT WHAT YOU WANT?
DON'T TALK ABOUT HER!

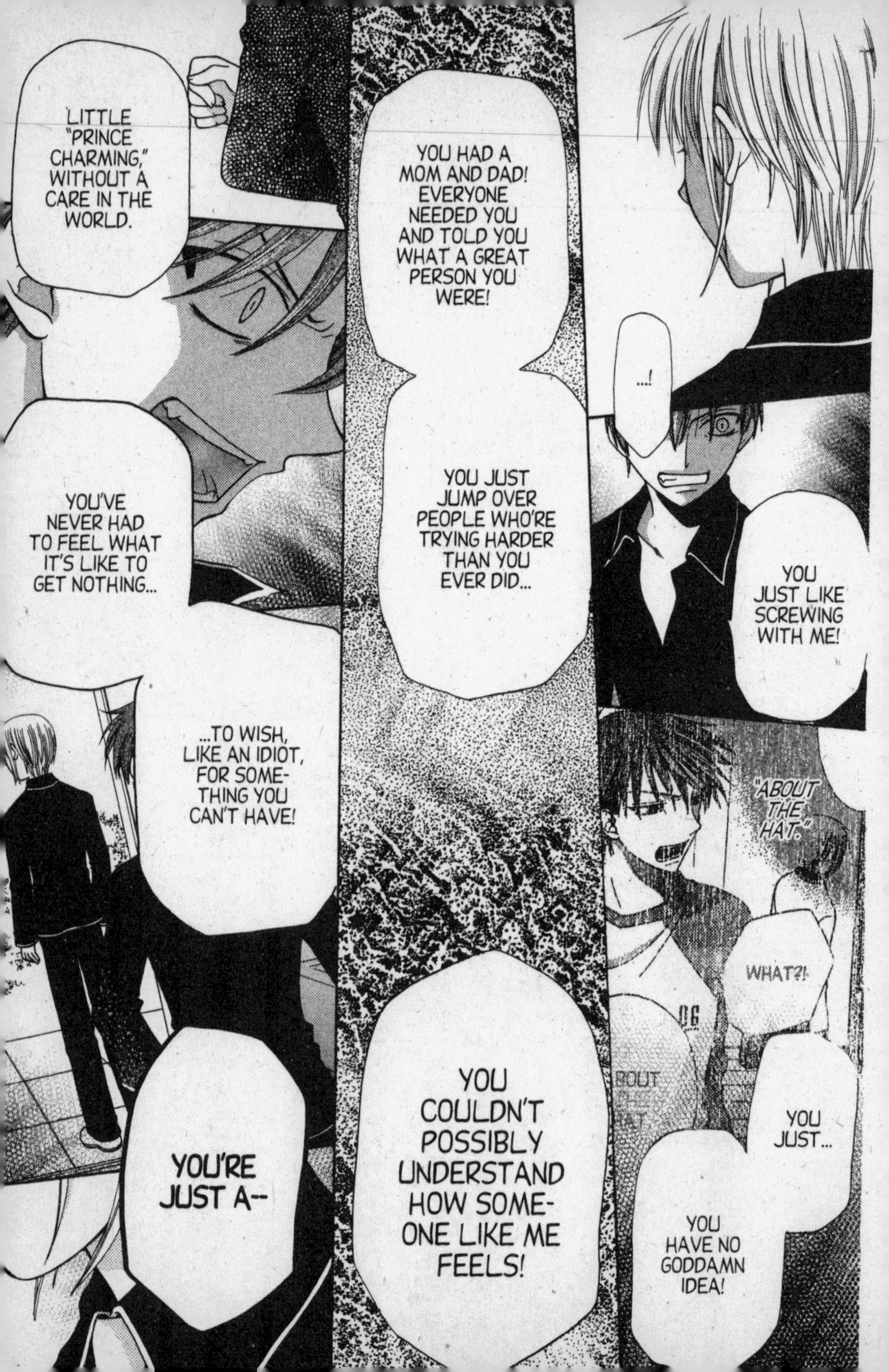
...!
YOU JUST LIKE SCREWING WITH ME!
"ABOUT THE HAT."
WHAT?!
YOU JUST...
YOU HAVE NO GODDAMN IDEA!
YOU HAD A MOM AND DAD! EVERYONE NEEDED YOU AND TOLD YOU WHAT A GREAT PERSON YOU WERE!
YOU JUST JUMP OVER PEOPLE WHO'RE TRYING HARDER THAN YOU EVER DID...
YOU COULDN'T POSSIBLY UNDERSTAND HOW SOME-ONE LIKE ME FEELS!
LITTLE "PRINCE CHARMING," WITHOUT A CARE IN THE WORLD.
YOU'VE NEVER HAD TO FEEL WHAT IT'S LIKE TO GET NOTHING...
...TO WISH, LIKE AN IDIOT, FOR SOME-THING YOU CAN'T HAVE!
YOU'RE JUST A--

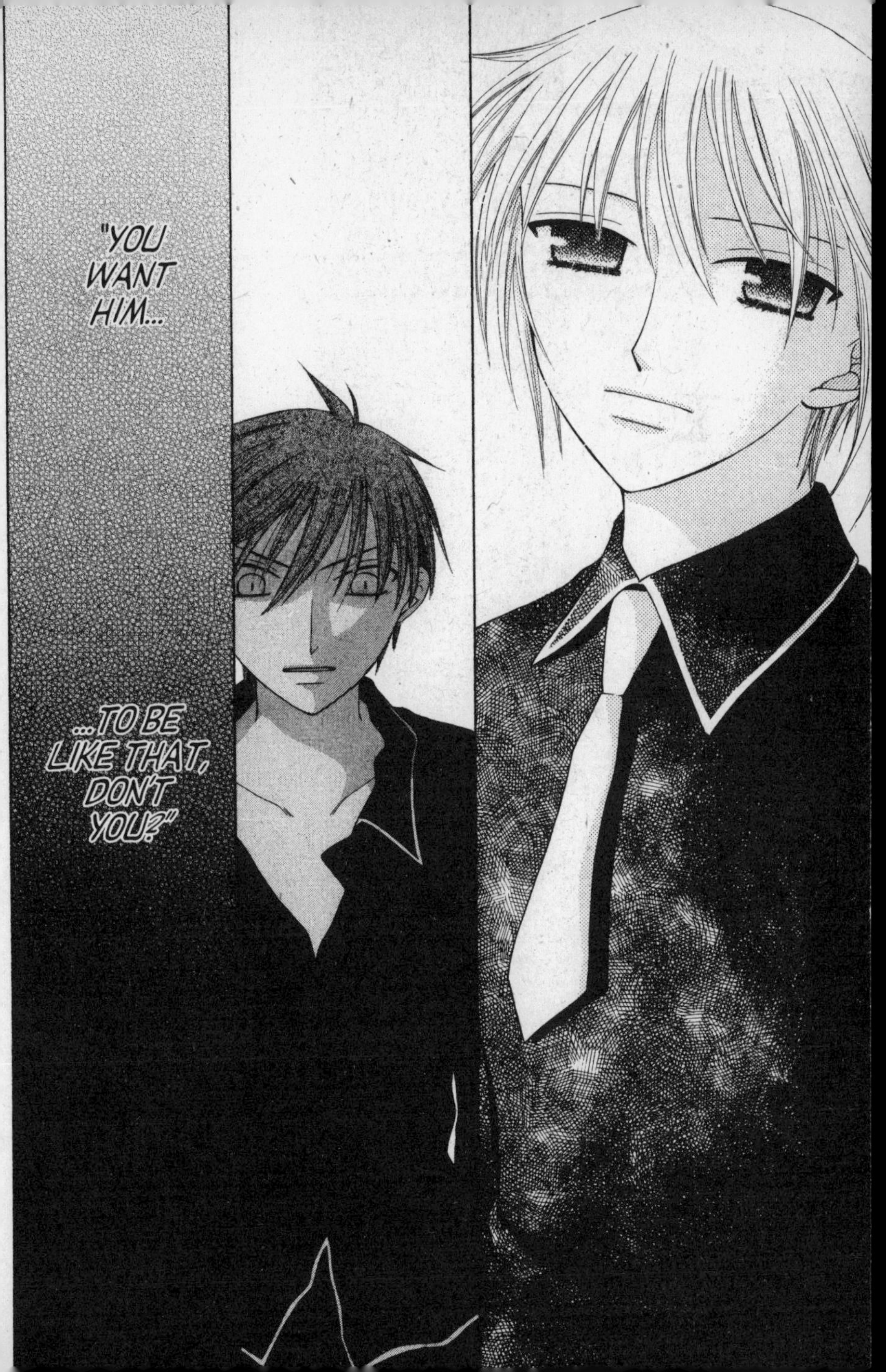
"YOU WANT HIM...
...TO BE LIKE THAT, DON'T YOU?"

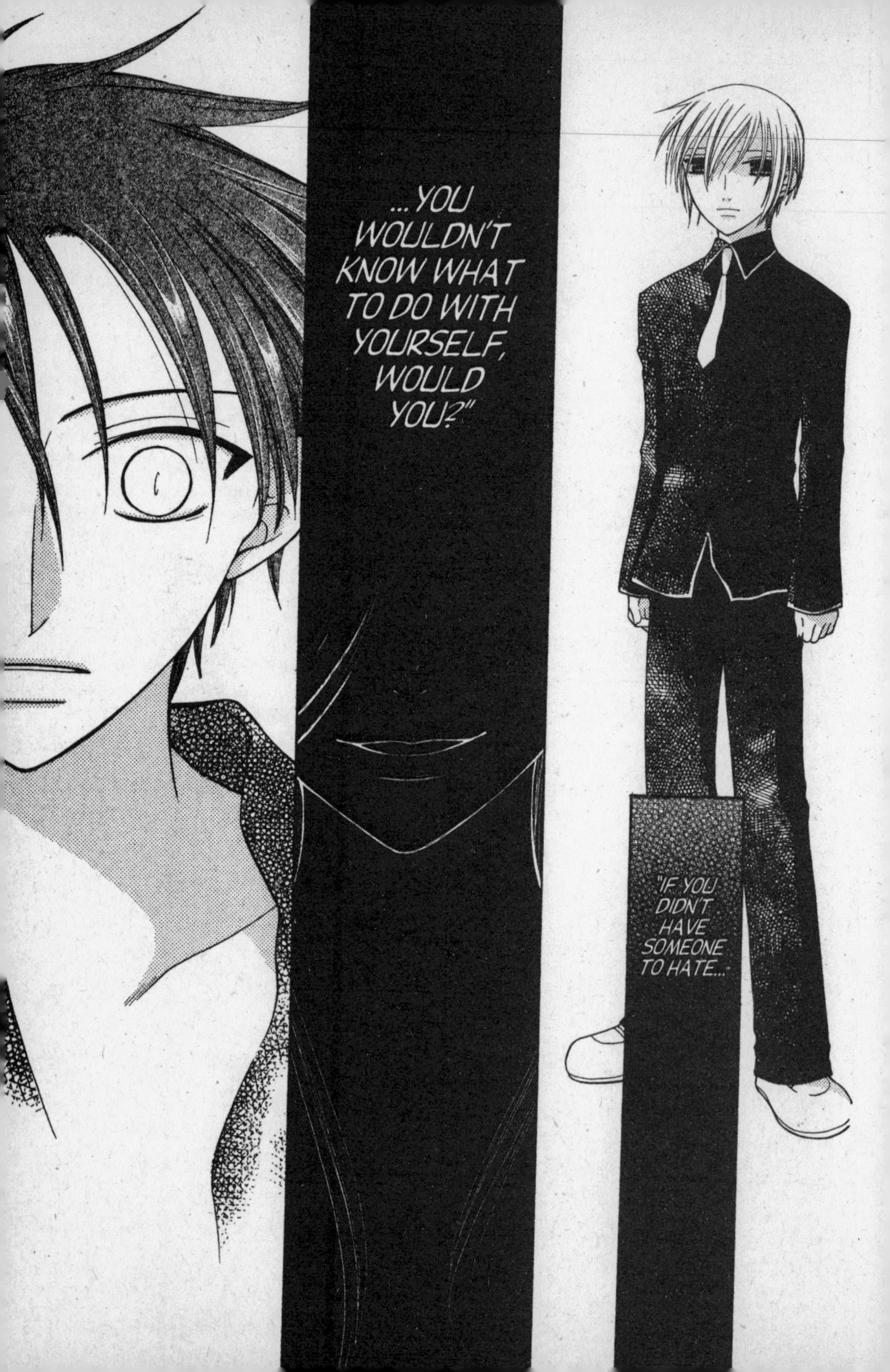
"IF YOU DIDN'T HAVE SOMEONE TO HATE...
...YOU WOULDN'T KNOW WHAT TO DO WITH YOURSELF, WOULD YOU?"

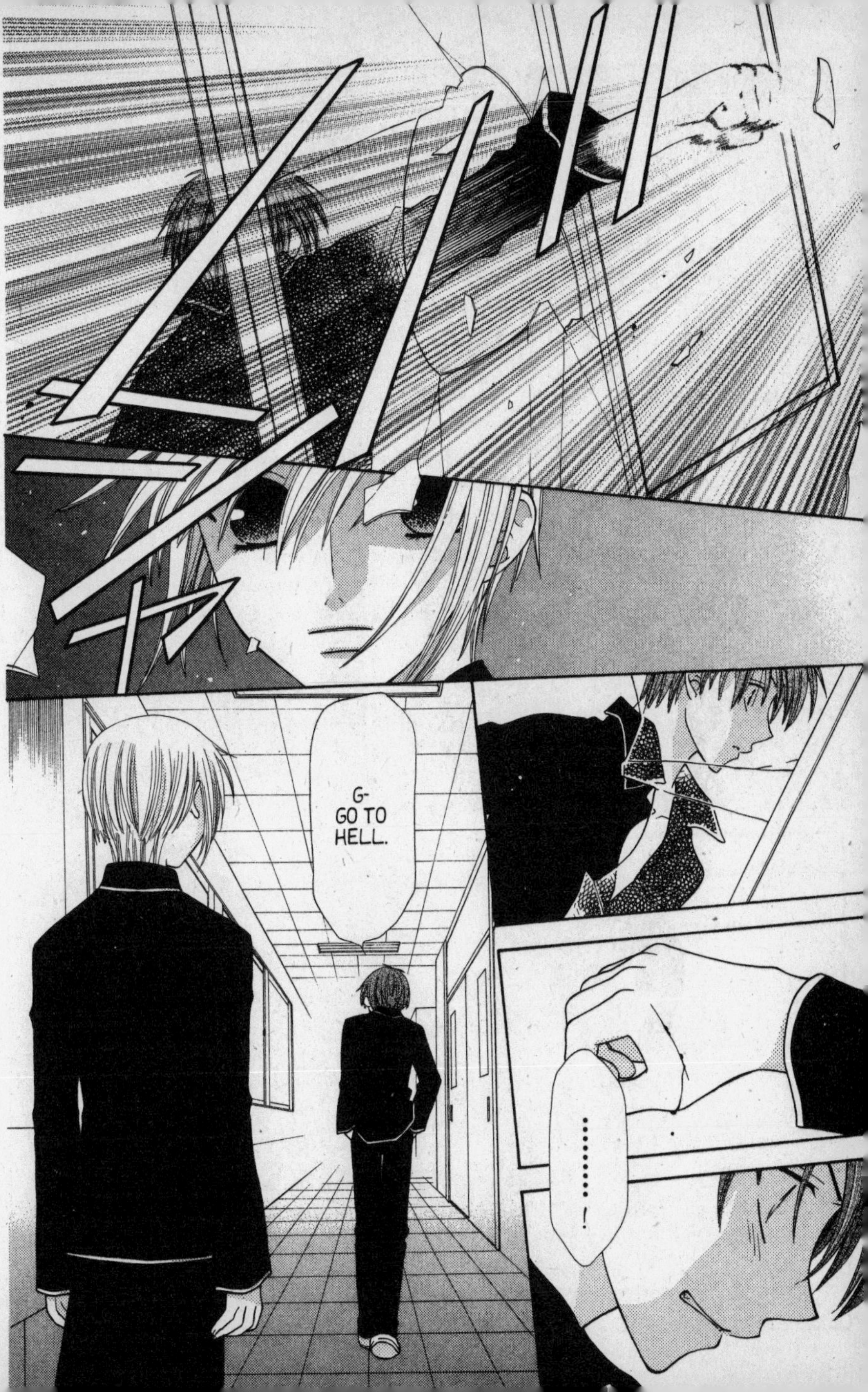
G-
GO TO
HELL.
.........!

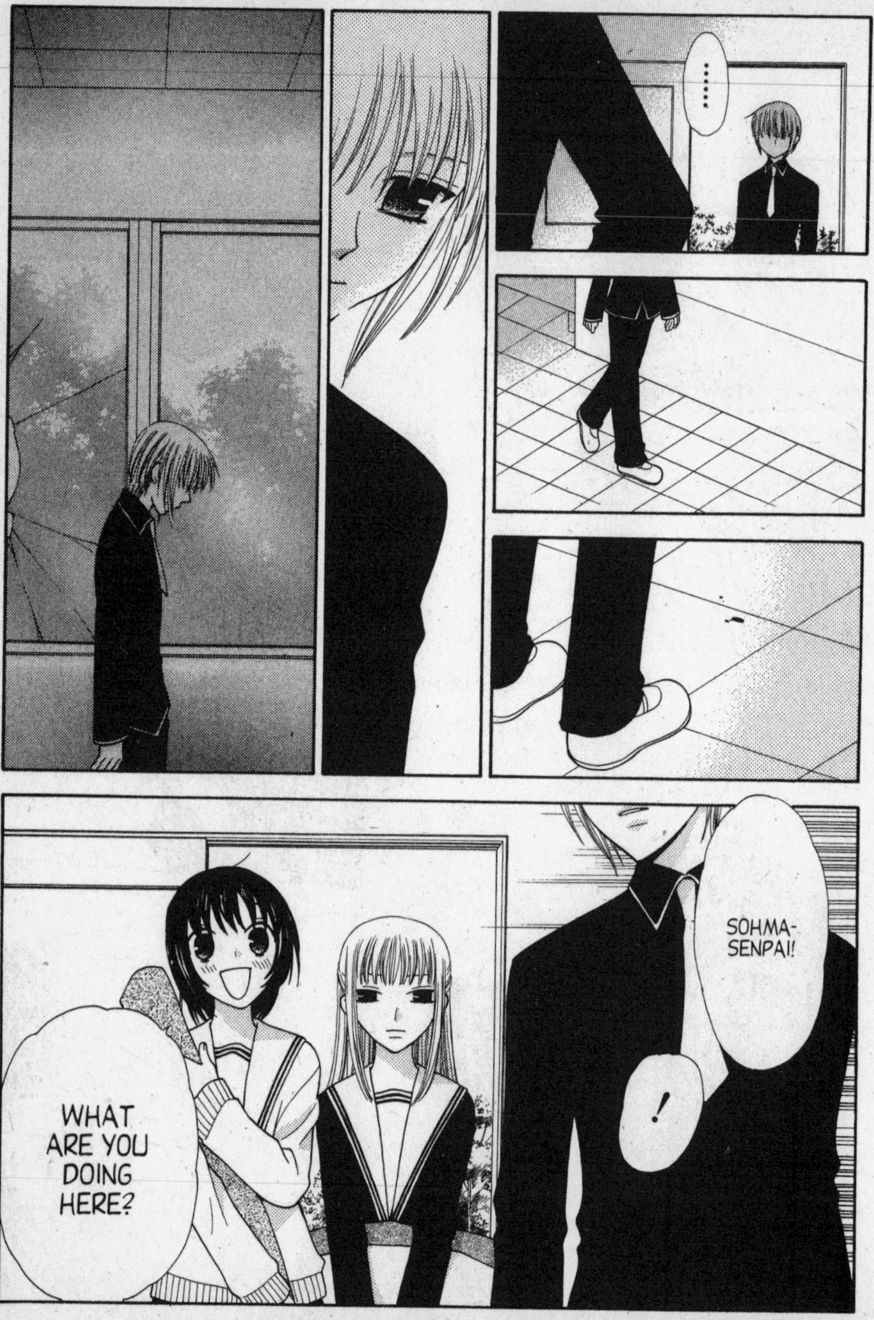
......
SOHMA-SENPAI!
!
WHAT ARE YOU DOING HERE?

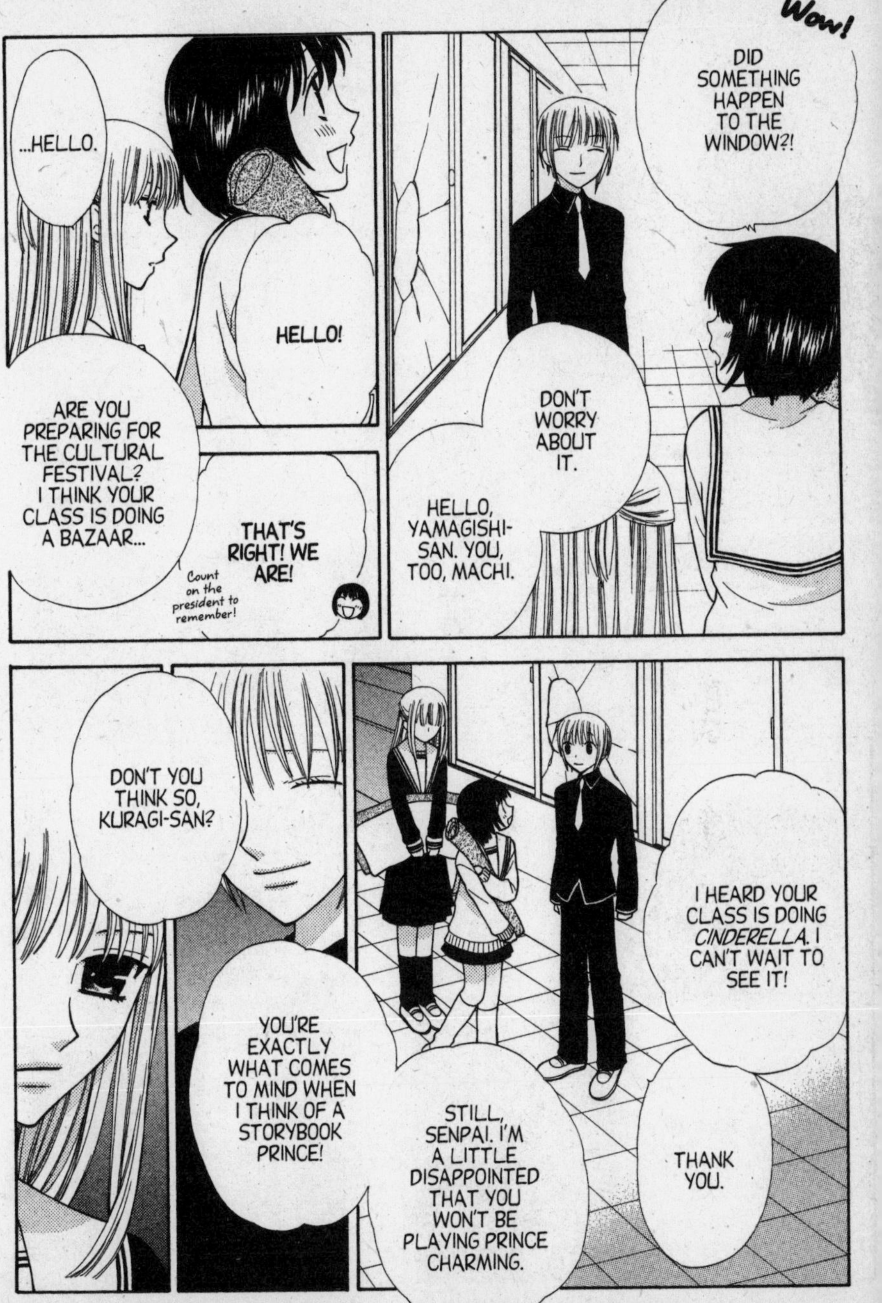
Wow!
DID SOMETHING HAPPEN TO THE WINDOW?!
DON'T WORRY ABOUT IT.
HELLO, YAMAGISHI-SAN. YOU, TOO, MACHI.
HELLO!
...HELLO.
ARE YOU PREPARING FOR THE CULTURAL FESTIVAL? I THINK YOUR CLASS IS DOING A BAZAAR...
THAT'S RIGHT! WE ARE!
Count on the president to remember!
I HEARD YOUR CLASS IS DOING *CINDERELLA*. I CAN'T WAIT TO SEE IT!
THANK YOU.
STILL, SENPAI. I'M A LITTLE DISAPPOINTED THAT YOU WON'T BE PLAYING PRINCE CHARMING.
YOU'RE EXACTLY WHAT COMES TO MIND WHEN I THINK OF A STORYBOOK PRINCE!
DON'T YOU THINK SO, KURAGI-SAN?

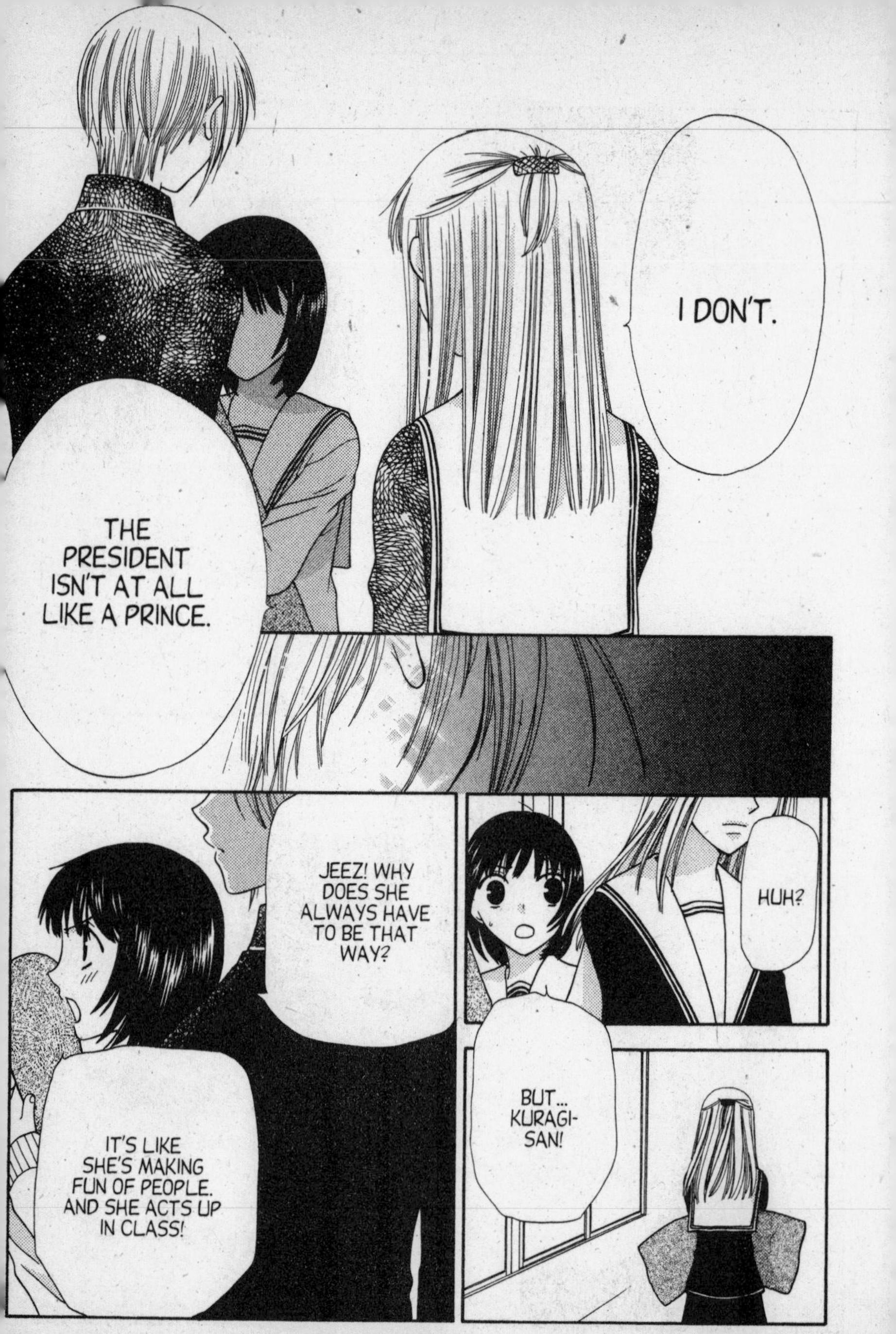
I DON'T.
THE PRESIDENT ISN'T AT ALL LIKE A PRINCE.
HUH?
BUT... KURAGI-SAN!
JEEZ! WHY DOES SHE ALWAYS HAVE TO BE THAT WAY?
IT'S LIKE SHE'S MAKING FUN OF PEOPLE. AND SHE ACTS UP IN CLASS!

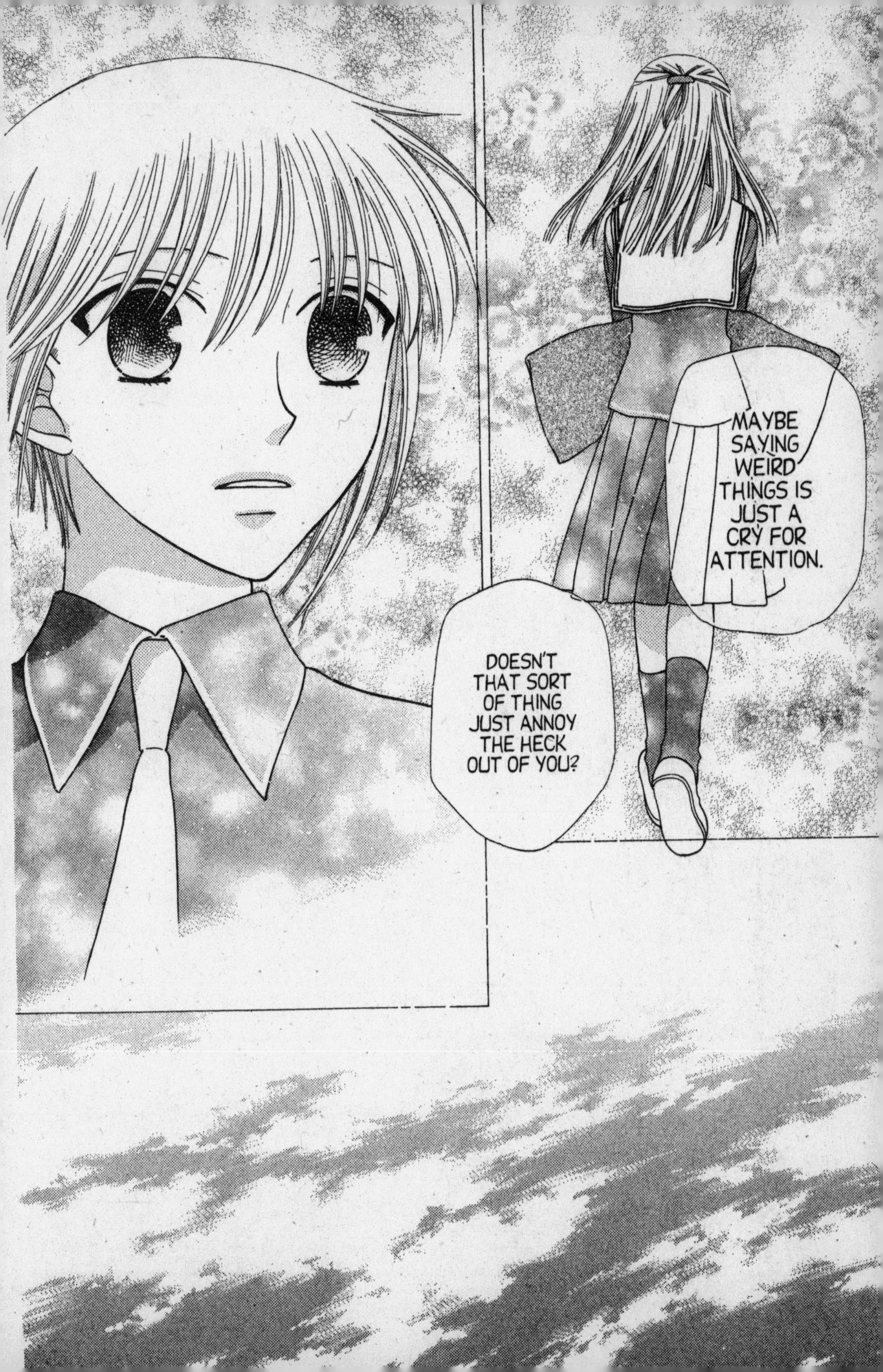
MAYBE SAYING WEIRD THINGS IS JUST A CRY FOR ATTENTION.
DOESN'T THAT SORT OF THING JUST ANNOY THE HECK OUT OF YOU?

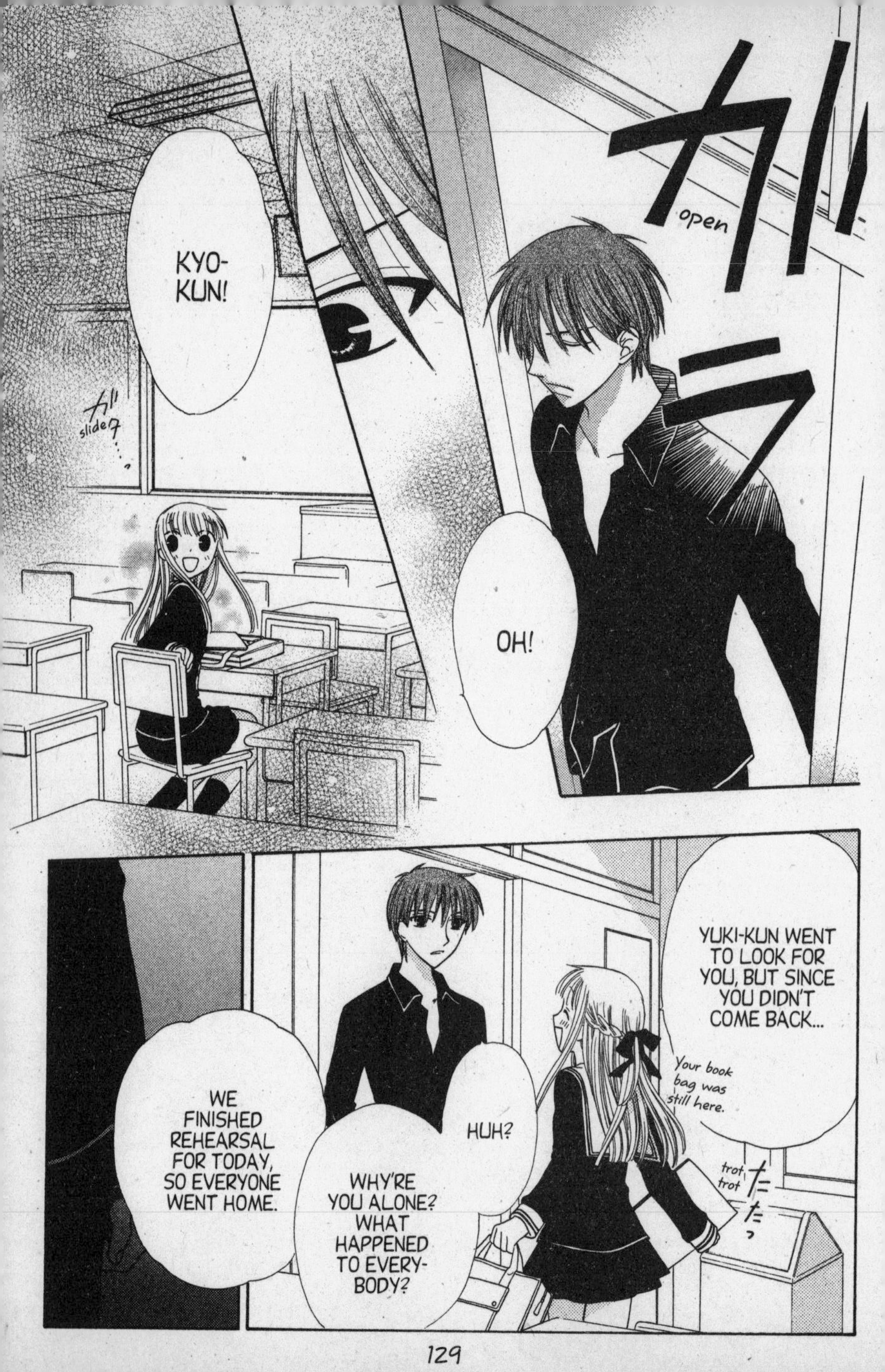

カラ
open
OH!
KYO-KUN!
slide
YUKI-KUN WENT TO LOOK FOR YOU, BUT SINCE YOU DIDN'T COME BACK...
Your book bag was still here.
trot trot
HUH?
WHY'RE YOU ALONE? WHAT HAPPENED TO EVERY-BODY?
WE FINISHED REHEARSAL FOR TODAY, SO EVERYONE WENT HOME.

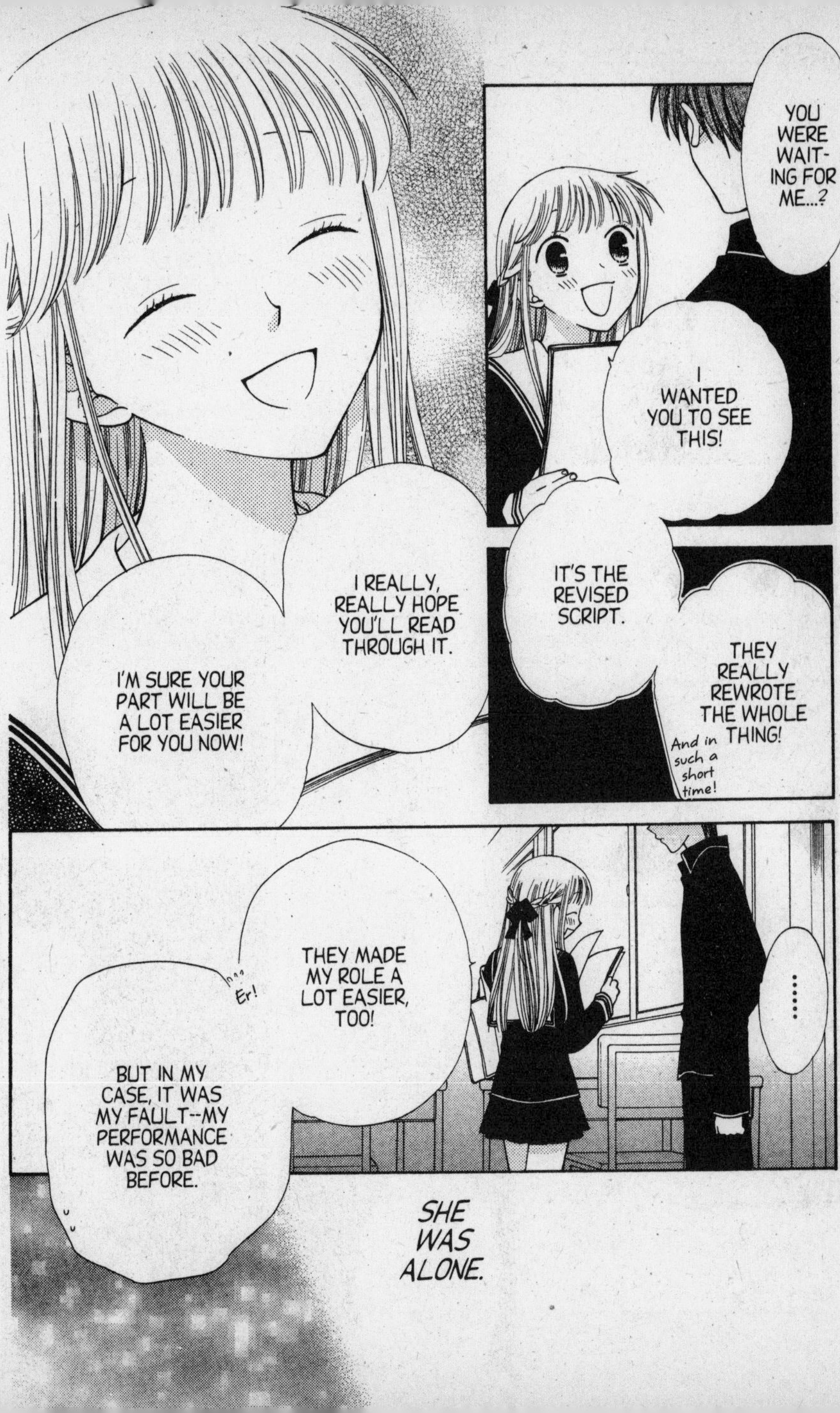
YOU WERE WAIT-ING FOR ME...?
I WANTED YOU TO SEE THIS!
IT'S THE REVISED SCRIPT.
THEY REALLY REWROTE THE WHOLE THING!
And in such a short time!
I REALLY, REALLY HOPE YOU'LL READ THROUGH IT.
I'M SURE YOUR PART WILL BE A LOT EASIER FOR YOU NOW!
......
THEY MADE MY ROLE A LOT EASIER, TOO!
Er!
BUT IN MY CASE, IT WAS MY FAULT--MY PERFORMANCE WAS SO BAD BEFORE.
SHE WAS ALONE.

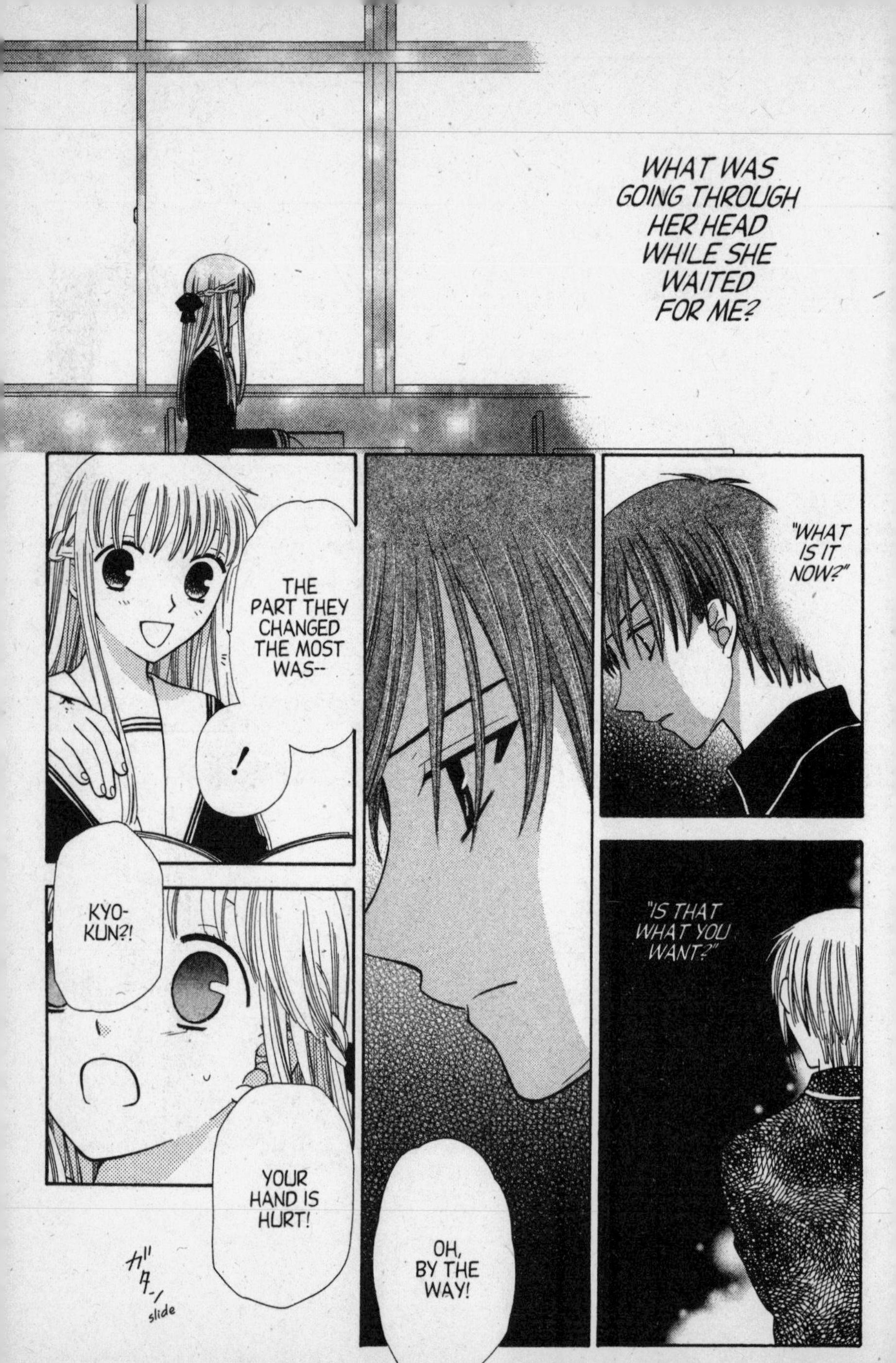
WHAT WAS GOING THROUGH HER HEAD WHILE SHE WAITED FOR ME?
"WHAT IS IT NOW?"
"IS THAT WHAT YOU WANT?"
OH, BY THE WAY!
THE PART THEY CHANGED THE MOST WAS--
!
KYO-KUN?!
YOUR HAND IS HURT!
slide

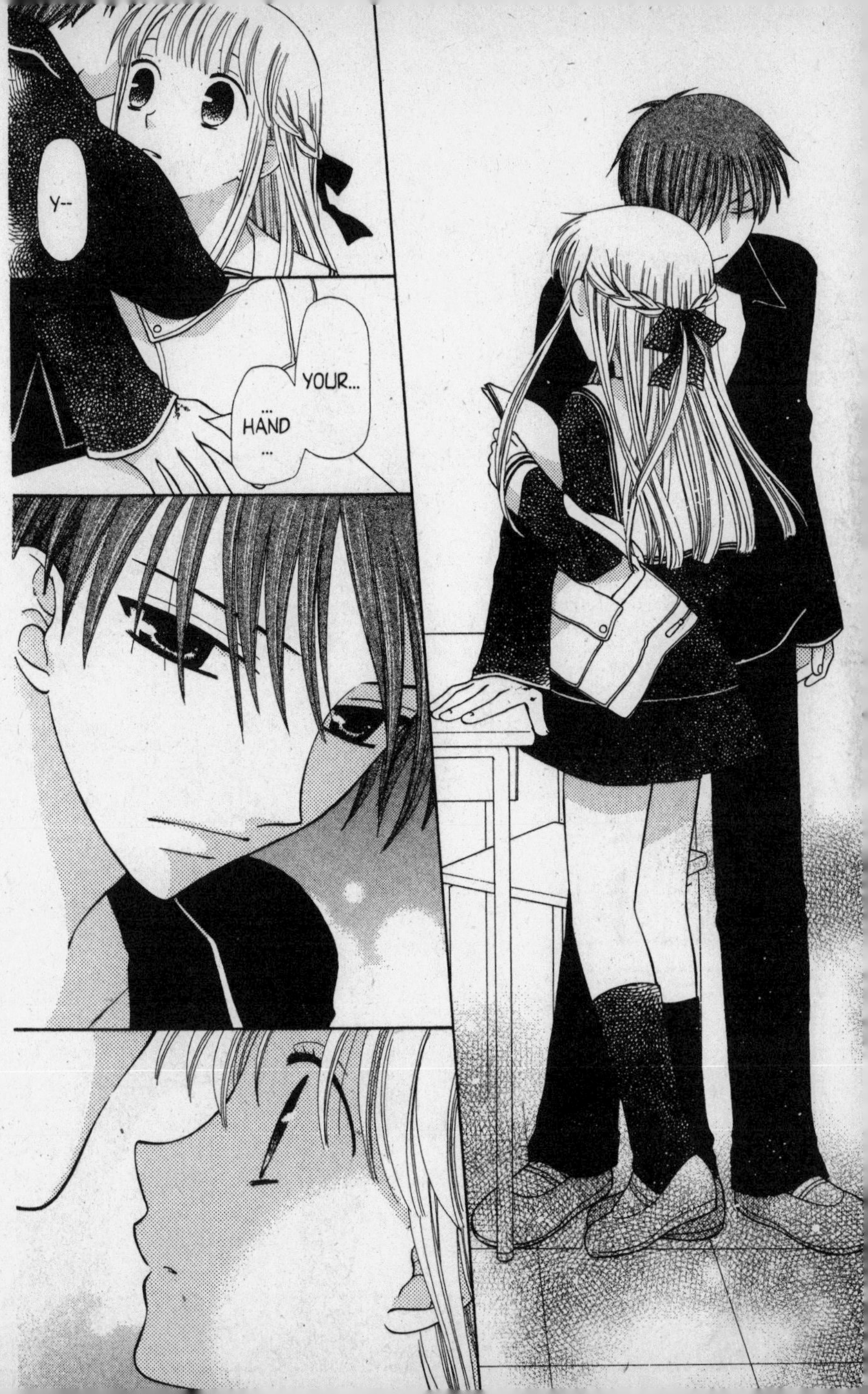
Y--
YOUR...
...HAND...

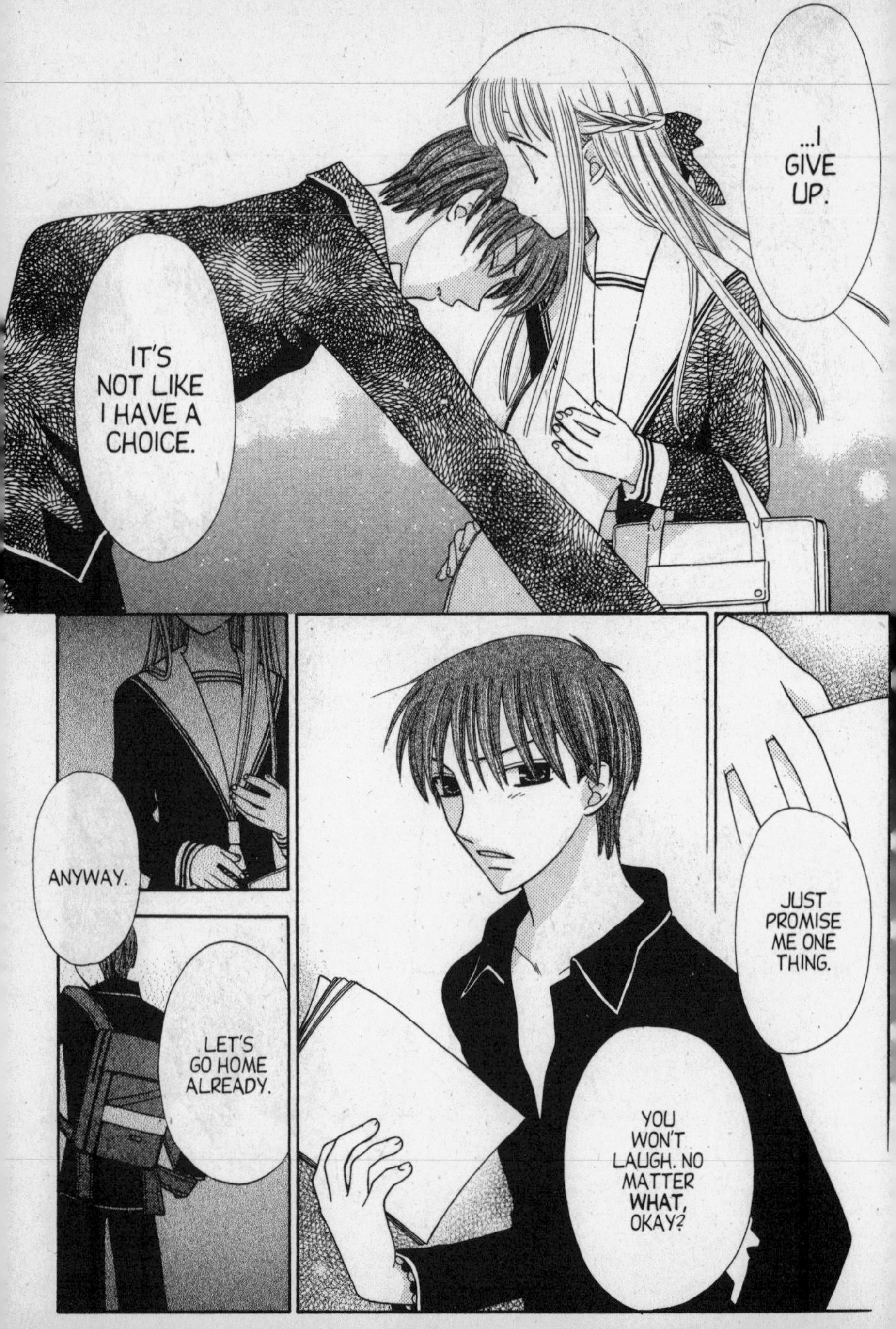
...I GIVE UP.
IT'S NOT LIKE I HAVE A CHOICE.
JUST PROMISE ME ONE THING.
YOU WON'T LAUGH. NO MATTER WHAT, OKAY?
ANYWAY.
LET'S GO HOME ALREADY.

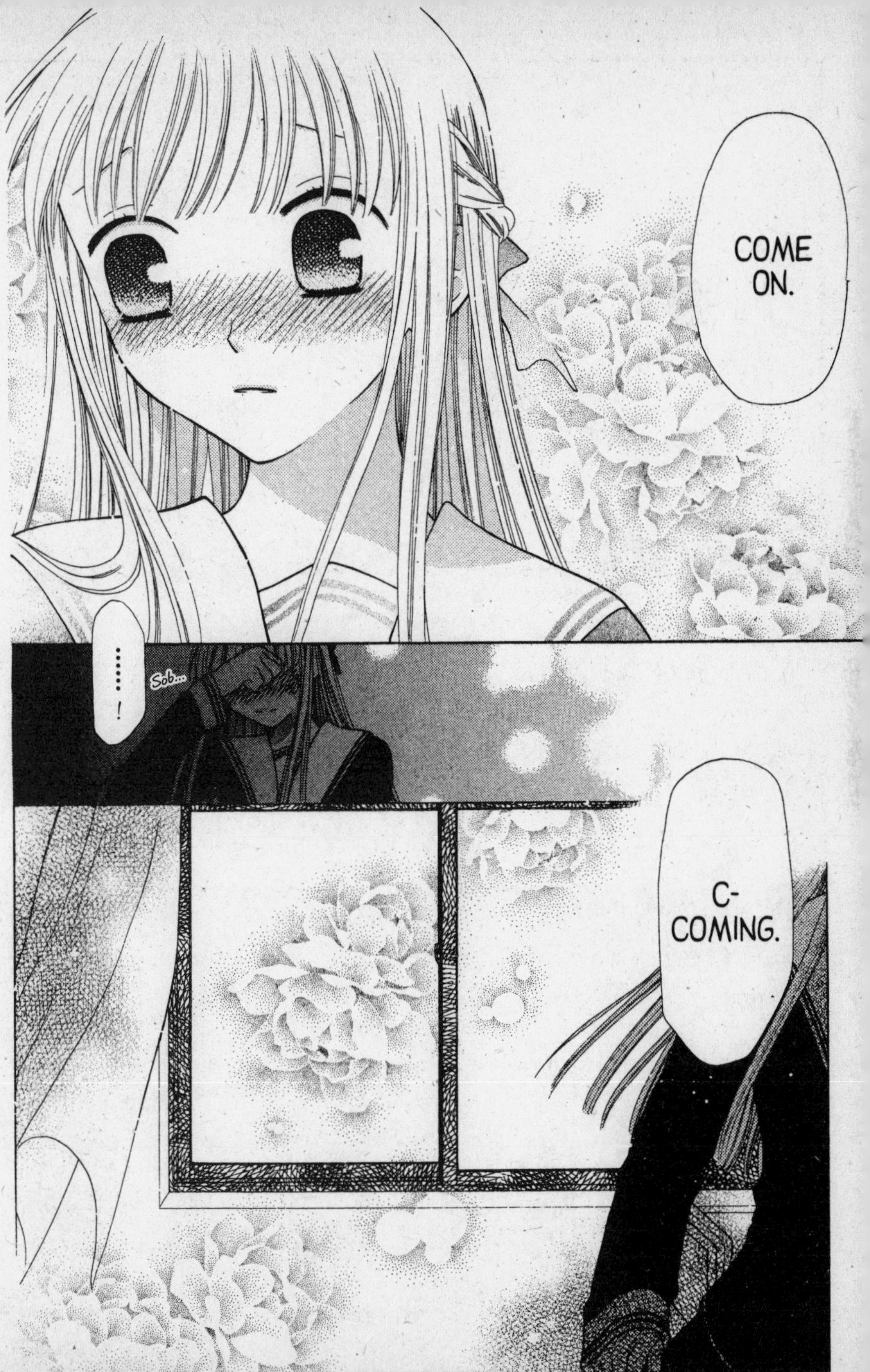
COME ON.
......!
Sob...
C- COMING.

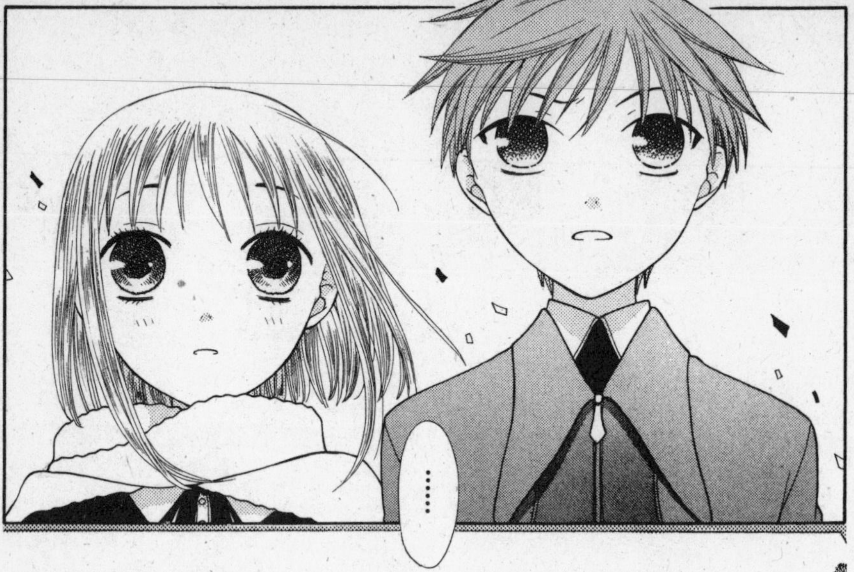
......

Kaibara Public HIGH SCHOOL Cultural Festival

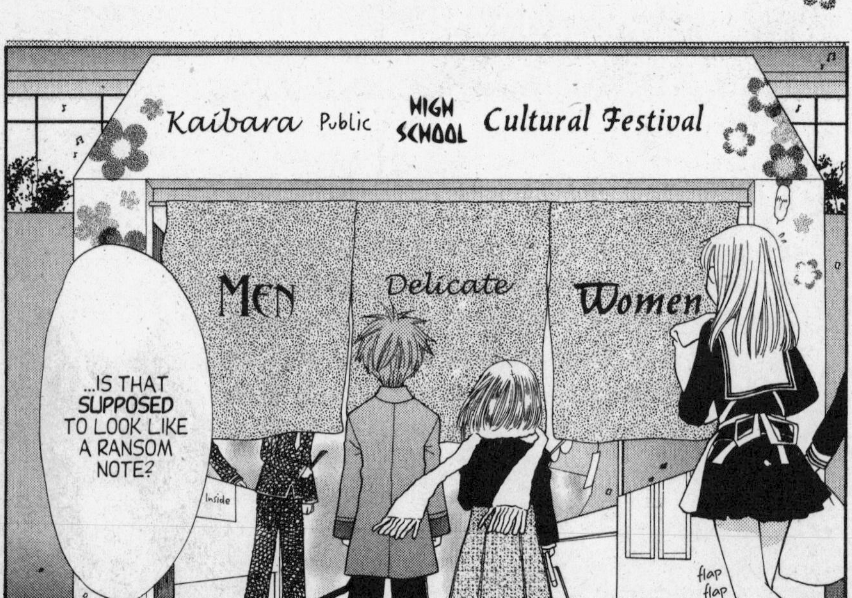
Kaibara Public HIGH SCHOOL Cultural Festival
Women
Delicate
MEN
flap flap
Inside
...IS THAT SUPPOSED TO LOOK LIKE A RANSOM NOTE?

Chapter 88

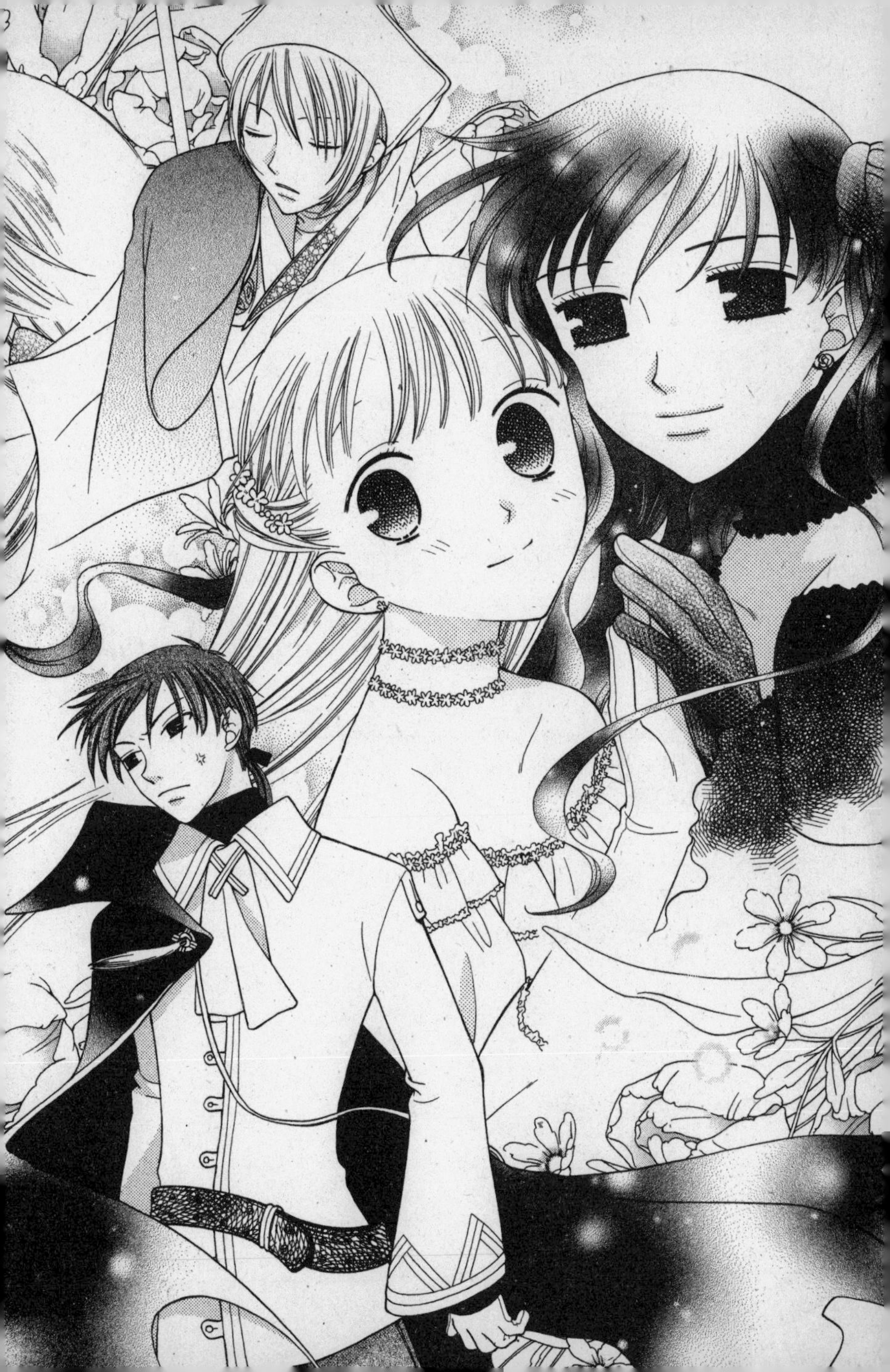

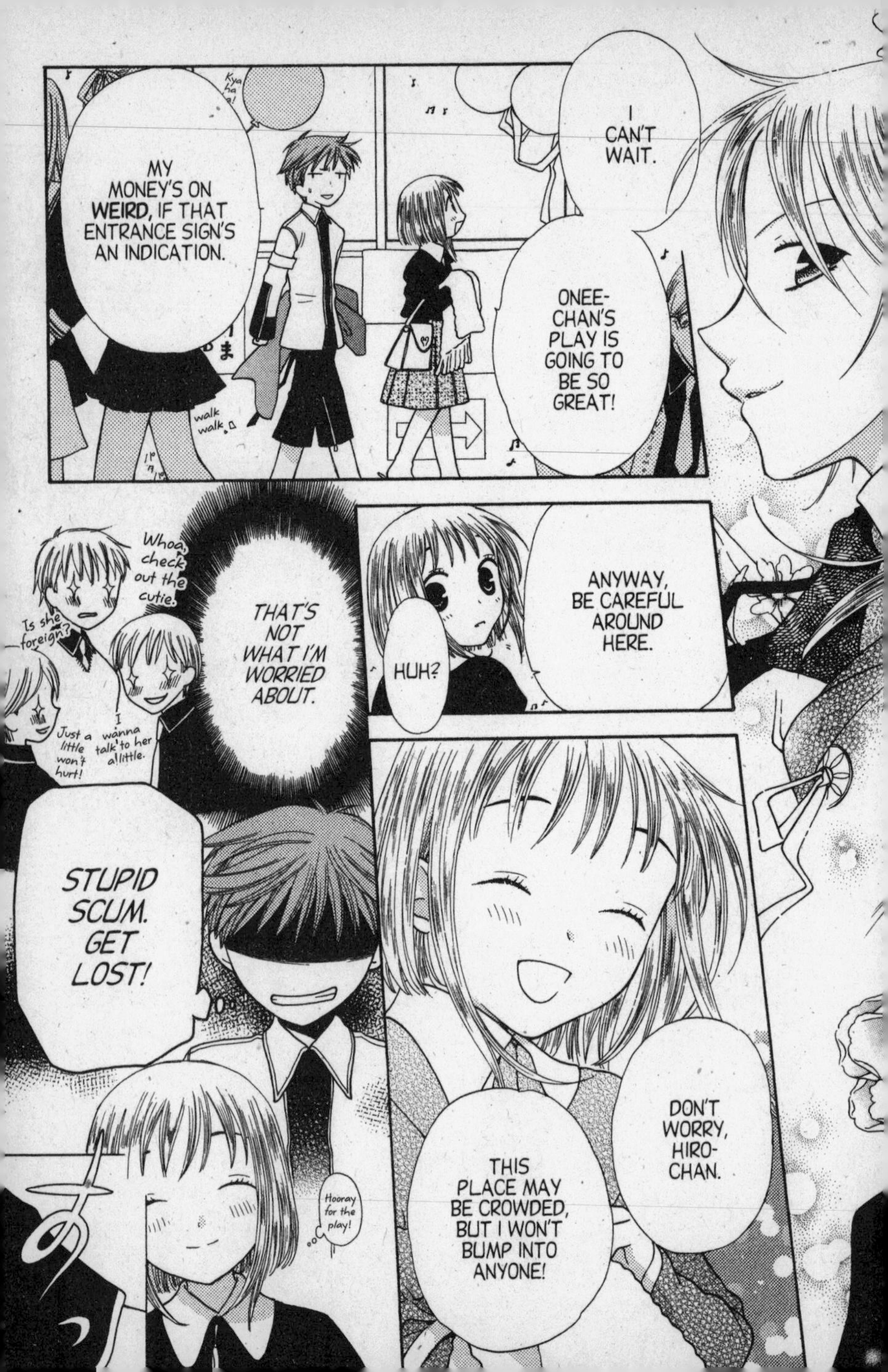
I CAN'T WAIT.
ONEE-CHAN'S PLAY IS GOING TO BE SO GREAT!
Kya ha ha!
MY MONEY'S ON **WEIRD,** IF THAT ENTRANCE SIGN'S AN INDICATION.
walk walk
ANYWAY, BE CAREFUL AROUND HERE.
HUH?
THAT'S NOT WHAT I'M WORRIED ABOUT.
Whoa, check out the cutie.
Is she foreign?
I wanna talk to her a little.
Just a little won't hurt!
DON'T WORRY, HIRO-CHAN.
THIS PLACE MAY BE CROWDED, BUT I WON'T BUMP INTO ANYONE!
STUPID SCUM. GET LOST!
Hooray for the play!

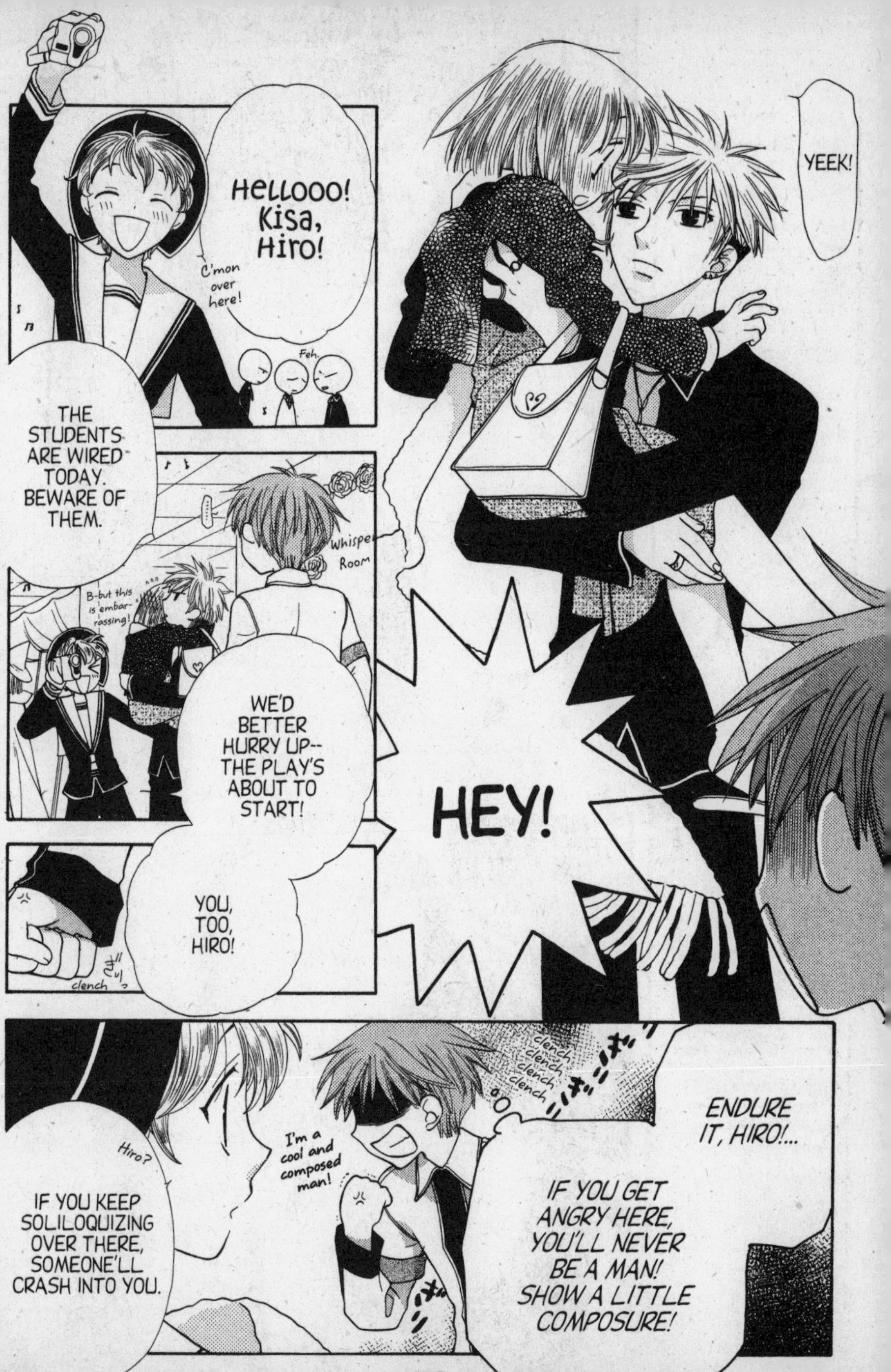

YEEK!
HEY!
Helllooo! Kisa, Hiro!
C'mon over here!
Feh.
THE STUDENTS ARE WIRED TODAY. BEWARE OF THEM.
......
Whisper Room
B-but this is embar-rassing!
WE'D BETTER HURRY UP-- THE PLAY'S ABOUT TO START!
YOU, TOO, HIRO!
clench
ENDURE IT, HIRO!...
IF YOU GET ANGRY HERE, YOU'LL NEVER BE A MAN! SHOW A LITTLE COMPOSURE!
clench clench clench clench
I'm a cool and composed man!
Hiro?
IF YOU KEEP SOLILOQUIZING OVER THERE, SOMEONE'LL CRASH INTO YOU.

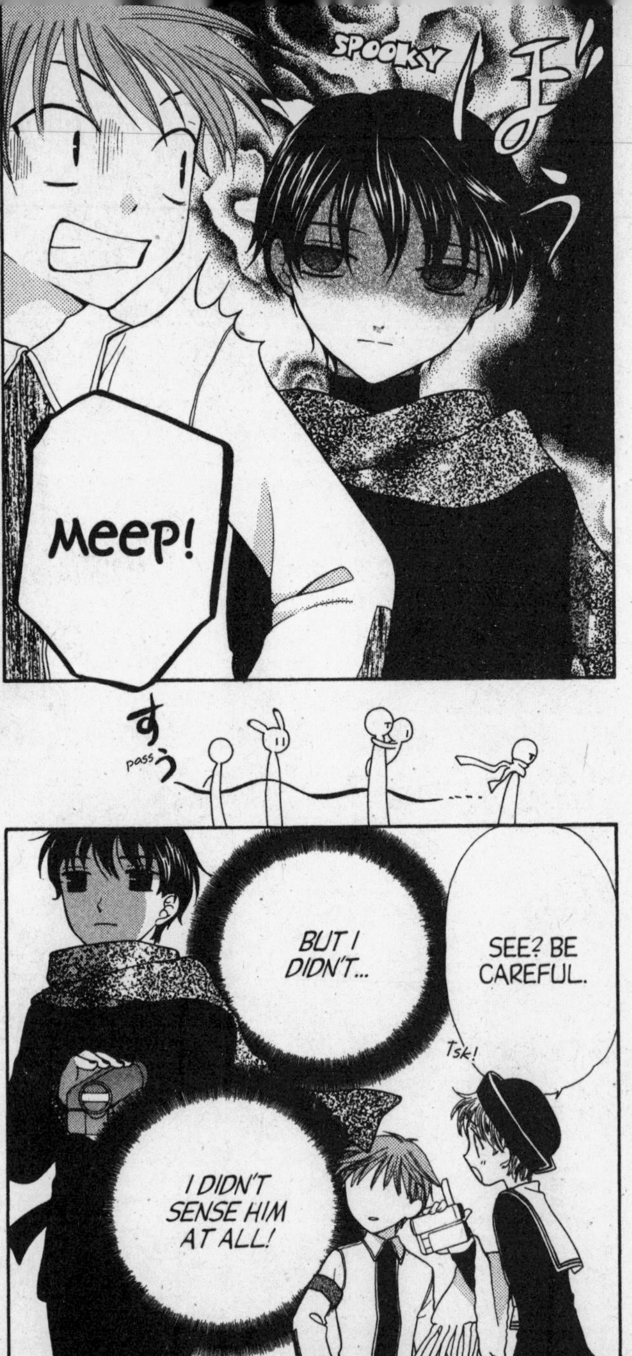
SPOOKY
MEEP!
pass
SEE? BE CAREFUL.
Tsk!
BUT I DIDN'T...
I DIDN'T SENSE HIM AT ALL!

Continued →

Hatori didn't date anyone. Hatori didn't, anyway.

At this moment in time, he's forming a close friendship with Mayu-chan...although that doesn't mean they don't still argue from time to time.

And, obviously, Hatori's still got issues to work through.

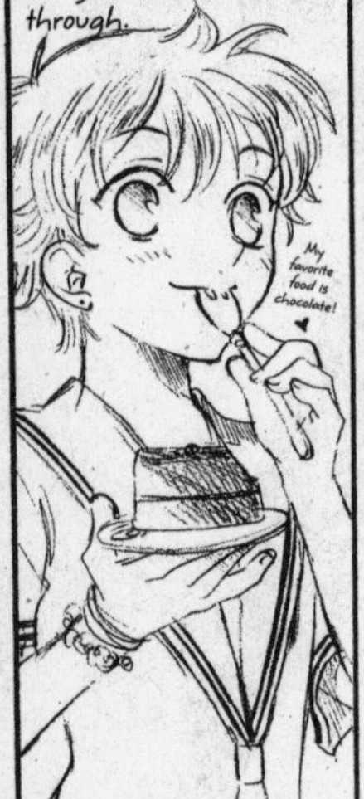
My favorite food is chocolate!

And now we have the boy often described as "a scene-calming agent":

Momiji.

Momiji's family consists of four people: Papa, Mama, his little sister Momo, and himself.

He's currently living alone (sort of). He has several servants.

To be
← continued

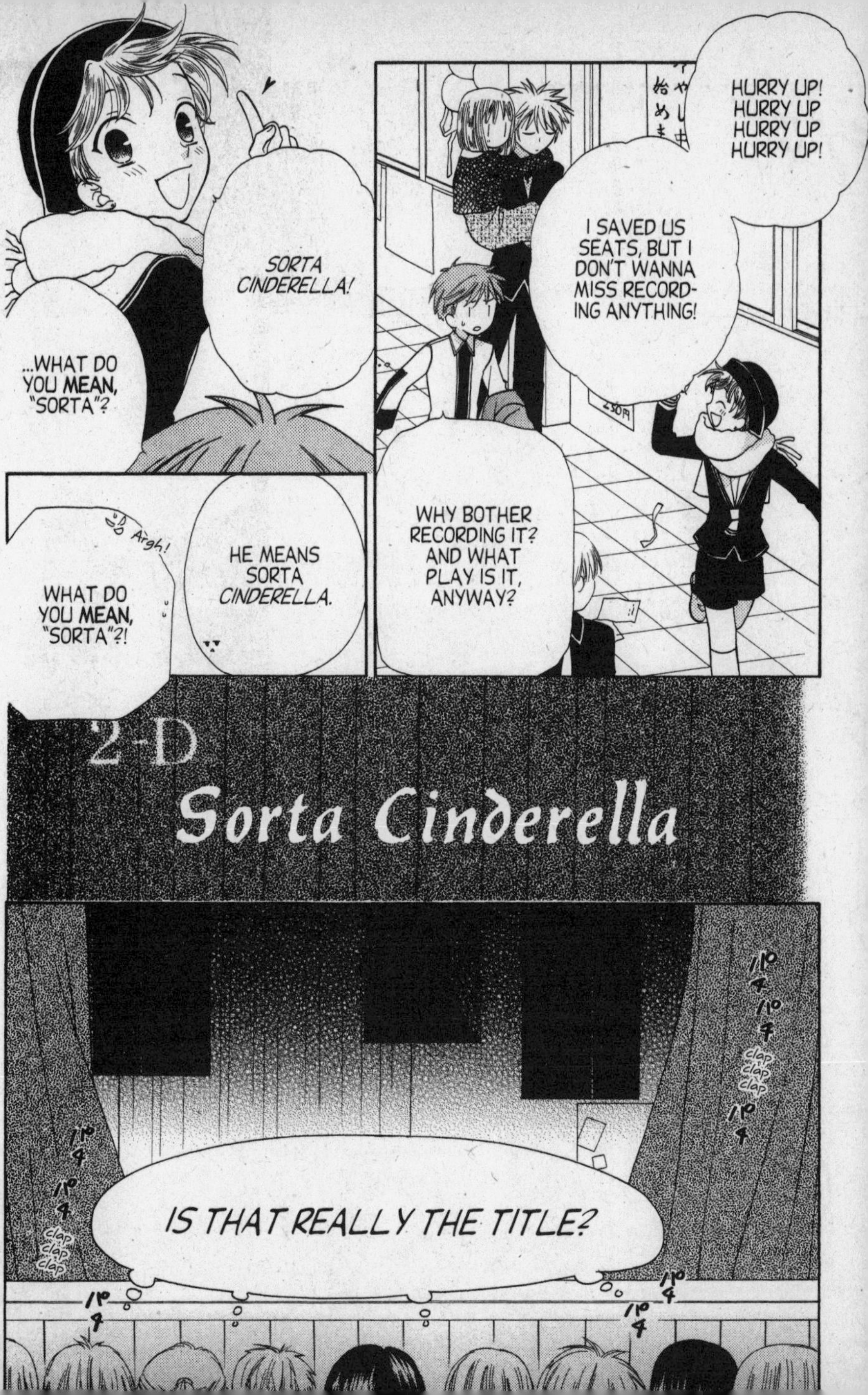
HURRY UP! HURRY UP HURRY UP HURRY UP!
I SAVED US SEATS, BUT I DON'T WANNA MISS RECORDING ANYTHING!
WHY BOTHER RECORDING IT? AND WHAT PLAY IS IT, ANYWAY?
SORTA CINDERELLA!
...WHAT DO YOU MEAN, "SORTA"?
HE MEANS SORTA CINDERELLA.
Argh!
WHAT DO YOU MEAN, "SORTA"?!
2-D
Sorta Cinderella
パチパチ
clap clap clap
パチ
IS THAT REALLY THE TITLE?
パチパチ
clap clap clap
パチ

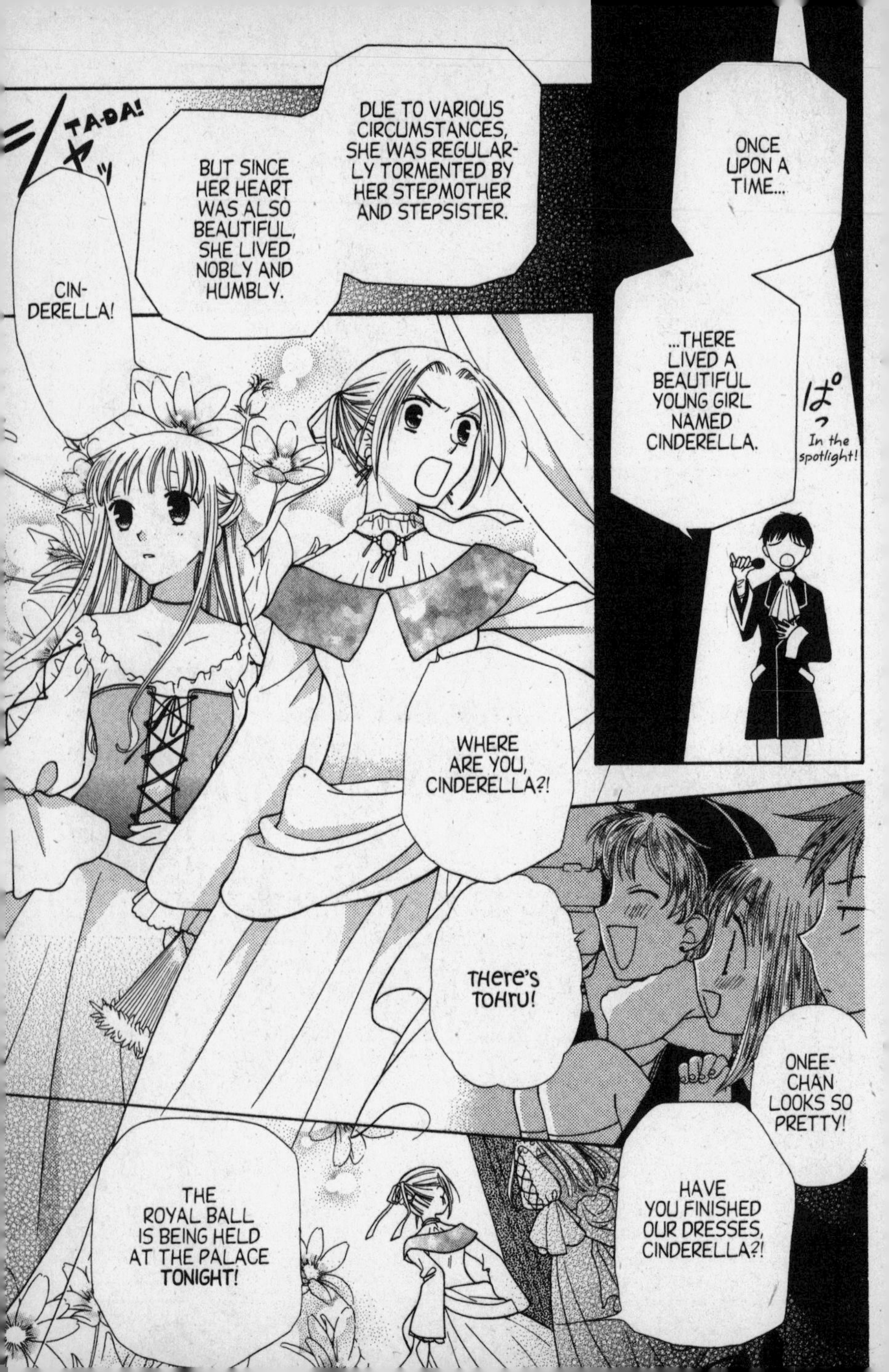
ONCE UPON A TIME...
...THERE LIVED A BEAUTIFUL YOUNG GIRL NAMED CINDERELLA.
ぱっ
In the spotlight!
DUE TO VARIOUS CIRCUMSTANCES, SHE WAS REGULARLY TORMENTED BY HER STEPMOTHER AND STEPSISTER.
BUT SINCE HER HEART WAS ALSO BEAUTIFUL, SHE LIVED NOBLY AND HUMBLY.
TA-DA!
ヤッ
CINDERELLA!
WHERE ARE YOU, CINDERELLA?!
ONEE-CHAN LOOKS SO PRETTY!
There's Tohru!
HAVE YOU FINISHED OUR DRESSES, CINDERELLA?!
THE ROYAL BALL IS BEING HELD AT THE PALACE TONIGHT!

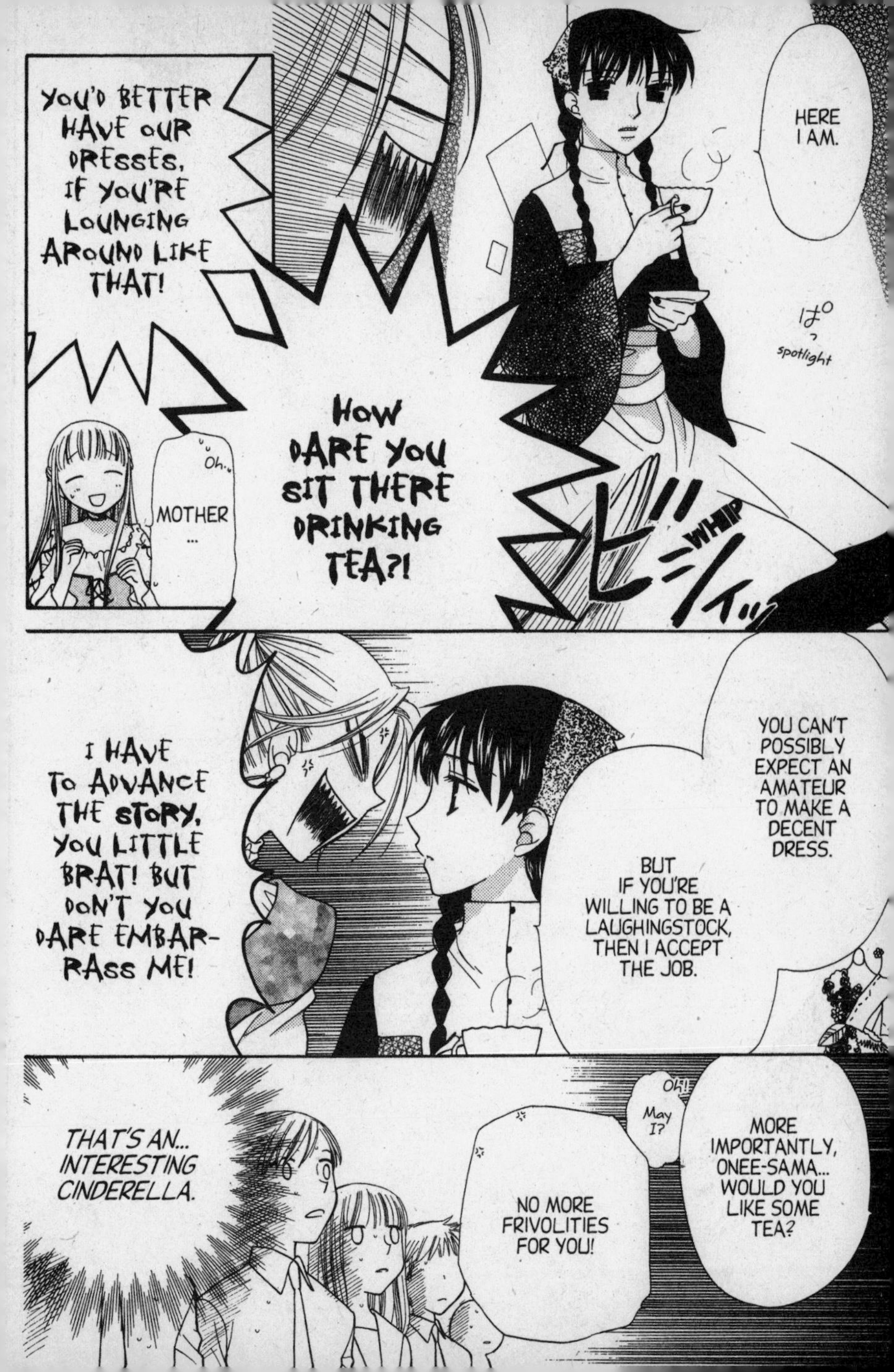

HERE I AM.
ぱっ
spotlight
WHIP
HOW DARE YOU SIT THERE DRINKING TEA?!
YOU'D BETTER HAVE OUR DRESSES, IF YOU'RE LOUNGING AROUND LIKE THAT!
Oh... MOTHER...
YOU CAN'T POSSIBLY EXPECT AN AMATEUR TO MAKE A DECENT DRESS.
BUT IF YOU'RE WILLING TO BE A LAUGHINGSTOCK, THEN I ACCEPT THE JOB.
I HAVE TO ADVANCE THE STORY, YOU LITTLE BRAT! BUT DON'T YOU DARE EMBARRASS ME!
MORE IMPORTANTLY, ONEE-SAMA... WOULD YOU LIKE SOME TEA?
Oh! May I?
NO MORE FRIVOLITIES FOR YOU!
THAT'S AN... INTERESTING CINDERELLA.

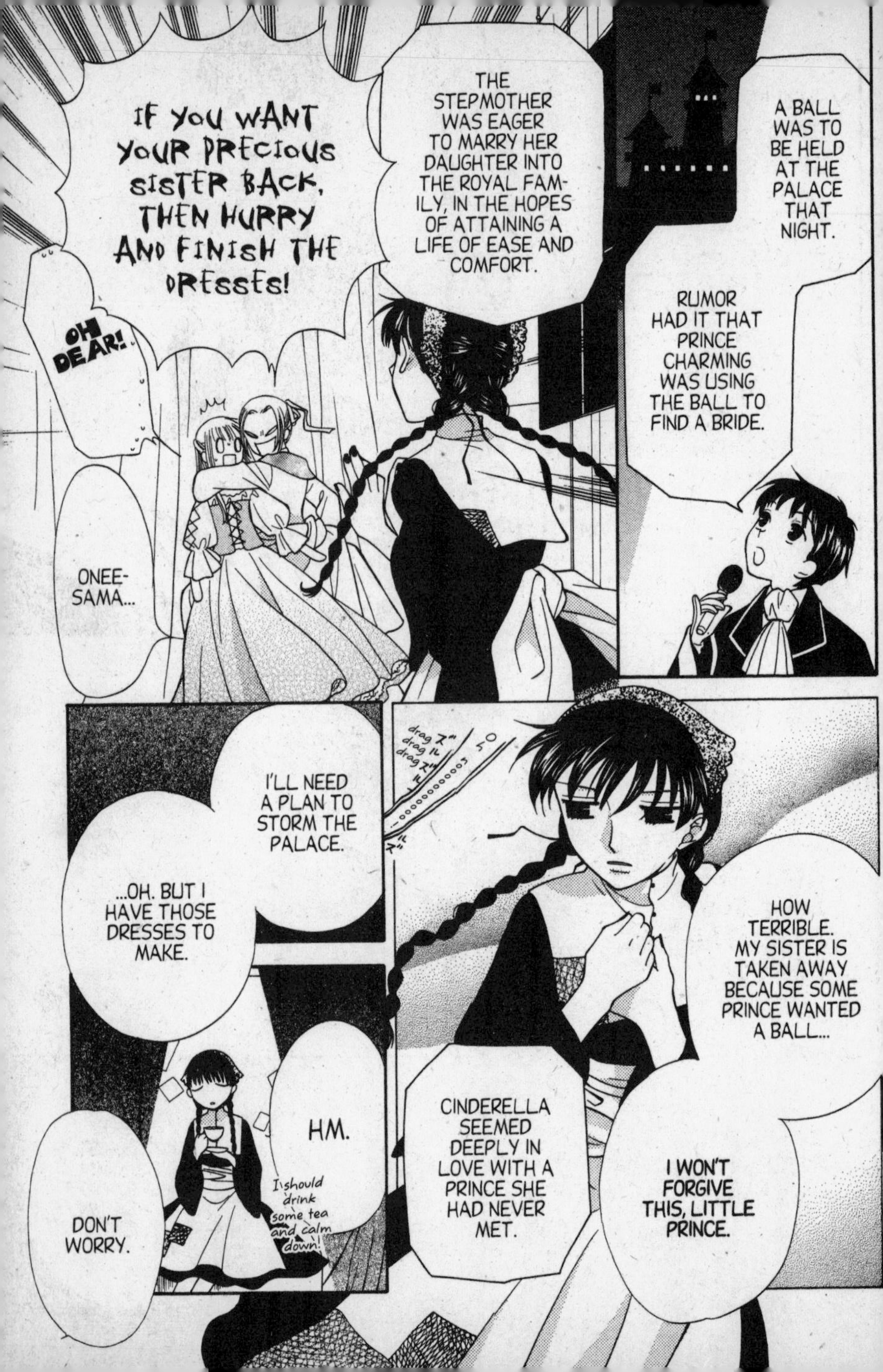
A BALL WAS TO BE HELD AT THE PALACE THAT NIGHT.
RUMOR HAD IT THAT PRINCE CHARMING WAS USING THE BALL TO FIND A BRIDE.
THE STEPMOTHER WAS EAGER TO MARRY HER DAUGHTER INTO THE ROYAL FAMILY, IN THE HOPES OF ATTAINING A LIFE OF EASE AND COMFORT.
IF YOU WANT YOUR PRECIOUS SISTER BACK, THEN HURRY AND FINISH THE DRESSES!
OH DEAR!
ONEE-SAMA...
HOW TERRIBLE. MY SISTER IS TAKEN AWAY BECAUSE SOME PRINCE WANTED A BALL...
I WON'T FORGIVE THIS, LITTLE PRINCE.
CINDERELLA SEEMED DEEPLY IN LOVE WITH A PRINCE SHE HAD NEVER MET.
drag drag drag
I'LL NEED A PLAN TO STORM THE PALACE.
...OH. BUT I HAVE THOSE DRESSES TO MAKE.
HM.
I should drink some tea and calm down!
DON'T WORRY.

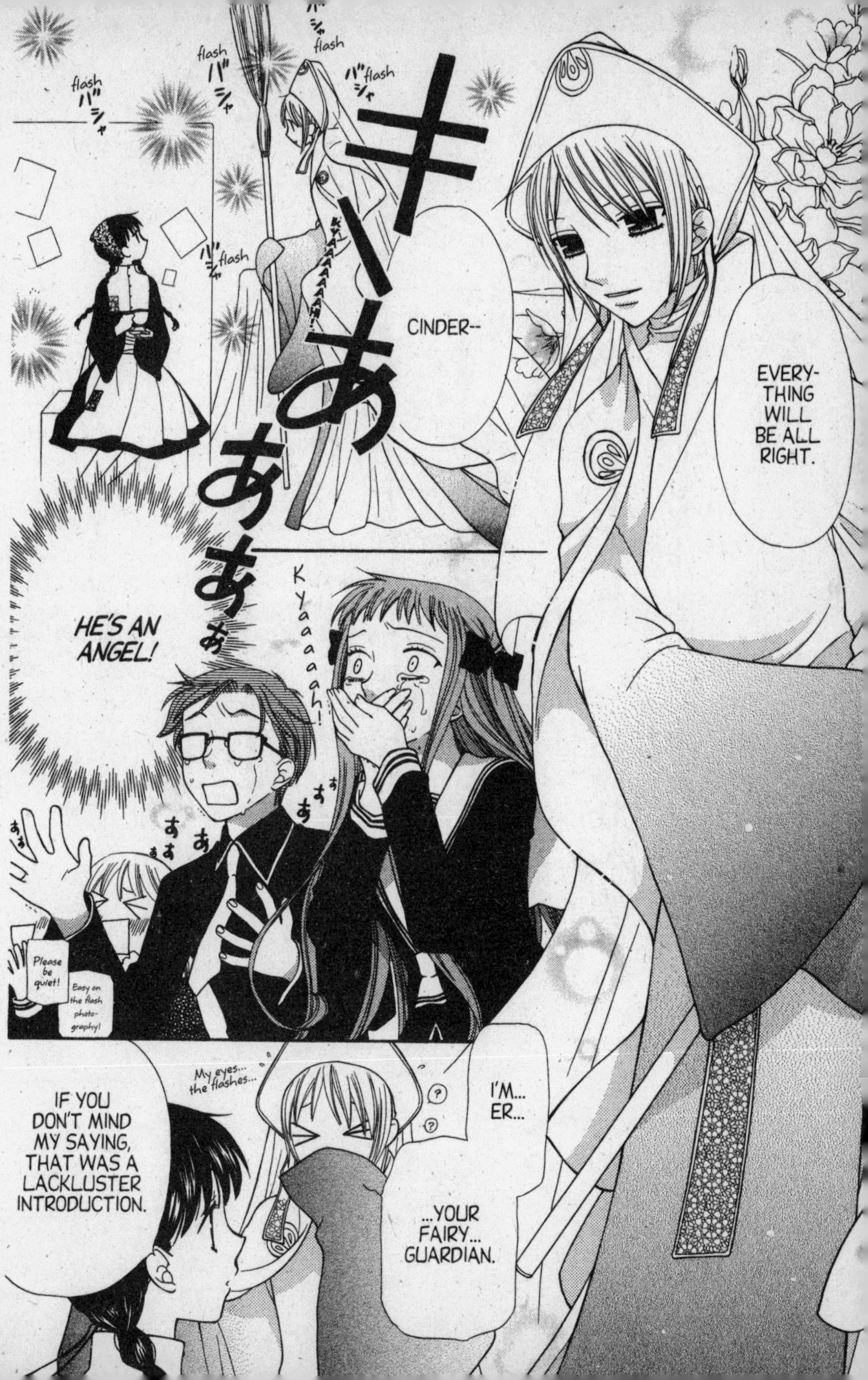
EVERYTHING WILL BE ALL RIGHT.
CINDER--
キャあああぁ
KYAAAAAAAH!
バシャ flash
バシャ flash
バシャ flash
バシャ flash
バシャ flash
HE'S AN ANGEL!
Kyaaaaah!
Please be quiet!
Easy on the flash photography!
I'M... ER...
...YOUR FAIRY... GUARDIAN.
My eyes... the flashes...
IF YOU DON'T MIND MY SAYING, THAT WAS A LACKLUSTER INTRODUCTION.

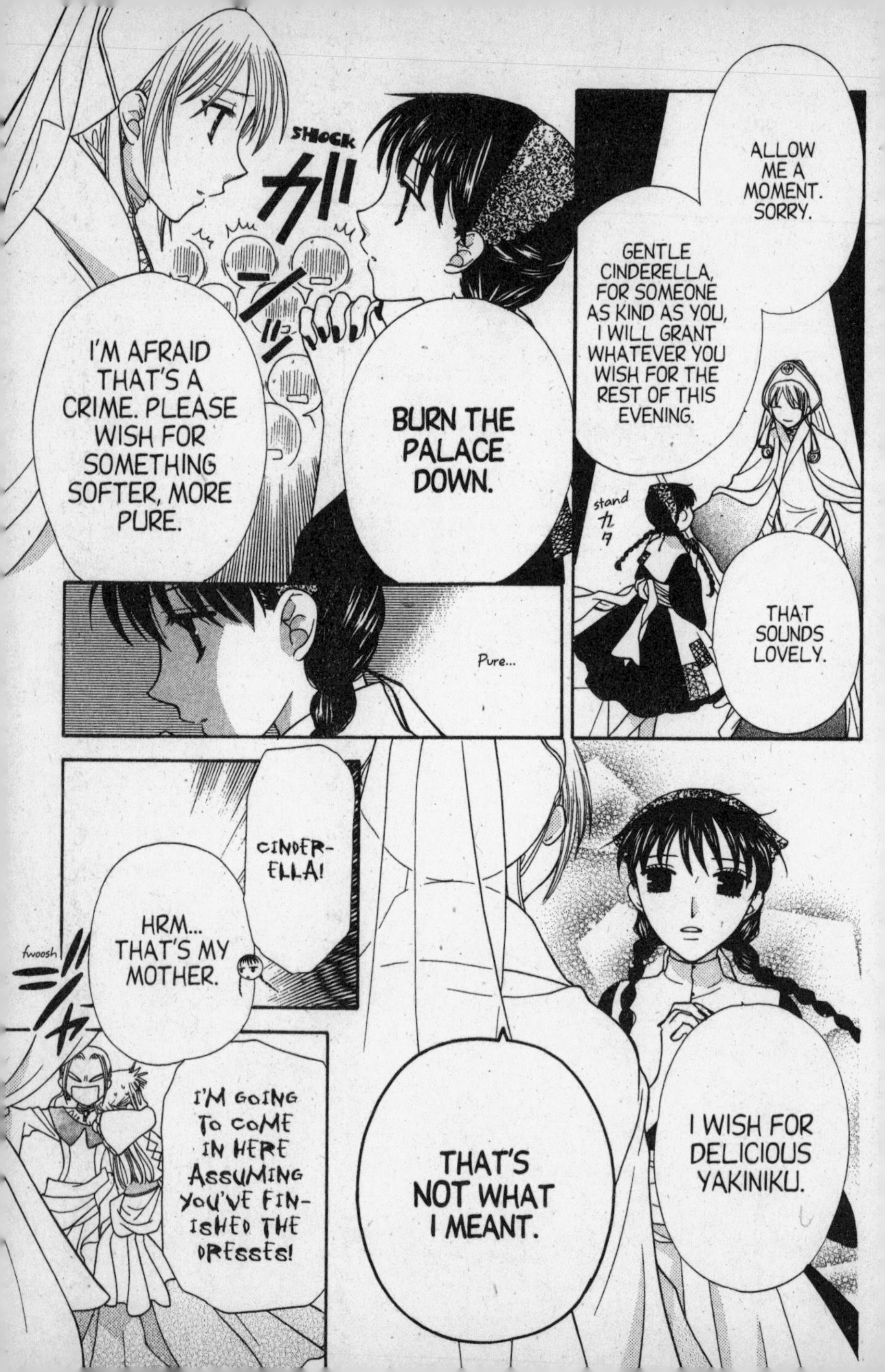
ALLOW ME A MOMENT. SORRY.
GENTLE CINDERELLA, FOR SOMEONE AS KIND AS YOU, I WILL GRANT WHATEVER YOU WISH FOR THE REST OF THIS EVENING.
THAT SOUNDS LOVELY.
stand カタ
BURN THE PALACE DOWN.
SHOCK ガ
I'M AFRAID THAT'S A CRIME. PLEASE WISH FOR SOMETHING SOFTER, MORE PURE.
Pure...
I WISH FOR DELICIOUS YAKINIKU.
THAT'S NOT WHAT I MEANT.
CINDER-ELLA!
HRM... THAT'S MY MOTHER.
fwoosh
I'M GOING TO COME IN HERE ASSUMING YOU'VE FIN-ISHED THE DRESSES!

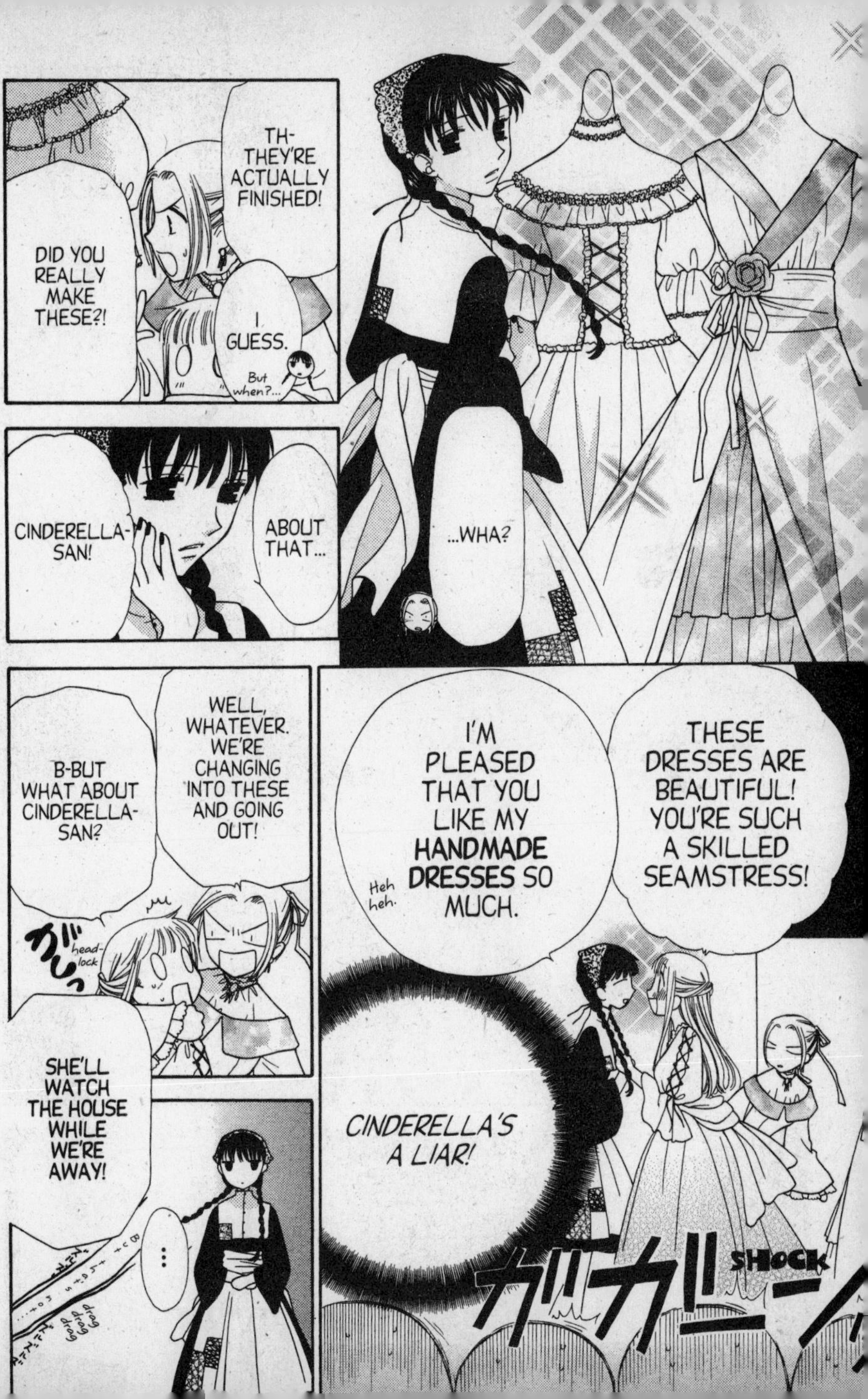
...WHA?
TH- THEY'RE ACTUALLY FINISHED!
DID YOU REALLY MAKE THESE?!
I GUESS.
But when?...
ABOUT THAT...
CINDERELLA-SAN!
THESE DRESSES ARE BEAUTIFUL! YOU'RE SUCH A SKILLED SEAMSTRESS!
I'M PLEASED THAT YOU LIKE MY **HANDMADE DRESSES** SO MUCH.
Heh heh.
CINDERELLA'S A LIAR!
SHOCK
WELL, WHATEVER. WE'RE CHANGING INTO THESE AND GOING OUT!
B-BUT WHAT ABOUT CINDERELLA-SAN?
head-lock
SHE'LL WATCH THE HOUSE WHILE WE'RE AWAY!
...
But that's not...
drag drag drag

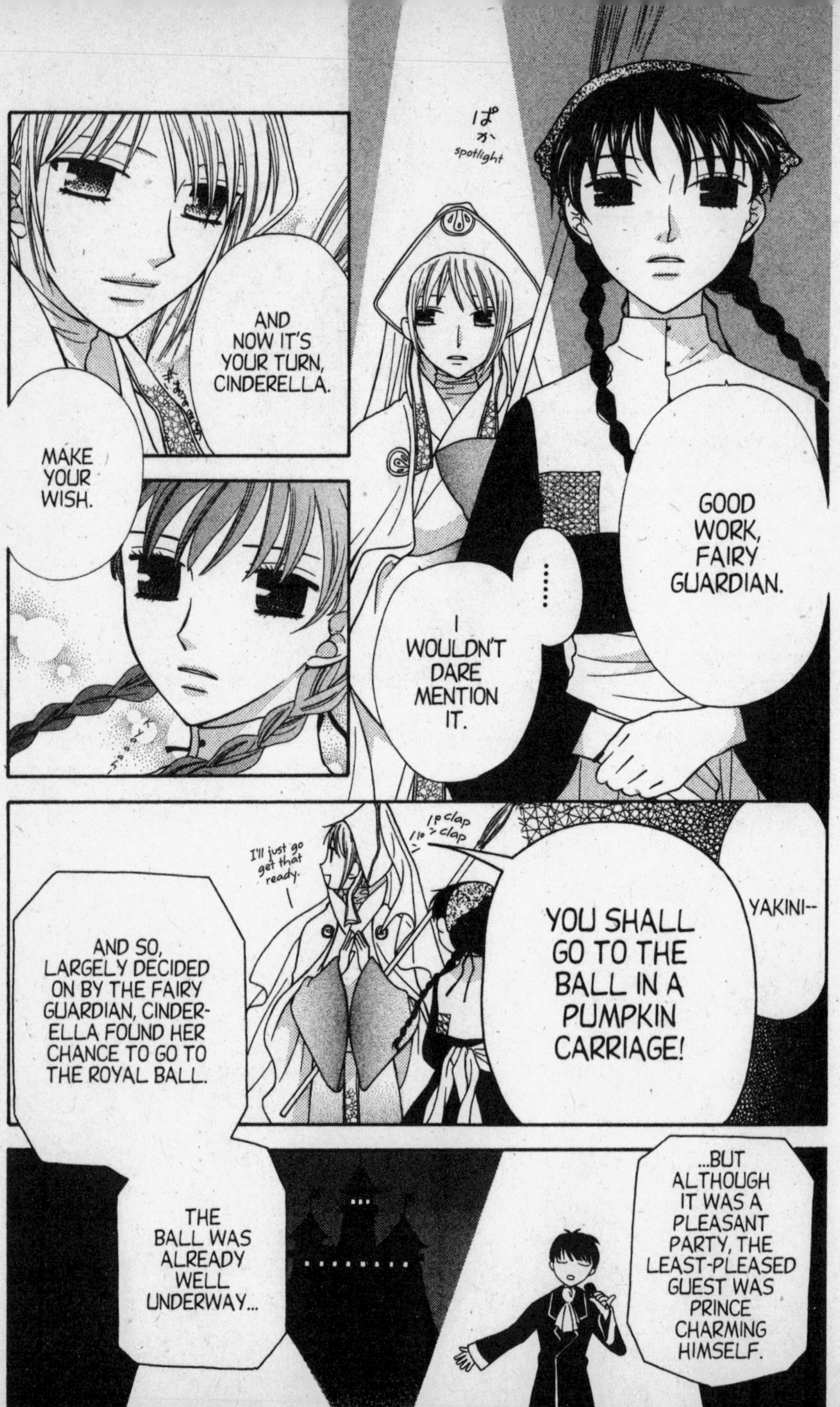
ぱか
spotlight
GOOD WORK, FAIRY GUARDIAN.
......
I WOULDN'T DARE MENTION IT.
AND NOW IT'S YOUR TURN, CINDERELLA.
MAKE YOUR WISH.
YAKINI--
YOU SHALL GO TO THE BALL IN A PUMPKIN CARRIAGE!
clap clap
I'll just go get that ready.
AND SO, LARGELY DECIDED ON BY THE FAIRY GUARDIAN, CINDERELLA FOUND HER CHANCE TO GO TO THE ROYAL BALL.
THE BALL WAS ALREADY WELL UNDERWAY...
...BUT ALTHOUGH IT WAS A PLEASANT PARTY, THE LEAST-PLEASED GUEST WAS PRINCE CHARMING HIMSELF.

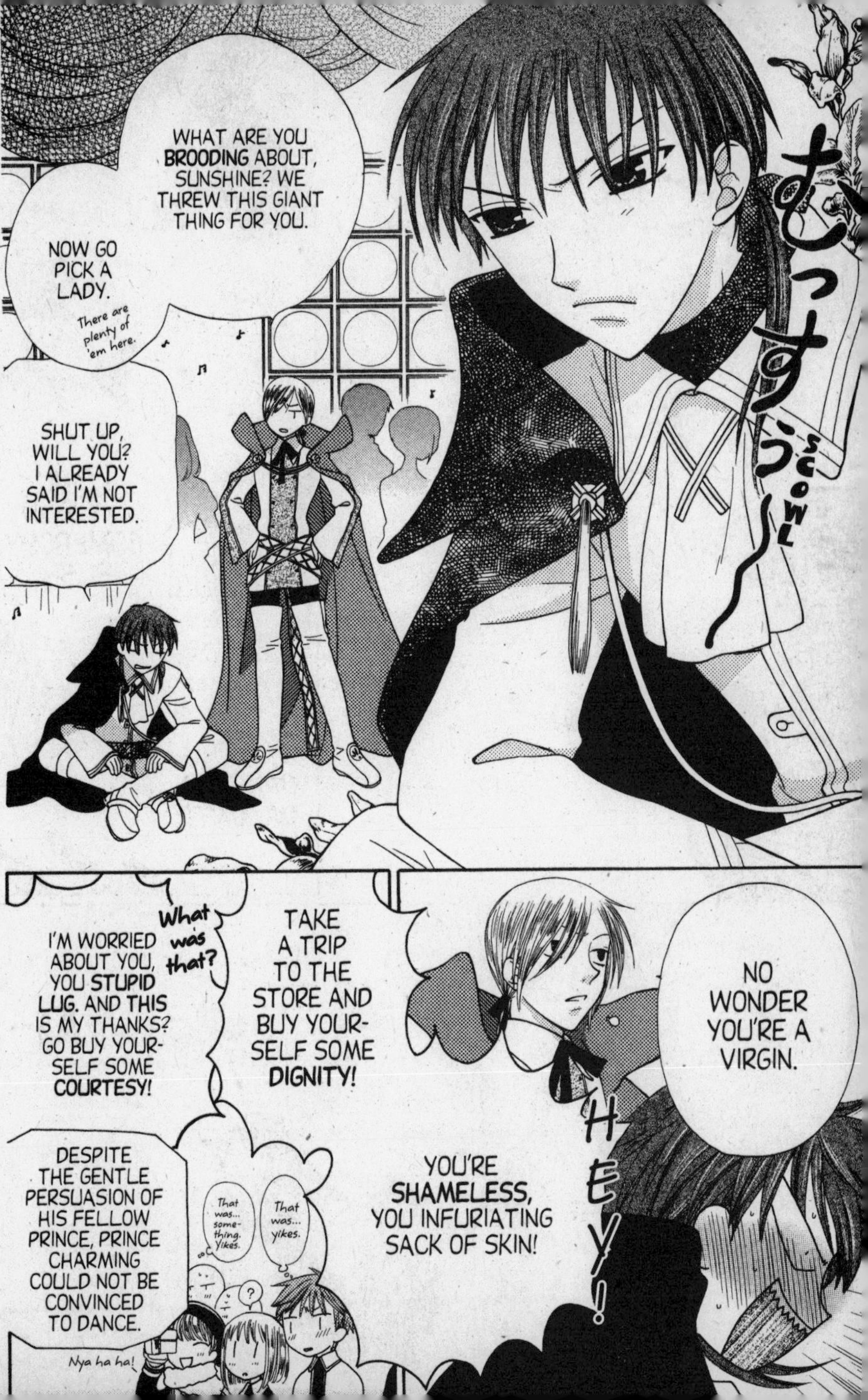

むっすぅ~
SCOWL
WHAT ARE YOU BROODING ABOUT, SUNSHINE? WE THREW THIS GIANT THING FOR YOU.
NOW GO PICK A LADY.
There are plenty of 'em here.
SHUT UP, WILL YOU? I ALREADY SAID I'M NOT INTERESTED.
NO WONDER YOU'RE A VIRGIN.
HEY!
YOU'RE SHAMELESS, YOU INFURIATING SACK OF SKIN!
TAKE A TRIP TO THE STORE AND BUY YOURSELF SOME DIGNITY!
What was that?
I'M WORRIED ABOUT YOU, YOU STUPID LUG. AND THIS IS MY THANKS? GO BUY YOURSELF SOME COURTESY!
That was... yikes.
That was... something. Yikes.
DESPITE THE GENTLE PERSUASION OF HIS FELLOW PRINCE, PRINCE CHARMING COULD NOT BE CONVINCED TO DANCE.
Nya ha ha!

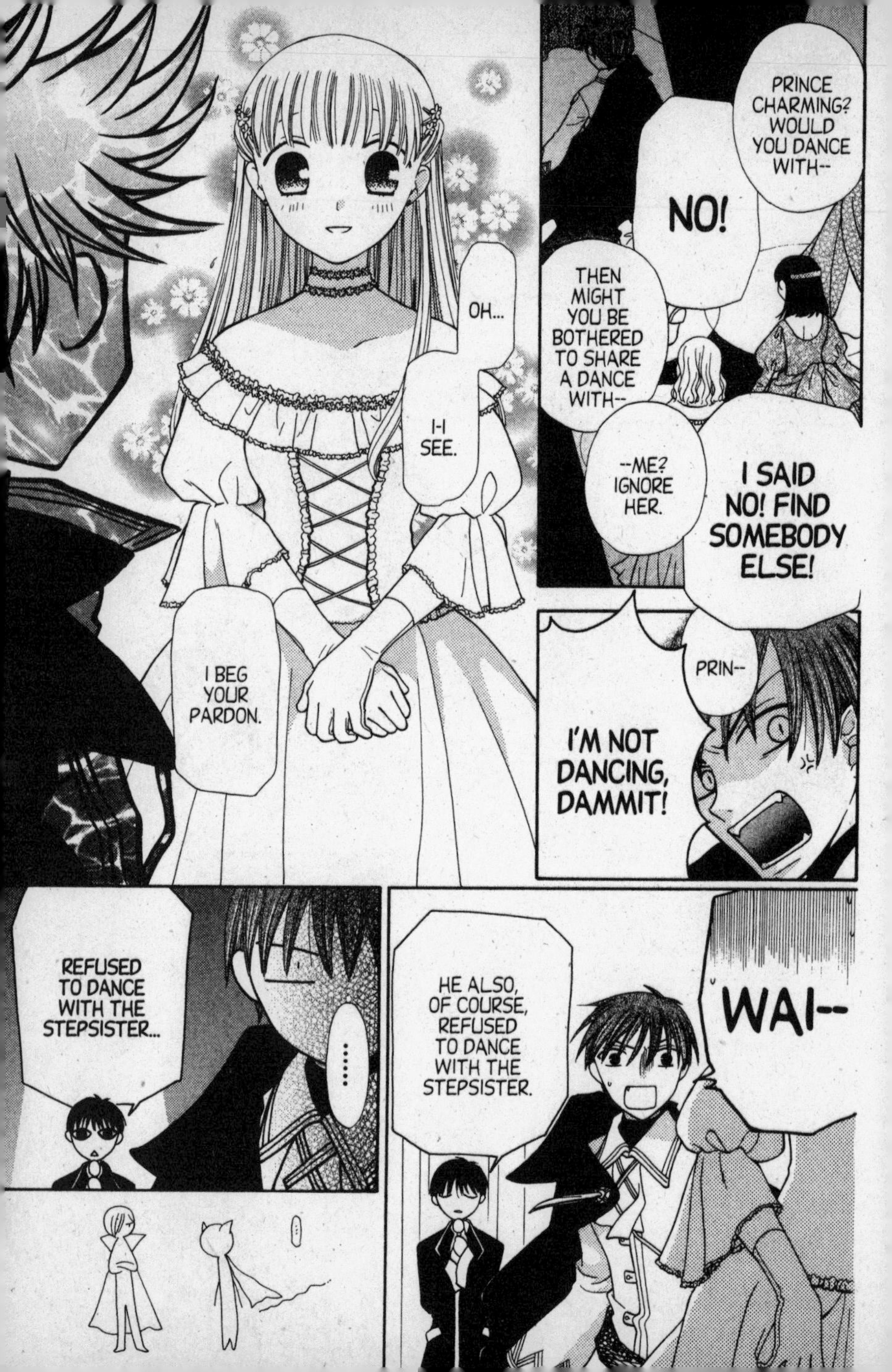
PRINCE CHARMING? WOULD YOU DANCE WITH--
NO!
THEN MIGHT YOU BE BOTHERED TO SHARE A DANCE WITH--
--ME? IGNORE HER.
I SAID NO! FIND SOMEBODY ELSE!
PRIN--
I'M NOT DANCING, DAMMIT!
OH...
I-I SEE.
I BEG YOUR PARDON.
WAI--
HE ALSO, OF COURSE, REFUSED TO DANCE WITH THE STEPSISTER.
REFUSED TO DANCE WITH THE STEPSISTER...
......

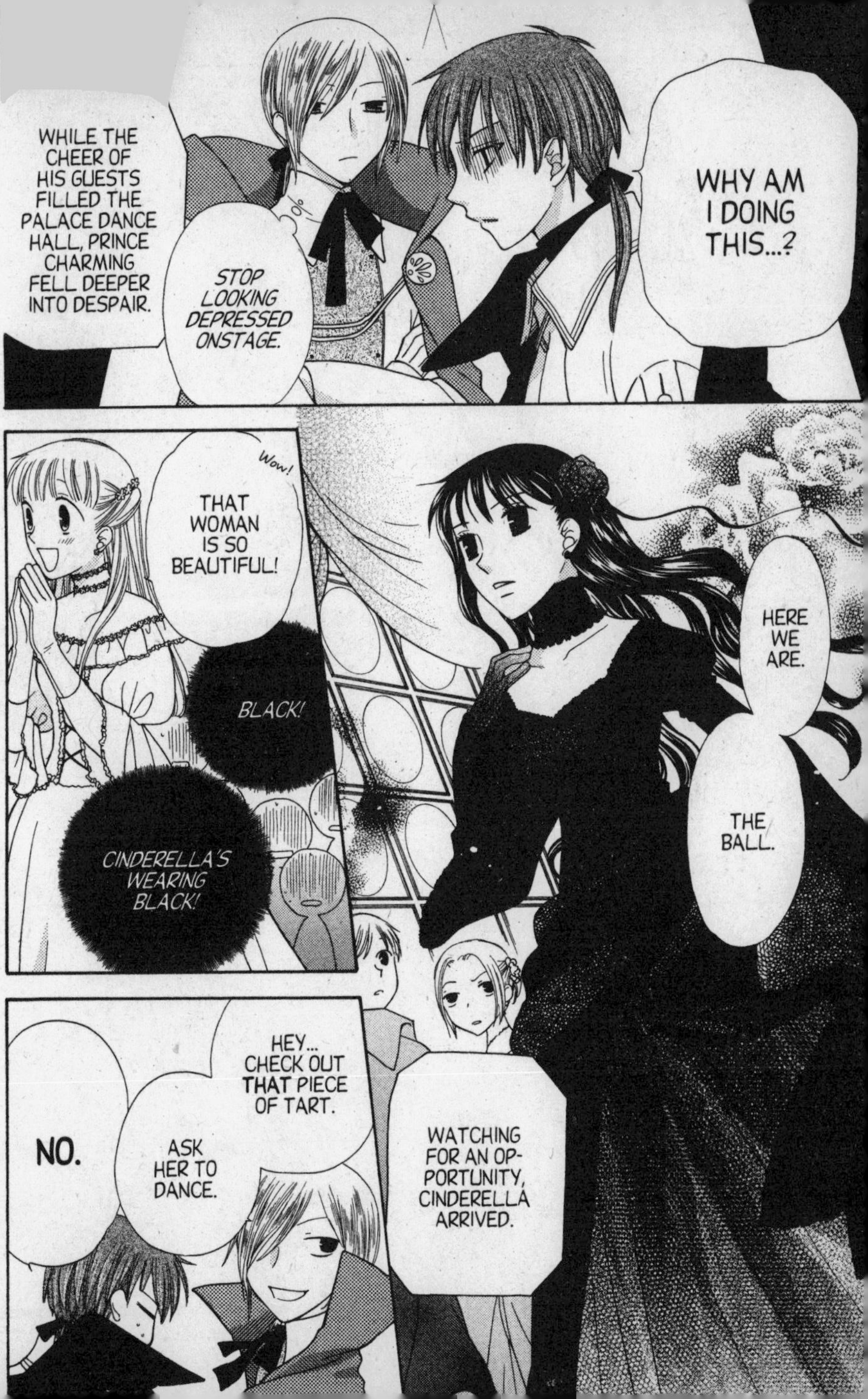
WHY AM I DOING THIS...?
WHILE THE CHEER OF HIS GUESTS FILLED THE PALACE DANCE HALL, PRINCE CHARMING FELL DEEPER INTO DESPAIR.
STOP LOOKING DEPRESSED ONSTAGE.
HERE WE ARE.
THE BALL.
Wow!
THAT WOMAN IS SO BEAUTIFUL!
BLACK!
CINDERELLA'S WEARING BLACK!
WATCHING FOR AN OP-PORTUNITY, CINDERELLA ARRIVED.
HEY... CHECK OUT **THAT** PIECE OF TART.
ASK HER TO DANCE.
NO.

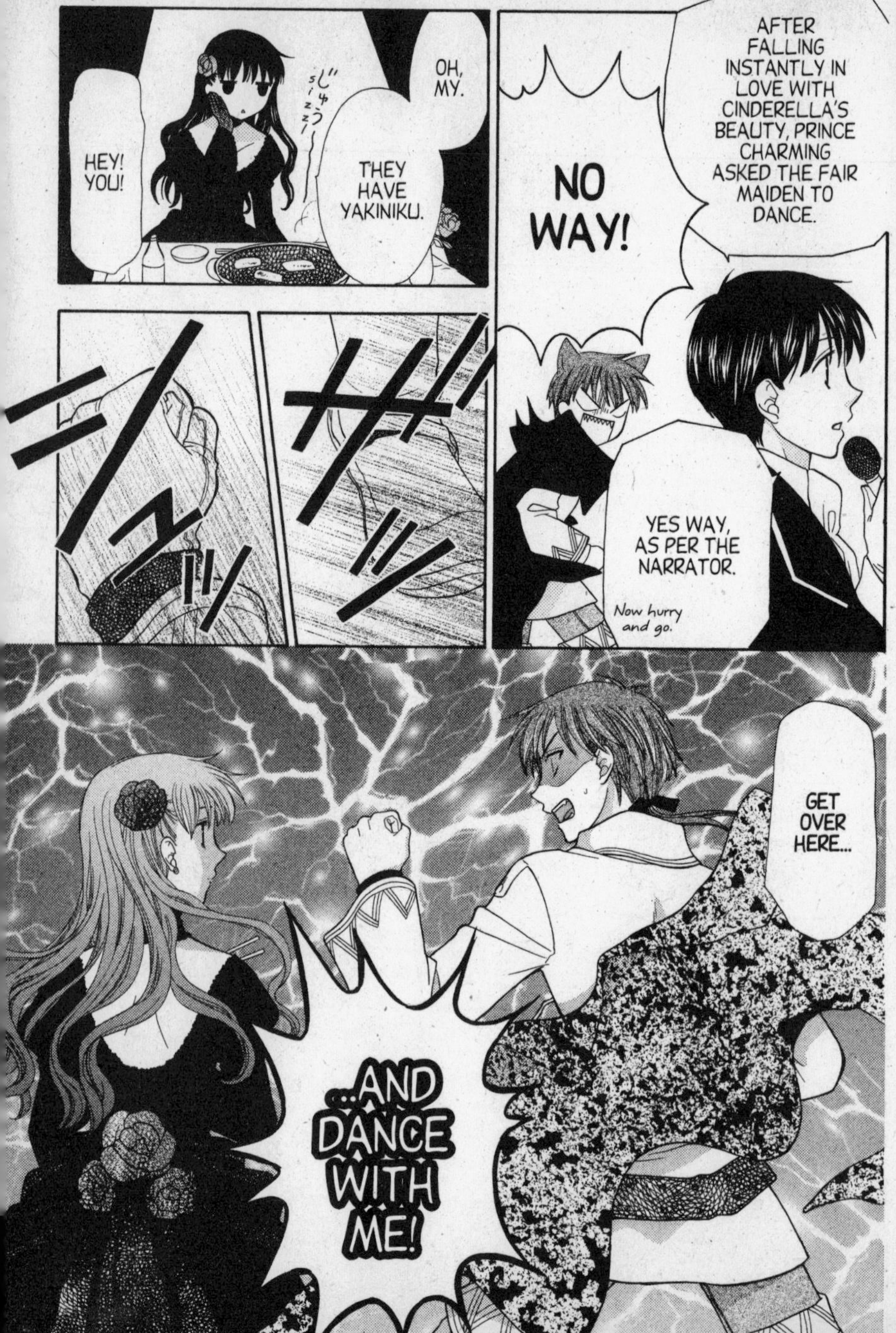

AFTER FALLING INSTANTLY IN LOVE WITH CINDERELLA'S BEAUTY, PRINCE CHARMING ASKED THE FAIR MAIDEN TO DANCE.
NO WAY!
YES WAY, AS PER THE NARRATOR.
Now hurry and go.
OH, MY.
THEY HAVE YAKINIKU.
じゅう sizzz
HEY! YOU!
GET OVER HERE...
...AND DANCE WITH ME!

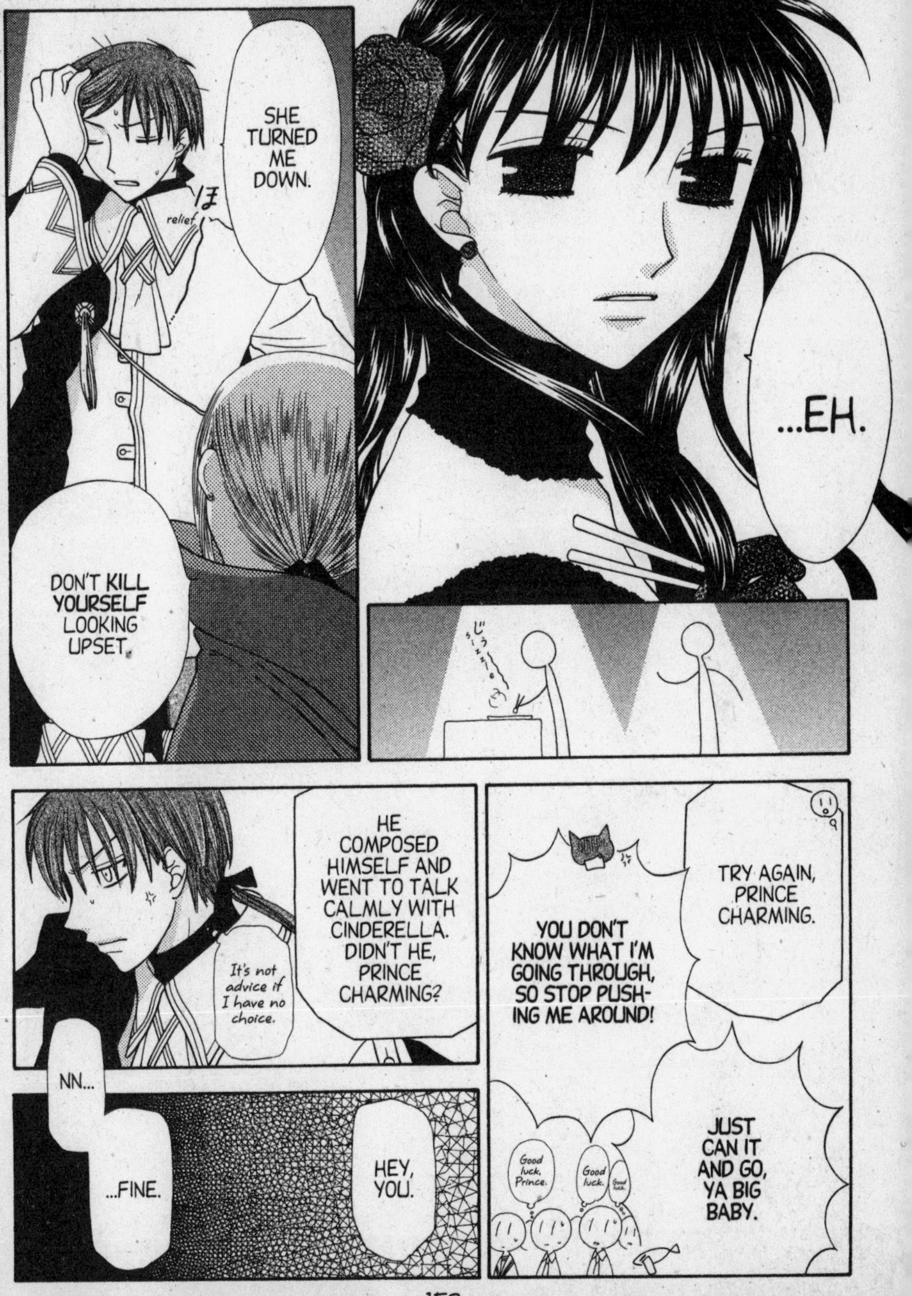
...EH.
sizzle
SHE TURNED ME DOWN.
relief
DON'T KILL YOURSELF LOOKING UPSET.
TRY AGAIN, PRINCE CHARMING.
YOU DON'T KNOW WHAT I'M GOING THROUGH, SO STOP PUSHING ME AROUND!
JUST CAN IT AND GO, YA BIG BABY.
Good luck, Prince.
Good luck.
Good luck.
HE COMPOSED HIMSELF AND WENT TO TALK CALMLY WITH CINDERELLA. DIDN'T HE, PRINCE CHARMING?
It's not advice if I have no choice.
HEY, YOU.
NN...
...FINE.

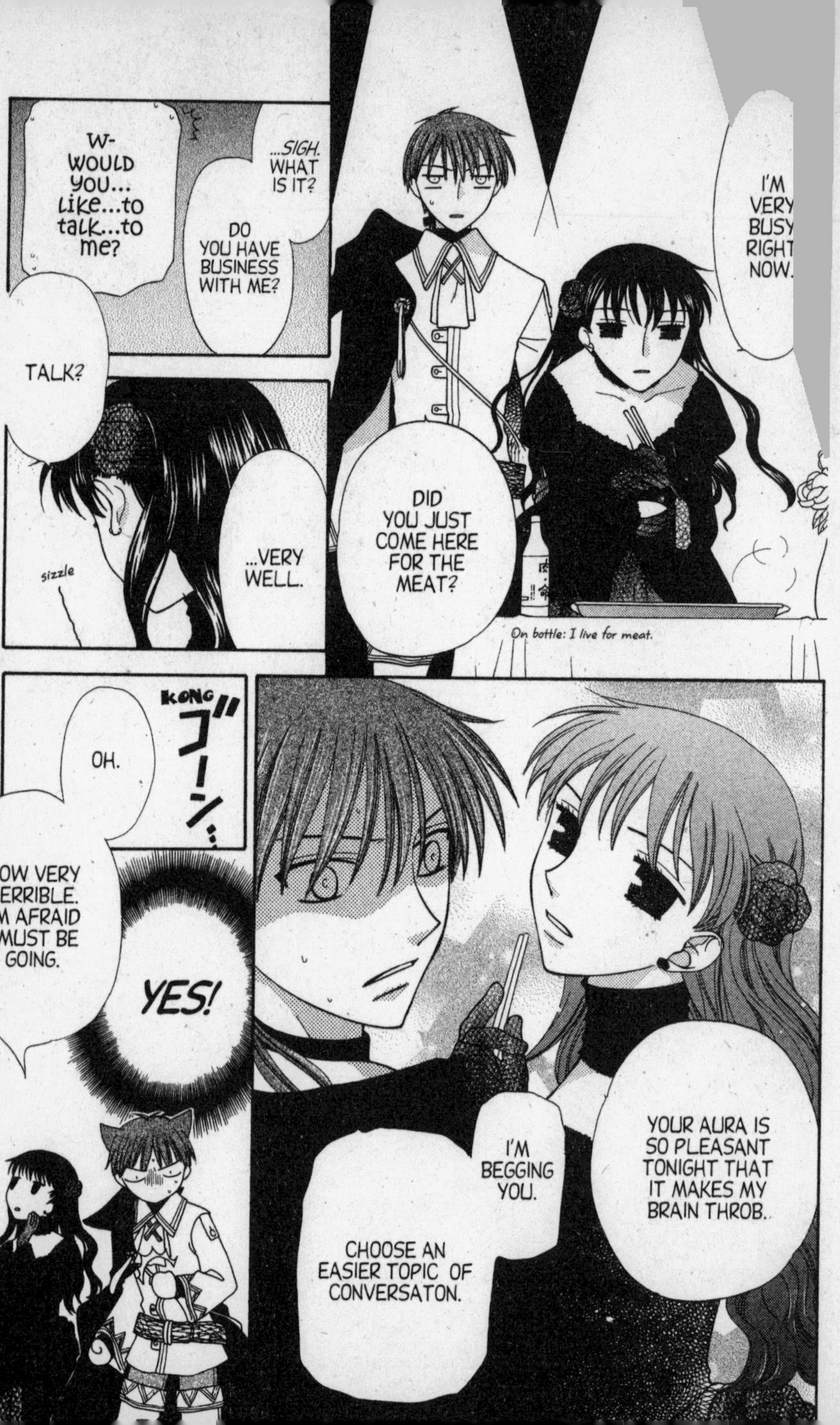
I'M VERY BUSY RIGHT NOW.
DID YOU JUST COME HERE FOR THE MEAT?
On bottle: I live for meat.
...SIGH. WHAT IS IT?
DO YOU HAVE BUSINESS WITH ME?
W-WOULD YOU... LIKE...to talk...to me?
TALK?
...VERY WELL.
sizzle
YOUR AURA IS SO PLEASANT TONIGHT THAT IT MAKES MY BRAIN THROB.
I'M BEGGING YOU.
CHOOSE AN EASIER TOPIC OF CONVERSATON.
KONG
OH.
HOW VERY TERRIBLE. I'M AFRAID I MUST BE GOING.
YES!

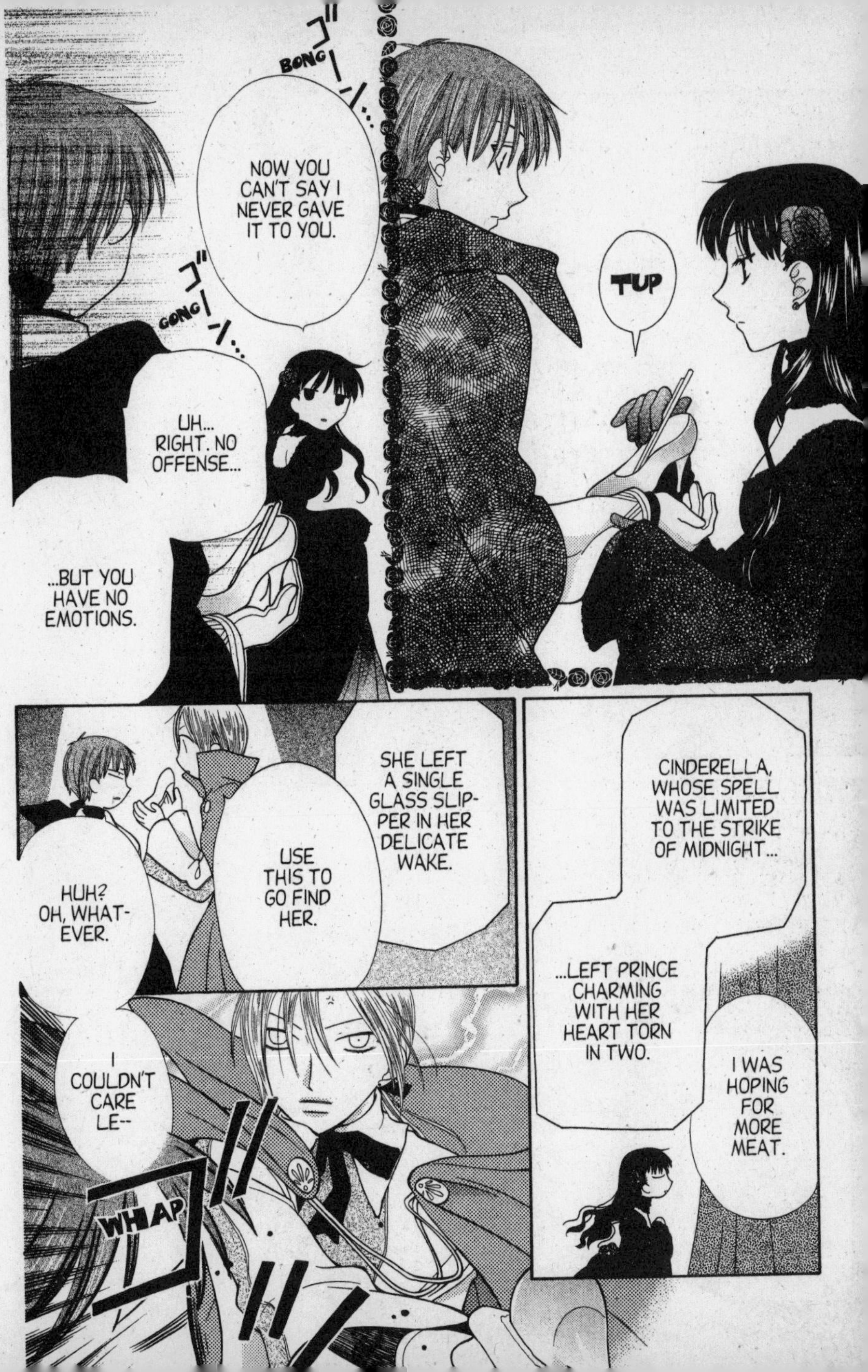
TUP
BONG
NOW YOU CAN'T SAY I NEVER GAVE IT TO YOU.
GONG
UH... RIGHT. NO OFFENSE...
...BUT YOU HAVE NO EMOTIONS.
CINDERELLA, WHOSE SPELL WAS LIMITED TO THE STRIKE OF MIDNIGHT...
...LEFT PRINCE CHARMING WITH HER HEART TORN IN TWO.
I WAS HOPING FOR MORE MEAT.
SHE LEFT A SINGLE GLASS SLIP-PER IN HER DELICATE WAKE.
USE THIS TO GO FIND HER.
HUH? OH, WHAT-EVER.
I COULDN'T CARE LE--
WHAP

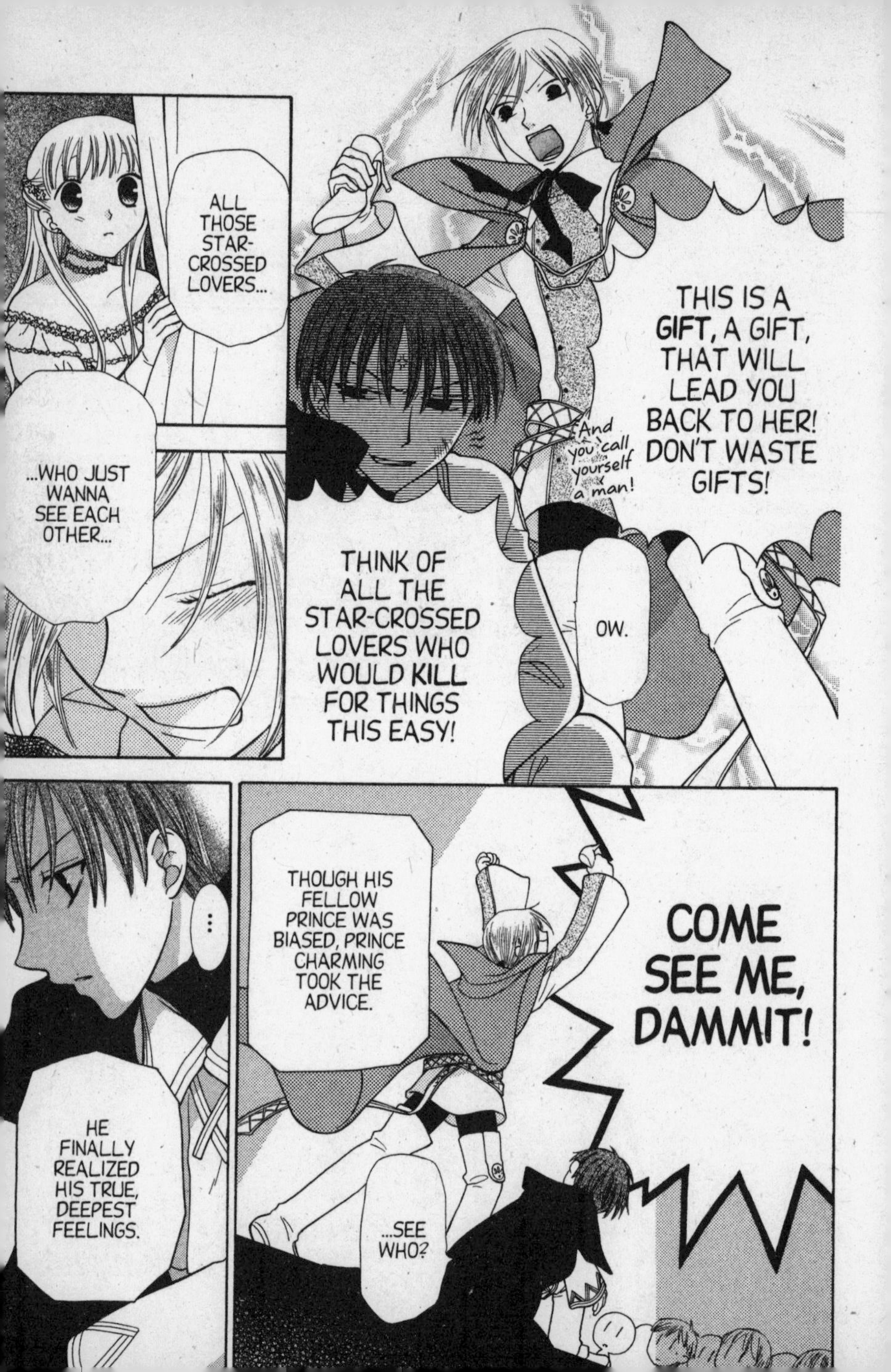
THIS IS A GIFT, A GIFT, THAT WILL LEAD YOU BACK TO HER! DON'T WASTE GIFTS!
And you call yourself a man!
THINK OF ALL THE STAR-CROSSED LOVERS WHO WOULD KILL FOR THINGS THIS EASY!
OW.
ALL THOSE STAR-CROSSED LOVERS...
...WHO JUST WANNA SEE EACH OTHER...
THOUGH HIS FELLOW PRINCE WAS BIASED, PRINCE CHARMING TOOK THE ADVICE.
COME SEE ME, DAMMIT!
...SEE WHO?
...
HE FINALLY REALIZED HIS TRUE, DEEPEST FEELINGS.

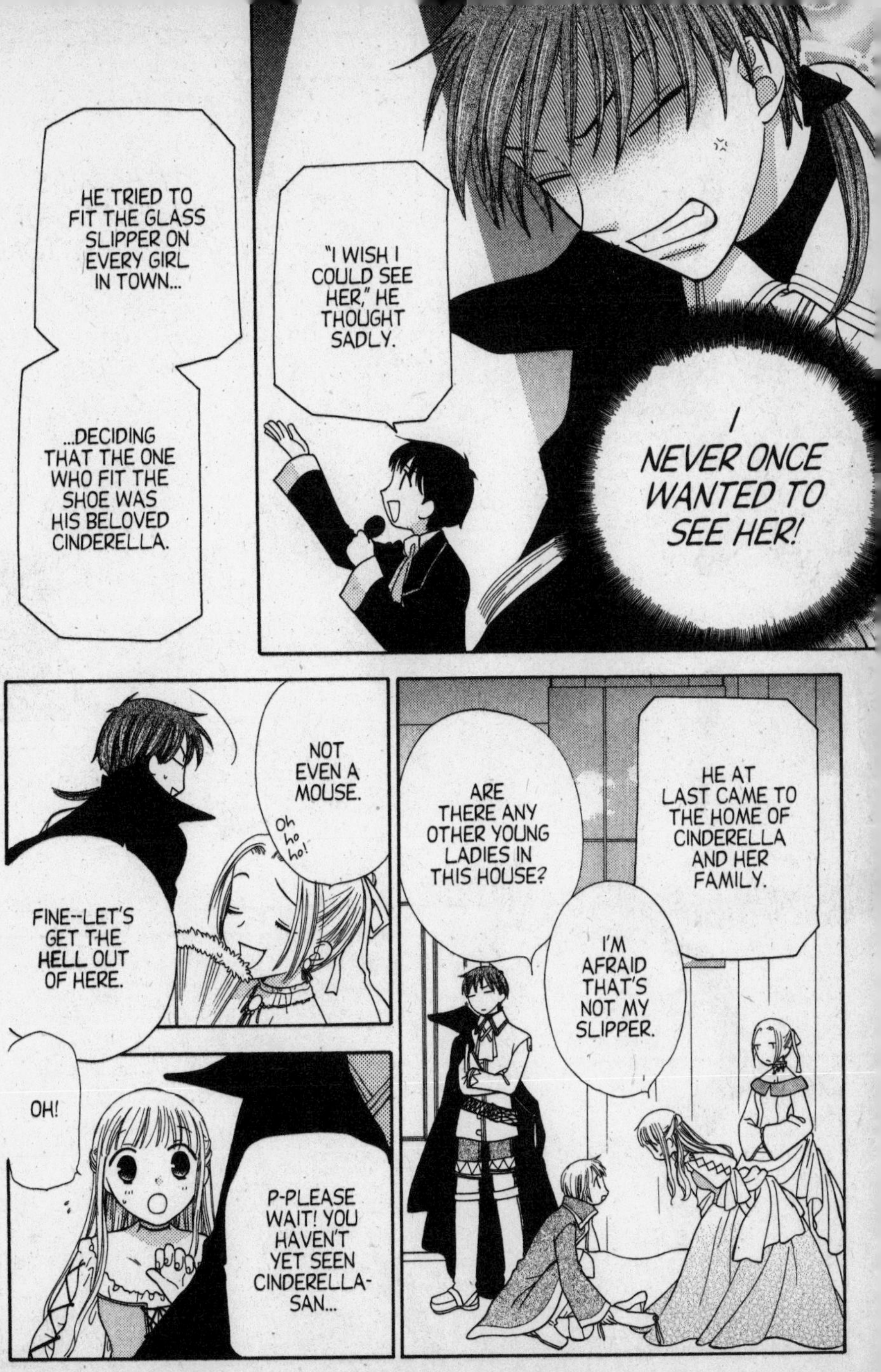
"I WISH I COULD SEE HER," HE THOUGHT SADLY.
I NEVER ONCE WANTED TO SEE HER!
HE TRIED TO FIT THE GLASS SLIPPER ON EVERY GIRL IN TOWN...
...DECIDING THAT THE ONE WHO FIT THE SHOE WAS HIS BELOVED CINDERELLA.
HE AT LAST CAME TO THE HOME OF CINDERELLA AND HER FAMILY.
ARE THERE ANY OTHER YOUNG LADIES IN THIS HOUSE?
I'M AFRAID THAT'S NOT MY SLIPPER.
NOT EVEN A MOUSE.
Oh ho ho!
FINE--LET'S GET THE HELL OUT OF HERE.
OH!
P-PLEASE WAIT! YOU HAVEN'T YET SEEN CINDERELLA-SAN...

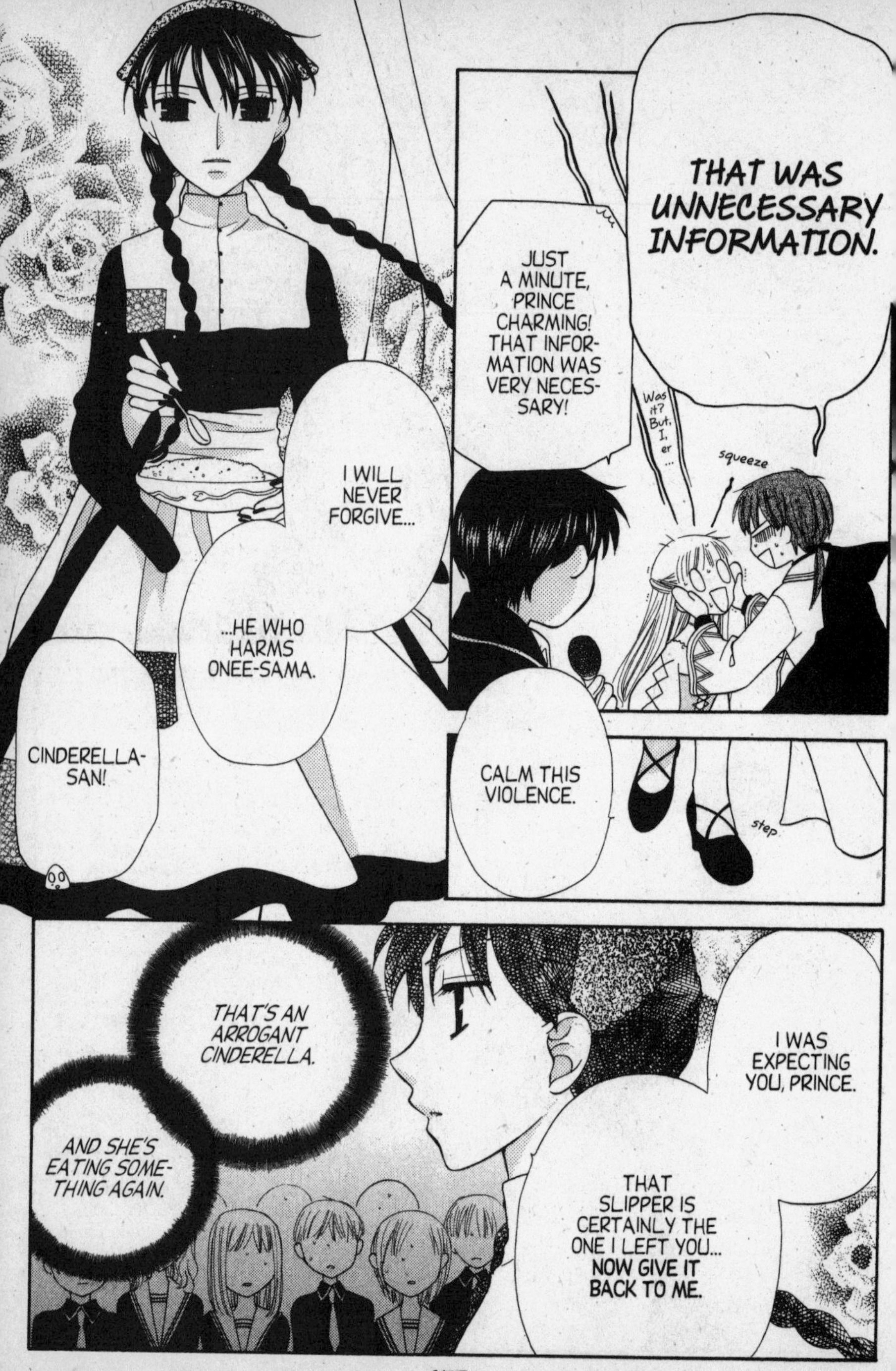
THAT WAS UNNECESSARY INFORMATION.
JUST A MINUTE, PRINCE CHARMING! THAT INFORMATION WAS VERY NECESSARY!
Was it? But, I, er ...
squeeze
CALM THIS VIOLENCE.
step
I WILL NEVER FORGIVE...
...HE WHO HARMS ONEE-SAMA.
CINDERELLA-SAN!
I WAS EXPECTING YOU, PRINCE.
THAT SLIPPER IS CERTAINLY THE ONE I LEFT YOU... NOW GIVE IT BACK TO ME.
THAT'S AN ARROGANT CINDERELLA.
AND SHE'S EATING SOMETHING AGAIN.

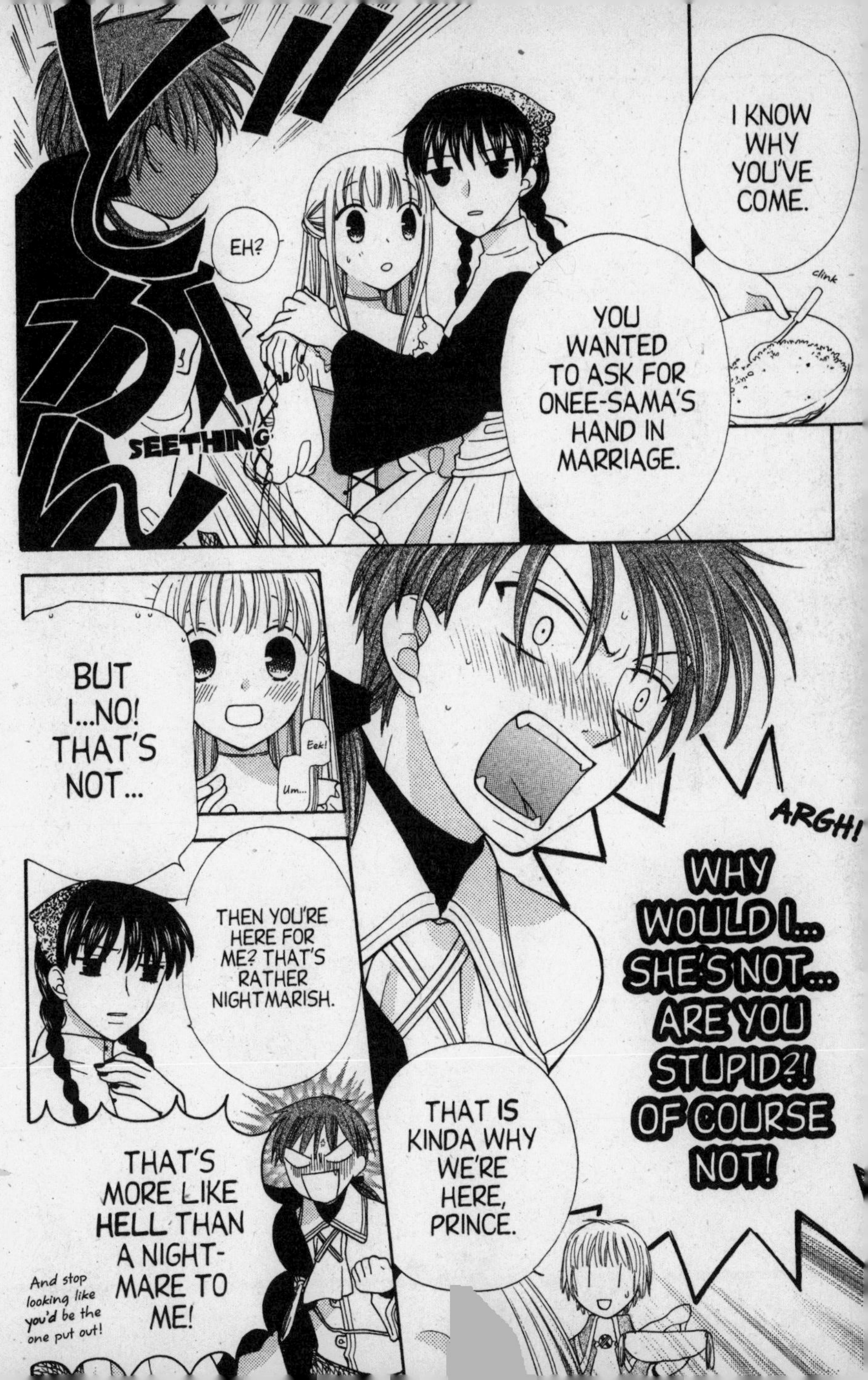
I KNOW WHY YOU'VE COME.
clink
YOU WANTED TO ASK FOR ONEE-SAMA'S HAND IN MARRIAGE.
EH?
SEETHING
ARGH!
WHY WOULD I... SHE'S NOT... ARE YOU STUPID?! OF COURSE NOT!
BUT I...NO! THAT'S NOT...
Eek!
Um...
THEN YOU'RE HERE FOR ME? THAT'S RATHER NIGHTMARISH.
THAT IS KINDA WHY WE'RE HERE, PRINCE.
THAT'S MORE LIKE HELL THAN A NIGHT-MARE TO ME!
And stop looking like you'd be the one put out!

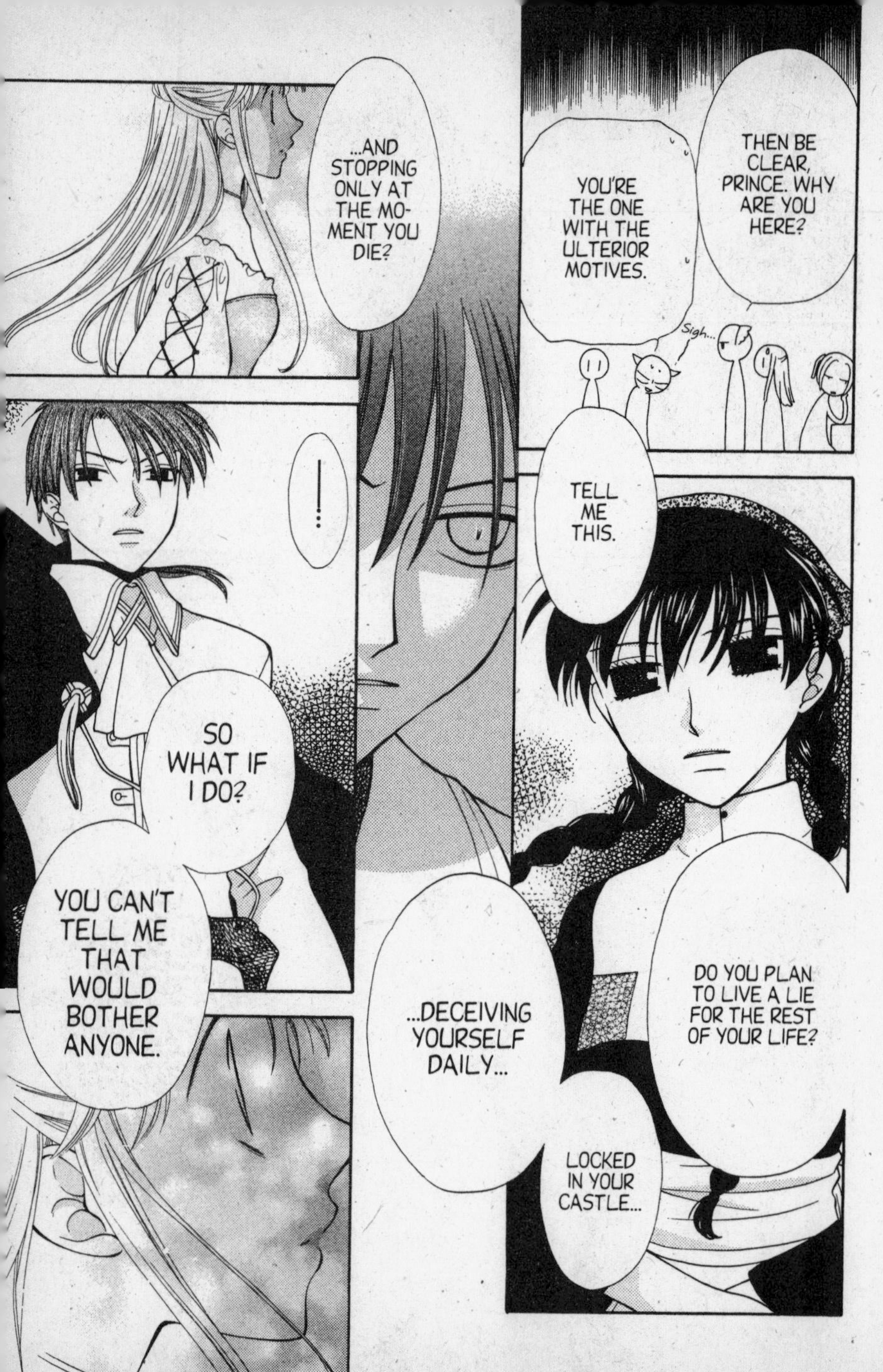
THEN BE CLEAR, PRINCE. WHY ARE YOU HERE?
YOU'RE THE ONE WITH THE ULTERIOR MOTIVES.
Sigh...
TELL ME THIS.
DO YOU PLAN TO LIVE A LIE FOR THE REST OF YOUR LIFE?
LOCKED IN YOUR CASTLE...
...DECEIVING YOURSELF DAILY...
...AND STOPPING ONLY AT THE MOMENT YOU DIE?
!...
SO WHAT IF I DO?
YOU CAN'T TELL ME THAT WOULD BOTHER ANYONE.

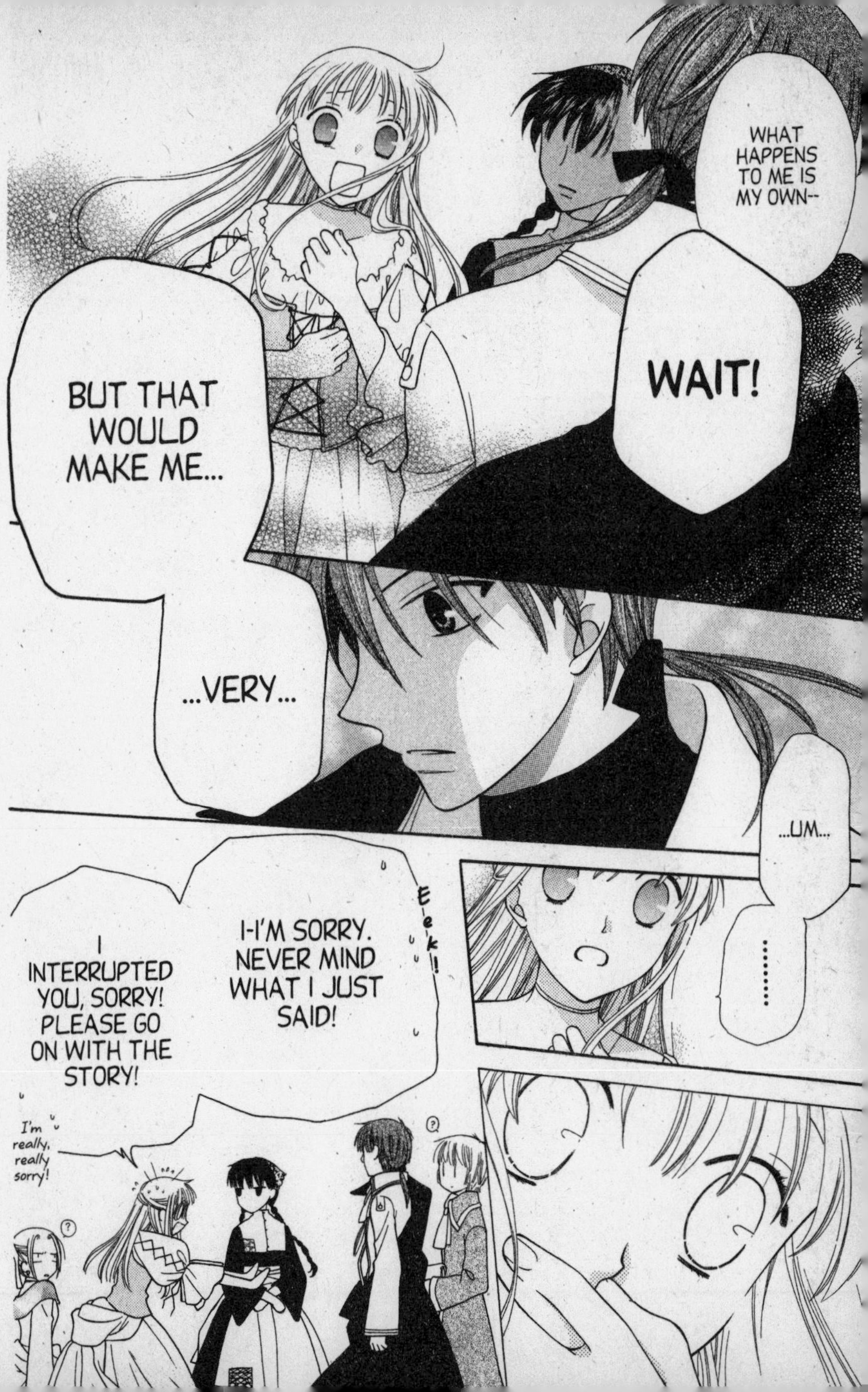

WHAT HAPPENS TO ME IS MY OWN--
WAIT!
BUT THAT WOULD MAKE ME...
...VERY...
...UM...
......
Eek!
I-I'M SORRY. NEVER MIND WHAT I JUST SAID!
I INTERRUPTED YOU, SORRY! PLEASE GO ON WITH THE STORY!
I'm really, really sorry!

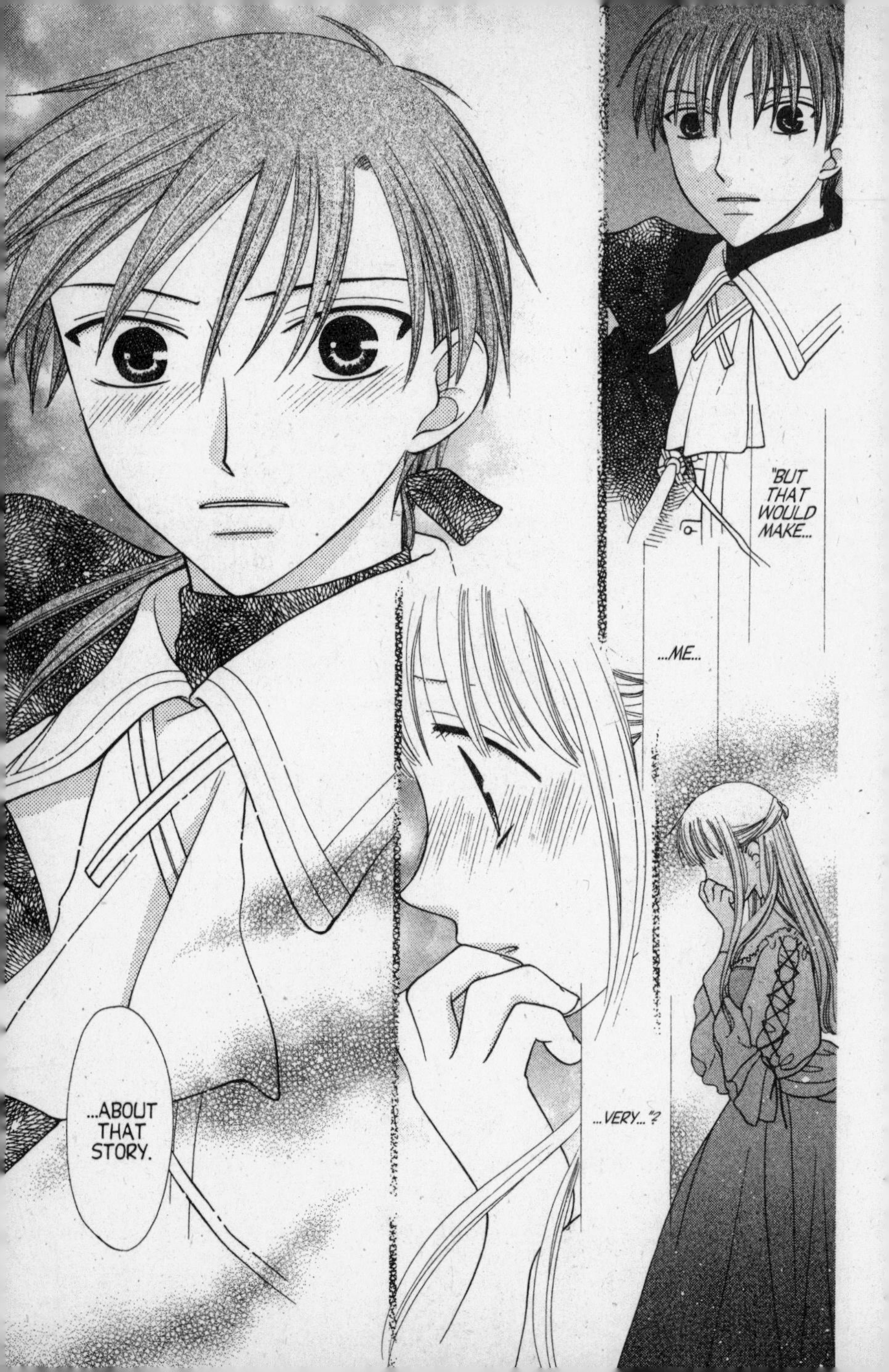
"BUT THAT WOULD MAKE...
...ME...
...VERY..."?
...ABOUT THAT STORY.

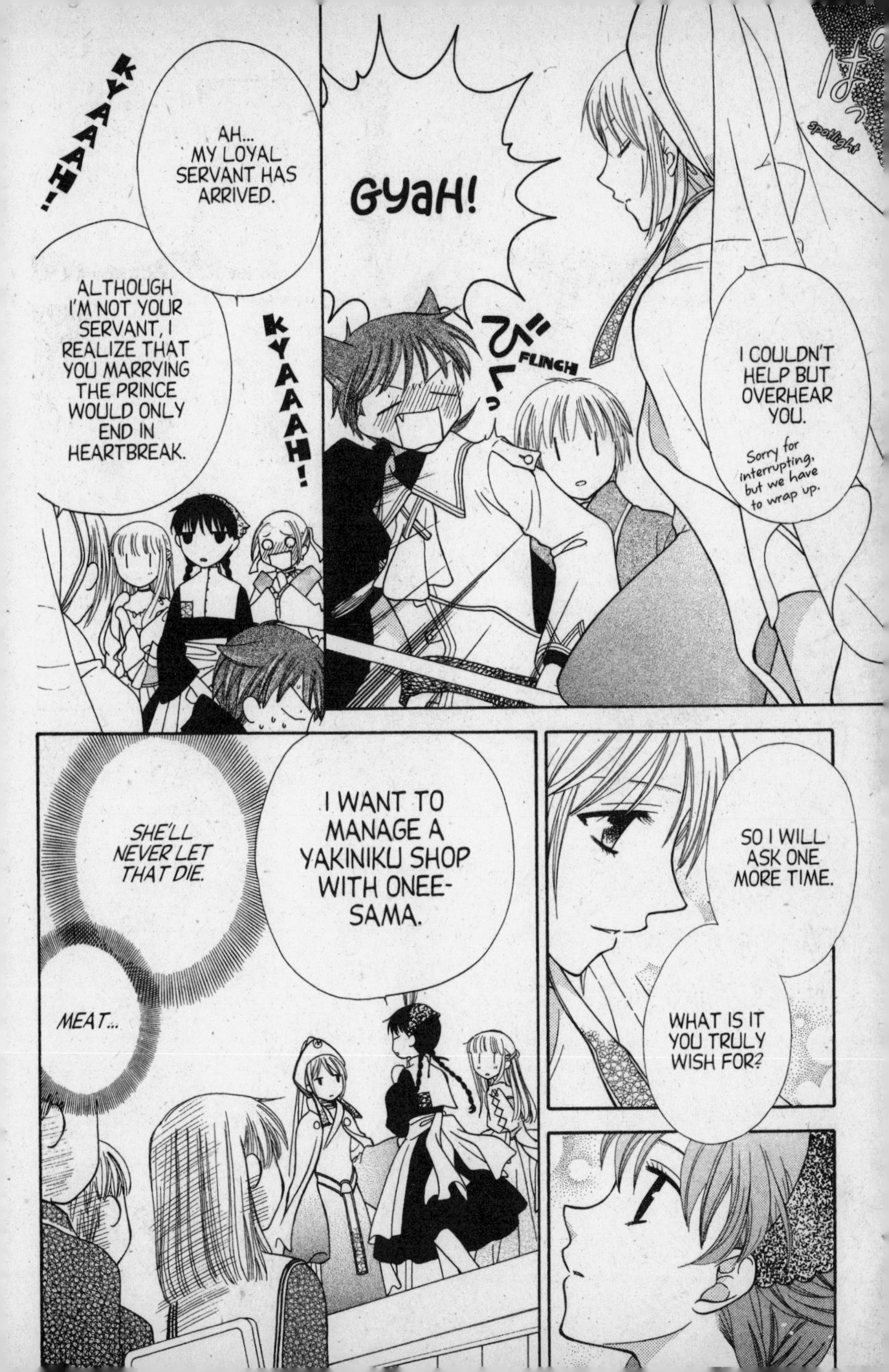
spotlight
I COULDN'T HELP BUT OVERHEAR YOU.
Sorry for interrupting, but we have to wrap up.
GYAH!
FLINCH
AH... MY LOYAL SERVANT HAS ARRIVED.
KYAAAH!
ALTHOUGH I'M NOT YOUR SERVANT, I REALIZE THAT YOU MARRYING THE PRINCE WOULD ONLY END IN HEARTBREAK.
KYAAAH!
SO I WILL ASK ONE MORE TIME.
WHAT IS IT YOU TRULY WISH FOR?
I WANT TO MANAGE A YAKINIKU SHOP WITH ONEE-SAMA.
SHE'LL NEVER LET THAT DIE.
MEAT...

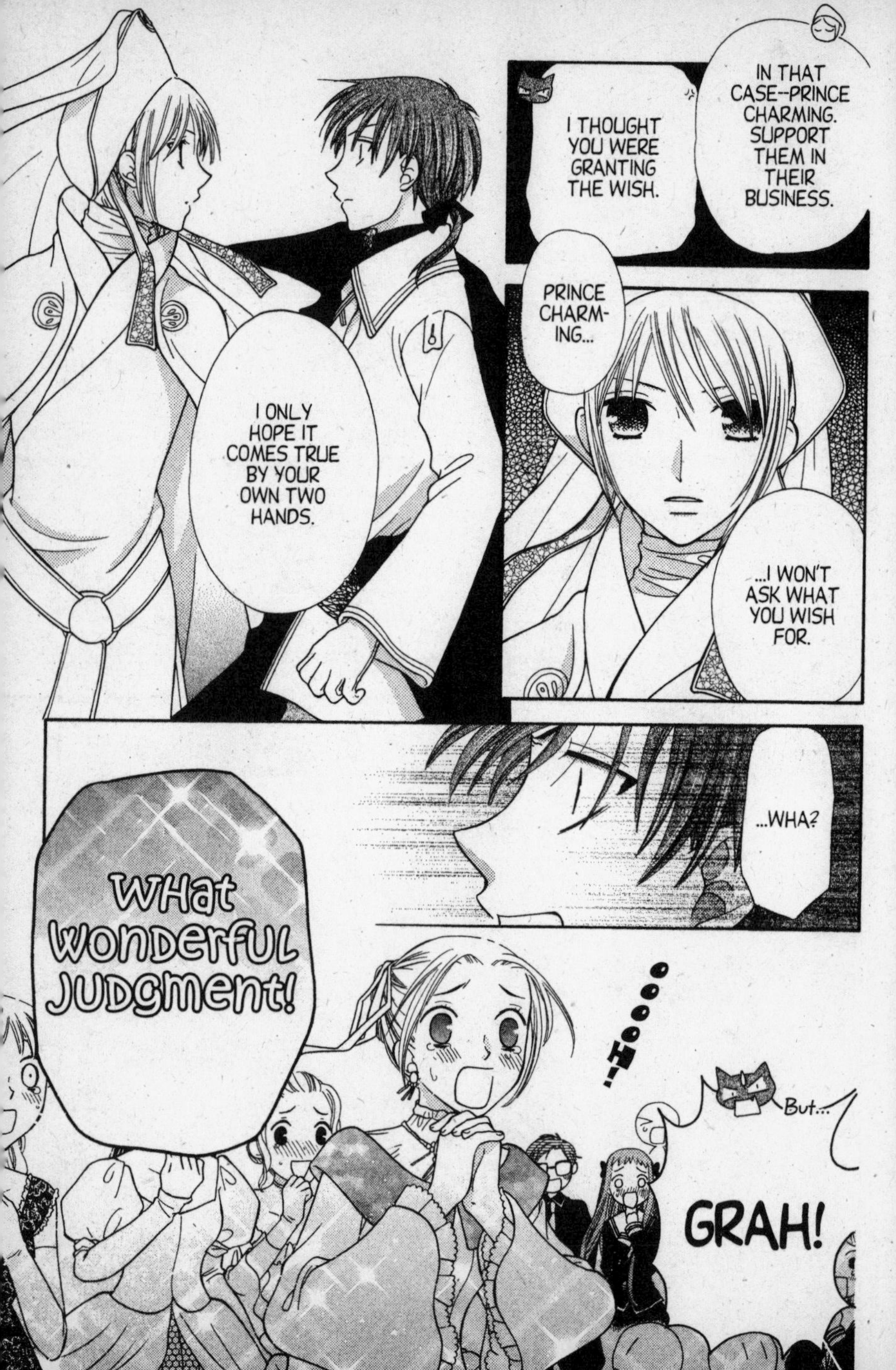
IN THAT CASE--PRINCE CHARMING. SUPPORT THEM IN THEIR BUSINESS.
I THOUGHT YOU WERE GRANTING THE WISH.
PRINCE CHARMING...
...I WON'T ASK WHAT YOU WISH FOR.
I ONLY HOPE IT COMES TRUE BY YOUR OWN TWO HANDS.
...WHA?
What wonderful judgment!
OOOOOH!
But...
GRAH!

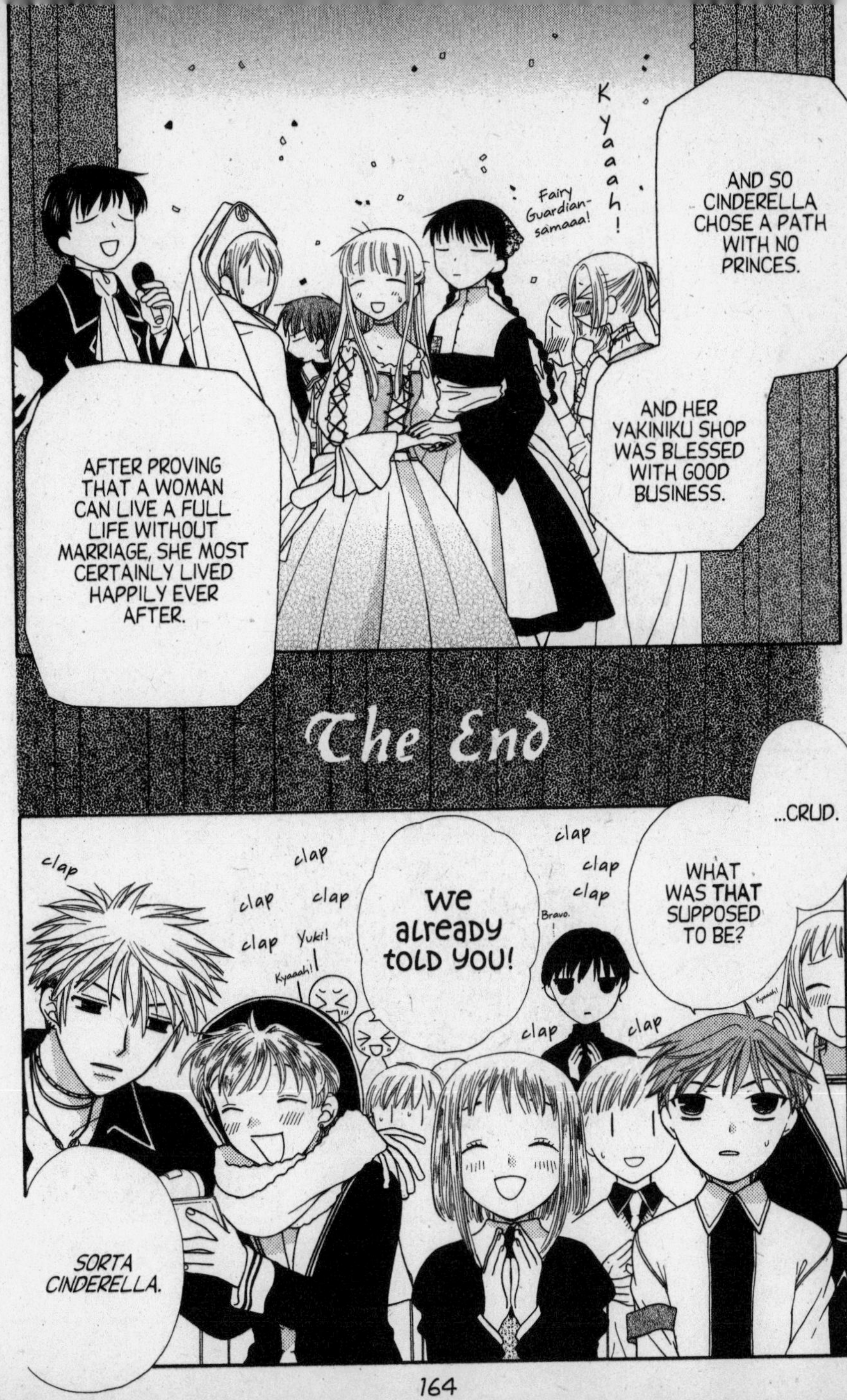
AND SO CINDERELLA CHOSE A PATH WITH NO PRINCES.
Kyaaah!
Fairy Guardian-samaaa!
AND HER YAKINIKU SHOP WAS BLESSED WITH GOOD BUSINESS.
AFTER PROVING THAT A WOMAN CAN LIVE A FULL LIFE WITHOUT MARRIAGE, SHE MOST CERTAINLY LIVED HAPPILY EVER AFTER.
The End
...CRUD.
WHAT WAS THAT SUPPOSED TO BE?
Kyaaah!
clap
clap
clap
clap
clap
Bravo.
We already told you!
clap
clap
clap
clap
Yuki!
Kyaaah!
SORTA CINDERELLA.

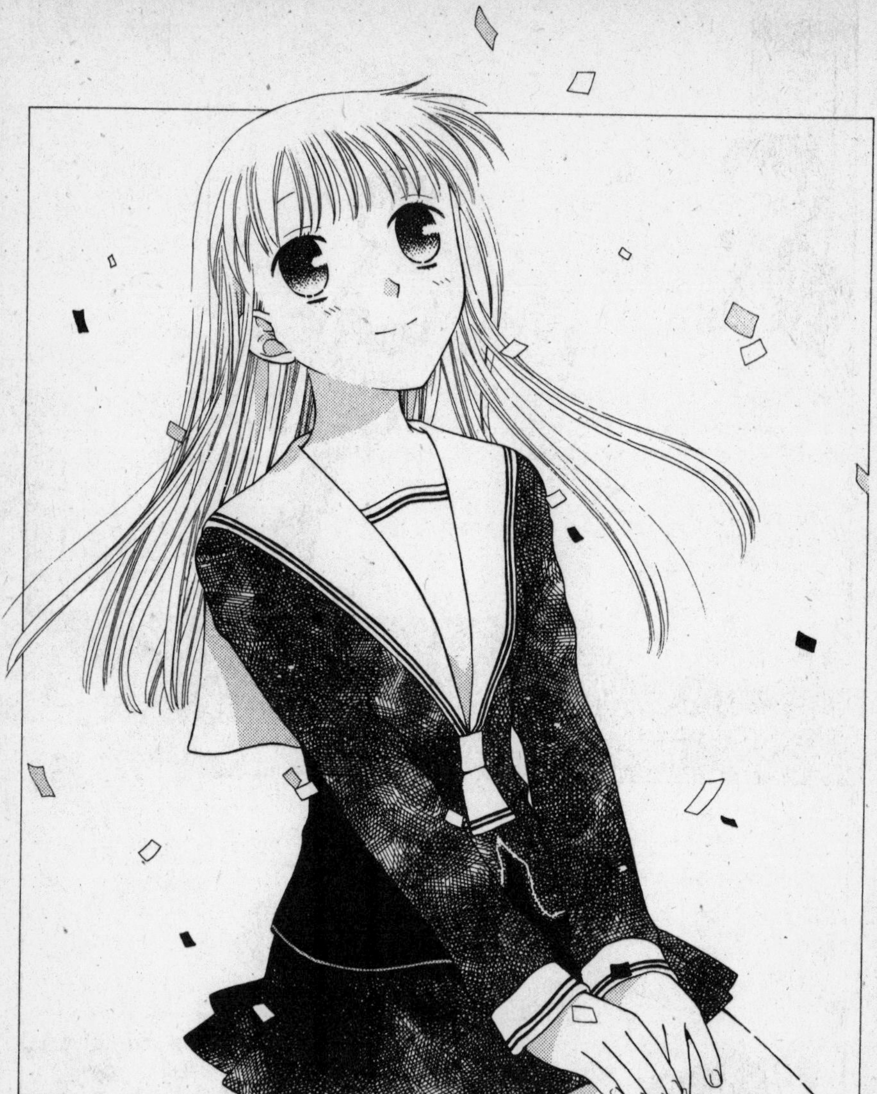

Chapter 89

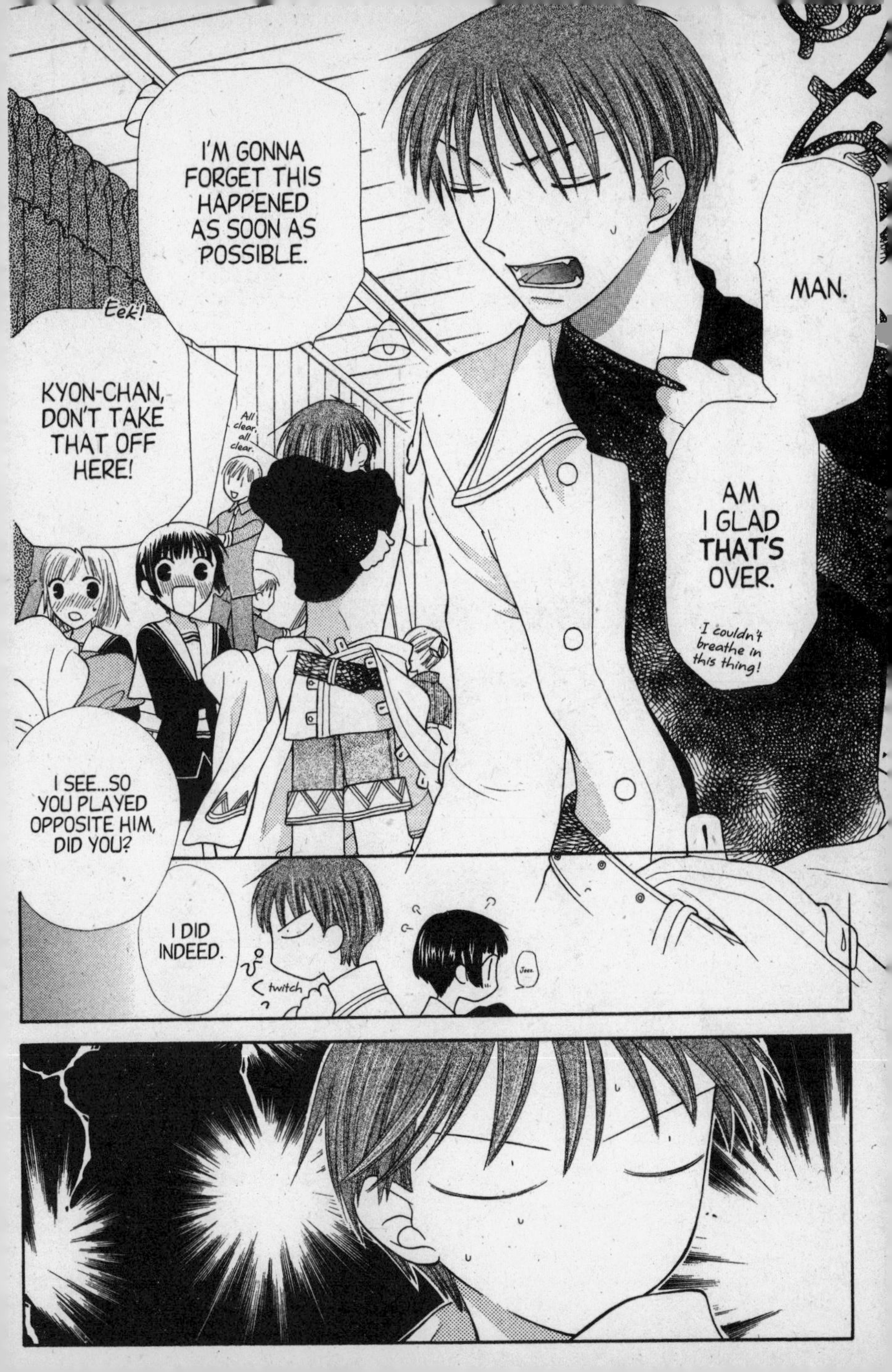
MAN.
AM I GLAD THAT'S OVER.
I couldn't breathe in this thing!
I'M GONNA FORGET THIS HAPPENED AS SOON AS POSSIBLE.
Eek!
KYON-CHAN, DON'T TAKE THAT OFF HERE!
All clear, all clear.
I SEE...SO YOU PLAYED OPPOSITE HIM, DID YOU?
Jeez.
I DID INDEED.
twitch

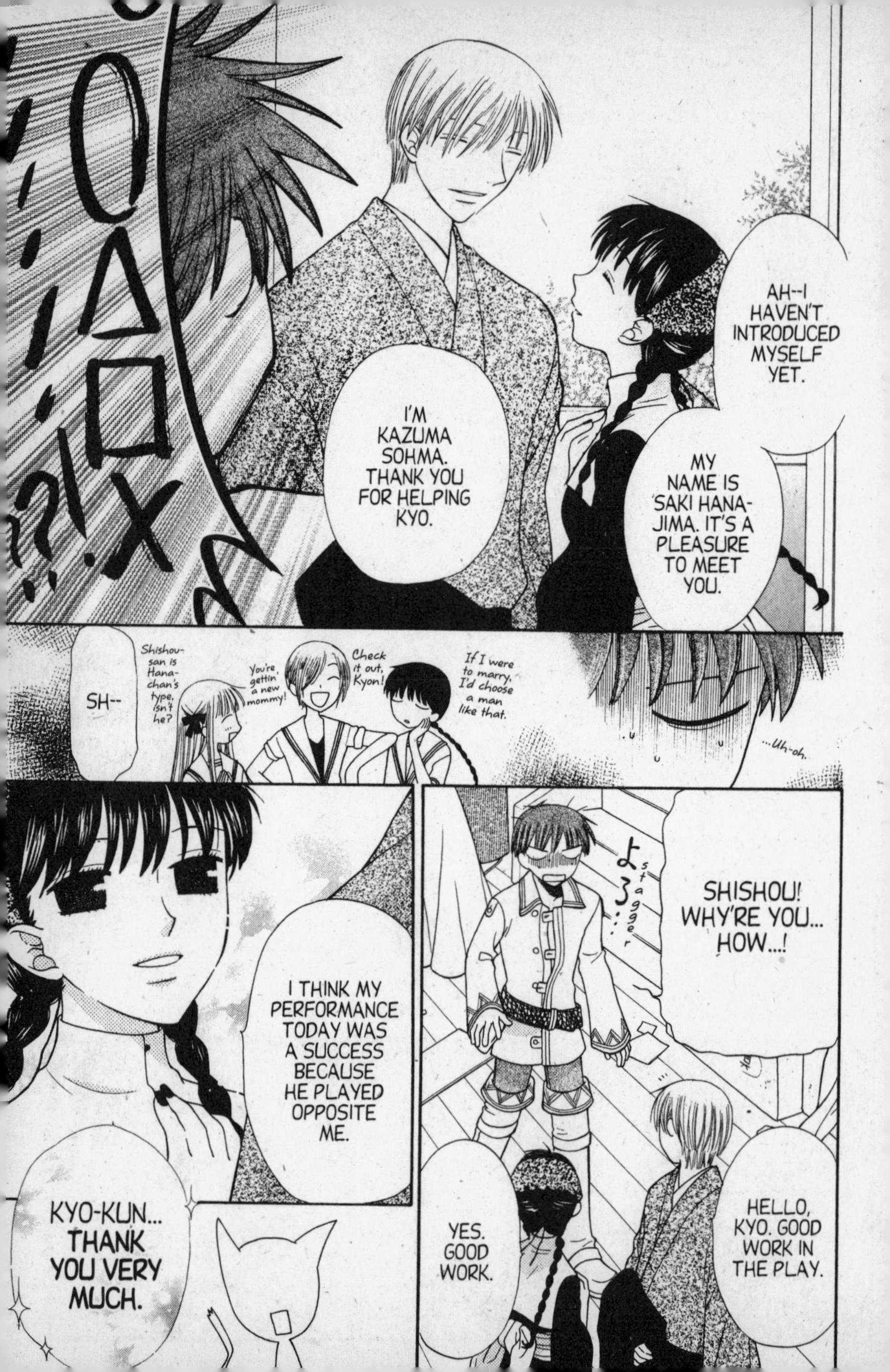
AH--I HAVEN'T INTRODUCED MYSELF YET.
MY NAME IS SAKI HANA-JIMA. IT'S A PLEASURE TO MEET YOU.
I'M KAZUMA SOHMA. THANK YOU FOR HELPING KYO.
...Uh-oh.
If I were to marry, I'd choose a man like that.
Check it out, Kyon!
You're gettin' a new mommy!
Shishou-san is Hana-chan's type, isn't he?
SH--
SHISHOU! WHY'RE YOU... HOW...!
stagger
HELLO, KYO. GOOD WORK IN THE PLAY.
YES. GOOD WORK.
I THINK MY PERFORMANCE TODAY WAS A SUCCESS BECAUSE HE PLAYED OPPOSITE ME.
KYO-KUN... THANK YOU VERY MUCH.

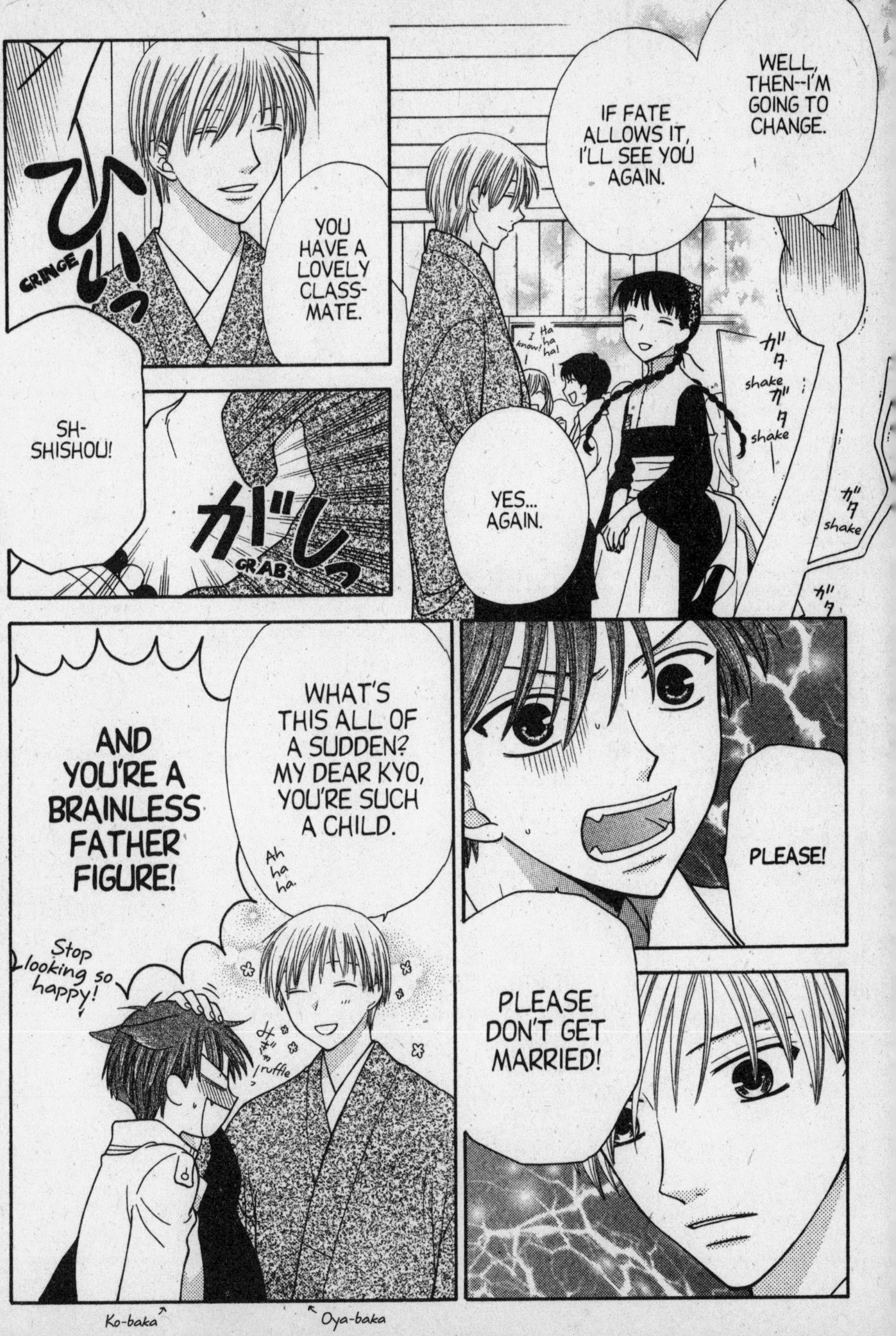
WELL, THEN--I'M GOING TO CHANGE.
IF FATE ALLOWS IT, I'LL SEE YOU AGAIN.
shake
shake
shake
I know!
Ha ha ha!
YES... AGAIN.
YOU HAVE A LOVELY CLASS-MATE.
CRINGE
SH-SHISHOU!
GRAB
PLEASE!
PLEASE DON'T GET MARRIED!
WHAT'S THIS ALL OF A SUDDEN? MY DEAR KYO, YOU'RE SUCH A CHILD.
Ah ha ha.
AND YOU'RE A BRAINLESS FATHER FIGURE!
Stop looking so happy!
ruffle

Ko-baka ↑ ↖ Oya-baka

Continued →

Momiji's Papa lives "outside," but he still comes to see his son every once in a while.

Since the incident with his Mama, Momitchi and Hatori have grown closer; they sympathize with each other, and worry about the other's feelings.

Unlike the other members of the Zodiac, Momiji went to international elementary and middle schools. He's also the member of the Zodiac most comfortable with his spirit possession.

Now matter how much he clings to Tohru, he still never gets in trouble...so I guess, in a way, he's the most successful of the boys.

I remember talking with my editor about how it would've been nice if I could have said that Momiji's song in Chapter 72 was "For Fruits Basket."

I hope that Ritsuko Okazaki-san may be happy in the next world.

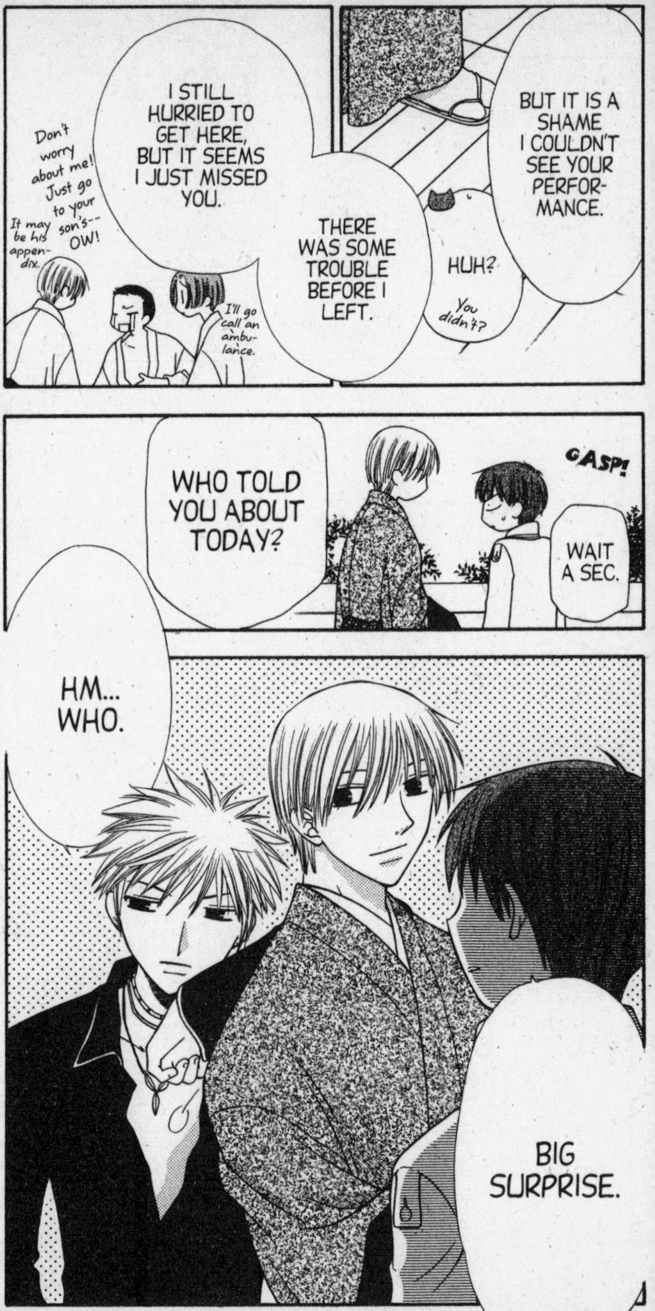
BUT IT IS A SHAME I COULDN'T SEE YOUR PERFORMANCE.
HUH?
You didn't?
THERE WAS SOME TROUBLE BEFORE I LEFT.
I STILL HURRIED TO GET HERE, BUT IT SEEMS I JUST MISSED YOU.
Don't worry about me! Just go to your son's-- OW!
It may be his appendix.
I'll go call an ambulance.
GASP!
WAIT A SEC.
WHO TOLD YOU ABOUT TODAY?
HM... WHO.
BIG SURPRISE.

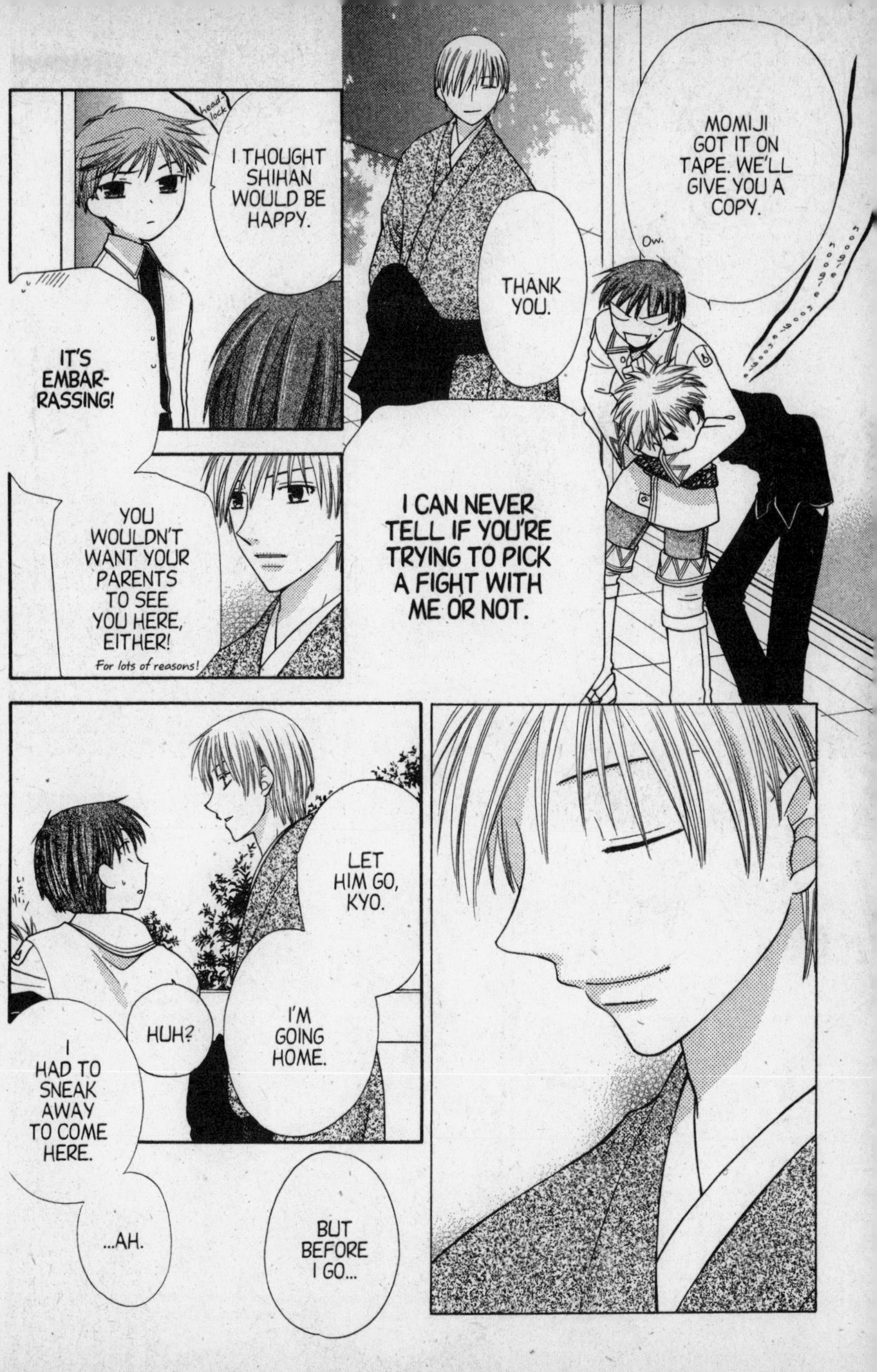
MOMIJI GOT IT ON TAPE. WE'LL GIVE YOU A COPY.
Ow.
THANK YOU.
I CAN NEVER TELL IF YOU'RE TRYING TO PICK A FIGHT WITH ME OR NOT.
head-lock
I THOUGHT SHIHAN WOULD BE HAPPY.
IT'S EMBARRASSING!
YOU WOULDN'T WANT YOUR PARENTS TO SEE YOU HERE, EITHER!
For lots of reasons!
LET HIM GO, KYO.
I'M GOING HOME.
HUH?
I HAD TO SNEAK AWAY TO COME HERE.
...AH.
BUT BEFORE I GO...

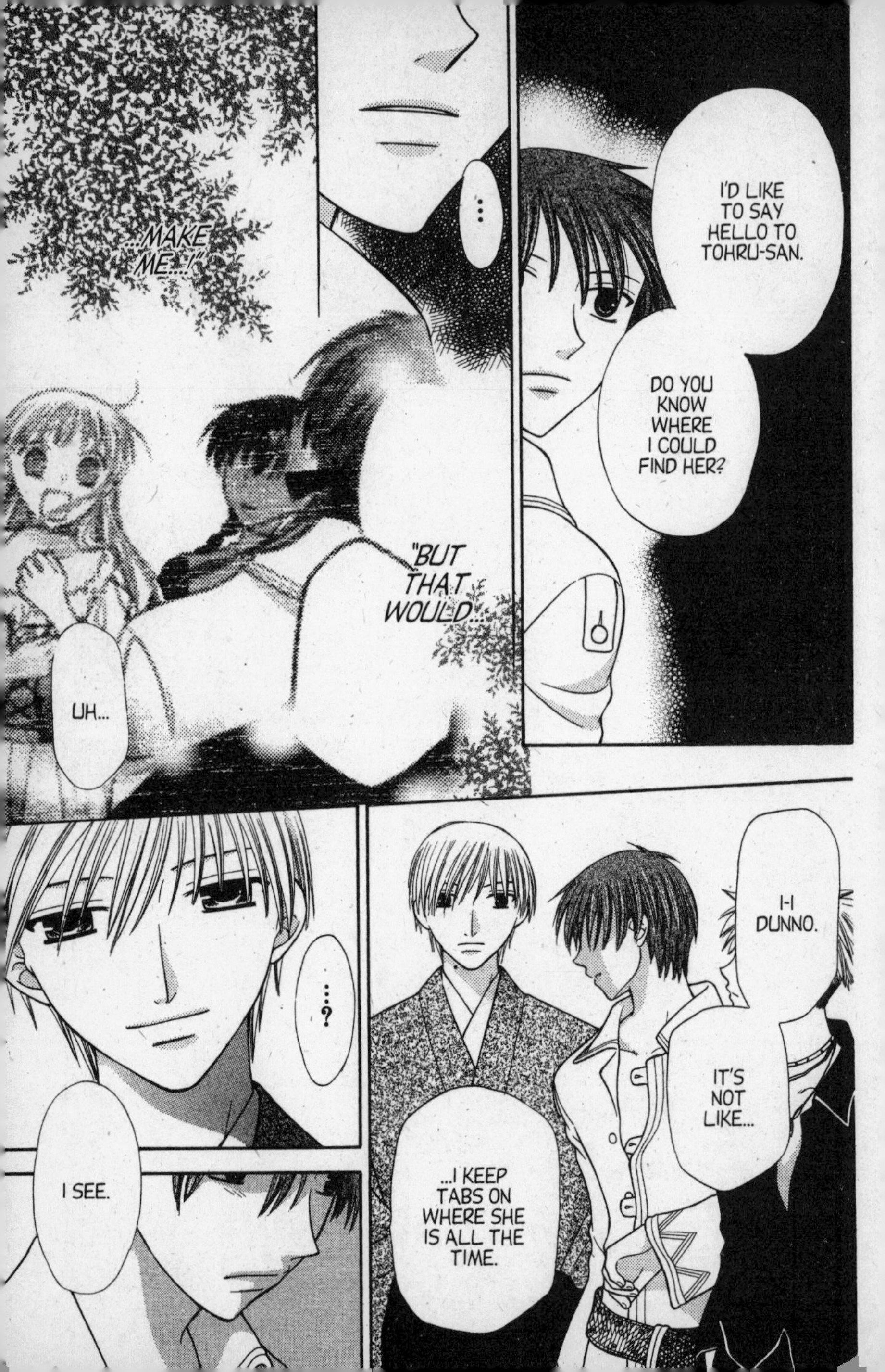
I'D LIKE TO SAY HELLO TO TOHRU-SAN.
DO YOU KNOW WHERE I COULD FIND HER?
...
"...MAKE ME...!"
"BUT THAT WOULD...
UH...
I-I DUNNO.
IT'S NOT LIKE...
...I KEEP TABS ON WHERE SHE IS ALL THE TIME.
...?
I SEE.

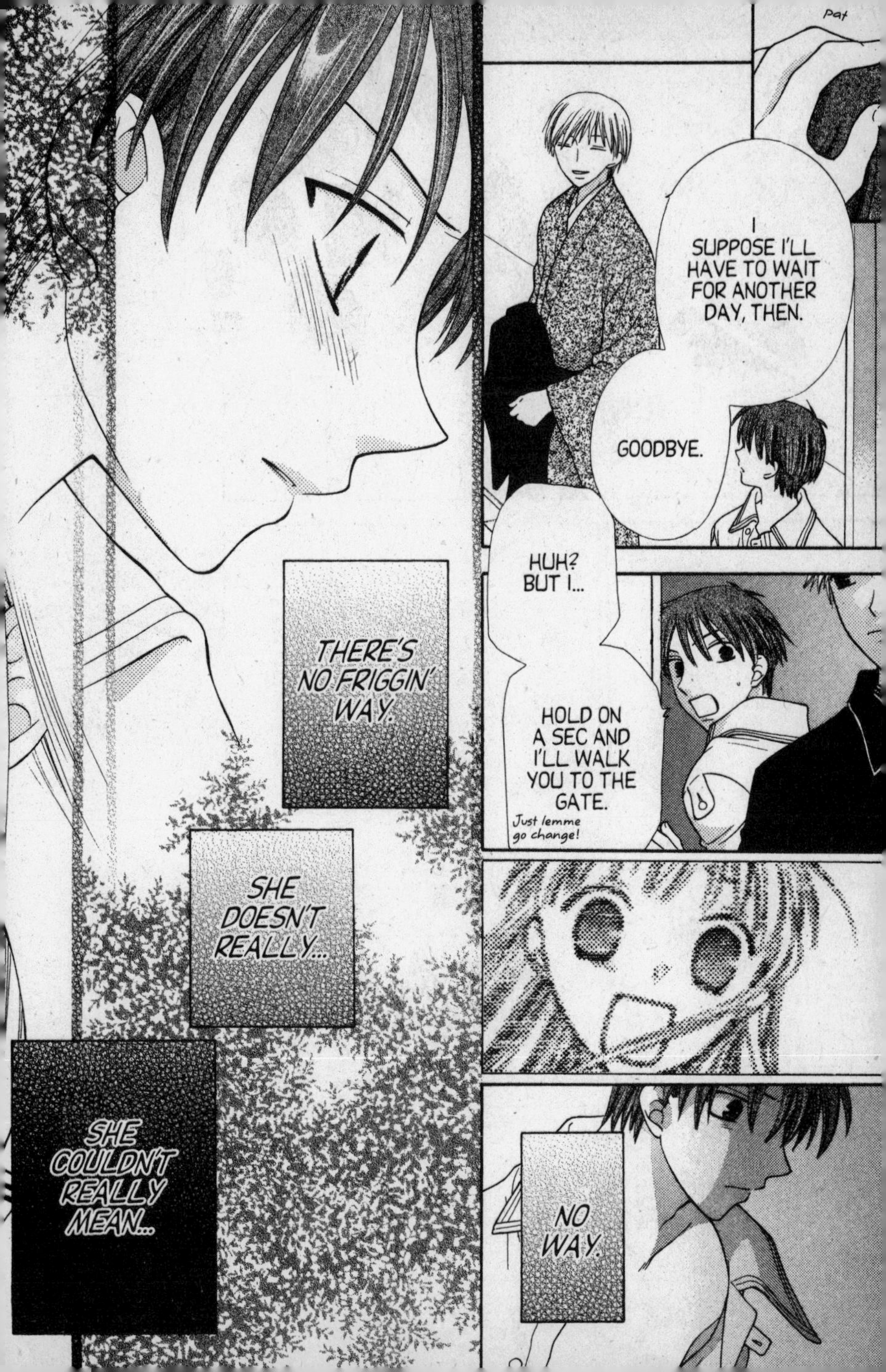
Pat
I SUPPOSE I'LL HAVE TO WAIT FOR ANOTHER DAY, THEN.
GOODBYE.
HUH? BUT I...
HOLD ON A SEC AND I'LL WALK YOU TO THE GATE.
Just lemme go change!
NO WAY.
THERE'S NO FRIGGIN' WAY.
SHE DOESN'T REALLY...
SHE COULDN'T REALLY MEAN...

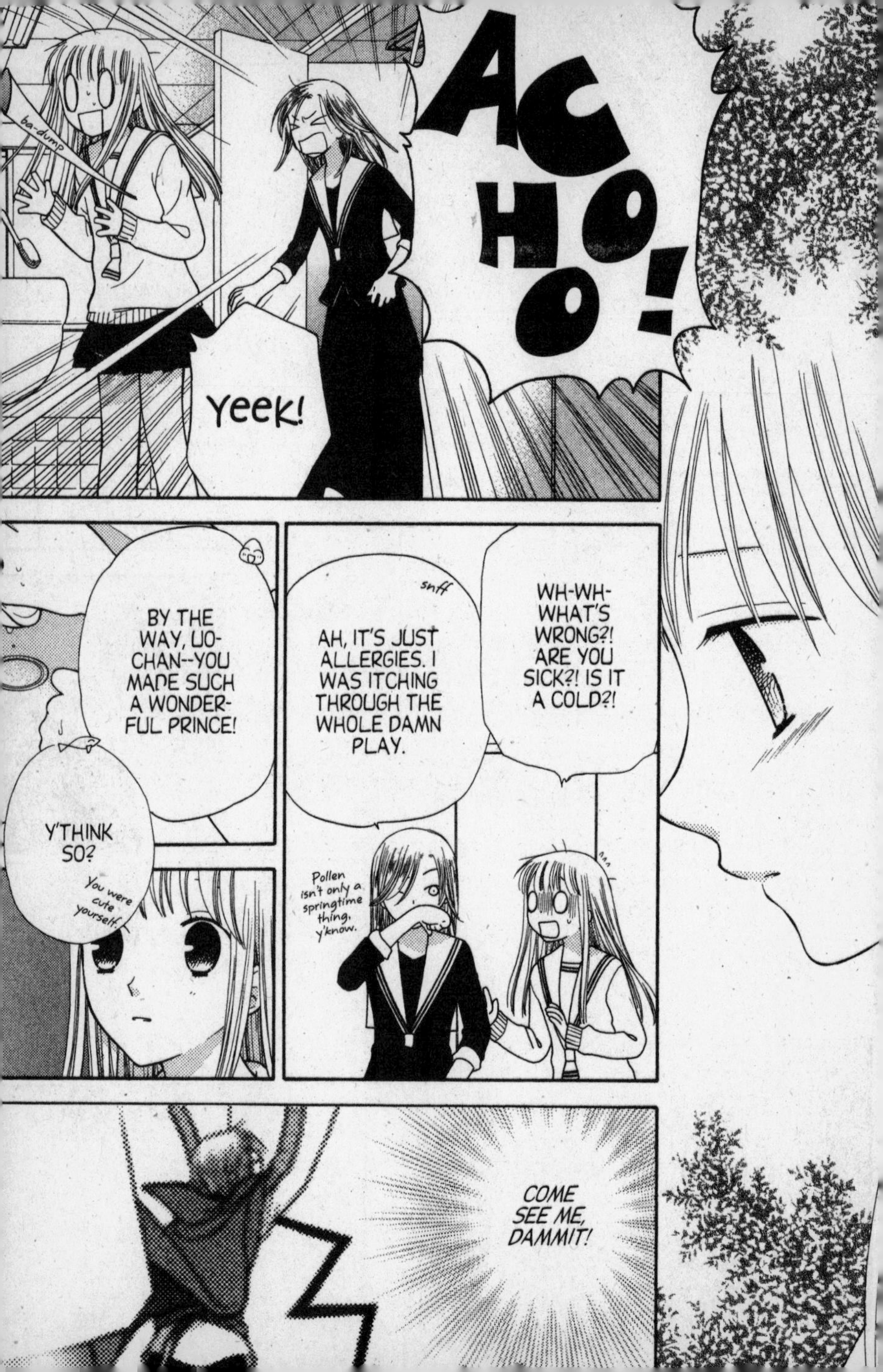
ACHOO!
YEEK!
ba-dump
WH-WH-WHAT'S WRONG?! ARE YOU SICK?! IS IT A COLD?!
snff
AH, IT'S JUST ALLERGIES. I WAS ITCHING THROUGH THE WHOLE DAMN PLAY.
Pollen isn't only a springtime thing, y'know.
BY THE WAY, UO-CHAN--YOU MADE SUCH A WONDER-FUL PRINCE!
Y'THINK SO?
You were cute yourself.
COME SEE ME, DAMMIT!

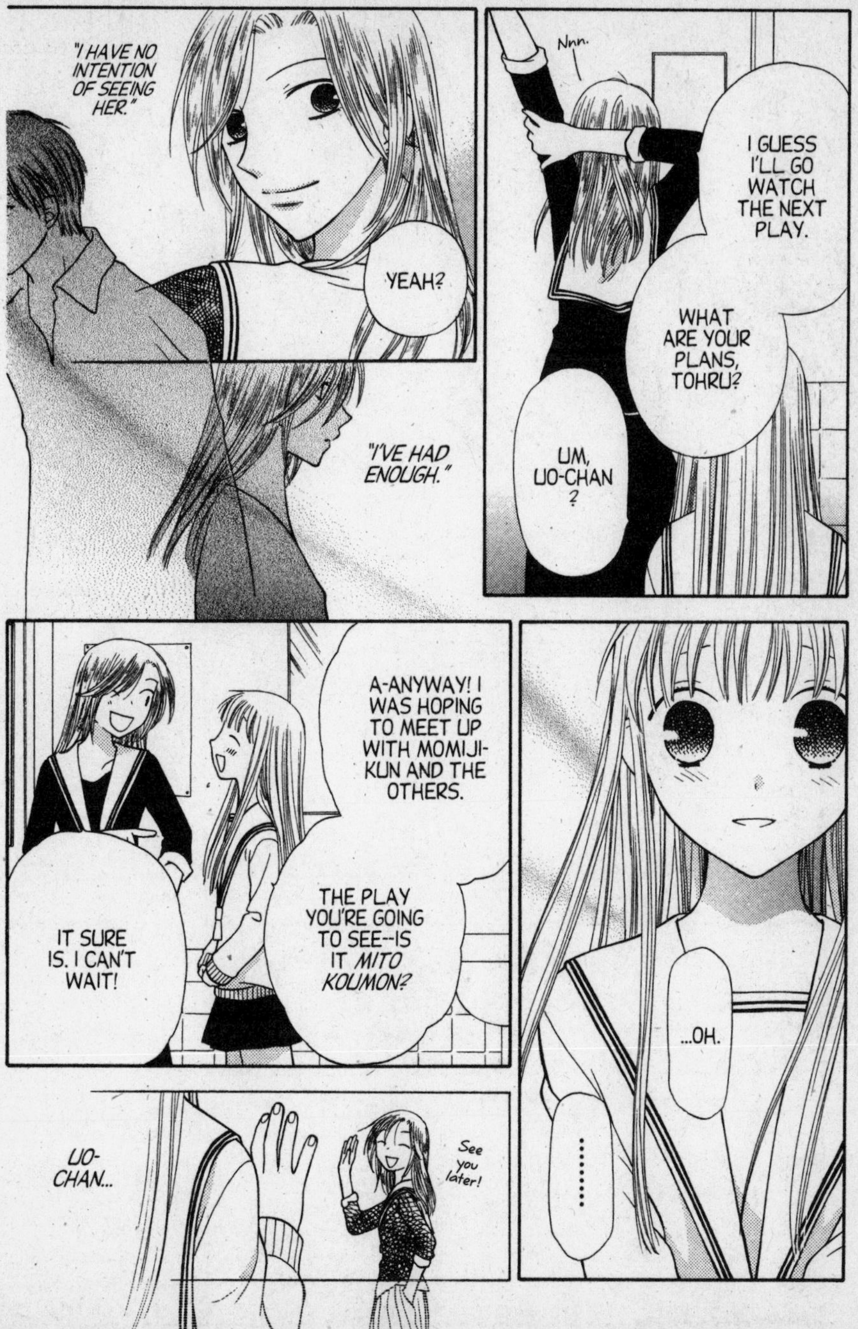
Nnn.
I GUESS I'LL GO WATCH THE NEXT PLAY.
WHAT ARE YOUR PLANS, TOHRU?
UM, UO-CHAN?
"I HAVE NO INTENTION OF SEEING HER."
YEAH?
"I'VE HAD ENOUGH."
...OH.
......
A-ANYWAY! I WAS HOPING TO MEET UP WITH MOMIJI-KUN AND THE OTHERS.
THE PLAY YOU'RE GOING TO SEE--IS IT *MITO KOUMON*?
IT SURE IS. I CAN'T WAIT!
See you later!
UO-CHAN...

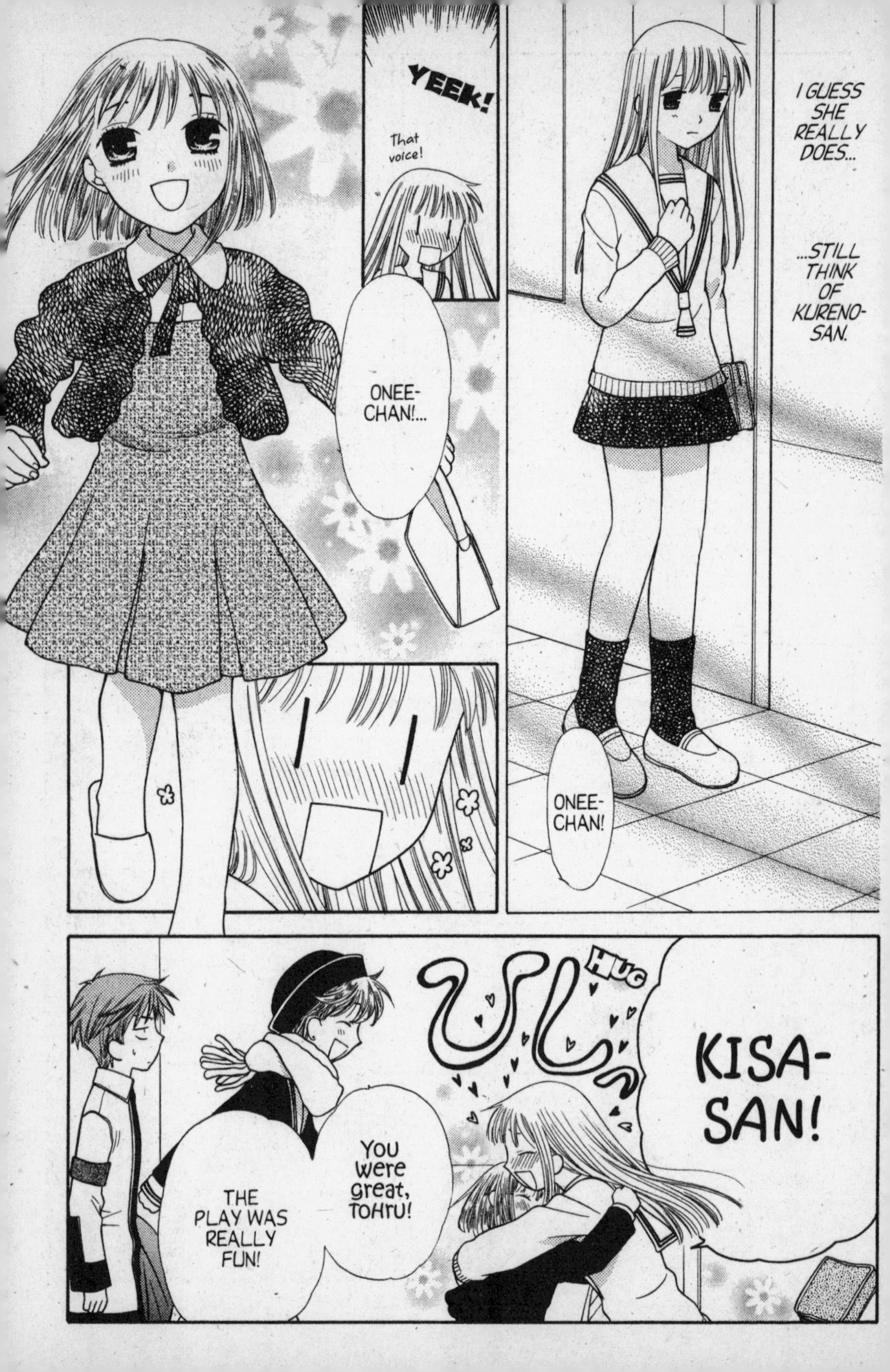
I GUESS SHE REALLY DOES...
...STILL THINK OF KURENO-SAN.
ONEE-CHAN!
YEEK!
That voice!
ONEE-CHAN!...
HUG
KISA-SAN!
You were great, TOHRU!
THE PLAY WAS REALLY FUN!

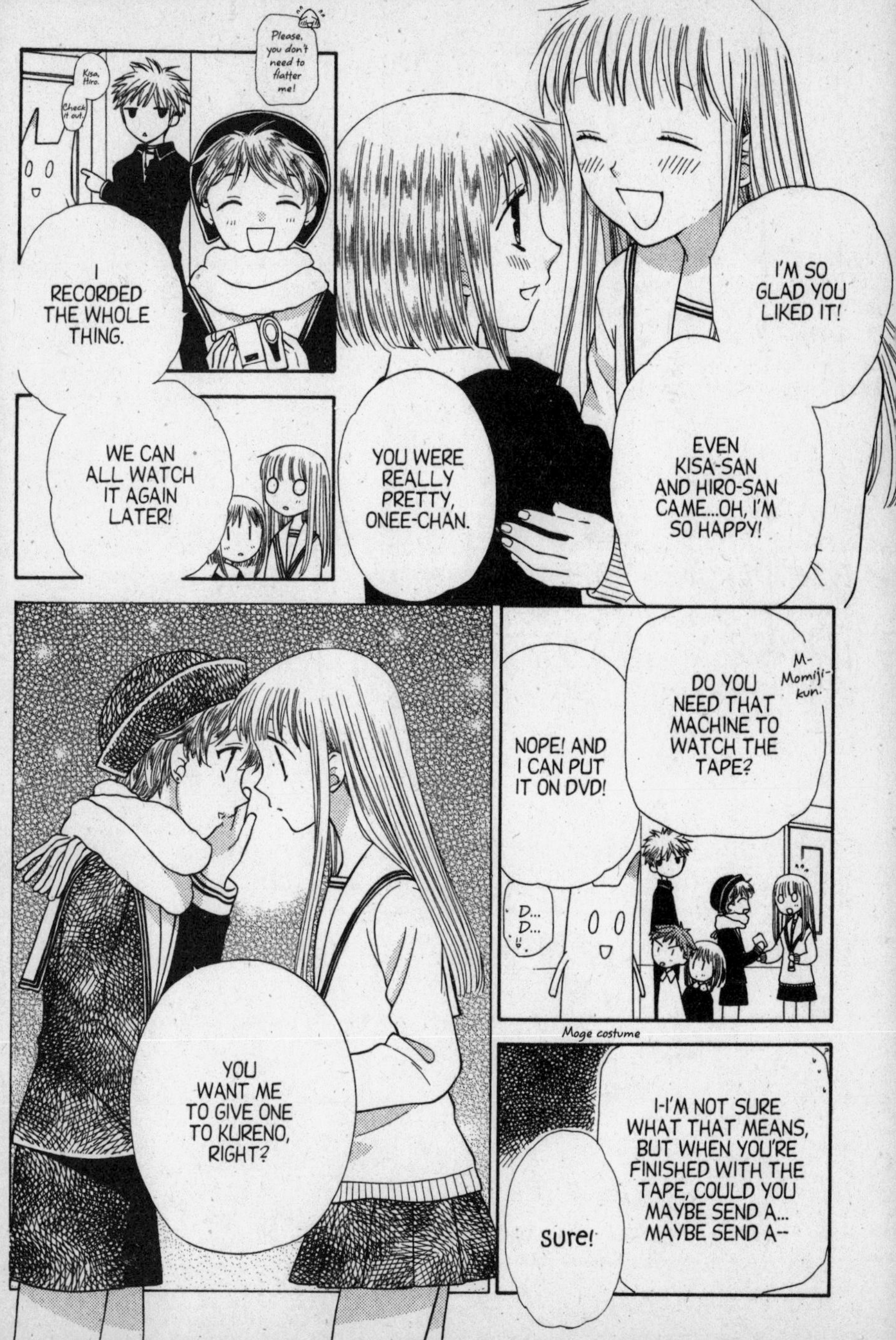
I'M SO GLAD YOU LIKED IT!
EVEN KISA-SAN AND HIRO-SAN CAME...OH, I'M SO HAPPY!
YOU WERE REALLY PRETTY, ONEE-CHAN.
Please, you don't need to flatter me!
Kisa, Hiro.
Check it out.
I RECORDED THE WHOLE THING.
WE CAN ALL WATCH IT AGAIN LATER!
M-Momiji-kun.
DO YOU NEED THAT MACHINE TO WATCH THE TAPE?
NOPE! AND I CAN PUT IT ON DVD!
D... D...!!
Moge costume
I-I'M NOT SURE WHAT THAT MEANS, BUT WHEN YOU'RE FINISHED WITH THE TAPE, COULD YOU MAYBE SEND A... MAYBE SEND A--
Sure!
YOU WANT ME TO GIVE ONE TO KURENO, RIGHT?

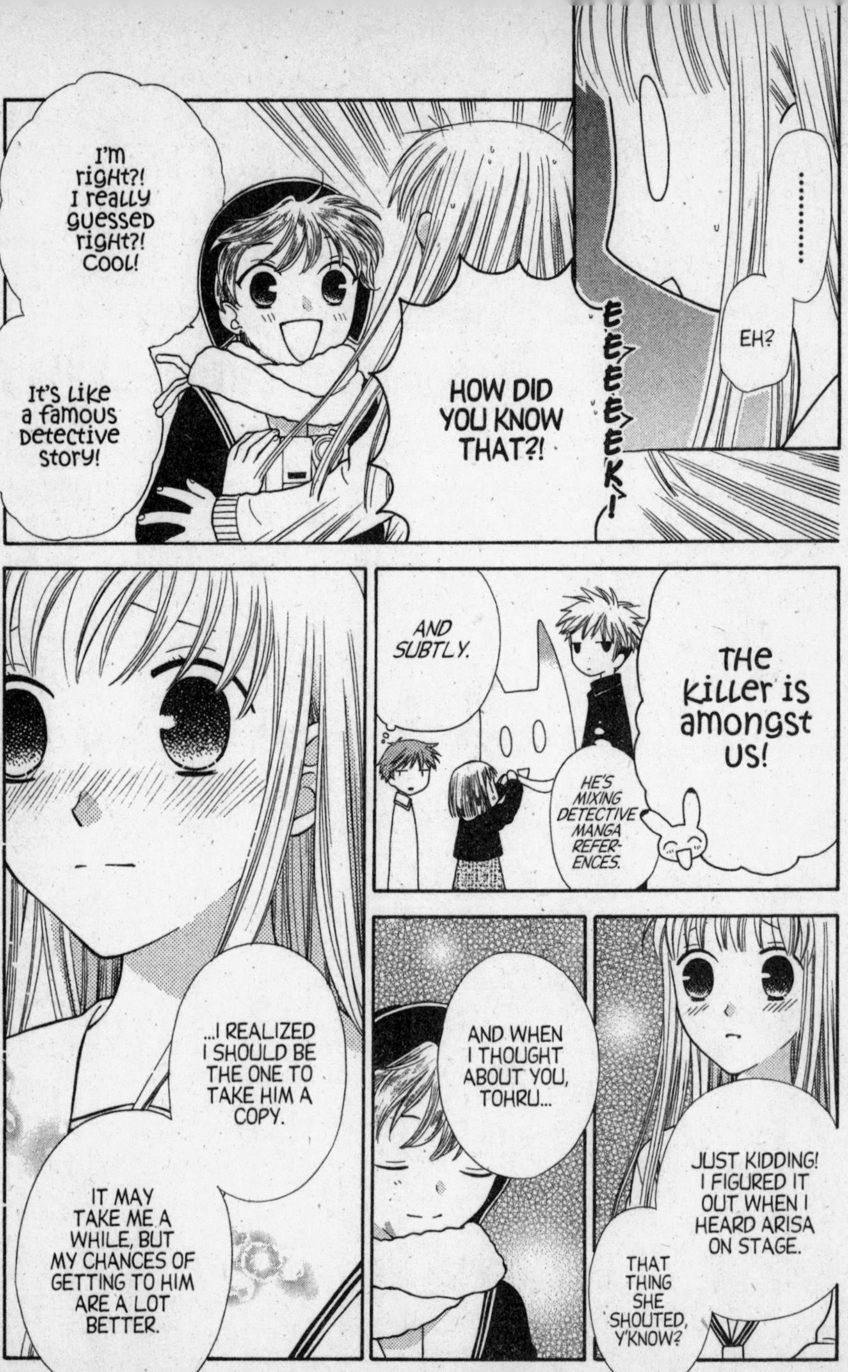
......
EH?
EEEEEK!
HOW DID YOU KNOW THAT?!
I'm right?! I really guessed right?! Cool!
It's like a famous detective story!
The killer is amongst us!
HE'S MIXING DETECTIVE MANGA REFERENCES.
AND SUBTLY.
JUST KIDDING! I FIGURED IT OUT WHEN I HEARD ARISA ON STAGE.
THAT THING SHE SHOUTED, Y'KNOW?
AND WHEN I THOUGHT ABOUT YOU, TOHRU...
...I REALIZED I SHOULD BE THE ONE TO TAKE HIM A COPY.
IT MAY TAKE ME A WHILE, BUT MY CHANCES OF GETTING TO HIM ARE A LOT BETTER.

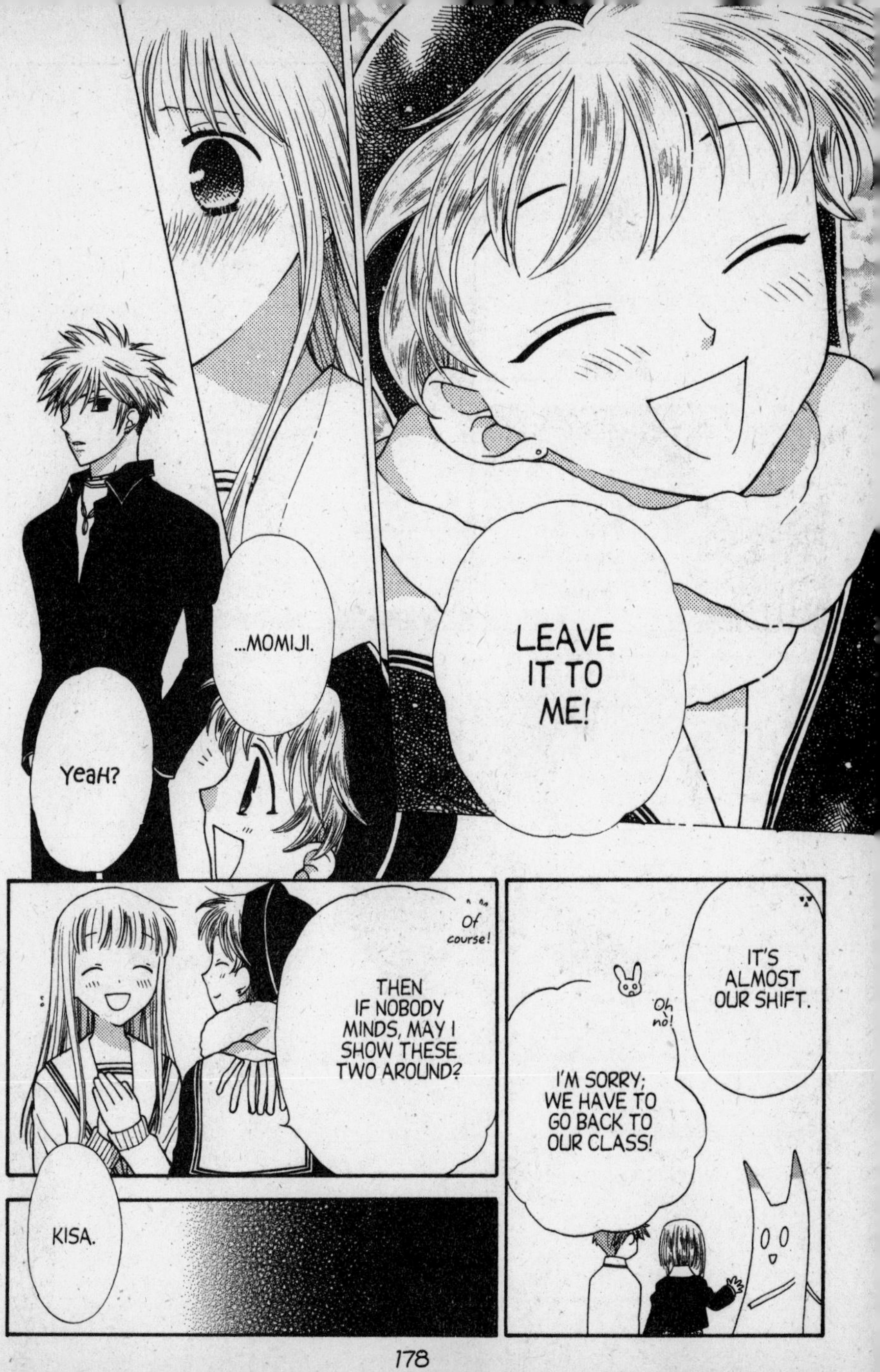
LEAVE IT TO ME!
...MOMIJI.
YeaH?
IT'S ALMOST OUR SHIFT.
Oh no!
I'M SORRY; WE HAVE TO GO BACK TO OUR CLASS!
Of course!
THEN IF NOBODY MINDS, MAY I SHOW THESE TWO AROUND?
KISA.

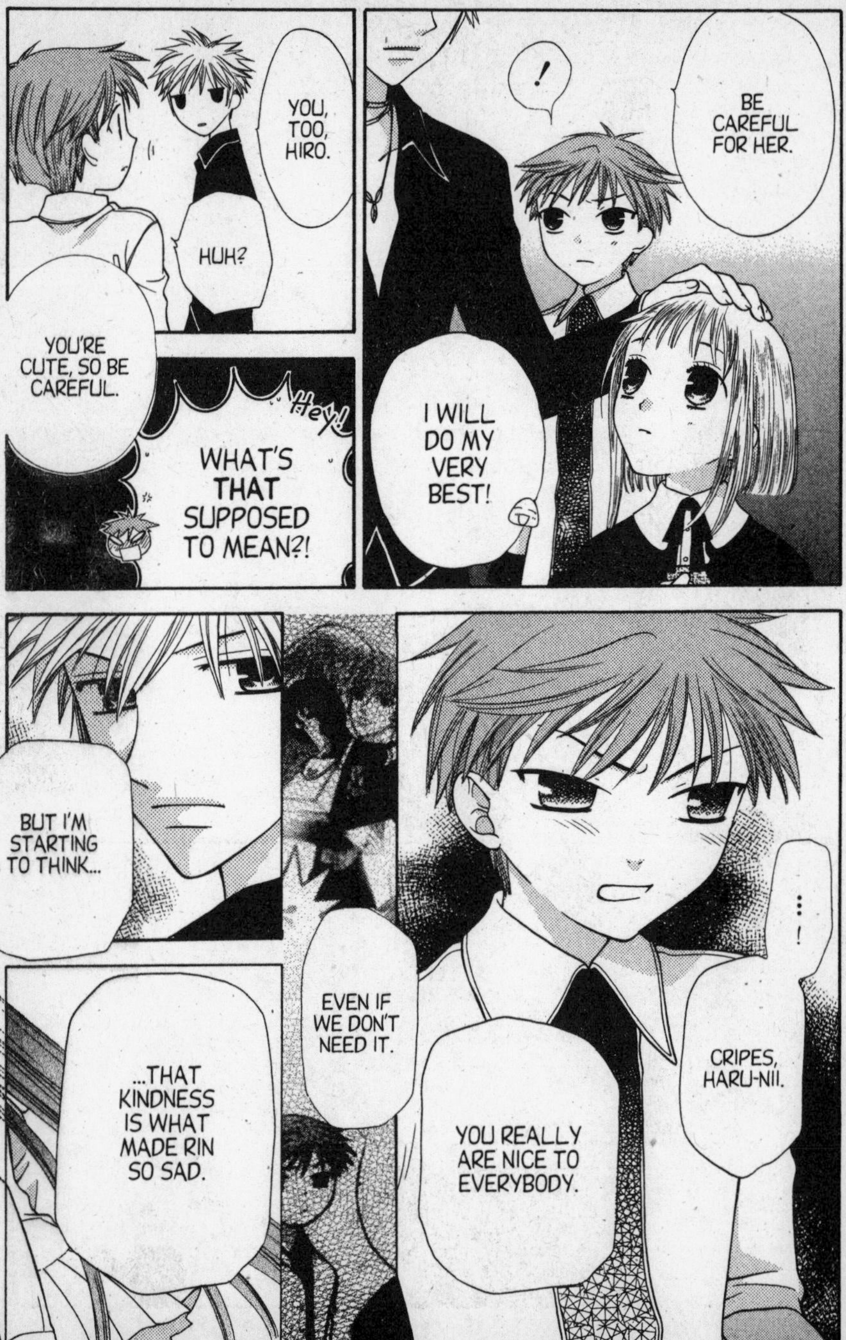
BE CAREFUL FOR HER.
!
I WILL DO MY VERY BEST!
YOU, TOO, HIRO.
HUH?
YOU'RE CUTE, SO BE CAREFUL.
Hey!
WHAT'S THAT SUPPOSED TO MEAN?!
...!
CRIPES, HARU-NII.
YOU REALLY ARE NICE TO EVERYBODY.
EVEN IF WE DON'T NEED IT.
BUT I'M STARTING TO THINK...
...THAT KINDNESS IS WHAT MADE RIN SO SAD.

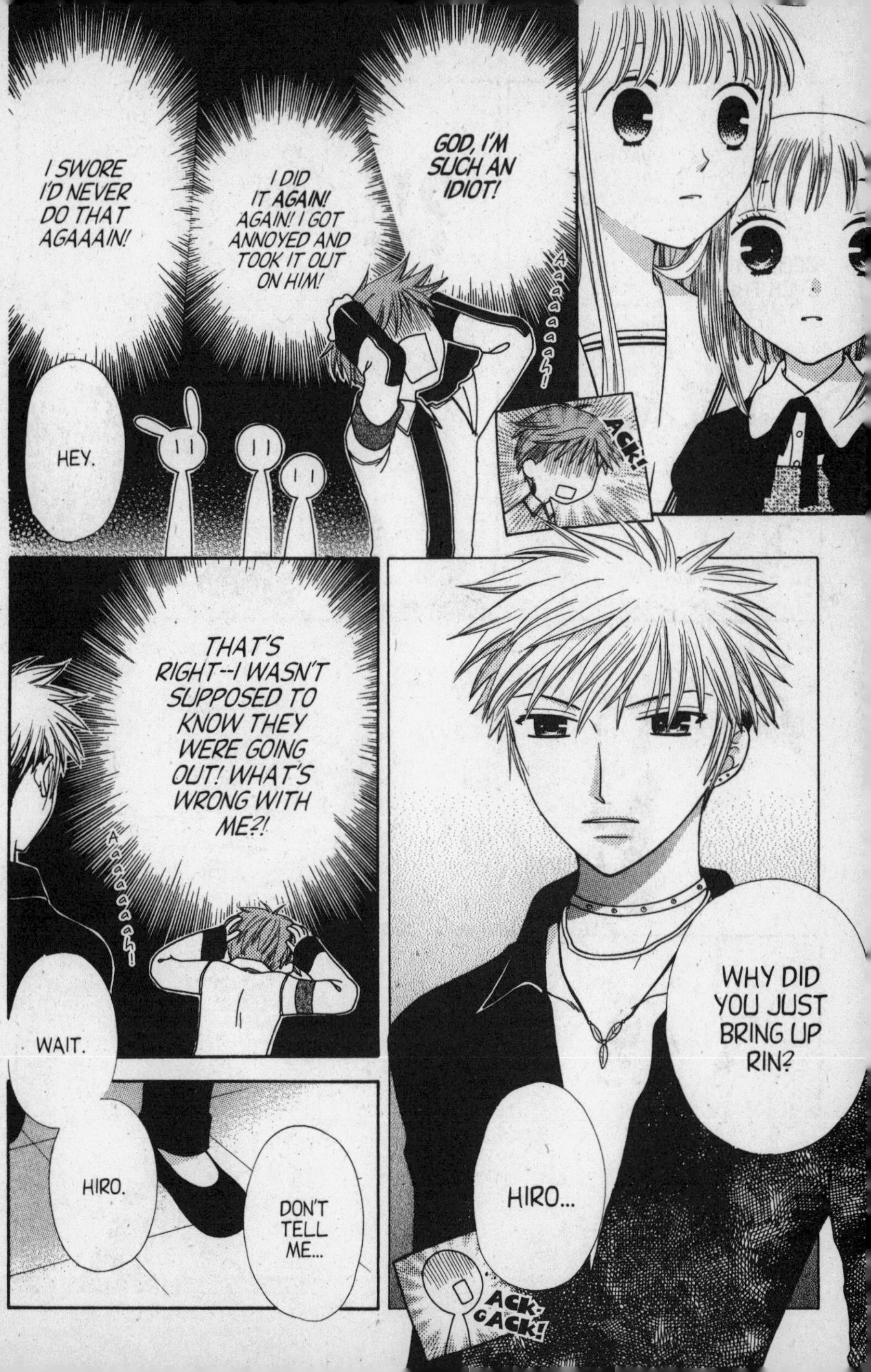
ACK!
GOD, I'M SUCH AN IDIOT!
I DID IT AGAIN! AGAIN! I GOT ANNOYED AND TOOK IT OUT ON HIM!
Aaaaaaaaaah!
I SWORE I'D NEVER DO THAT AGAAAIN!
HEY.
WHY DID YOU JUST BRING UP RIN?
HIRO...
ACK GACK!
THAT'S RIGHT--I WASN'T SUPPOSED TO KNOW THEY WERE GOING OUT! WHAT'S WRONG WITH ME?!
Aaaaaaaaah!
WAIT.
HIRO.
DON'T TELL ME...

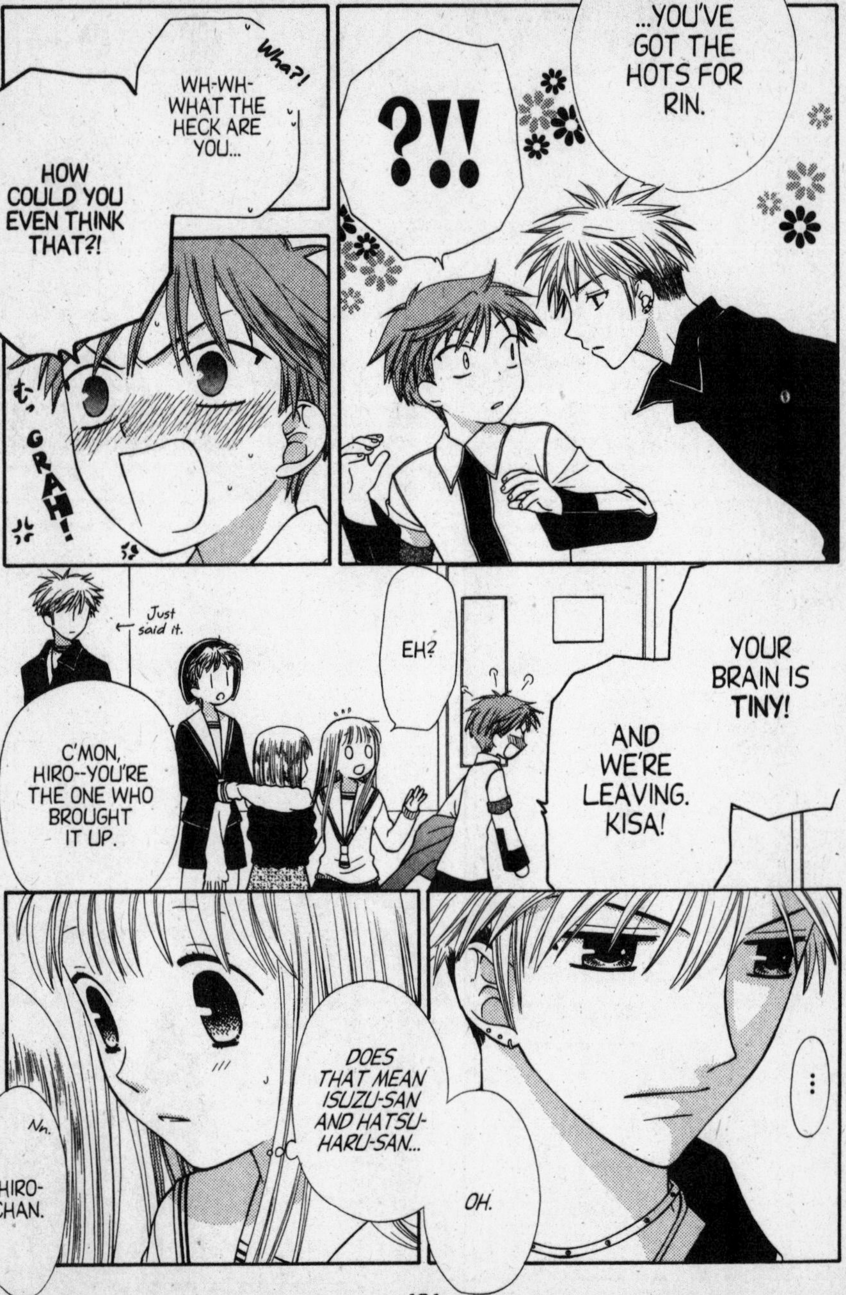
...YOU'VE GOT THE HOTS FOR RIN.
?!!
Wha?!
WH-WH-WHAT THE HECK ARE YOU...
HOW COULD YOU EVEN THINK THAT?!
GRAH!
YOUR BRAIN IS TINY!
AND WE'RE LEAVING. KISA!
EH?
C'MON, HIRO--YOU'RE THE ONE WHO BROUGHT IT UP.
Just said it.
...
OH.
DOES THAT MEAN ISUZU-SAN AND HATSUHARU-SAN...
Nn.
HIRO-CHAN.

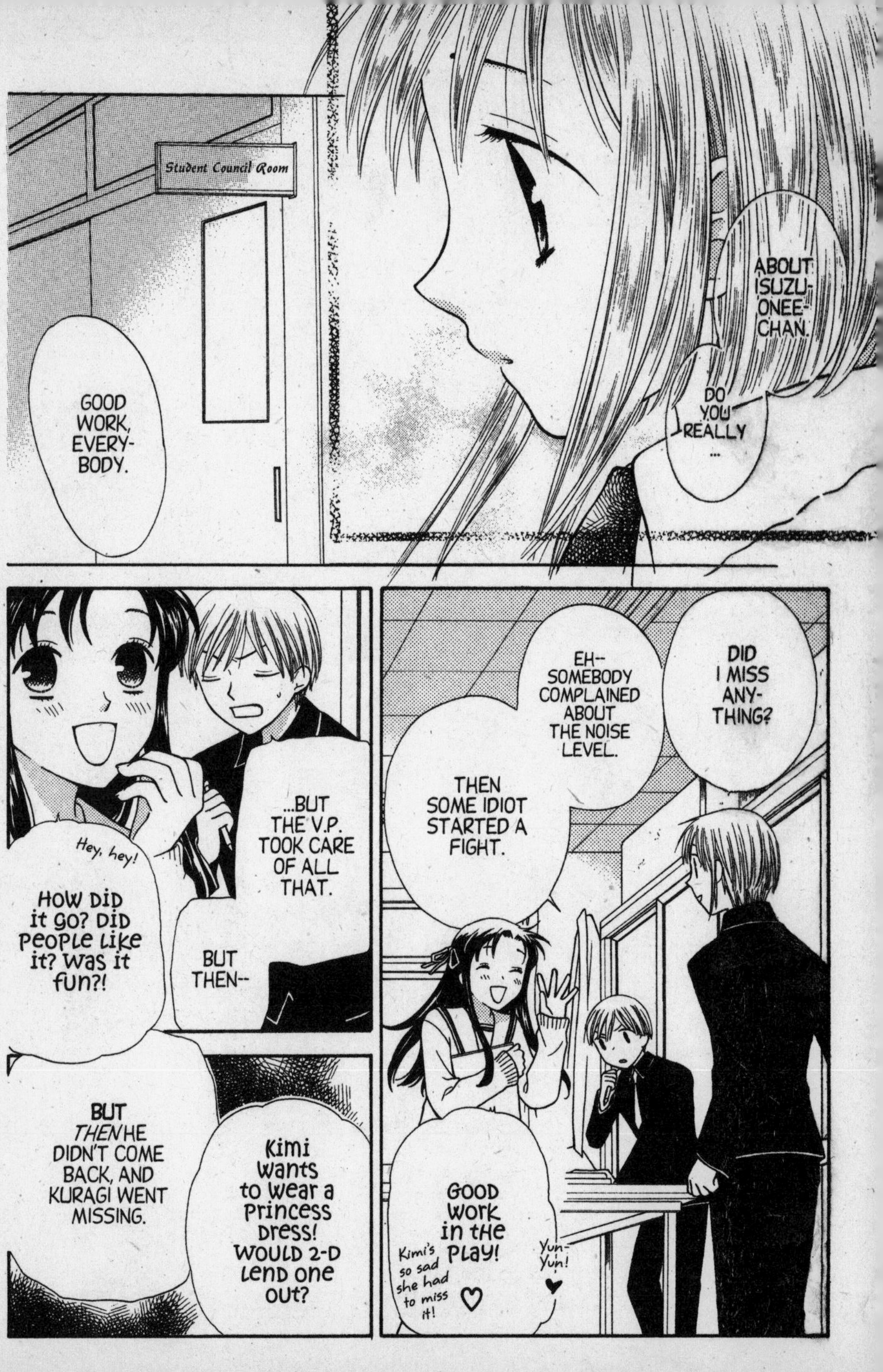
ABOUT ISUZU-ONEE-CHAN.
DO YOU REALLY ...
Student Council Room
GOOD WORK, EVERYBODY.
DID I MISS ANYTHING?
EH-- SOMEBODY COMPLAINED ABOUT THE NOISE LEVEL.
THEN SOME IDIOT STARTED A FIGHT.
GOOD WORK IN THE PLAY!
Kimi's so sad she had to miss it! ♡
Yun-Yun! ♥
...BUT THE V.P. TOOK CARE OF ALL THAT.
BUT THEN--
Hey, hey!
HOW DID IT GO? DID PEOPLE LIKE IT? WAS IT FUN?!
BUT *THEN* HE DIDN'T COME BACK, AND KURAGI WENT MISSING.
KIMI WANTS TO WEAR A PRINCESS DRESS! WOULD 2-D LEND ONE OUT?

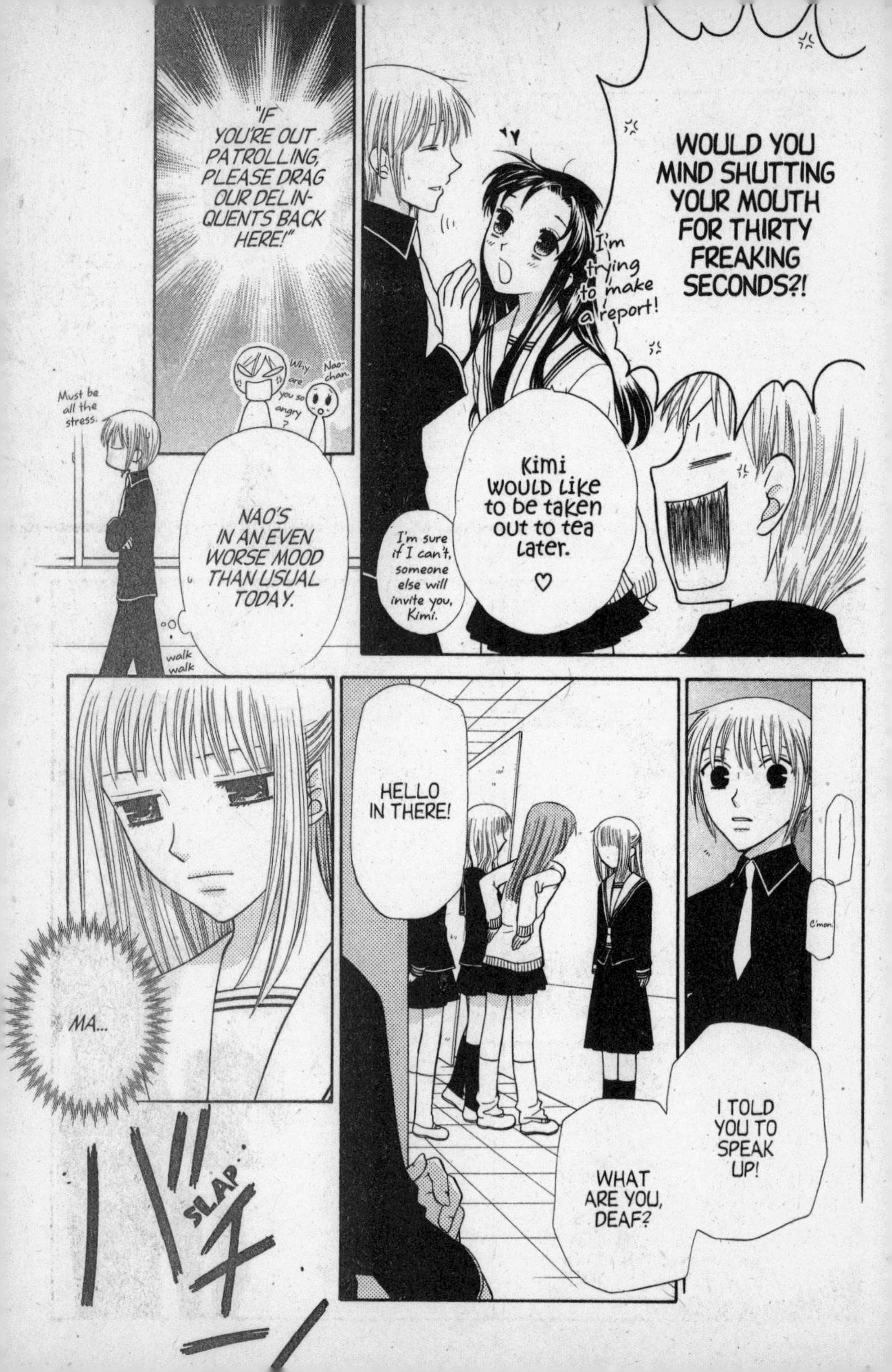
WOULD YOU MIND SHUTTING YOUR MOUTH FOR THIRTY FREAKING SECONDS?!
I'm trying to make a report!
Kimi WOULD LIKE to be taken out to tea later. ♡
I'm sure if I can't, someone else will invite you, Kimi.
"IF YOU'RE OUT PATROLLING, PLEASE DRAG OUR DELIN-QUENTS BACK HERE!"
Nao-chan.
Why are you so angry?
NAO'S IN AN EVEN WORSE MOOD THAN USUAL TODAY.
Must be all the stress.
walk walk
I TOLD YOU TO SPEAK UP!
WHAT ARE YOU, DEAF?
C'mon.
HELLO IN THERE!
MA...
SLAP

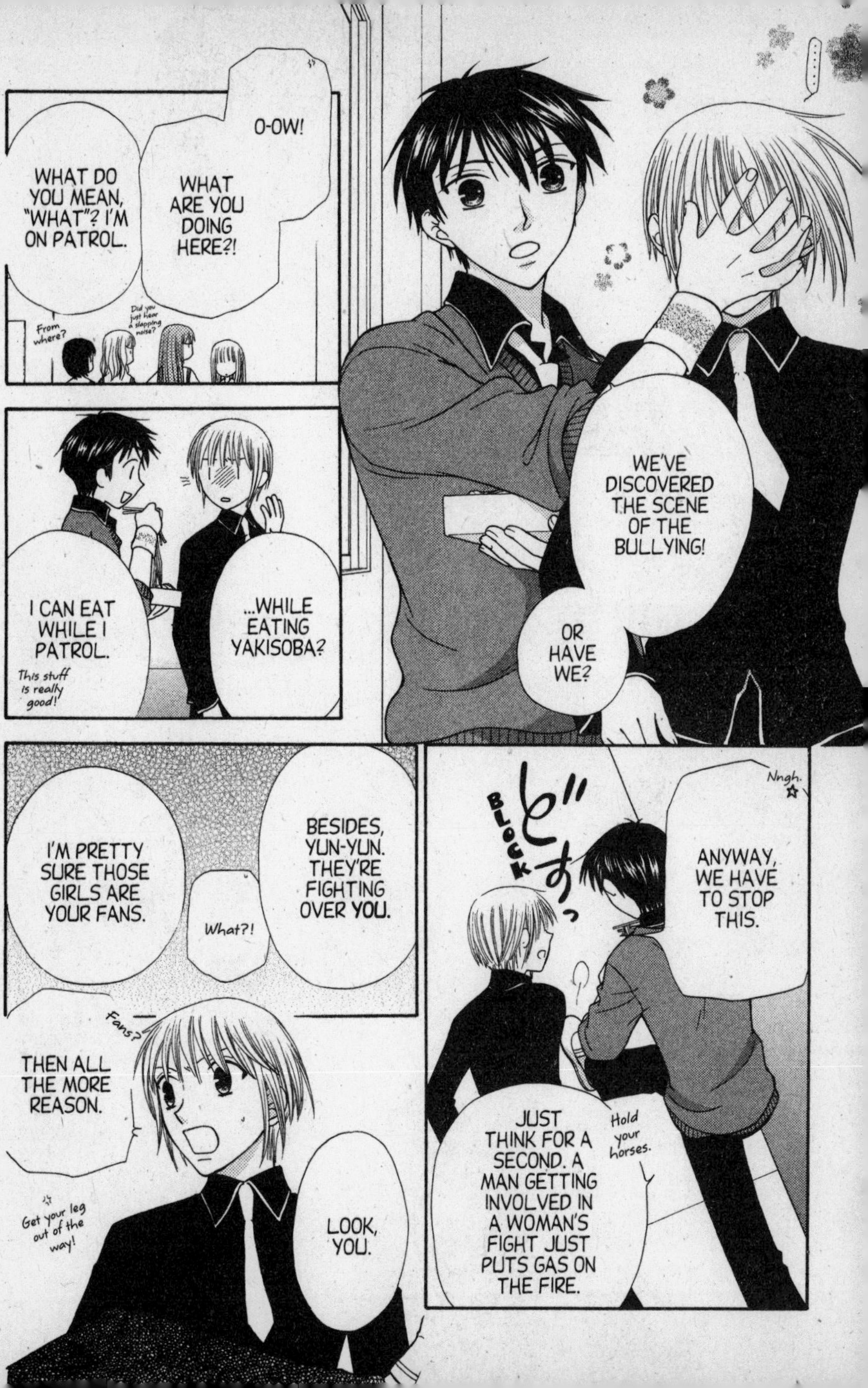
......!
WE'VE DISCOVERED THE SCENE OF THE BULLYING!
OR HAVE WE?
O-OW!
WHAT ARE YOU DOING HERE?!
WHAT DO YOU MEAN, "WHAT"? I'M ON PATROL.
Did you just hear a slapping noise?
From where?
...WHILE EATING YAKISOBA?
I CAN EAT WHILE I PATROL.
This stuff is really good!
どすっ
BLOCK
Nngh.☆
ANYWAY, WE HAVE TO STOP THIS.
Hold your horses.
JUST THINK FOR A SECOND. A MAN GETTING INVOLVED IN A WOMAN'S FIGHT JUST PUTS GAS ON THE FIRE.
BESIDES, YUN-YUN. THEY'RE FIGHTING OVER YOU.
What?!
I'M PRETTY SURE THOSE GIRLS ARE YOUR FANS.
Fans?
THEN ALL THE MORE REASON.
LOOK, YOU.
Get your leg out of the way!

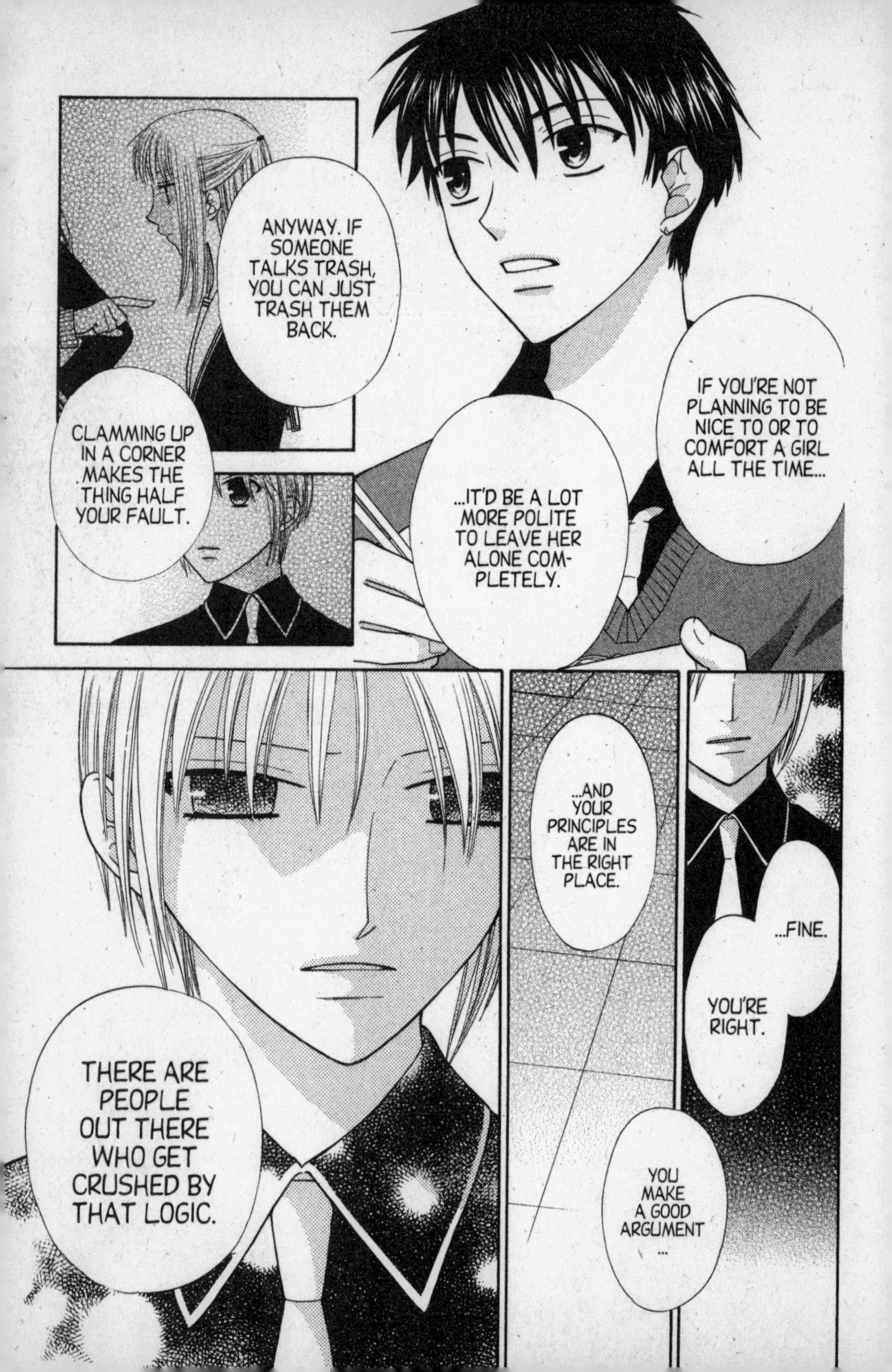
IF YOU'RE NOT PLANNING TO BE NICE TO OR TO COMFORT A GIRL ALL THE TIME...
...IT'D BE A LOT MORE POLITE TO LEAVE HER ALONE COM-PLETELY.
ANYWAY. IF SOMEONE TALKS TRASH, YOU CAN JUST TRASH THEM BACK.
CLAMMING UP IN A CORNER MAKES THE THING HALF YOUR FAULT.
...FINE.
YOU'RE RIGHT.
YOU MAKE A GOOD ARGUMENT ...
...AND YOUR PRINCIPLES ARE IN THE RIGHT PLACE.
THERE ARE PEOPLE OUT THERE WHO GET CRUSHED BY THAT LOGIC.

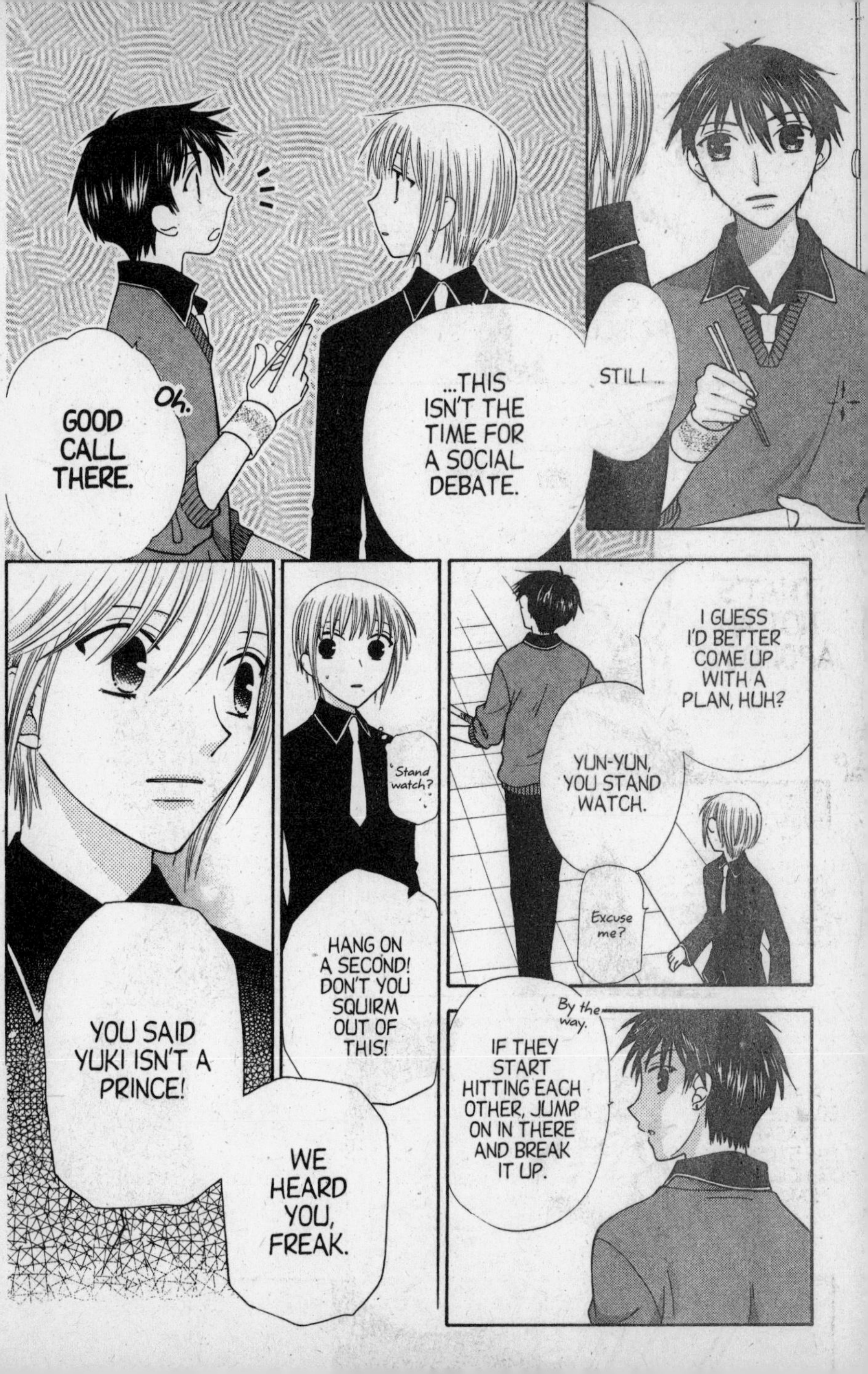
STILL...
...THIS ISN'T THE TIME FOR A SOCIAL DEBATE.
Oh.
GOOD CALL THERE.
I GUESS I'D BETTER COME UP WITH A PLAN, HUH?
YUN-YUN, YOU STAND WATCH.
Excuse me?
By the way.
IF THEY START HITTING EACH OTHER, JUMP ON IN THERE AND BREAK IT UP.
"Stand watch?"
HANG ON A SECOND! DON'T YOU SQUIRM OUT OF THIS!
YOU SAID YUKI ISN'T A PRINCE!
WE HEARD YOU, FREAK.

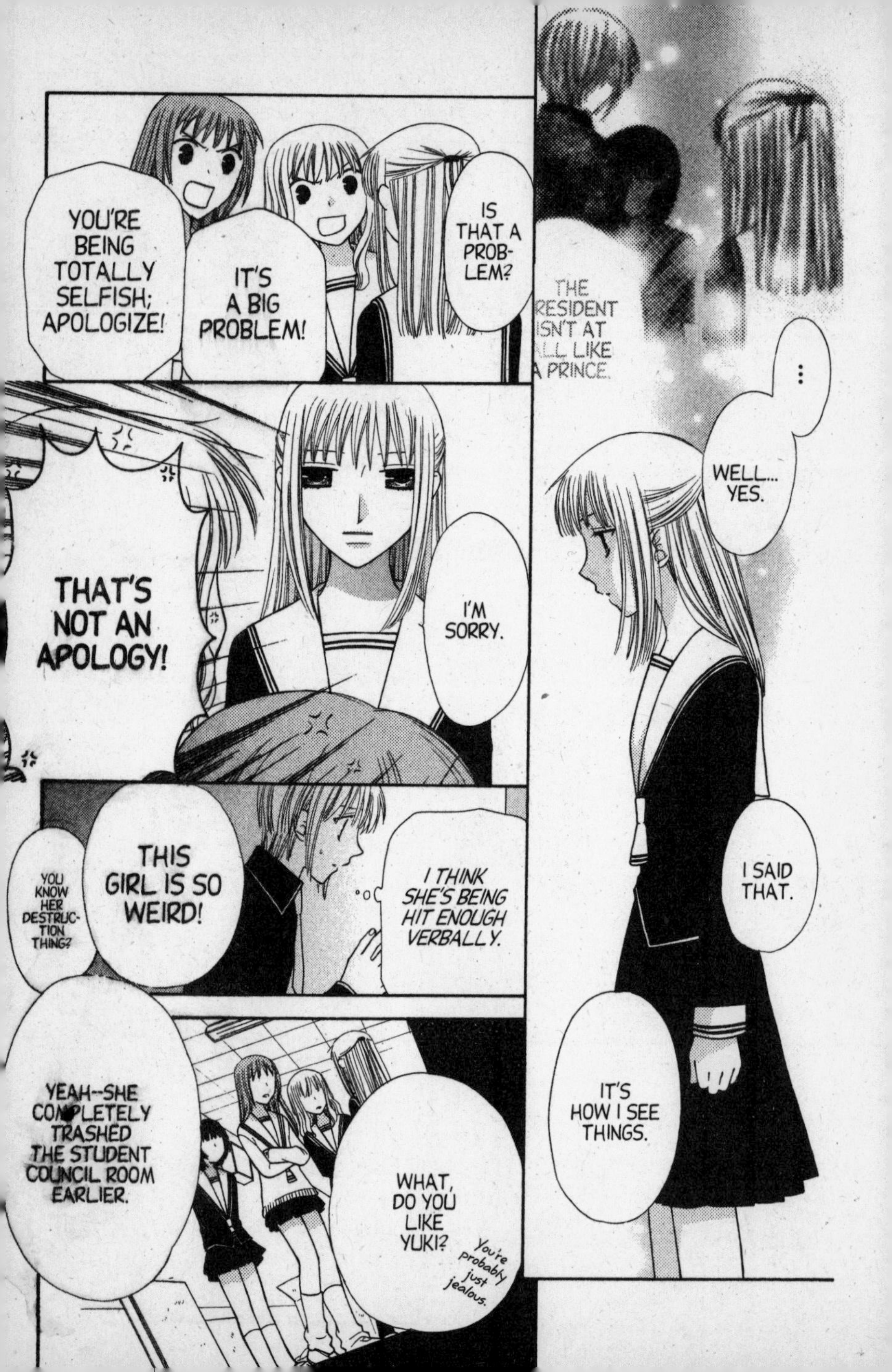
THE RESIDENT ISN'T AT LL LIKE A PRINCE.
...
WELL... YES.
I SAID THAT.
IT'S HOW I SEE THINGS.
IS THAT A PROBLEM?
IT'S A BIG PROBLEM!
YOU'RE BEING TOTALLY SELFISH; APOLOGIZE!
I'M SORRY.
THAT'S NOT AN APOLOGY!
I THINK SHE'S BEING HIT ENOUGH VERBALLY.
THIS GIRL IS SO WEIRD!
YOU KNOW HER DESTRUCTION THING?
WHAT, DO YOU LIKE YUKI?
You're probably just jealous.
YEAH--SHE COMPLETELY TRASHED THE STUDENT COUNCIL ROOM EARLIER.

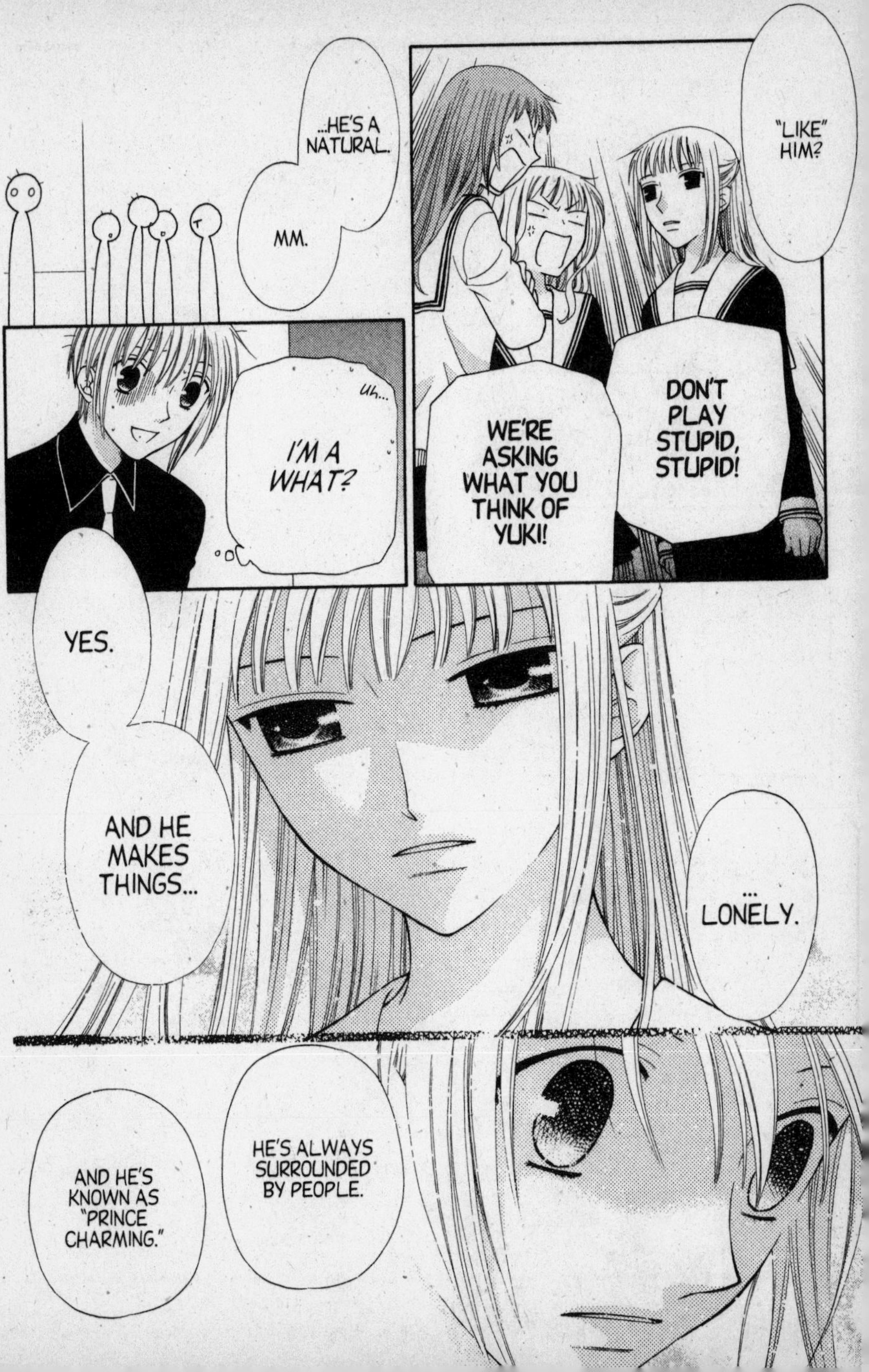
"LIKE" HIM?
DON'T PLAY STUPID, STUPID!
WE'RE ASKING WHAT YOU THINK OF YUKI!
...HE'S A NATURAL.
MM.
uh...
I'M A WHAT?
...LONELY.
YES.
AND HE MAKES THINGS...
HE'S ALWAYS SURROUNDED BY PEOPLE.
AND HE'S KNOWN AS "PRINCE CHARMING."

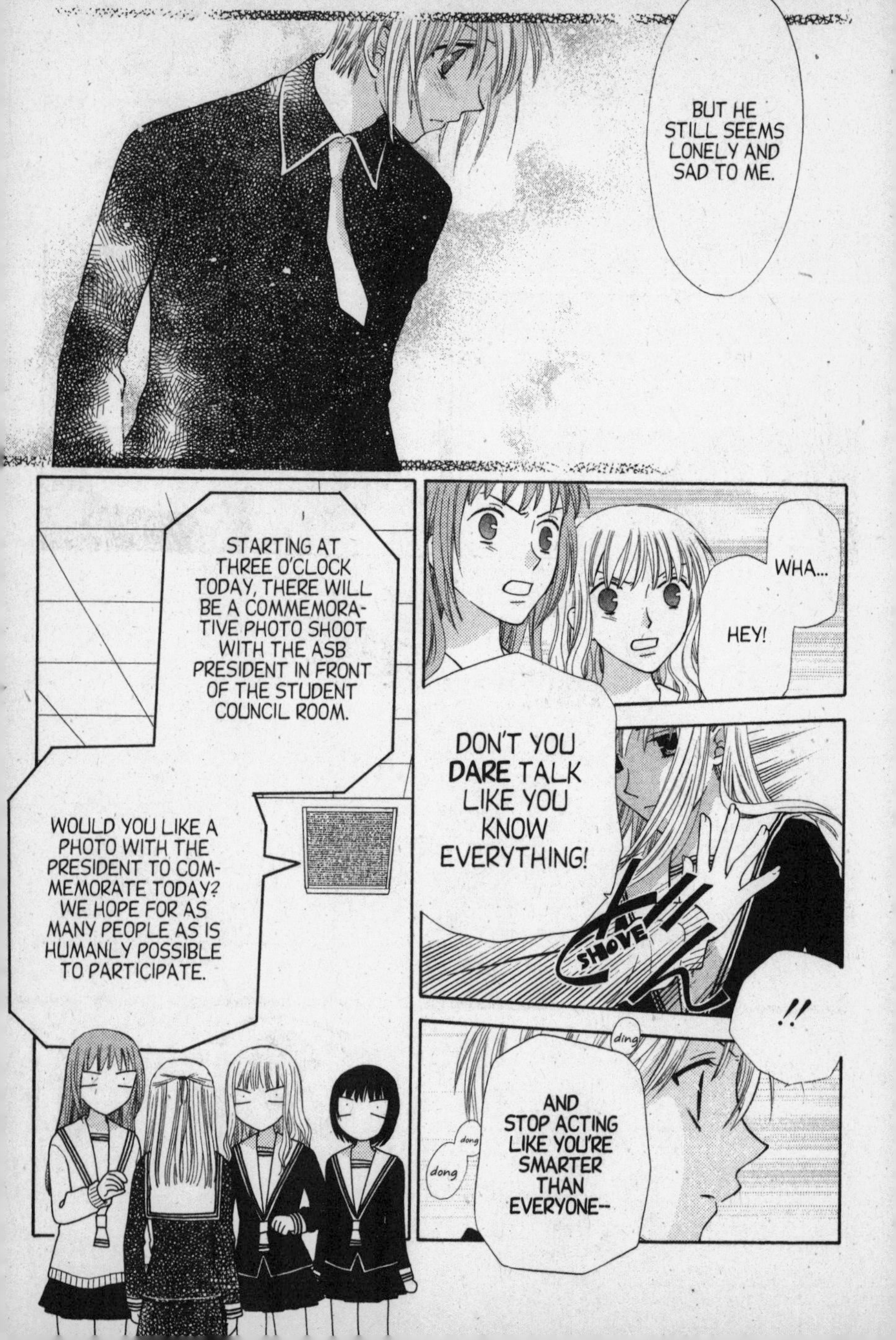

BUT HE STILL SEEMS LONELY AND SAD TO ME.
WHA...
HEY!
DON'T YOU **DARE** TALK LIKE YOU KNOW EVERYTHING!
SHOVE
!!
ding
dong
dong
AND STOP ACTING LIKE YOU'RE SMARTER THAN EVERYONE--
STARTING AT THREE O'CLOCK TODAY, THERE WILL BE A COMMEMORATIVE PHOTO SHOOT WITH THE ASB PRESIDENT IN FRONT OF THE STUDENT COUNCIL ROOM.
WOULD YOU LIKE A PHOTO WITH THE PRESIDENT TO COMMEMORATE TODAY? WE HOPE FOR AS MANY PEOPLE AS IS HUMANLY POSSIBLE TO PARTICIPATE.

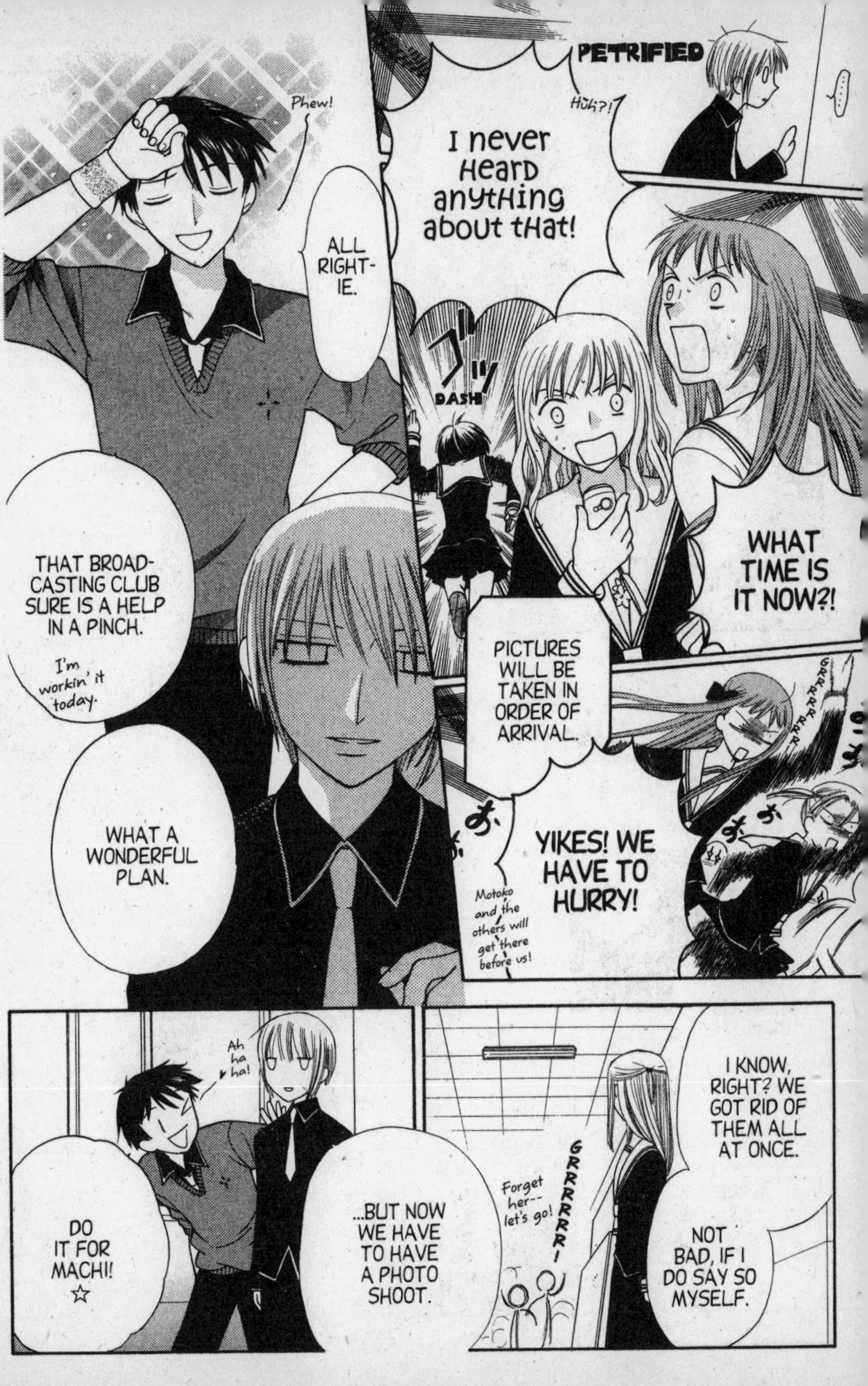

PETRIFIED
...
Huh?!
I never heard anything about that!
WHAT TIME IS IT NOW?!
DASH
PICTURES WILL BE TAKEN IN ORDER OF ARRIVAL.
GRRRRRRR
YIKES! WE HAVE TO HURRY!
Motoko and the others will get there before us!
Phew!
ALL RIGHT-IE.
THAT BROAD-CASTING CLUB SURE IS A HELP IN A PINCH.
I'm workin' it today.
WHAT A WONDERFUL PLAN.
I KNOW, RIGHT? WE GOT RID OF THEM ALL AT ONCE.
NOT BAD, IF I DO SAY SO MYSELF.
GRRRRRRR!
Forget her-- let's go!
Ah ha ha!
...BUT NOW WE HAVE TO HAVE A PHOTO SHOOT.
DO IT FOR MACHI! ☆

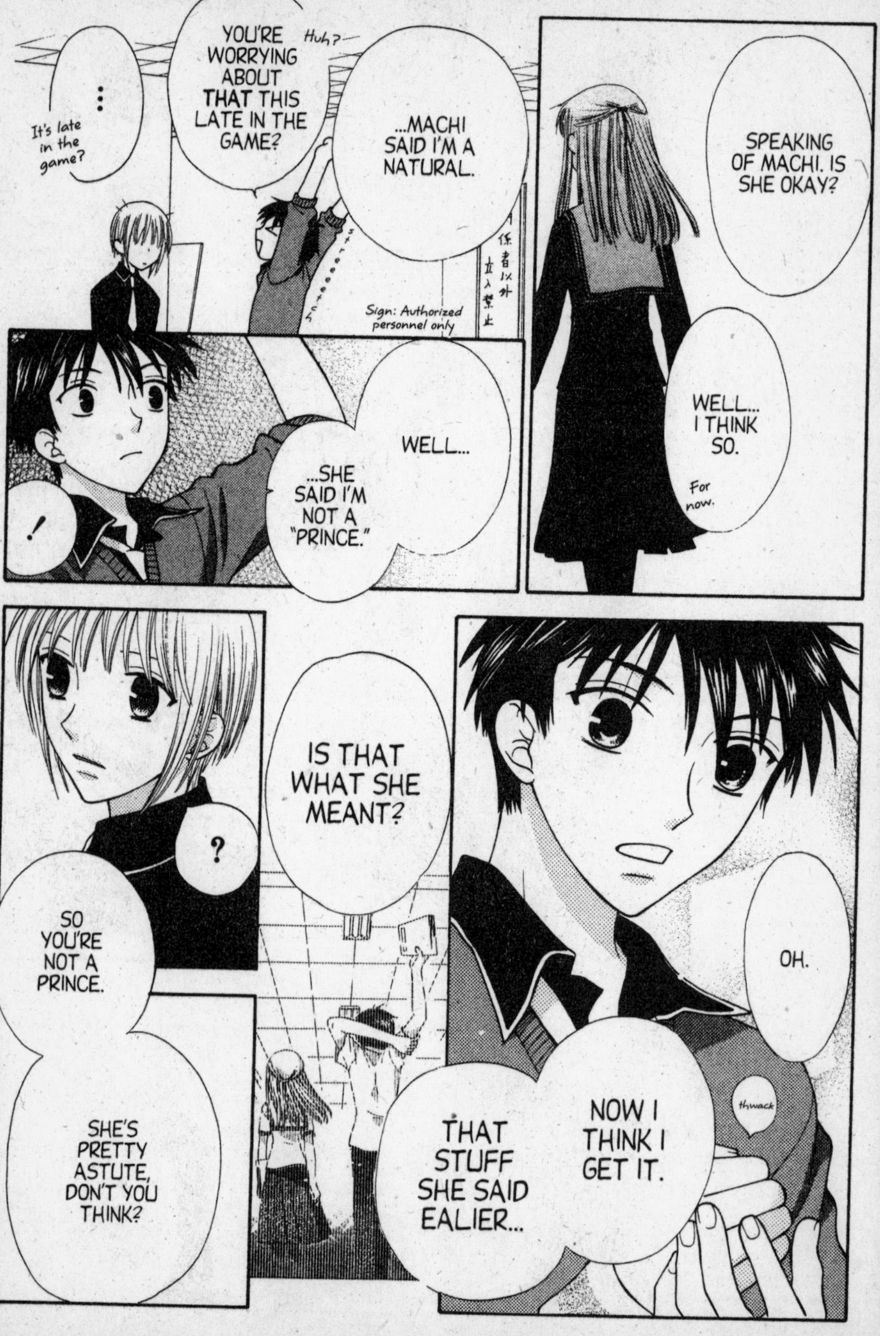
SPEAKING OF MACHI. IS SHE OKAY?
WELL... I THINK SO.
For now.
...MACHI SAID I'M A NATURAL.
Huh?—
YOU'RE WORRYING ABOUT THAT THIS LATE IN THE GAME?
streeeetch
係者以外
立入禁止
Sign: Authorized personnel only
...
It's late in the game?
WELL...
...SHE SAID I'M NOT A "PRINCE."
!
OH.
NOW I THINK I GET IT.
THAT STUFF SHE SAID EALIER...
thwack
IS THAT WHAT SHE MEANT?
?
SO YOU'RE NOT A PRINCE.
SHE'S PRETTY ASTUTE, DON'T YOU THINK?

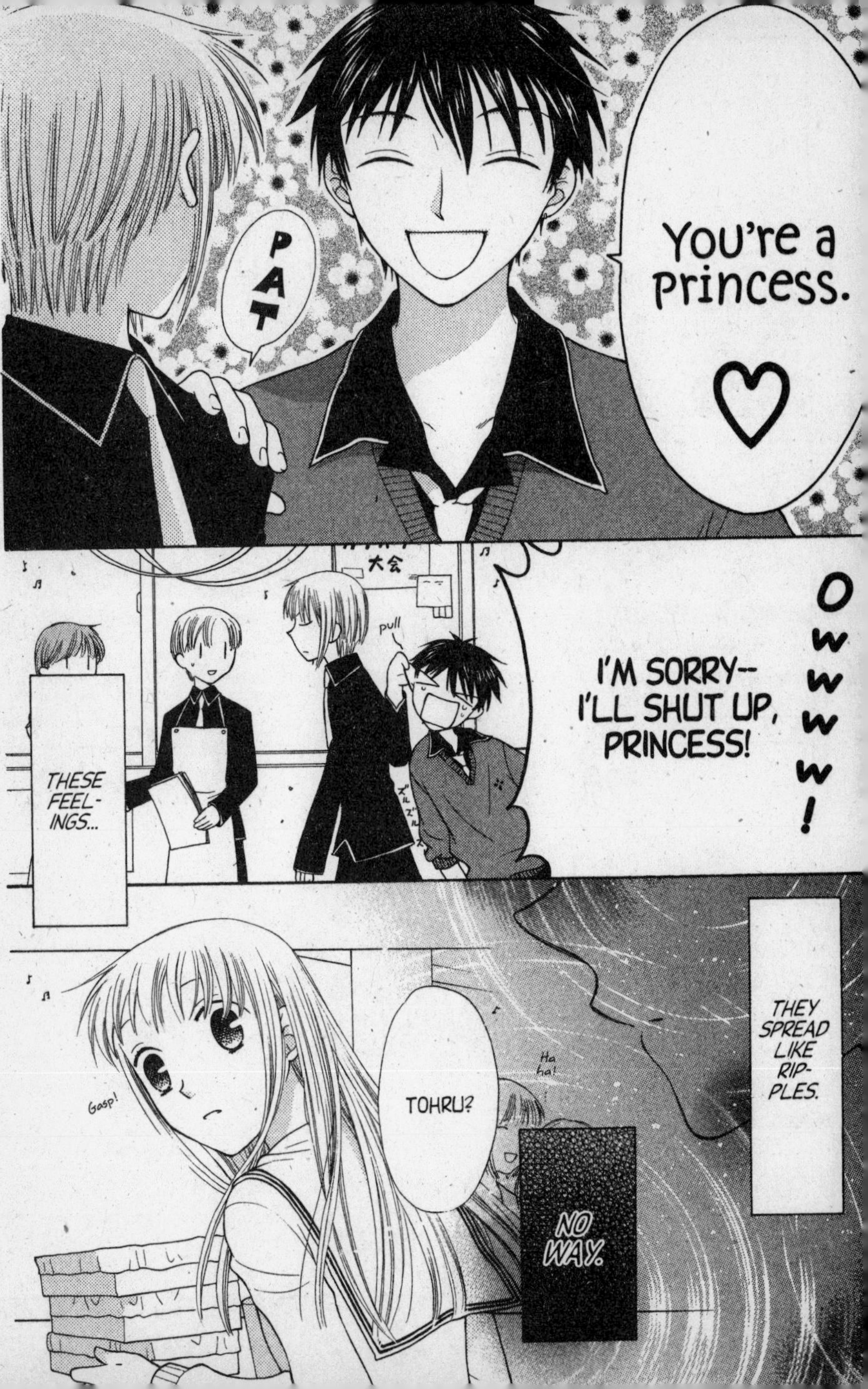
You're a princess. ♡
PAT
Owwwww!
I'M SORRY-- I'LL SHUT UP, PRINCESS!
pull
THESE FEEL-INGS...
THEY SPREAD LIKE RIP-PLES.
NO WAY.
Ha ha!
TOHRU?
Gasp!

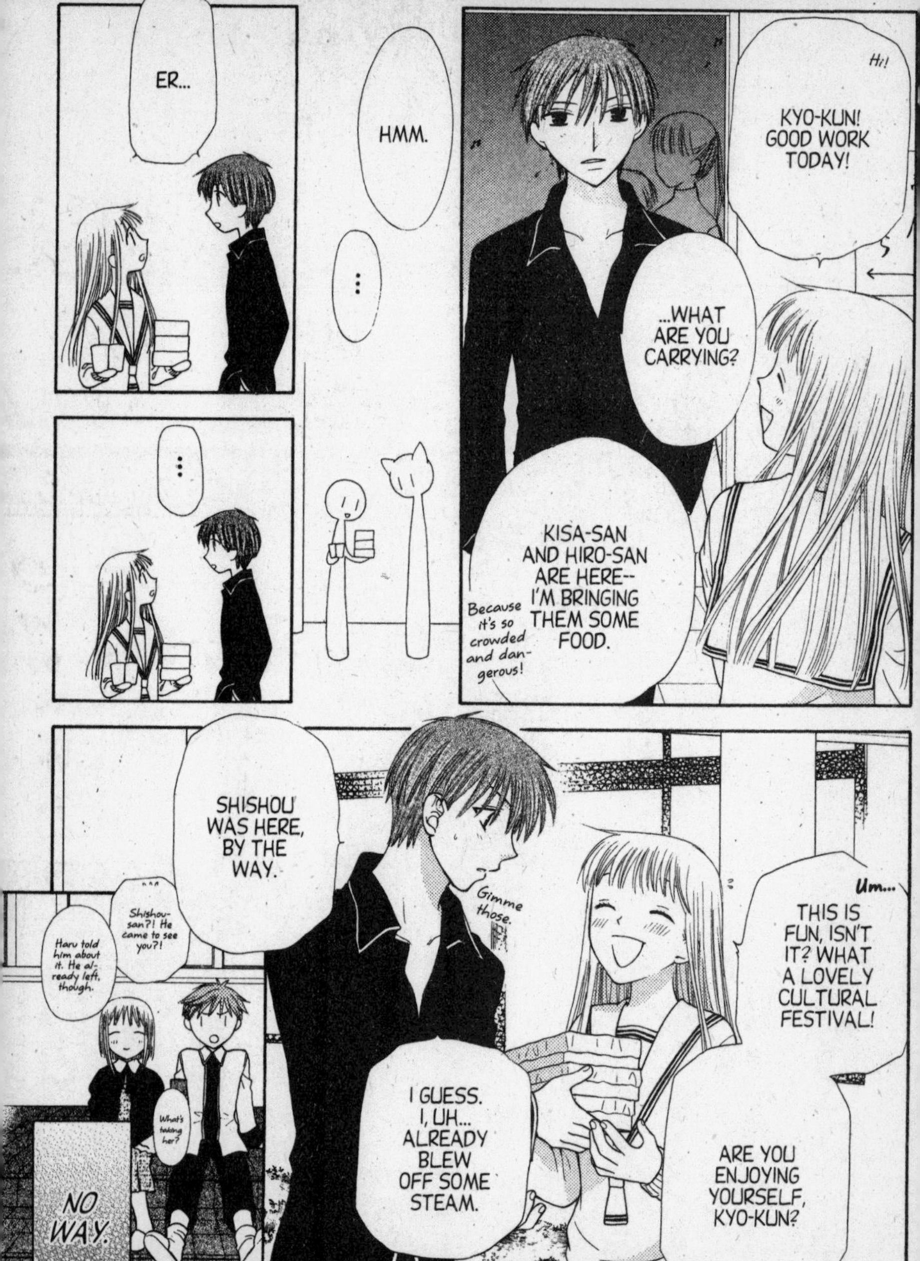
Hi!
KYO-KUN! GOOD WORK TODAY!
...WHAT ARE YOU CARRYING?
KISA-SAN AND HIRO-SAN ARE HERE-- I'M BRINGING THEM SOME FOOD.
Because it's so crowded and dangerous!
HMM.
...
ER...
...
Um...
THIS IS FUN, ISN'T IT? WHAT A LOVELY CULTURAL FESTIVAL!
ARE YOU ENJOYING YOURSELF, KYO-KUN?
Gimme those.
I GUESS. I, UH... ALREADY BLEW OFF SOME STEAM.
SHISHOU WAS HERE, BY THE WAY.
Shishou-san?! He came to see you?!
Haru told him about it. He already left, though.
What's taking her?
NO WAY.

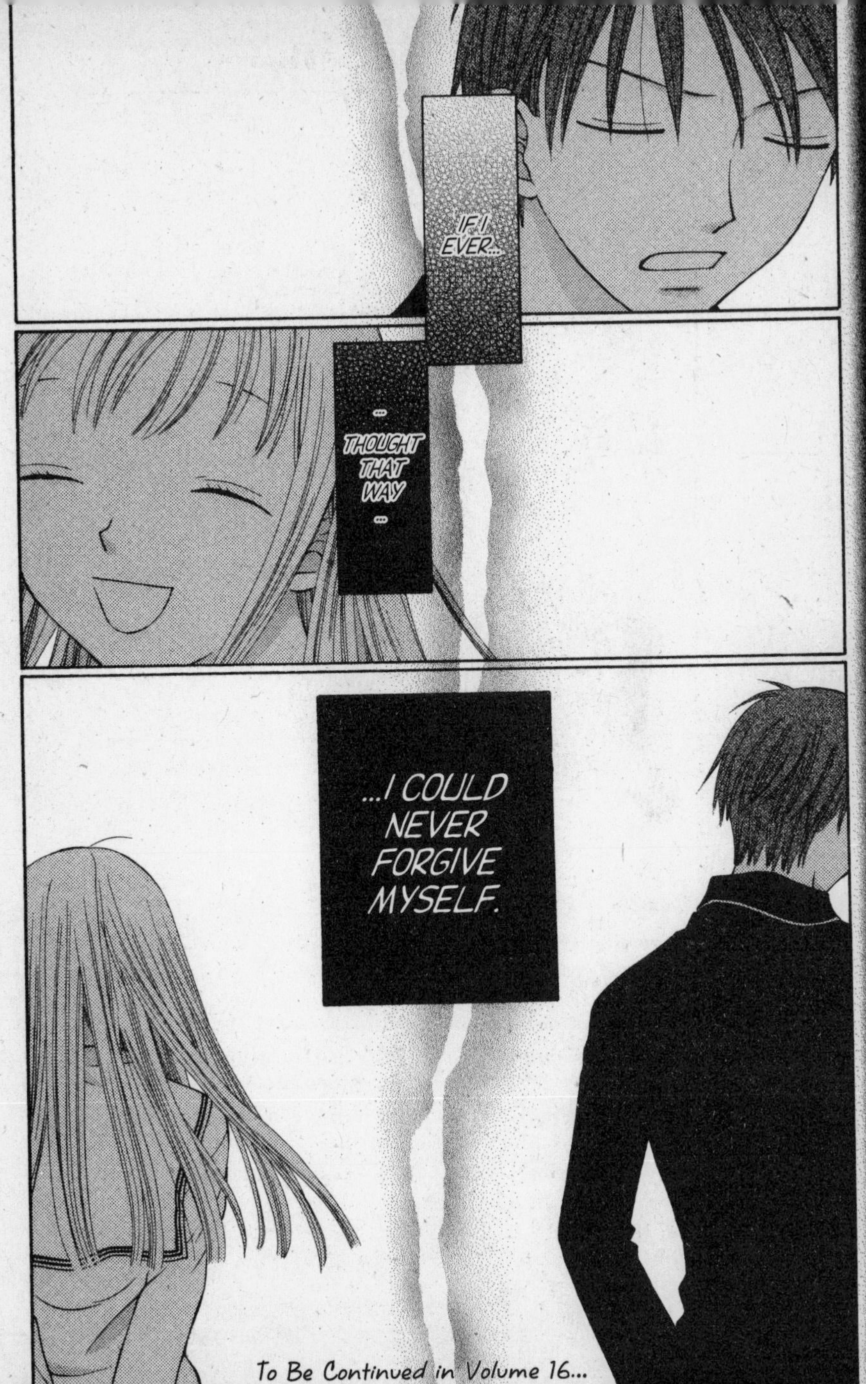
IF I EVER...
...THOUGHT THAT WAY...
...I COULD NEVER FORGIVE MYSELF.
To Be Continued in Volume 16...

Next time in...

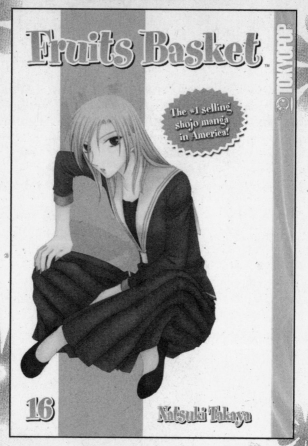

Fruits Basket

The #1 selling shojo manga in America!

TOKYOPOP

16

Natsuki Takaya

The Curse Knows No Bounds...

The world's best shojo manga opens a new chapter in the Sohma family's story. Tragedy continues to smother the Sohmas—and it seems to be spreading to those souls unlucky enough to be connected to this cursed family. It seems that Kyo met Tohru's mother in the past. His memory involves Tohru's birth...and the sad events that shortly followed. Is she ready to hear the truth about her mother and father? Meanwhile, Yuki announces that he's going to take responsibility for his own problems...instead of blaming everyone else. But how will Akito react to Yuki's declaration?

Fruits Basket Volume 16
Available April 2007

Fans Basket

We meet again, loyal *Furuba* readers. I think we have a particularly impressive Fans Basket section for Volume 15. I am continually impressed by the fan mail you all send. And it just breaks my heart that I won't be able to print it all. We just don't have enough pages left in the series! Lately, I've been getting a lot of jewelry for Takaya-san. This might shock some of you, but I've never even met Takaya-san. Rest assured, though, we've been sending some of your fan mail to Japan! I can't promise you'll get a response, though. But I do know this: Takaya-san is staggered by how many fans she has worldwide!

–Paul Morrissey, Editor

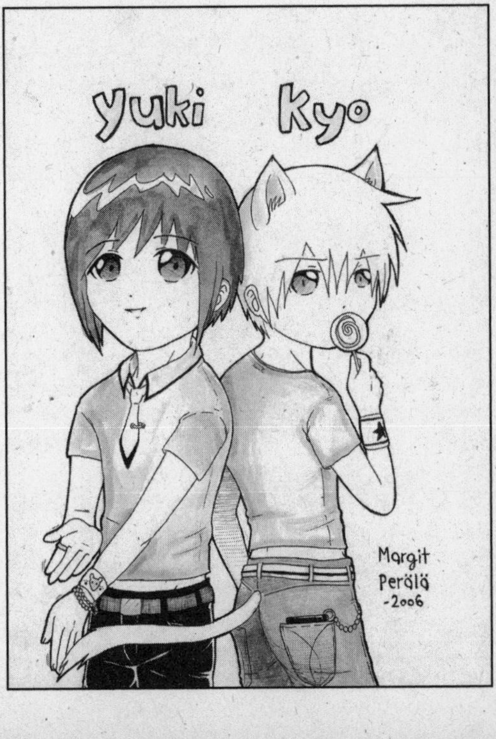

Yuki
Kyo
Margit Perälä -2006

Margit Perälä
Age 19
Finland

Whoa! Margit is from Finland! That's so cool. I wonder how many people read *Fruits Basket* in Finland. I really like your art style, Margit. It's very emo/indie rock.

Tia Ramirez
Tijeras, NM

Tohru's bedroom looks fantastically decorated, Tia! I absolutely love all the *Furuba* merchandise!

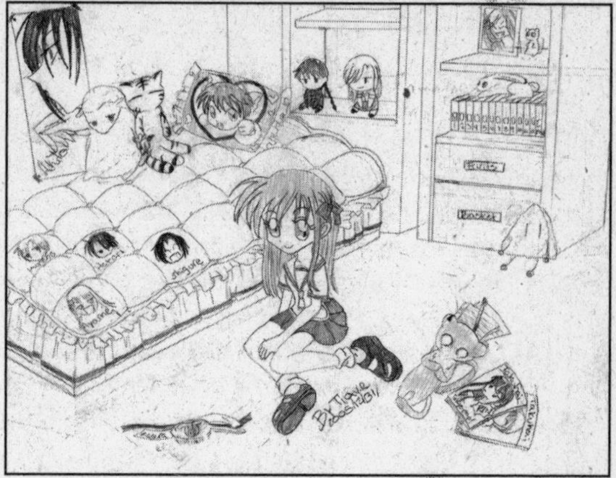

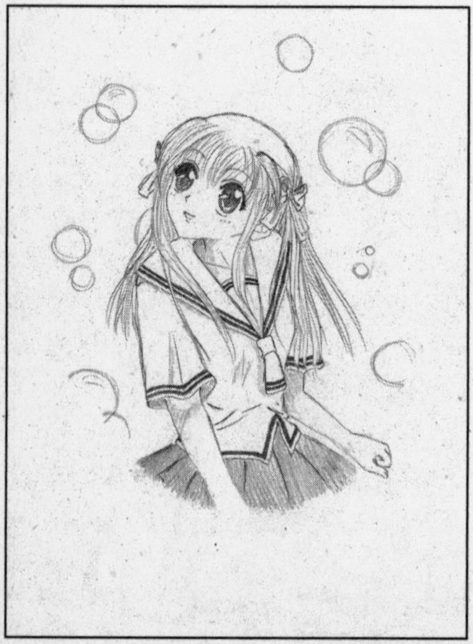

Riku
Age 13
Northridge, CA

How adorable does Tohru look in this sketch? Nice work, Riku!

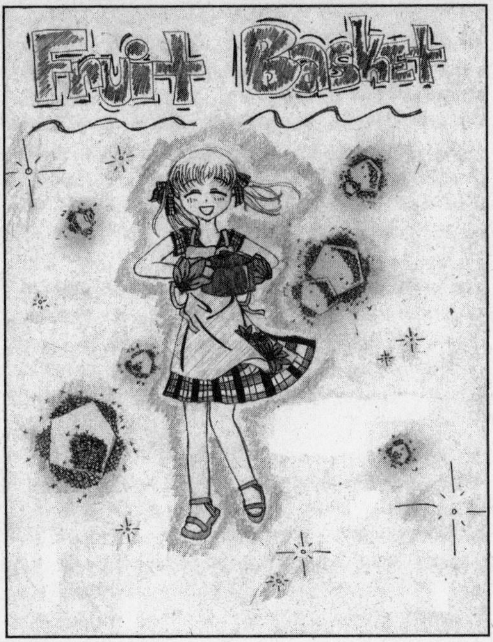
Fruit Basket

Stephanie Thomas
Age 12
Columbia, MD

Tohru should wear gingham more often! And take a close look at her over mitts–they totally match her outfit!

Maggie McGrattan
Age 22
Paris, Ontario
- Canada

Hey, Maggie. I haven't played *Star Ocean.* (I'm too busy reading fan mail to play videogames.) But it's a total blast seeing our *Fruits Basket* characters cosplaying in these awesome outfits.

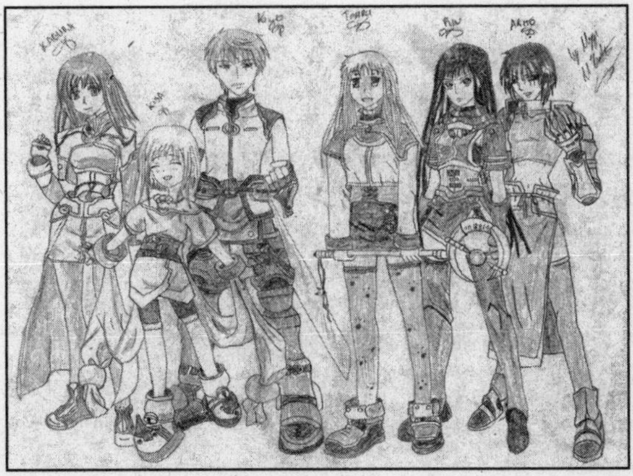

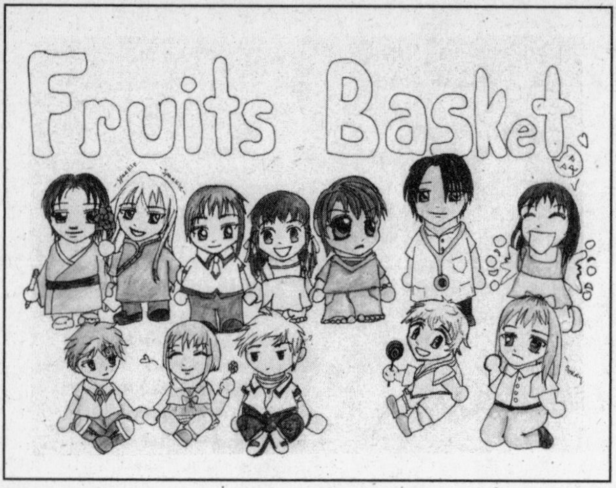
Fruits Basket

Sheila Syroka
Age 18
Erie, PA

It's *Furuba* Babies! They all look so cuddly and adorable!

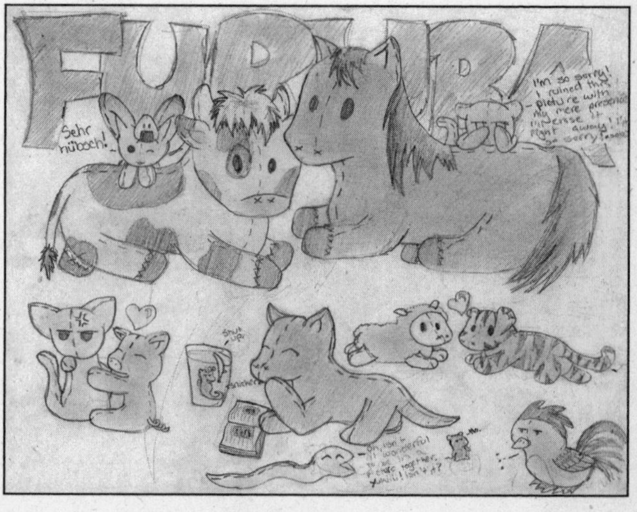
FURUBA
Sehr hübsch!
I'm so sorry!

Chelsea Hensbergen
Macomb, MI

More plush toys! Seriously, wouldn't you all buy *Furuba* plush toys if you could get your hands on them? This sketch made me laugh, Chelsea. My favorite part: Ritsu freaking out in the corner!

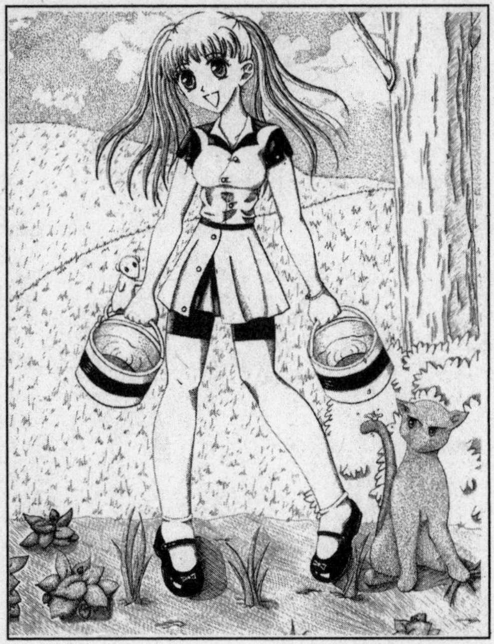

Shelley Davis
Age 17
St. Anthony, ID

Shelly, your art is terrific! I'm amazed at the way you used your pen to mimic tones. And the little splash of water on Kyo's tail is priceless! Keep drawing, and good luck!

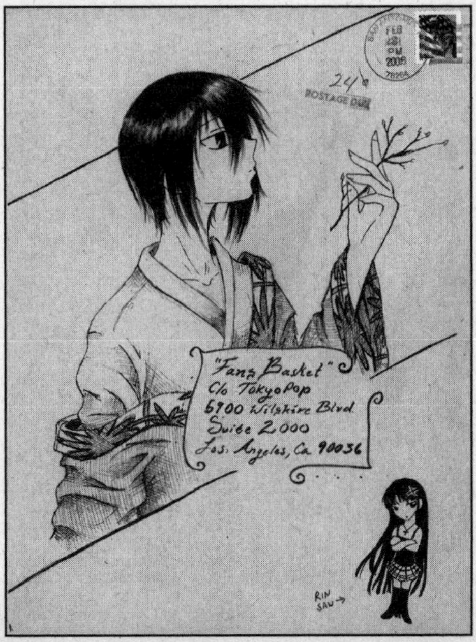

"Fans Basket"
C/o TokyoPop
5900 Wilshire Blvd
Suite 2,000
Los Angeles, Ca 90036
RIN SAN →

Claire Ramirez
Age 16
San Antonio, TX

Hey, Claire. Your envelope art is absolutely gorgeous! I wonder if the mail carrier was as impressed as I was.

Do you want to share your love for *Fruits Basket* with fans around the world? "Fans Basket" is taking submissions of fan art, poetry, cosplay photos, or any other Furuba fun you'd like to share!

How to submit:

1) Send your work via regular mail (NOT e-mail) to:

"Fans Basket"
c/o TOKYOPOP
5900 Wilshire Blvd.
Suite 2000
Los Angeles, CA 90036

2) All work should be in black-and-white and no larger than 8.5" x 11". (And try not to fold it too many times!)

3) Anything you send will not be returned. If you want to keep your original, it's fine to send us a copy.

4) Please include your full name, age, city and state for us to print with your work. If you'd rather us use a pen name, please include that, too.

5) IMPORTANT: If you're under the age of 18, you must have your parent's permission in order for us to print your work. Any submissions without a signed note of parental consent cannot be used.

6) For full details, please check out our web-site: http://www.tokyopop.com/aboutus/fanart.php

Disclaimer: Anything you send to us becomes the exclusive property of TOKYOPOP Inc. and, as we said before, will not be returned to you. We will have the right to print, reproduce, distribute, or modify the artwork for use in future volumes of *Fruits Basket* or on the web royalty-free.

Alexandra Minazuki
Age 19
Orem, UT

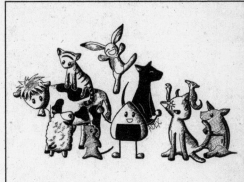

Hey, Alexandra. I bet there aren't a lot of Minazukis in Utah! This is a great piece of art. I love the fact that you used your own unique style. I think you perfectly captured the essence of Momiji, by the way!

Rosalie Meli Tam
Age 18
Silver Spring, MD

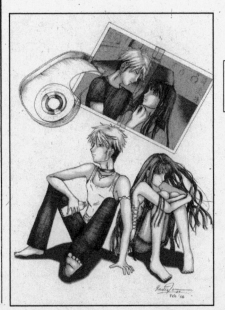

Lovely work, Rosalie. This piece of art actually tells a story... I wonder why that photo was torn in half... And when did it get taped back together? In any case, I hope Rin and Hatsuharu can find happiness together!

TOKYOPOP®.com

WHERE MANGA LIVES!

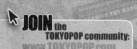

JOIN the
TOKYOPOP community:
www.TOKYOPOP.com

LIVE THE MANGA LIFESTYLE!

CREATE...
UPLOAD...
DOWNLOAD...
BLOG...
CHAT...
VOTE...
LIVE!!!!

WWW.TOKYOPOP.COM HAS:

- Exclusives
- News
- Columns
- Special Features
  and more...

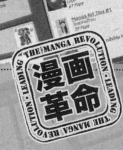

Mail Order Ninja © Joshua Elder, Erich Owen and TOKYOPOP Inc.

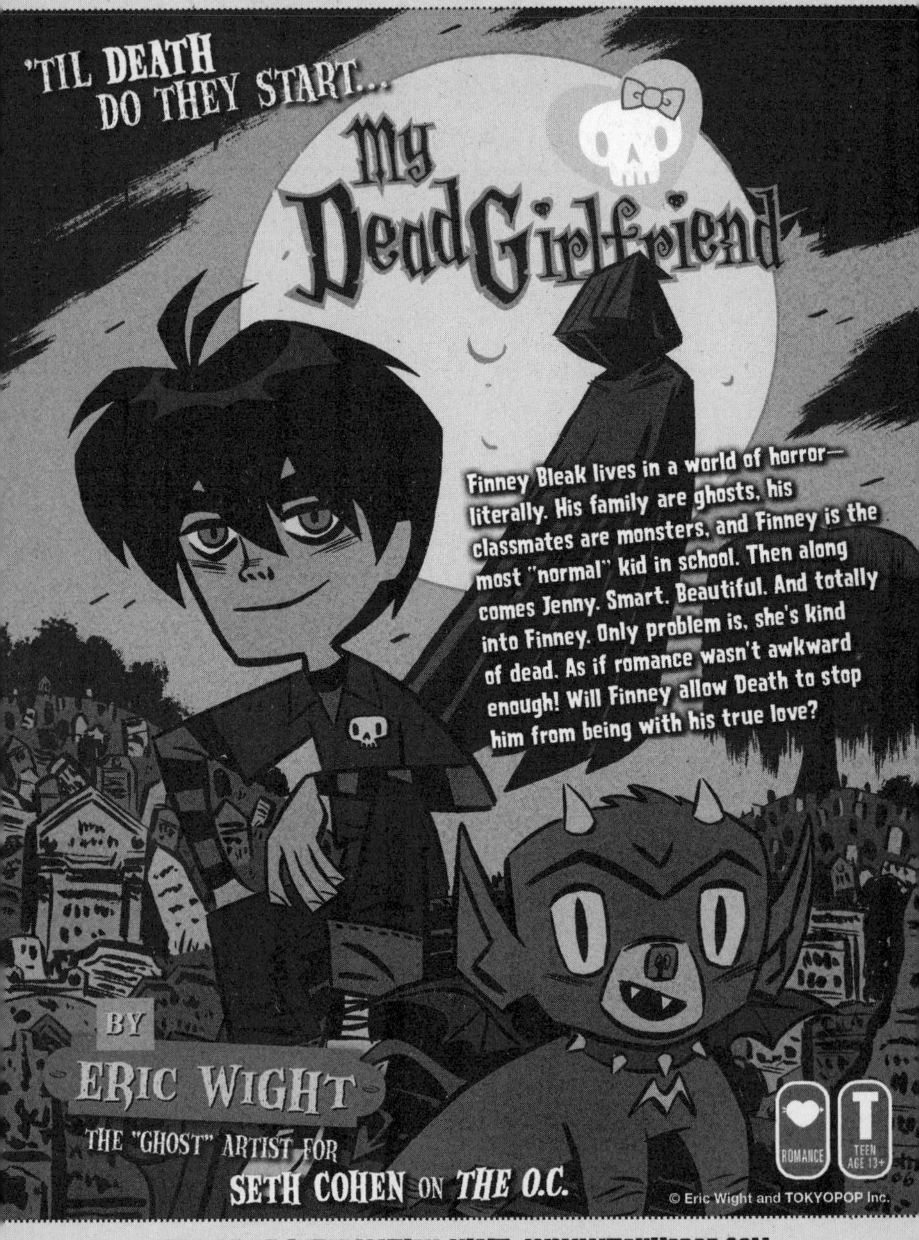
'TIL DEATH DO THEY START...
My Dead Girlfriend
Finney Bleak lives in a world of horror—literally. His family are ghosts, his classmates are monsters, and Finney is the most "normal" kid in school. Then along comes Jenny. Smart. Beautiful. And totally into Finney. Only problem is, she's kind of dead. As if romance wasn't awkward enough! Will Finney allow Death to stop him from being with his true love?
BY
ERIC WIGHT
THE "GHOST" ARTIST FOR SETH COHEN ON THE O.C.
ROMANCE
T
TEEN AGE 13+
© Eric Wight and TOKYOPOP Inc.

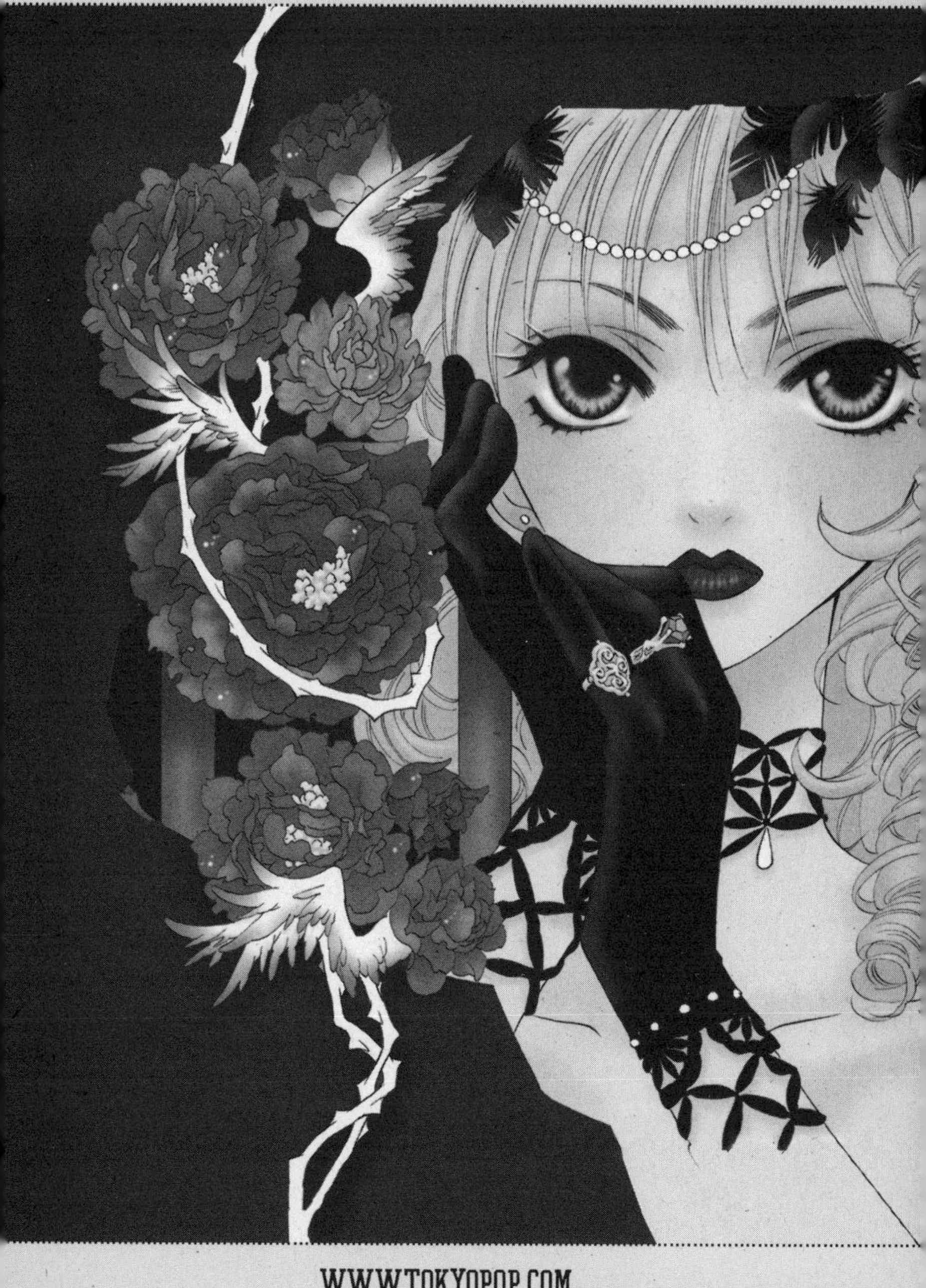

PRINCESS AI: ROSES AND TATTOOS

A DIVA TORN FROM CHAOS...

A SAVIOR DOOMED TO LOVE.

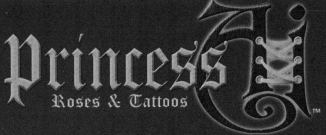

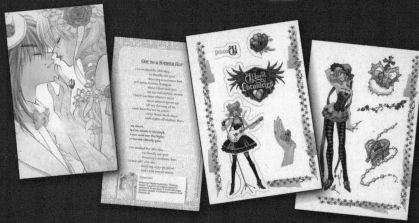

Princess Ai like you've never seen her before in this limited edition art and poetry book!

Take home more of the gorgeous art of Princess Ai! Your favorite art from the manga, new poetry from D.J. Milky, and never-before-seen illustrations are now available as stickers and mini-posters that you can use anywhere.

© & ™ TOKYOPOP Inc. and Kitty Radio, Inc.

FOR MORE INFORMATION VISIT:

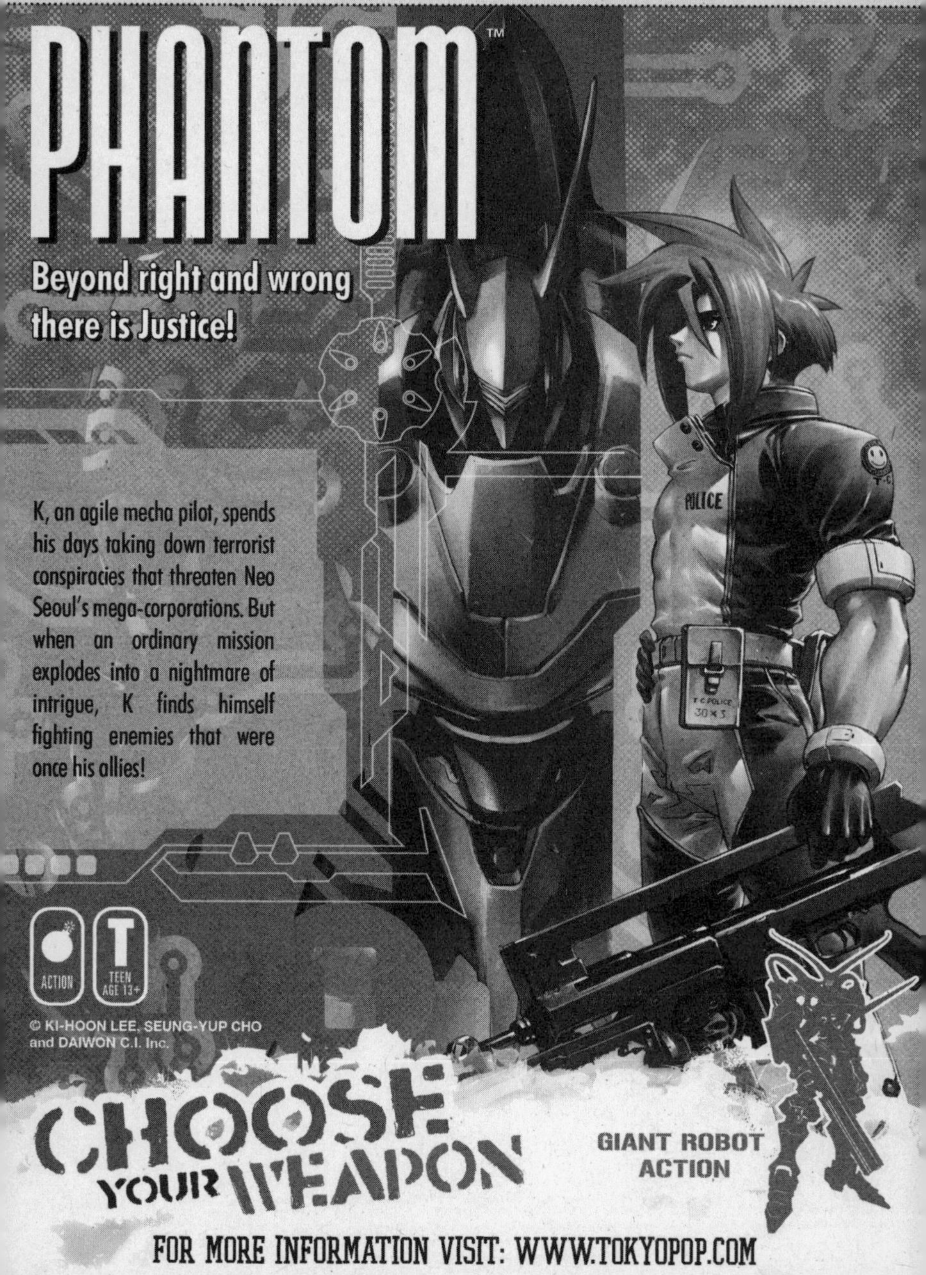

TOKYOPOP MANGA SUPPLEMENT

PHANTOM™

Beyond right and wrong there is Justice!

K, an agile mecha pilot, spends his days taking down terrorist conspiracies that threaten Neo Seoul's mega-corporations. But when an ordinary mission explodes into a nightmare of intrigue, K finds himself fighting enemies that were once his allies!

ACTION

T TEEN AGE 13+

© KI-HOON LEE, SEUNG-YUP CHO and DAIWON C.I. Inc.

CHOOSE YOUR WEAPON

GIANT ROBOT ACTION

FOR MORE INFORMATION VISIT: WWW.TOKYOPOP.COM

TOKYOPOP MANGA SUPPLEMENT

Black Magic + Cat boys =
a WILD ride!

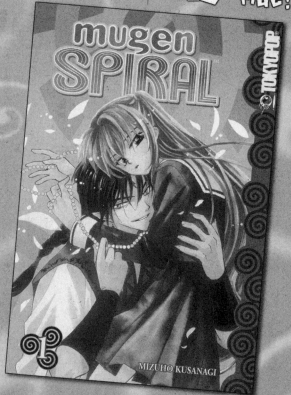

MIZUHO KUSANAGI

Yayoi, a spunky high school girl, has inherited incredible powers which she uses to protect others. While battling the devil Ura, Yayoi turns him into an adorable black kitten. Although Ura is bent on "eating" Yayoi's power, the unlikely pair find themselves caught up in a magical adventure beyond their imagination!

© Mizuho Kus

FOR MORE INFORMATION VISIT: WWW.TOKYOPOP.COM

P9-CFS-742

STOP!

This is the back of the book.
You wouldn't want to spoil a great ending!

This book is printed "manga-style," in the authentic Japanese right-to-left format. Since none of the artwork has been flipped or altered, readers get to experience the story just as the creator intended. You've been asking for it, so TOKYOPOP® delivered: authentic, hot-off-the-press, and far more fun!

DIRECTIONS

If this is your first time reading manga-style, here's a quick guide to help you understand how it works.

It's easy... just start in the top right panel and follow the numbers. Have fun, and look for more 100% authentic manga from TOKYOPOP®!

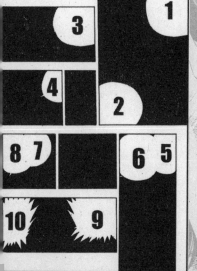

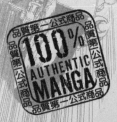